PENGUIN BOOKS

NONE BUT A BLOCKHEAD

Larry L. King has won the Stanley Walker Journalism
Award for general excellence in reporting and a
television "Emmy" for documentary writing; he has
been nominated for a National Book Award and a
Broadway "Tony." Mr. King began his writing career
working for small newspapers in New Mexico and
Texas, later becoming a columnist for the *Washington
Star* and a features writer for *The Washington Post*. He
has been a contributing editor at *Harper's, New Times,
The Texas Observer,* and *Texas Monthly,* and he
currently serves *Parade* in that role. He is the author of
many books, including *Confessions of a White Racist,
The Old Man and Lesser Mortals,* and *Of Outlaws, Con
Men, Whores, Politicians, and Other Artists,* and
coauthor of the Broadway hit *The Best Little
Whorehouse in Texas.* His new play, *The Night Hank
Williams Died,* is currently in production. Mr. King
lives in Washington, D.C.

NONE BUT A BLOCKHEAD

On Being a Writer

By LARRY L. KING

Penguin Books

PENGUIN BOOKS
Viking Penguin Inc., 40 West 23rd Street,
New York, New York 10010, U.S.A.
Penguin Books Ltd, Harmondsworth,
Middlesex, England
Penguin Books Australia Ltd, Ringwood,
Victoria, Australia
Penguin Books Canada Limited, 2801 John Street,
Markham, Ontario, Canada L3R 1B4
Penguin Books (N.Z.) Ltd, 182–190 Wairau Road,
Auckland 10, New Zealand

First published in the United States of America by
Viking Penguin Inc. 1986
Published in Penguin Books 1987

Portions of this book first appeared in the following publications, some in
slightly different form: *Playboy*, *Esquire*, *The Harvard Crimson*,
The Washington Post, *Parade*, and *The Washington Post Magazine*.

Grateful acknowledgment is made for permission to reprint the following
copyrighted material:
Excerpts from *Ernest Hemingway: Selected Letters 1917–1961*
by Carlos Baker.
Copyright © 1981 The Ernest Hemingway Foundation, Inc., and Carlos Baker.
Reprinted with the permission of Charles Scribner's Sons.
Excerpts from *Sorties* by James Dickey. Copyright © 1971 by James Dickey.
Reprinted by permission of Doubleday & Company, Inc.
Letter from Billie Lee Brammer to the author. Permission granted
by the children of Billie Lee Brammer.
Letters from Lanvil Gilbert and Elroy Bode to the author.

LIBRARY OF CONGRESS CATALOGING IN PUBLICATION DATA
King, Larry L.
None but a blockhead.
1. King, Larry L. — Biography.   2. Authors, American
— 20th century — Biography.   3. Authorship.   I. Title.
[PS3561.I48Z47   1987]   818'.5409   [B]   86-20514
ISBN 0 14 00.9918 2

Printed in the United States of America by
R. R. Donnelley & Sons Company, Harrisonburg, Virginia
Set in Century Expanded

For Lanvil and Glenda Gilbert,
who offered shelter and comfort
in the darkest days of many
uncertain wars.

And

For those dear home folks now in
gentle custody of the writing body:
Barbara, Lindsay and Blaine.

No man but a blockhead
ever wrote except for money.
—Dr. Samuel Johnson

***

Writers . . . as a class have
distinguished themselves as
barroom brawlers, drawing-room
wolves, breakers of engagements,
defaulters of debts, crying
drunks, and suicidal maniacs.
—Malcolm Cowley

Introduction

Though I do not instruct you to place this book back on the shelf if you are a mere reader, it is primarily directed toward neophyte writers, struggling writers, would-be writers young or old—those hopeful wordsmiths who harbor dreams yet unfulfilled.

Sometimes I estimate that group at 92 percent of the world population; I am forever encountering sweet little old ladies, real estate magnates, blind beggars and retired corporals who offer to let me help with their life stories and then split the profits. What they don't realize is that relatively few books show any profit. I will be absolutely astounded if this one does.

Large numbers of people apparently want to write, or think they do. They speak as if they are going out to catch a bus or whip up a batch of fudge: "One of these days I'm gonna sit down and write a book," or "I got a Uncle Carl, he's real funny; if he'd just come spend a long weekend then me and him could write a book."

Writing looks much easier than trapeze work, I know, until you sit before a typewriter long enough to realize it won't speak back unless spoken to. But I am not directing these remarks at idle dreamers; what I have to say is for the citizen who is locked in serious combat with his or her typewriter, and who may be wondering when, or if, the battle will be won. I want to give that hopeful some idea of what to expect. So this is not a book intended to quarrel over rules of grammar or quibble about vocabulary selections; rather, its purpose is to deal at the nuts-and-bolts level with the working writer's experiences in the marketplace.

In those long fruitless years while trying to break into print, and during my early apprenticeship, I wondered in times of discouragement how anyone could make a living writing or sustain—over a lifetime—the agonies of uncertainty or the fears of rejection accompanying almost any writing project. Conversely, my more innocent and romantic parts believed published writers to be rich to the last in number or on smooth paths to quick riches; that they lived charmed lives unafflicted by the head colds or barking dogs visited upon the rest of us. Many times I wondered about that special magic or chaos made by writers, agents, editors, critics, contracts: what *really* went on in the inner workings of this crazy literary business?

In reciting the ups and downs of my own career, I hope to rise slightly above the egomaniacal; my purpose is to show what working writers may encounter—the triumphs and the setbacks—and I simply know more of my own story than of the stories of others. In reading the autobiographies of many writers, I have often found certain gaps as to how the author felt about a certain story, break, editor, fee. What had his relationships been with his writing contemporaries, or his family? Did he drink too much? Did he fight with his wife? How much money had he made, or how little, and did he feel adequately rewarded for his efforts or cheated? Writers telling about themselves rarely tell *on* themselves. Within the limits of a certain selective discretion, I hope to go beyond the usual confessions—though you may be certain I shall suppress any revelations that might send me to jail or domestic court.

In the final section I have used some recycled materials, articles earlier published elsewhere, to illustrate how or why a certain piece gets done as a working writer grinds and pounds away at a livelihood. Most of those pieces were written for fun and/or money; I have found it is better to be a busy writer than a proud one.

A lady once visited me from Texas, expecting in New York to hear my writer friends talk of their Art, their creative processes, their private secretions and visions or motives. "But," she later complained, "all they talked about was money. They might have been Texas oilmen." That writers often seem preoccupied by money is evident in the published missives of many who attained prominence enough for their old letters to have been collected. Dickens, Hemingway, Faulkner, O'Hara, Steinbeck, Twain—to name but a few—seem to have spent astonishing amounts of time imploring their agents, editors and publishers to rush shipment of their next batch of gold, or to grant advances against future work, or to make them personal loans. Those same writers often railed to their friends or families about the terrible price of living, and how many people expected the writer to assist in their upkeep or schemes. One receives the impression that no matter how much the writer earned, he almost always seemed to skate on thin financial ice.

There are logical reasons for this. No writer I personally know—with the exception of John Kenneth Galbraith, an economist—has the slightest inkling of how to manage money. Writers' fees or royalties usually are paid in lump sums with no taxes withheld; few trouble to establish an adequate tax reserve to deal with that inevitable day when the IRS man knocks to demand payment plus penalties and rapidly accumulating interest. I know whereof I speak: the tax boys placed a garnishment against my box-office earnings, the moment they suspected I had a hit musical, to satisfy Uncle Sam's claim on more than $13,000 I had not gotten around to paying. Such a poor record might embarrass a doctor, a minister or even a congressman; in writers' circles it is considered the norm.

More impractical stargazers than businessmen, writers often squander fortunes in private obsessions. Mark Twain lost huge sums investing in a typesetter never perfected. Norman Mailer has dropped a couple of bundles making his own movies. I myself once lost a year's wages in a get-rich-quick scheme attempting to exploit the popularity of President Dwight D. Eisenhower—the foolish specifics of which will be found later in this book—and of recent years only the foot-stomping disapproval of my wife-lawyer-agent and her meddling financial advisers prevented my investing heavily in a professional football team that went belly-up bankrupt in two years after losing twenty-nine of thirty-six games.

Interesting personal lives prove costly. Half the writers I know pay multiple alimony penalties for their hearts' old misjudgments, and have two or more batches of children to support. Most writers have no dependable steady income: no check in the mailbox each Friday. Their money arrives erratically, not at the convenience of their creditors or cash-flow needs. A fat season almost surely was preceded by many lean ones, and may be followed by seasons leaner still. Writers travel—another costly proposition—to accomplish research, to find that hideaway where perfect working conditions exist, or simply because their restless feet urge them to move on and no nine-to-five obligations exist to stay them.

When writers are earning good money, they tend to spend as if expecting to be robbed of every last dime. In fat times they obligate themselves to sustaining properties or projects put in dire risk the moment their incomes drop. Your present hero, when his musical comedy was doing hot business around the nation (and in more foreign ports than we were fighting or planning brush wars in), discovered he had always wanted to live in a castle. He went out and bought one, so to speak. When the big weekly royalty checks abruptly ended, the big bills for house payments, help, utilities, maintenance costs and property taxes did not. Now he must come up with more money each month than would be required to support boatloads of refugees putting up at the Waikiki Hilton. Yes, there are days I understand what Dr. Samuel Johnson was talking about when he said, "No man but a blockhead ever wrote except for money."

Those of us who decide to make a career of words and storytelling begin, I think, with the notion of equaling Twain or Faulkner or whatever Old Dead Great we most admire. Comes a time when the realities touch us, and we must make the damaging admission that such honors are not in our stars. Even after this painful surrender it is possible to go on doing decent work—though, once the sights are lowered, the prideful writer must guard against sliding all the way down to television sit-coms. Once the soul has admitted to the shadows that Shakespeare's work is quite likely to last a bit longer than one's own, there may be a tendency to grumble, pout or indulge in self-pity. It is of little avail to curse Dr. Oppenheimer for the bomb he built, which may one day blow up all the libraries harboring one's hard-wrought books. Take away the prospect of Immortality, yes, and you have robbed the writer of a helpful and fueling illusion.

As writers age and gain experience they are likely to find that accomplishing their work isn't as exhilarating as formerly. Some of the fun simply goes. This discovery need not be fatal if the writer pauses to recognize it as a normal progression; indeed, it may signal the arrival of a new and deeper professionalism. If unthinking or unwary, however, the writer may become careless or cynical enough to question not only his own talent or commitment but that of others who seem to be faring better. I suspect that Dr. Johnson, for all his accomplishments, may have uttered his crass creed on a day when his words wouldn't properly parade themselves and he had learned of some coveted honor freshly heaped upon a hated rival.

When I taught writing at Princeton, I found my students terribly contemptuous each time they discovered I had published a new article in *Cosmopolitan* or *New Times* or *Playboy*. Their inference, never concealed, was that I had sold out; that I didn't have the stuff to starve in some cold garret while waiting for my creative juices to boil over and produce at least a quart of bottled-in-bond Great Literature. They were right, to the extent that I never have believed poverty to assist Art, as the old myth insists. Show me a man who prefers to be tattered, hungry and wretched, on the theory these conditions will improve his performance, and I will show you a madman no matter his vocation.

I might have told my Princeton kids—but, being a kindly old gent, did not—that perhaps my biggest "sellout" had been accomplished in taking $26,000 annually to teach writing to a bunch of young richies who likely would never become writers of any sort. I *did* tell them that almost to a person they did not belong in my class and, given a choice, should become dentists or train themselves to work in Daddy's bank. Though they did not then take warmly to such advice, I am unaware—with the exception of two students, each of whom has produced one book in the ensuing decade—that any of them has published anything or spent any meaningful energies or time trying; of the two who did publish, neither is primarily a writer: one is a psychologist and the other a lawyer dabbling in politics. Other ex-students I have heard from became Wall Street workers, State Department types, self-starting entrepreneurs, corporate lawyers and—sure enough—good burghers who took their places in established family businesses.

The point is not that those Princeton kids were not bright enough to write or that they somehow lacked character, but that they simply didn't *want* to write strongly enough to put up with the financial uncertainties, disappointments and rejections of a long apprenticeship when they had other, more immediate and surely easier options. What they did with their lives was predictable and probably the best for them. It was for those exact reasons, you see, that I long ago advised them—nay, implored them!—to vacate my classes and make room for some young man or young woman whose guts were on fire. Some kid, yes, who wanted to be the next Twain or the next Faulkner and wouldn't rest until he had taken a shot.

You would-be Thomas Wolfes and Gertrude Steins out there should understand one thing above all: likely you ain't gonna make no money as a writer. *Real* money, I mean. The kind of money that makes a mother clap hands when her progeny marries you, and that places one above traffic with common collection agencies. Some few of us get lucky and reap a bundle perhaps once in our careers; an even smaller and more elite group can depend on satisfactory water almost every time they dip in the well. When one of us does make a big score you may count on reading and hearing about it again and again. Though we may be ignored by the serious pucker-brows of academe, or attacked by the *New York Review of Books* for having polluted the literary creek, we are almost certain to be temporarily deified by *People, Women's Wear Daily, Entertainment Tonight* and the gossip columnists. That is why you have the illusion that members of the Writers Guild also belong to the Millionaires Club. But make no mistake: we are a distinct minority, if we have made big bucks, in this fascinating—if often frustrating—old word game.

What they do not tell you about are those hundreds or thousands of writers who earn so little at their chosen craft they qualify for welfare gratuities, or those many thousands more who find it necessary to work straight jobs and are forced to settle for writing as an avocation. I don't have any statistics to back up what I am about to allege, but here it is: I contend—in what may be loosely termed the Arts—that only artists who paint, toe dancers, and musicians too talented to play rock or punk show marginally higher rates of unemployment, and marginally lower average annual incomes, than their poor cousin the writer.

This fact won't make one whit of difference—and it shouldn't—to the writer, especially if young, who dares to dream and has that fire in the belly. This book is for that haunted soul; may the Good Lord at once bless and pity him, as I do. I hope these tales may somehow instruct, warn and entertain him—even if falling short of the truly inspirational.

Part One

REFLECTIONS OF
A FREE-LANCE
OLD WORDSMITH

Chapter One

STARTING OUT

*** One way or another—as working newspaperman, political ghost or free-lance opportunist—I have been writing for a living all of my adult life. Oh, periodically I have pretended to teach, dabbled in television or flirted fitfully with the lecture circuit; but those were temporary aberrations and sprang, indeed, from the fact that I first was a writer. Neither Princeton nor Duke would have welcomed me to their classrooms to instruct would-be scriveners had I not earned a writer's spurs out in the field, nor would lecture agents and network producers have beckoned.

Even as I met classes, eyed cameras or droned for pay from podiums, my heart and my head remained at the typewriter. Writing was all I ever truly wanted to do. I never seriously thought of seeking honest toil. Should the wordsmith's trade somehow make me wealthy and famous and fulfilled, fine and dandy; even if it should not, I suspected, it offered more than the time clock and anonymous gray days marching in lockstep one behind the other nine-to-five or worse.

For more than twenty years, now, I have led the rum life (no guaranteed salary or pension, no comfortable perks, no automatic prestige in a social pecking order as might be granted a syndicated columnist or some noted drone from the *New York Times*) of the free lance: pounding away to produce magazine pieces, nonfiction books, novels, musical comedies, straight plays, a screenplay, television documentaries, book reviews, bad poetry and even—Lord help us—a few poor country-western songs mercifully known only to a handful of former barstool cronies. In short, I have written everything from hot checks (plural) to a hit musical comedy (singular) in an effort to stay ahead of the financial hounds and in the good cause of continuing to dodge conventional work. I have the smallest possible appreciation for bossmen, regular hours or heavy lifting; writing has permitted me largely to evade all three.

My late father, the hardest-working man I ever knew, died old and with precious little save the satisfaction of having surrendered a lifetime of sweat. As a dirt farmer, blacksmith, railway repairman, oilfield grunt, nightwatchman, dock loader, yardman, poultry plucker, cotton-gin hand, stump grubber and carpenter of sorts he gave his all, in causes that mystified me, so that others might prosper where he merely survived. Occasionally he lashed out in private at Wall Street or those rich, pus-gutted politicians "who don't give a shit for the little man"; otherwise, he kept his fires well banked. No leader of revolutions ruled the itinerant houses where I grew up. Indeed, my father so fully subscribed to the work ethic that he took what I thought to be a perverse joy in arduous tasks and found moral fault with all who did not. Night after night, once he had washed off the day's grimes and odors, he settled down with his post-supper home-rolled cigarettes to relate the weight he had borne that day, or the amount of earth his shovel had moved, while decrying others on the job who had proved less dedicated to back-breaking toil. It was a litany that soon made me weary, and one I judged foolish even in the face of his obvious pride: who the hell knew, or cared, that he was Mr. Productivity behind the shovel or the forge or the jackhammer or the plow? "*I* do," the old man would snap, his eyes fiercely burning, at once angered and puzzled by such a question coming from his own bloodline.

I loved that old man, and in time would grudgingly respect the tenacity with which he clung to his outmoded values, though it required only a few of my youthful years in the cotton fields or the oil patch to grow a stubborn determination not to emulate him. The way I reckoned it, he had grubbed and grunted and toted enough in his hardscrabble life for the both of us. By personal inclination and by family history, I felt, at least one King was entitled to work indoors aided by thermostats, refreshing liquids and soft lights.

That alone, however, would not suffice: I wanted to keep no ledgers, clerk no store, wear no man's white collar. The only occupation ever to tempt me, other than becoming a writer, was that of the trial lawyer. I even went so far, while a young Capitol Hill aide in Washington, to talk officials of American University into admitting me to their law school—but never troubled to show up for registration, much less a single class; one of the reasons I became a writer, rather than a trial lawyer, was an impatience with the classroom and its routine, boring requirements: one who had dropped out of high school a year shy of a diploma, and who later quit college after suffering only slightly more than one semester of undergraduate joys, did not judge himself a good bet to survive three years of such ritualistic tediums as are guaranteed by law schools. Had I been able to simply declare myself a lawyer—as with self-ordained tent preachers—and go out into the legal world ranting and raving my special point of view, then civilization might have been spared *The Best Little Whorehouse in Texas* and given, instead, the gift of another windy ambulance chaser.

My mother hoped I would be a minister of the Gospel. She could not get enough of church, of hymns, of scriptures committed to memory and recited by rote; my earliest memories include waking each morning to her singing of pie-in-the-sky hymns—promising streets of gold and some vague billowy smothering eternal bliss—while she baked biscuits, fried ham, or stirred gravy. She taught me to read long before school age, so that I might better appreciate the Bible and gain a running jump on other young saints slated for a life of service in the cause of Jesus. She would sit and rock contentedly, quilting or shelling peas or churning butter, while my four-year-old voice attempted to ring the rafters of our unpainted old farmhouse in preaching hellfire-and-damnation sermons against pig thieves, those who took the Lord's name in vain or other crimes my young imagination could conceive. When baby chicks died or rats were murdered in traps or by poisons placed in and about our rude plank house, I was encouraged to give them individual Christian burials with scriptural quotations and prayers. Mother saw it as practice for the future. I got into the spirit of the thing by constructing a little dead critters' cemetery complete with individual rocks or twig crosses for headstones. Billy Graham must shudder to realize how close he came to serious competition.

My father never outgrew his disappointment at having been denied a minister's license by the Methodist hierarchy, at the age of seventeen, on the grounds that his third-grade education constituted insufficient training. In my youth he served as a lay preacher, sporadically filling pulpits in backwoods churches or conducting summertime brush-arbor revivals where old ladies talked in tongues and sinners wailed for forgiveness at the mourners' bench or rolled and writhed like mad snakes in the dusty red-dirt aisles. These excesses—which both frightened and repelled me—combined with the well-meaning, foul-breathed old women who circled up and attempted to persuade me with embarrassing tears, prayers and tugs on my overalls to make a public profession for Jesus Christ effectively sabotaged Mother's efforts to turn me into a man of the cloth. Early on I developed an active, if unspoken, distaste for the short-fused, high-tempered, vengeful Old Testament God who seemed to delight in catching folks out and then tossing the erring into lakes of fire. By the time I reached puberty I could be driven to church only by shouts and main force. Soon after, I developed a preference for barstool beer over sacramental grape juice; after that, heaven had to search elsewhere for its missionaries.

I had earlier discovered, too, that I much preferred the writings of one Samuel Clemens (*The Adventures of Tom Sawyer* and *The Prince and the Pauper* did the trick) to the jottings of Matthew, Mark, Luke or John. Soon I was trying to imitate Mr. Twain and just about any other author whose books I could find in the tiny school library. Visiting cousins, or neighboring farmers ambushed in their fields, shifted uncertainly while I doggedly read them my dispatches in the shade of our farmhouse or under the broiling Texas sun: alleged short stories; harangues proving that any number of white men could whip the black heavyweight champion, Joe Louis; arguments for yet another reelection of the sainted Franklin D. Roosevelt; formless yarns drawn from Dick Tracy or Buck Rogers or whatever inspirational source had recently fallen under my eyes.

Sam Yeager, a kindly old soul who published the weekly *Putnam News*, permitted me to hang about his cluttered little shop when I could avoid farm chores. When I was seven or eight he published my first work—an alleged poem, "The Indian Squaw"—and my young heart had trouble containing its bliss. When I was perhaps nine he said one day, "Lonnie, we just got a big rain. How about writing me a weather story?" I wanted to do that more than can be said even now, but how to go about it? Mr. Yeager advised me to hit the street and talk to farmers and ranchers, in town for Saturday socializing and shopping, to learn what effect the rain had upon their crops and grasslands. I sought out the khaki-clad ranchers and denim-overalled farmers in grocery stores, on the sidewalks and in the domino parlor behind Loren Everette's Ice House and came back to report, "They all said the rain done good." Mr. Yeager smiled and said that would do just fine, though I suspected my first effort somehow had fallen a tad short of prize-winning journalism.

In the absence of competition I became the undisputed poet laureate of my rural school; no holiday celebration was safe from my sketches, poems or stories, which I doggedly pushed to public airings on that little school's poor stage. Some schoolmates, less literarily inclined, engaged me in fisticuffs by way of taxing my Art and collecting on the time they had been forced to invest in suffering it; I now tardily thank them for having prepared me for the later darts of professional critics. Several times my creative urges spasmed out a hand-printed "newspaper," with four or five smudged carbon copies. When classmates or neighbors refused to buy or even rent them, I gave them away rather than lose readers.

Still, I could not crack the Big Time. The Big Time then was represented by a page each month in *Farm and Ranch* magazine, the only periodical to which my parents subscribed, and in which lucky youngsters might find their stories or poems published provided they were no more than eighteen years old and stuck to rural themes. The staggering reward for attaining such literary prominence was, I believe, $2; I wanted the money not only for the candy jawbreakers and Big Little Books it would buy, but also because I knew that selling an article or poem would elevate me to the status of Professional Writer. I wanted, too, the heady thrill of seeing my name in print and the adulation I was certain would follow from unattainable country princesses named Lena Ruth, Dorothy Fae and Thelma Lodene once word got around that I had achieved publication in the Big Time.

For three or four years I stuffed the mailbags at *Farm and Ranch* with essays on hog raising or the benefits of crop rotation—much of which had been cribbed from agricultural textbooks at school—or hot doggerel enthusing of those sunsets, woods or creeks indigenous to bucolic latitudes. As each new issue of the magazine arrived I ripped it open hastily to turn to the Young Contributor's Page—there to suffer fresh disappointment. Ultimately, it became my conviction the magazine was edited by men of such small literary judgments I no longer wished to be associated with them. It may be that I sent a letter of resignation.

All through high school and a brief flirtation with college, during three years in the Army and for five years as a reporter on small daily newspapers in New Mexico and Texas, I banged out short stories and mailed them to the major magazines of the day. Each story, I knew, had the potential to put me on a footing with Scott Fitzgerald and William Faulkner. Imagine my surprise when those stories bounced back as if attached to rubber bands. Not for what seemed eons did I receive more than curt, preprinted labels saying *Not suitable for Collier's* or *Sorry, not for Esquire.* When, finally, a *Saturday Evening Post* editor was kind enough to actually write a personal note indicating his interest in seeing my future stories, I buried the poor fool under such a paper avalanche he may have given up his trade. That's what I assumed at the time, anyway, since he neither bought my masterpieces nor felt the need ever again to encourage me. These early, persistent writing attempts constitute the only secret I ever managed to keep; I was sore afraid of ridicule, and so confessed to friends no more of my ill-received submissions than I did of chronic masturbation.

In high school I accomplished in the school paper, the *Bulldog*, a column I fancied full of sophisticated wit as well as occasional overwrought attacks upon the school administration for its failure to provide a jukebox for noon-hour dancing (though I, personally, danced not a step) or its rule against smoking on the school grounds. (I did smoke, though to fool my football coach my column claimed a highminded concern for the civil liberties of smokers other than myself). At a small Army base on Long Island I wrote sports and, again, a column I presumed to be outstanding for its humor; no weekly issue of that mimeographed little post "newspaper" was permitted to roll without my byline.

I landed my first "real" newspaper job in Hobbs, New Mexico, by lying. While hitchhiking through the little village of 10,000, I spotted a sign in the window of the decrepit offices of the *Hobbs Daily Flare* announcing the need for a "reporter-editor," and the notation flashed in my brain—*God wants me to have that job!* I repaired to a nearby mom 'n' pop café, where, with the aid of a couple of beers, I assisted the Lord's will by inventing a background as a former reporter for newspapers in Red Bank and Long Branch, New Jersey—publications I had only fleetingly glimpsed while fighting the Battle of Fort Monmouth. My presumption, in 1949, was that the New Mexico publisher would not telephone my alleged sources in distant New Jersey to check me out. Fortunately, she did not. Fired five months later for coming dangerously close in a front-page story to libeling a federal judge with whose legal decision I disagreed, I worked briefly as a telephone lineman until a fear of electricity and untimely seizures of acrophobia brought me down the pole for good and all; for a few months I was a maladroit counterman at my brother's drive-in restaurant, often sending out steak fingers to those who had ordered the shrimp basket and vice versa, until—fortunately for family relations—the sportswriter for my hometown newspaper was called back to military service to help the Air Force tie North Korea in a war. Bill Collyns, editor of the *Midland Reporter-Telegram*, hired me to replace Shorty Shelburne at a dazzling $55 per week before deducts. This was in September 1950, and I was twenty-one years old; a couple of years later I went to the *Odessa American*, after a brief fling in local radio.

I reveled in daily newspapering with its deadline excitements, the feeling of being "in" on events as they happened and, of course, the bonus of seeing my wonderful byline blinking from the page each day and knowing that *people were actually reading my stuff!* Once in a while in the barbershop, courthouse or some scruffy café some old Nestor might say, "That 'uz a purty good article you wrote yestiddy, boy," and the mild praise would fuel me for days. In retrospect, I believe I was fortunate to work for small dailies where young reporters had the opportunity to cover everything: city hall, murder trials, sports, labor disputes, oilwell fires, state and regional politics, the police beat with its hard-boiled cops and hard-nosed crooks. One learned—as David Halberstam would say of his youthful service on a small-town daily in Mississippi before going on to stardom with the *Nashville Tennessean* and the *New York Times*—that the same lies told in city hall or the police station by "official spokesmen" would later be repeated on a larger scale from the White House and the Pentagon.

I was also permitted to write feature stories on subjects largely of my own choosing and infrequently could wheedle an editor into allowing me to critique a community theater play or review a book— no small feat where armed robberies, spectacular car wrecks, vicious barroom killings or winning high school football teams excited more comment, both among editors and the reading public, than did the announcement of Pulitzer Prize winners. Though having day-to-day fun, I was not truly happy. No, I wanted to be a lordly Writer and not a mere reporter: I might have had trouble defining the difference, but I knew there was one.

I also developed the strange and revolutionary notion, for the time and place, that my labors should be rewarded with a living wage. Though within four years I had risen from the *Flare*'s $40 per week to the *American*'s $100 per week, that sum seemed insufficient as to both hours worked and how far the money would go. Like everyone who knows nothing of the harsh economic realities of the average writer's life, I was convinced that magazine writers—and particularly those who had graduated to the making of books—earned vast sums, kept Harvard-tooled accountants and perhaps were served by liveried footmen. After all, an observant lad could hardly pick up a newspaper or magazine without noting pictures of Hemingway tracking a pride of lions in far-off Africa, or reading of stupendous sums being paid by Hollywood to Budd Schulberg or by Broadway to Arthur Miller, or becoming aware that a young Virginian—William Styron—had freshly broken through the publishing barrier, was being heralded as the next Faulkner and even then was lounging over wine in Paris or Rome until he felt the urge to deliver a second *Lie Down in Darkness*. Dragging home each night from covering a tedious school-board meeting or the latest killer car crash, to my bare and ruined walk-up apartment on the desert's edge, or trying to stretch $3 and change to feed a wife and baby in the final twenty-four hours before yet another meager payday, I wondered at the inability of New York editors to see that I clearly belonged in the company of more-heralded men and fatter rewards. Here I was, stuck in the Texas boonies, discouraged and aging—going on *twenty-six*, for God's sake!—while getting nowhere fast.

Somehow I had to get East to call attention to myself! Surely then blinding scales would fall from the eyes of unseeing editors and publishers. They would recognize my special qualities on sight, stand me to drinks and offer contracts almost as soon as I had my bags unpacked.

But how to *get* to the mystic East? For several years I had cheekily written all newspapers in New York (starting with the august *Times*, then reluctantly going through all other, if inferior, Manhattan daily outlets before finally lowering my sights to include the

Brooklyn Eagle and the *Long Island Star-Journal*), shipping them my best byline clippings and confidently volunteering to become each newspaper's Star Reporter. Despite this dogged diligence, I had not so much as received the courtesy of a single response—leading to the conclusion that New York editors were perhaps incorrigibly prejudiced against ill-educated youngsters who could not spell well and who occasionally dangled a few participles or split the stray infinitive.

So how to get where the action was? I hooked up with a tall young cowboy-type state senator, J. T. Rutherford, and encouraged his ambition to run for the United States Congress. This was not out of character; I had been marginally involved in local and state political races since my father first took me to a political pie supper when I was about nine or ten, and I knew something of political trade-offs. My goal was to impress candidate Rutherford with my political sagacity, if any, in the hope of riding on his back from Texas to Washington.

Washington was not, I knew, a place where many books were published. But it was on the Eastern Seaboard and surely would provide more opportunities and helpful contacts than the desert village where I then vainly dreamed. Perhaps, after somehow being exposed to my clear, crisp prose, Senator Lyndon Johnson might pick up the phone to call Mr. McGraw or Mr. Hill or one of the Harper Brothers up there in New York and say, "You fellers missin' a bet in not signin' up this King kid to write y'all a batch of books. He's a can-do man." If my young mind then had not worked out the specifics, my instinct was that the closer I got to New York, then the closer I would be to becoming a concern to Old Man Hemingway and that young Norman Mailer guy who looked to be threatening for the title.

I crassly used my newsman's position to promote the candidacy of J. T. Rutherford. The *Odessa American* was so rabidly antigovernment it never had named a "political correspondent"; I convinced an unwary editor, who perhaps had shipped aboard excessive wet goods, to give me that job in addition to my other duties. Then I used it to see that Rutherford received more and better coverage in our pages than did his incumbent opponent. I wrote press releases for my candidate, then flattered or cajoled other media people into publishing or airing them. Purists may charge that I became a propagandist rather than a reporter. Guilty as Thomas Paine, your honor. I lost not a wink of sleep over the ethics of the thing: all was fair, I had heard, in love, war or politics; I took to that credo as unthinkingly as members of the Watergate Gang later would. An impossible objectivity has never been my forte.

Remarkably, my gambit paid off. Perhaps because J. T. Rutherford was the decided underdog to the veteran incumbent congressman, few rivals contested me for the coveted staff job. When he won a close election, the upset victor was kind enough to hire me.

I arrived in Washington in late 1954 ready for the main chance, certain I would spend much of my time pounding out novels soon to be advertised in the *Book-of-the-Month Club News*. There came a quick, rude awakening. My job required twelve-hour days Monday through Friday, a half-day or more on Saturday, some Sunday-afternoon conferences with my young, eager boss and endless tedious hours on the telephone with faceless bureaucrats and constituents. My reward was the kind of "passion for anonymity" FDR had recommended to his palace guard. My spear carrier's job required, in short, all the energy and concentration I could muster to assist in the unfamiliar processes of democracy. Once I had innocently imagined attending President Eisenhower's press conferences (where, I assumed, I would ask at least 20 percent of the questions), breaking bread with Senate Majority Leader LBJ, advising Speaker Sam Rayburn on policies both foreign and domestic, and, in general, taking over the town. In reality, my days were spent responding to the most mundane constituent requests and demands. I saw President Eisenhower only on television; it was months before I got close enough to Lyndon Johnson or Sam Rayburn to greet them without a megaphone.

Though the days dragged by, the years somehow sped—two, three, four. I had yet to find time to begin the first of what surely would prove to be a string of triumphant novels. Little personal satisfaction reposed in seeing my contributions to the weekly congressional newsletter published under the byline of another, or in hearing someone else utter the lines or paragraphs I had inserted in speeches. That was the way the game was played, I knew, but I chafed under the rules. My life could not be forever lived in shadows. Any writer who tells you that ego isn't a factor in his or her drive is not to be believed under oath.

I began anew seeking a big-city newspaper job. The editors of the *Washington Post, Washington Evening Star* and *Washington Daily News* proved exactly as interested in my services as had New York newspaper editors. I told myself, *To hell with 'em. I'm a novelist, not some little pissant nickel newspaperman.*

The problem was, nobody else knew I was a novelist. Those who didn't know included the many New York publishing-house editors who soon began receiving my unsolicited manuscripts—pounded out in the attic at night and on weekends, or in motel rooms catch-as-catch-can when political drudgeries called me back to Texas. I spent almost five years concocting two and one-half tortured, mutilated works of genius with only one instance of more than routine rejection.

An editor at what we shall call St. Vitus Press thought he saw possibilities in a novel of boyhood, *The Back of a Bear*, and rang me up. I was faint and tongue-tied at the prospect of actually speaking to a real-life New York Editor. Veddy British he sounded: *Could we praps meet for drinks, doya think, when I'm down Washington way in a fortnight?* We could, even should World War III intervene; it would require more than atomic bombs to prevent that meeting. I pored over a smudged carbon of my unrecognized masterpiece and saw visions of front-page reviews in the Sunday *New York Times*.

The New York Editor brought along his girlfriend; they bought me many drinks and accommodatingly laughed at my political yarns and Texas tales. Marvelous companions—but, as the night wore on, not a word of my wonderful manuscript. Not long before daybreak, I breathed deeply and brought the question to the floor. "Not to worry," the New York Editor said with a limp wave. My book was great. He loved it. All that remained was for a couple of other in-house editors to gorge themselves on its poetic beauty, and then the formality of a contract.

Naturally, such news was too good to keep. I told all my friends, many bewildered strangers in bars or at bus stops and—you may be sure—a few enemies with special relish. Weeks passed. No word. I fretted, couldn't sleep, drank heavily. I began to grow churlish when well-meaning souls asked the latest publishing development. Ultimately, I risked a call to New York. "Not to worry," the St. Vitus editor again assured: this colleague had been on vacation, that colleague had been visiting writers in Europe; any day, now, they would gather to grant Official Approval so that my contract might go in the mail.

The St. Vitus editor came to town three or four more times during subsequent months. Each time I entertained him just short of tap-dancing on tables. Near the end of the evening I would be told not to worry: the thing was practically in the bag. Each such visit renewed my hopes and brags; I began to look forward to them as does the alcoholic contemplating the day's first drink, for they allowed me to reassure myself, my friends and my enemies that Fame indeed was gaining on me—if not at a gallop, then most certainly at a determined walk.

One Saturday morning as I thumped a typewriter in my Washington home, the mailman called with a huge package from St. Vitus Press in Magic City. Appended to the package—which I thought to be the fattest contract in all history; hell, it was as thick as a *book*— was a letter. I ripped it open to read something like this:

> Dear Larry:
>   Sorry, but the majority here feel that *The Back of a Bear* is not a St. Vitus book. Know I was your good and willing advocate.
>   Cordially,
>   Amos Gotfodgett

or whatever the sorry fucker's name was. Ten months—*ten months!*— that fake-limey chickenshit had held my manuscript while building up my hopes the better to dash them in twenty-five words or less. To this day, dear Lord, I pray that man suffers much pain and is permitted to die oh-so-slowly. Amen.

Wellsir, I issued as strangled and wounded a bull-beller as any Artist ever has. I flang that rejected manuscript and the rejecting letter against the handiest wall, then stomped on 'em and spit on 'em and doubtless would have pissed on 'em had not my wife cried pitiable warnings about the future of her carpet. Next I gathered up all my manuscripts and all copies thereof—including the half-finished novel then in progress—and held in my backyard the goddamnedest book burning since Hitler first came to power. Oh yes, I ranted and raved and cursed and cried and got so drunk I blame near fell in the fire. Alarmed neighbors called their children in from play, and my weeping wife took our three tykes to saner and safer precincts. On waking with as morose a hangover as history records, I still faced the shame of having to tell my friends—*and, God, please please please keep it from my enemies*—that for one reason and another I had decided against winning the Pulitzer Prize that particular year.

That particular year was 1962. A year earlier, old friend William Brammer *(The Gay Place)* and new friend David Halberstam *(The Noblest Roman)* had their first novels published to good reviews. They, along with a veteran novelist I had met through Brammer, Warren Miller *(The Cool World; The Sleep of Reason; Flush Times)*, encouraged my literary efforts by kind words. I am afraid I abused friendship in hounding them for their trade secrets, following them around like a stray puppy, begging them to forward my unformed manuscripts to their editors and, in general, making a pest of myself. They loyally sent their publishing connections *The Back of a Bear* and a second novel (inspired by American "turncoat" GIs who had refused repatriation during the Korean War, a subject about which I knew absolutely nothing save what I had read in newspaper dispatches) fancifully titled *The Secret Music*.

Indeed, a temporary rupture in friendship with Bill Brammer had occurred when on the return of my Korean War manuscript from his publisher I found stapled to it Brammer's transmittal note (which I obviously had not been meant to see) apologizing to his editor for sending along such a confused work, but explaining that he had no choice because of my aggressive persistence. I didn't really mean it when I threatened to kill Brammer, though a few months later when the St. Vitus Press turndown occurred there was murder enough in my heart for all. To hell with the New York Literary Establishment and its damnable conspiracy against me! Never again would I put pen to paper, unless to write a suicide note. I kept that vow for almost a year, utilizing time previously reserved for writing to become better acquainted with whiskey.

All it took to break my vow was a single letter from another New York Editor, in the early fall of 1963. Bob Gutwillig of McGraw-Hill said he had been told by Warren Miller that I might be capable of publishable work; did I have anything he could see? I did not, but was not above lying about such a small matter. In a letter to Mr. Gutwillig I spun out a rough plot for a political novel, finding a title—*The One-Eyed Man*—by flipping through Bartlett's *Familiar Quotations*. I claimed to have been slaving on the nonexistent book for about eight months; after ninety days of polishing I would send along representative chapters. Very truly yours.

I then retired to my favorite whiskey haunts to await developments. Mr. Gutwillig's quick response, by telephone, got me off my barstool: "If you write the novel like you wrote the letter, both of us may become rich and famous. For God's sake, don't wait ninety days! Let me see your manuscript now!" One thing I know of flattery is that it almost always works. I played sick from the office for a week and accomplished one thirty-six-page chapter. At Bob Gutwillig's invitation, I flew the truncated manuscript to New York at the expense of Misters McGraw and Hill. I arrived a couple of days before my appointment, the better to drink my friend Warren Miller's booze and give him the opportunity to look over my lone chapter so that I might jump off the Empire State Building should he find it wanting beyond repair.

"I'm going to tell you the truth," Miller warned.

I insisted that was what I wanted to hear, though I doubtless would have preferred comfort to honesty should the two conflict. Warren Miller locked himself in his study while I made desperate chit-chat with his wife, Jimmy, and manufactured nervous acids to eat on my stomach lining. We soon heard laughter escaping the novelist's study.

"Is he supposed to laugh?" Jimmy asked, worried.

"Depends on what page he's on," I said, twitching nervously. I leaped for a fresh drink, then another. Then Miller burst out the door, grinning, and said to his wife, "Honey, it looks as if we have another Texas novelist on our hands."

Miller picked up the phone and told Bob Gutwillig, "I think you'd better see King right away. I've just read his stuff and I think he may be on to something." Gutwillig consented. I stood dazed and suspicious, thinking, *Something's wrong. This is happening too fast.* Miller stuffed me into my coat, shoved me into a taxi and said, "Come on, cheer up! You look like you're going to the dentist." Actually, I felt as if I might be walking into some hairy ambush. After all those years of rejection slips and unanswered letters, I couldn't believe the battle might be so easily won.

At McGraw-Hill, atop a pea-green building on West 42nd Street, with the city crouching hungry and open-jawed below, I exchanged stiff pleasantries with Bob Gutwillig and surrendered my thin little manuscript. He advised me to return in two hours. I found the handiest bar, full of loud, drunk Irishmen knocking back a series of "balls and shots"—jiggers of whiskey chased by tap beers—and killed time. My mind was simply a blank. I was afraid to think of success and couldn't bring myself to dwell on another failure.

I think I just gaped at Bob Gutwillig when he said, "I've read it, our editor-in-chief has read it, and we'd like to offer you a contract." There was more, but I don't remember anything of it until Gutwillig said, sounding wispy and distant to my ears, "This *is* a first novel, so the advance money can't be large. Will you accept fifteen hundred dollars?" I would have accepted $1.98, and it was all I could do not to say so. Within moments I had signed a contract without reading a blessed word of it, except the line where they named the money. Then I shook the hands of a few smiling strangers on the way out and soon found myself wandering in a fog several blocks from the McGraw-Hill offices.

I honestly can't say whether I skipped and sang, shouted to the skies like the average New York street derelict or trudged along like a zombie—though my impression is that my emotions were turning backflips and shooting off firecrackers. The first landmark I recognized was the St. Regis Hotel at 55th Street and Fifth Avenue. I had never been in the high-toned place, where I imagined folks ate fancy things like snails and eggs Benedict, but reminded myself this was a special occasion. So I repaired to the hotel bar for a celebratory Scotch or three, stared into space and grinned awhile, stared into space and giggled awhile, and finally shed a few quiet, therapeutic tears while the bartender studied me out of the corner of his eye. Then I rushed to telephone the good news to Warren Miller, family, and perhaps no more than seventeen friends. After that I got as satisfyingly drunk as I ever had. Let those who cherish trivia note that it was late September 1963. I was thirty-four years old; counting my boyhood *Farm and Ranch* efforts, I had required only twenty-four years to make my first sale.

My assumption was that *The One-Eyed Man* would quickly jump me into the higher tax brackets and create the largest stir in literary circles since . . . well, maybe since Mark Twain tickled the nation's funnybone with his yarn of the celebrated jumping frog of Calaveras

County, or since Charles Dickens hacked out *A Christmas Carol* to satisfy creditors and instantly found himself the owner of a runaway classic. Styron had better move over a stool, if still hanging around those Paris and Rome bars, to make room for the new boy. It was perhaps better for Hemingway and Faulkner that they were no longer alive to suffer the inevitable comparisons between their work and mine. Mailer obviously was in big trouble for the rest of his life.

I window-shopped for my future Rolls-Royce, collected travel-agency folders on distant lands, priced diamonds and formed in my head the opening paragraphs of my acceptance speech in case they should wish the Pulitzer Prize on me. (The Nobel Prize for Litera-ture, I figured, would not come along for, say, five or six years, since it was rewarded for a *body* of work.) Now that I was a proven genius and so many people needed to hear my opinions on diverse matters, I found it necessary to spend more time in bars.

My work at the office deteriorated; I invested much time day-dreaming about when the Great American Novel would be pub-lished, and more time than was seemly working on it at my public servant's desk. Congressman Jim Wright of Texas, whose staff I joined following the defeat of Congressman Rutherford in 1962, was patient in the extreme; there came a day, however, when he felt compelled to quote Lincoln in suggesting that perhaps it was not altogether fitting and proper for me to write a novel during duty hours while accepting the taxpayers' money.

I had begun writing in the office because of an astounding discov-ery: I simply could not write at home at night or on weekends. All through those years when my manuscripts had been repeatedly re-jected, I had with mulelike diligence put in my hours at the type-writer—even, I later would realize, at the expense of spending only minimal time with my wife and children or worrying much about their needs or concerns. Each rejection, indeed, had seemed to spur me onward with a grimmer determination to prove the bastards wrong. But now that the dream was near, now that I had a contract, now that the world was waiting—however unknowingly—for my first published work, the words wouldn't come at the old time or place or pace. I stared at blank pages almost until blood popped out on my forehead or crumpled them into wadded balls after only a few ill-formed sentences, or, worse, avoided the typewriter altogether. Sixty days after signing with McGraw-Hill and getting my thrilling first check as a Professional Writer, I had not accomplished a half-dozen pages more—and feared that I might never. Though I pep-talked myself—*Dammit, Lawrence, just one measly page each night will give you 365 pages a year!*—next to nothing came of these inspirational orations.

This was disconcerting to one who had thought of himself as a rapid and energetic writer and who, in the first blush of his initial sale, had been confident that soaring flights of Inspiration would arrive as regularly as scheduled airlines and in record time bear him on gifted wings to the conclusion of his masterpiece-in-progress. Indeed, when Bob Gutwillig had inquired on that magical day in New York how long I might require to finish *The One-Eyed Man*, I had innocently, and perhaps arrogantly, boasted, "A year, tops. Maybe sooner."

To this moment I am uncertain whether I couldn't write at home because I feared, deep down where the lights don't shine, that I was incapable of producing a "real" book, or because my marriage was moving toward a breakup I long had known was inevitable, or whether other, more complex dogs barked and roisted in my psyche. Strangely, I *could* write at the office—though at a snail's pace when compared to the past, and while having to keep a wary eye out against the sudden appearance of my long-suffering boss or some outraged citizen who might rip my manuscript to shreds in the name of a taxpayers' revolt. I began staying at the office past midnight, working long after others had sensibly gone home and the phones had fallen silent. Only small progress was made on the novel, however, and my nightly absences from hearthside—usually extended by an hour or two in the bars—so strained my tattered marriage that I quit home between the assassination of John F. Kennedy and the Christmas season.

I took a tiny efficiency apartment on Capitol Hill in a building famed as "Heartbreak Hotel" (it always seemed to be jammed with transient failed husbands), determined to shut out the painful present and live only through the pages of my novel. Night after night, fortified by a few postwork drinks, I came to that cheerless, impersonal room to face a typewriter I had begun to fear incapable of the smallest utterances. My personal life was in such disorder that concentration became impossible: I had fallen in love with another woman after relations had cooled with my wife, and I felt keen guilt for that and pure agony over the hurt and confusion of my three young children. Nor did my fellow tenants at Heartbreak Hotel, themselves going through similar turmoil, assist the creative processes. Almost to a man they drank heavily, cried in the neighborhood bar, fell down in the lobby, raised their voices at all hours in anger and petulance or grief while talking on the hallway phones to their estranged wives or children or divorce lawyers. Of camaraderie there was none; indeed, more hostility than civility existed. Fistfights and cursing matches broke out on the slightest provocation; I don't think anybody in that crazed home of the homeless went to bed before four in the morning. It was, simply, the most depressing place I had ever been, and must have come close to living in a house for the officially deranged. Guess how much work I got done.

In that dismal time Willie Morris was a bright light when he periodically came down to Washington from New York, on business for *Harper's* magazine, where he was a new, young, up-and-coming editor. Morris had quit his native Mississippi at age seventeen to attend the University of Texas in Austin and there gained prominence as the crusading editor of the campus newspaper, the *Daily Texan*; when UT officials ordered one of his firebrand editorials killed, Morris had caused not only statewide but nationwide attention to be paid to the act of censorship by publishing on the front page a long, wide blank space where the editorial had been slated. He had gone on to become a Rhodes Scholar at Oxford. After four years at New College (he later would write it had not been "new" since 1386) he had returned from England to become the live-wire editor, and a fine and sensitive writer in his own right, for Ronnie Dugger's *Texas Observer*. The *Observer* was then the only voice of dissent (constant) or reason (occasionally) to be found in my native state. Daily newspapers were willing, tame lackeys and partners of the rich ruling Establishment. Morris and Dugger in those early years made the *Observer*'s excellent reputation with the help of a small cadre of low-paid staffers and unpaid volunteers who had the guts, hearts and pizzazz to gore, torment, harass and question those know-nothing Fatcats and Dixiecrats who then ran Texas as their private grand duchy and the public be damned.

Though I long had known his good reputation in the journalism trade, I knew Willie Morris the man only slightly until he shifted to *Harper's* and began visiting Washington. We immediately hit it off like brothers. Willie was the first editor to suggest that I belonged in writing rather than politics, and for some time had told me—after hearing another of my political anecdotes or some outrageous tale of life among Texas rednecks—"Larry, you really ought to be *writing* that stuff." I would lament that I could not because of the necessary political discretions; Willie, in turn, would quote Faulkner's comment to the effect that the "Ode on a Grecian Urn" was worth any number of little old ladies. He celebrated with me on learning I had at long last received a book contract, and he commiserated as I found it increasingly difficult to bring that novel closer to its realization.

One raw damp night in the early spring of 1964, as we drank in the Filibuster Room of the Congressional Hotel, Willie Morris said, "Maybe you should consider quitting your job and turning to writing full-time." I had been considering exactly that. I had lost all interest in, indeed had grown to detest, the grinding political chores and errands I had been running for almost a decade; the brutal assassination of President John F. Kennedy had caused me to take a personal inventory and find my own life largely without purpose, meaning or direction. Here was Kennedy at forty-six: young, rich, handsome and dead. But at least he had attained what he had gone after and had known many career satisfactions. I realized that should I suddenly come to some untimely demise, I would not have accomplished one dream or promise. Not only would I go out as a failure, but I would be remembered—if at all—as one who had lacked the courage to risk the full adventure of himself. Then freshly thirty-five, I felt much older and more used-up than I do these twenty years later.

Each time I thought of quitting to do my heart's bidding, however, the realities intruded. I had no money, save for a relatively small sum tied up in my government retirement fund; though my $17,000 annual salary did not provide much caviar or champagne, it *did* keep the wolf from the door and my kiddies in shoes and pizza. How would I support my children, or for that matter myself, should I abandon my paycheck? The $1,500 advance on my novel already had been spent in resettling my estranged wife and children in Texas, where our divorce lawyers were quibbling over the dividing of nickels and dimes.

"But if I stay with my job," I mourned that windy, rainy night to Willie Morris in that Capitol Hill bar, "I won't get a dollar ahead in the long run. That job is a dead end. I'll probably blow the novel, and for sure I'll go crazy." Willie said in that case, quit; don't keep doing what you know won't work. "I can't guarantee you much money if you write for me," he said, "or even that my *Harper's* bosses will like your stuff. But I think you can do it if you'll cut loose and try. Hell, it's for sure you won't if you don't try." Morris said he would do all he could to help me—edit articles I sent to him, push their sale on his superiors and talk me up for work assignments among editors at other publications.

For a week or two I debated whether to risk the gamble, coming down first on one side and then the other. One Monday morning in early May, I somehow came awake with my mind made up. I stared for a few moments at the chipped and soiled ceiling of my Heartbreak Hotel room and said aloud to the world, "Fuck it. I'm gone. As of today."

When I called Congressman Wright's office to tell his secretary, Kathy Mitchell, that I would be in late, she reminded me that our boss would be returning that night from a weekend in Fort Worth and expected me to drive him home from National Airport. I agreed, then went about packing my scant personal essentials—clothes, books, a few family photographs and personal mementos, my thin and neglected manuscript; the rest, consisting of Early Salvation Army furniture and a maladjusted old black-and-white television set that often whistled shrilly like a parrot, I would simply abandon in place.

I spent the rest of the morning on the telephone loosely arranging my immediate future. Willie Morris seemed startled that I had taken his advice so quickly, but rallied to suggest that as soon as settled I write an article for him on what it had been like being a faceless, powerless congressional assistant; assuming the article proved acceptable, he then would try to persuade his superiors to give me $500 for it; meanwhile, he would search his head for other suitable *Harper's* ideas.

My Austin cousin Lanvil Gilbert said I could stay with him and his wife, Glenda, until I had made more permanent arrangements. So far so good. But Bob Gutwillig at McGraw-Hill proved less than enthusiastic when I called New York to reveal my plans: "Goddammit, King, are you crazy? What will you live on? How will you feed your children? Do you know the odds against making a living as an unknown, *unpublished* writer?" I said I had no answers for his first three questions, and guessed maybe the odds against me might be oh, ten or fifteen to one. He snorted. "More like a goddamn million to one! Look, stick with your job until you finish *The One-Eyed Man*. If we like it, we'll give you a larger advance for a second novel. By then we should have a better notion of where you're going as a writer. But Jesus, you must be nuts to be doing this now!" I hung up for fear Mr. Gutwillig might talk me out of the silly thing I was bent on doing, but not before getting him to agree to make me a personal loan of $500 to be immediately mailed to my cousin's house in Austin.

Later in the day I cleared and cleaned my office desk of accumulated trivia, while staff members sneaked covert glances and whispered among themselves. Only to Kathy Mitchell did I confide that soon I would be a gone goose. Kathy was too ladylike to say it with her lips, though I fancied her eyes judged me more than moderately deranged.

Congressman Wright was at first mute and uncomprehending when I greeted him at National Airport with news of my desertion; he had to shove aside my boxed and lashed gear to find seating room in my car, and seemed not to believe my acute attack of foolhardiness. As I drove him to his Virginia home, Jim Wright made vague noises about whether I might be doing the proper thing. The more I insisted that I was, the less he insisted on my staying. In retrospect, I realize he became reconciled to the notion of my leaving with almost unbecoming speed and equanimity; presumably, between the airport and home, it dawned on him that I had been no great shakes as a hired hand for the past year anyway and would do little damage to himself, or to the Republic, by forcing Congress to stumble on without me. We had a couple of farewell drinks in his living room, shook hands, and wished each other luck. I appreciated then, and appreciate even more now, that Congressman Wright acted a gentleman about the whole sudden absurd process. He even said, "I think I know you, I think you're right, and I think you'll make it." Many, given the opportunity, would have called his bet.

My final leave-taking, before beginning the long midnight drive to Texas and a wobbly future, would not go as smoothly as had my unhitching from Jim Wright. I called on my ladylove, Rosemarie, hoping somehow to drop the brick gently. She did not, to put it charitably, take the news calmly. I could hardly stutter out my story and motivation (I had to get back to Texas to be near my children; I couldn't write my book in present circumstances; not one more day could I tote somebody's political water) for her tears, shouts and insults. Ultimately, she angrily ordered me out of her apartment and out of her life—which, when I later stopped to reflect on it, was what I had been trying to accomplish when she started all the commotion. As I morosely crawled into my packed car amid the clutter and debris—symbolic, I remember thinking, of my life—Rosemarie stuck her pretty head out a third-floor window and screamed: "You are crazy! Crazy! Crazy! Crazy!" That's what my tires seemed to hum across every paved mile on that long, lonely drive to Austin: *crazy, crazy, crazy, crazy.* . . .

Cousin Lanvil and wife Glenda lived in a rustic cottage with a big fireplace on the edge of East Austin; it was guarded by fine, big trees and wildflowers and was just off a country road appropriately named Blossom Lane. Though commodious, it was crowded; Glenda's recently divorced sister and her five-year-old son had repaired there for emergency shelter just before I had. I slept on a couch-bed in the kitchen, fighting for space with two senior house cats, Muff and Puff, who did not take kindly to an interloper stealing their private corner and using their favorite window ledge for his ashtrays and beer bottles. Each morning, when my relatives went to their jobs, I placed my junky old portable typewriter on their kitchen counter, straddled a tall stool and, surrounded by hostile cats, tried to make a book.

I began the article for *Harper's*, badgering Willie Morris by phone to make certain I was headed in the right direction. Warren Miller, who had just become book editor of *The Nation*, commissioned me to review a steady flow of books, and Ronnie Dugger solicited me for pieces for his *Texas Observer*. The money was criminally paltry— $40 per review from Miller, a zinging $15 per article from Dugger— and should have told me there was no way I could sustain myself and my children at the typewriter. Typically, I chose to ignore the facts and found myself elated in my work. "Small checks now, big checks later" was the way I looked at it. Thank God I didn't know the true odds against matters soon getting appreciably better; had I known, I might have made a decision to wear another man's yoke for the rest of my life. This would have guaranteed utter misery, a lifelong destructive rebelliousness, and—I truly believe—an ultimate act of suicide. But mine was the perfect case of ignorance begetting bliss. Though I always had read as widely and voraciously as time and conditions permitted, I knew nothing of the true mires and mucks of the literary world: its whimsical and sometimes cruel ebbs and flows of critical judgment, its capricious tricks of the marketplace, its helpful personal alliances or damaging cutting feuds, its chicken-shit little backbitings and generally stingy budgets, its desperate and cynical practitioners who had burned out along the way. I knew so little, in fact, as to be unable to truly imagine failure or even fear of failure. Hell, this was my chosen work! Let's *do* it!

Wrapped in my protective cloak of naiveté, secure in the armor of my simple country goddam dumbness, I figured the whole world was in my corner and cheering me on; should I keep pounding away, I was a certainty to muddle through until I reached that unmarked point where—somehow!—I would break through to rapidly outdistance the mediocre and leave the merely competent comfortably behind. Then it would be Star Time. *Hello there, Pulitzer. Nice to see you, Nobel.* I don't know if there is a Santa Claus, Virginia, but yes there certainly *is* a God; I know it, because He protected me from dangerous knowledge.

But my ignorance and optimism—combined with frequent entreaties by mail and by telephone from my children—led to a disastrous decision: to attempt a reconciliation with my wife. In deciding that since I had a promising writing career ahead I could handle anything, I forgot that you can't rekindle a fire from cold dead ashes. Impulsively, one morning, I agreed by telephone to drive from Austin to Midland and bring my family back with me. Even before I located a rented house marginally fit for them—borrowing $300 from Ronnie Dugger to swing it—I knew I had made a horrendous mistake, but I was too proud and too cowardly to recant. Going through with that charade was the most foolish decision I have ever made.

On the long, hot drive out to the West Texas desert to fetch my family I was glum and troubled; coming back, pulling a rented trailer full of furniture and household goods while my children and a small mutt frolicked in the car, I was painfully aware of crackling tensions; my wife and I attempted a desperate gaiety as false as a whore's kiss. We stopped for a picnic lunch beside the road in a remote, windblown part of that high, lonesome sagebrush country. As I watched my innocent children romp in a sandy field with their little dog—the sounds of laughter and shouts and joyous barking drifting back on the warm summer wind—I felt a weightier melancholy, a deeper sadness, than I had ever before known or ever want to know again. Jean and I had become two strangers, each alone, yet suffocatingly surrounded by the other; nothing shared.

We were broke. My wife originally couldn't find work in Austin, and I refused to seek it beyond my typewriter. We lived in a scruffy old house full of foul odors, armies of cockroaches and memories of too much sad, sorry, unrecallable history—and I was in love with someone who wasn't there. Tell me a more certain formula for failure. That wasted, desperate summer of '64 ended traumatically for all hands, reopening old wounds and slashing hurtful new ones.

Jean and the children, near summer's end, fled back to the West Texas desert and her divorce lawyer; I instructed my own lawyer to expedite matters. It soon was agreed that of the $6,000 in my retirement fund, all but $700 would go to my wife; I would pay $75 weekly for child support and agree to adjust it upward as my financial condition permitted; the debts we had mutually incurred, topping $16,000, would become mine alone to pay. So in my thirty-sixth year on earth I would start over with less than $1,000, no property, no job, no future pension, and badly in debt. Fine. All I wanted was out; to have done with the bad dream, and carve a new career.

Now that my plan to return to the land of my roots and settle into good work habits had gone kaput, I wanted nothing so much as to get away. Hide. Flee the past and all its baggage. My instinct was to head farther west, a latter-day pioneer following the wagonmasters of old, braving the frontier dangers of my day: exhaust fumes, neon villages, speed traps, concrete canyons, fast-food cafés, and— assuming one escaped poisoning in the latter—hitchhikers who might turn killer for the price of gumdrops. The West historically had always been America's jumping-off place, as far as one could run and yet retain a part of home, the place to pick up the pieces when the balloon went bust, the place where—although the sun sets there— Americans have traditionally seemed to seek their new dawns. My head and the tug of our migratory history told me to follow Horace Greeley's advice: *Go West, young man.*

But my heart urged me to retreat to the East and Rosemarie. We had covertly corresponded by phone and letter as my domestic situation worsened that terrible summer, and I knew I would be welcomed back. I made the drive from Austin to Washington on black coffee and amphetamines, never stopping to sleep. Rolling through the night while playing high-speed tag with huge lumbering trucks and listening to the twang and whine of country music on the car radio, I had ample time to brood on how little writing I had accomplished during the hectic summer: a couple of book reviews, a few political pieces for Dugger's *Observer*, a rough draft of perhaps half of the article for *Harper's*, and maybe forty pages more of my accursed novel.

Rosemarie, widowed young, had inherited a twenty-eight-foot powerboat—a Chris-Craft cabin cruiser—that would become my new home until cold weather. It was docked at Selby-on-the-Bay, near Annapolis. I moved aboard with my books, manuscripts and writing materials. This subtracted the cost of rent from my expenses and gave me a quiet place to work where—until the influx of weekend sailors—I might not sight a dozen people each week. I developed a schedule of writing in three- or four-day bursts, then working at odd jobs for a like number of days to keep myself in beer and cigarette money and to help toward the child support payments. Rosemarie, with a good-paying job as a Capitol Hill staffer, helped with my domestic obligations more than a little; we had decided by then to be married as soon as my divorce became final.

I looked forward to Friday nights when my lady would drive down from Washington and remain until dawn the following Monday. We sunned ourselves and took the *Prez* (named after a jazz musician admired by Rosemarie's late husband) out into Chesapeake Bay or up the twisting Severn River. We docked at waterfront joints for feasts of shrimp, crab and pizza washed down by cold beer. We tried our luck at the slot machines then to be found in almost every Maryland tavern, sought out places with jazz combos, drove through the lazy countryside, took walks on the beach or through the narrow, winding streets of old Annapolis. Sweet days.

I was content, too, during the week so long as I could remain at the typewriter. With seagulls screeching overhead and the bay waters slapping gently against the docked *Prez*, I tanned and slimmed as I wrote on short rations; the pages began to stack up. Those days when I found it necessary to perform mule work, however, I was less happy. I had not performed sustained hard labor in some fifteen years, and the sedentary life had left me ill equipped for rigors. My toughest job was installing and hand-screwing seats into the vast new football stadium rising up near the grounds of the United States

Naval Academy. One worked all day, under a broiling August sun, bent over like some acutely crippled arthritic; by the end of the work-day, that description was close to my true condition. The other grunts on the job, none older than twenty, called me Pops; sometimes when I couldn't keep the pace they covertly came to my aid, keeping a wary eye out for the tough, unlettered old redneck foreman who couldn't understand what I was doing there. "You seem to me like a eddicated man," he would say. "Why you got to do this here shit work?" Or, "I swear, you got hands soft as any girl. Why don'tcha git a job playing the pie-anna?" I parried his thrusts with fake good-natured laughter and sweated on in my coolie's crouch, silently curs-ing, while the old foreman regarded me suspiciously. I believe he had me figured as a white-collar criminal on the lam; some dangerous spy, perhaps, or a former bank functionary who had embezzled a bit too lightly to reach Brazil.

Each afternoon at workday's end, raging with thirst, I would race to the nearest beer joint and there spend half of my $20 earnings in an effort to slake it. When the football stadium job played out, I worked delivering produce to Annapolis markets from the flatbed of a gas-fumy old truck and, later, busboyed in a dank and dirty water-front café. One Saturday night in Annapolis as Rosemarie and I toured the taverns, I put a quarter in a slot machine and caused a merry silver avalanche: I had hit the jackpot for almost $260. We hugged and danced as if we had won the Irish Sweepstakes. By carefully husbanding the money, I didn't have to work at odd jobs anymore until cold weather forced me off the *Prez* and back to Washington.

I made the move in mid-November, assuming as I packed that I would be moving into Rosemarie's small apartment in Southwest Washington near the Potomac River waterfront and directly across the street from Arena Stage. But on the drive back to the city she was uncharacteristically silent, tense and preoccupied; as the Capi-tol's dome came into view, my lady blurted that she had rented me a room in an old hotel at the foot of Capitol Hill. I was baffled, stunned and angry and demanded to know why. She offered a variety of rea-sons, none of which I liked.

(1) She didn't want her Washington-area relatives to know she was serious about anyone so recently after the death of her husband. *Goddammit, Rosie, that's been two years!* (2) Her boss, a straitlaced Midwestern Republican, would be sure to frown on any unconven-

tional living arrangement. *Well, goddammit, don't tell him! He doesn't come around making door-to-door inspections of his employees' homes, does he?* (3) There was her landlord and the people in her building: she didn't want them to think her a person of loose habits. *Oh, Jesus Christ! When I've stayed over at your place before, do you think they thought you'd called in an all-night plumber or that I was your cousin?* (4) Her place was too small for two people. *Oh, I see! It appears to be shrinking? It's smaller than when I stayed there a week before going to the boat, right?* (5) She didn't think my young children should know their father was living, unmarried, with a woman. *How will they find out? I'm not gonna tell 'em! It'll just be the latest in a series of changes of address to them. Besides, we'll be married in a matter of weeks.* (6) Well, there was this, too: she was not exactly certain she wanted to be tied down just yet. She wanted to retain her freedom, didn't want to be fenced in. (This accompanied by a nervous drumming of her fingers, and no eye contact.) *Goddammit, baby, have you been jacking around on me while I've been stuck in isolation down in the goddam Maryland boonies?*

Well, no. Not exactly.

What the blankety-blank double-cussword fornicating hell do you mean, "Not exactly"? Either you did or you didn't!

Well, maybe she'd had a few, you know, casual dinner dates. They hadn't really meant anything.

Then why all the goddam secrecy? Why haven't you told me?

She just had.

Don't be a damn smartass with me, Rosie! Dammit, who are these "casual dinner date" bastards who don't "mean anything"?

She didn't think I knew him.

Him? Him! What do you mean, "him"? Just one guy you're telling me? Oh, this is real sweet, Rosie! This is peachy! This is really wonderful goddam news! I'll kill the fucker! How long have you been seeing the half-faggot probably Republican son of a bitch?

When she snapped, "Since you deserted me on about two minutes' notice," she started a serious quarrel.

I unloaded my gear in front of the dreary old Dodge House hostelry, ranting and cussing and grumbling. As the last ragged bundle hit the sidewalk Rosemarie suddenly sped away, burning rubber and leaving smoke. I ran along the sidewalk screaming, "Come back here, goddammit! That's *my* car!" It was, too, Rosie having been driven to the *Prez* for the weekend by her friend Ella Ward, and then having ridden back to the city with me.

One look at the Dodge House conveyed that if it had known grand days they must have occurred during the reign of the first Roosevelt. Bent old ladies and palsied old men huddled in the lobby on worn stuffed couches and soiled chairs as if for warmth, cupping their ears or turning up their hearing devices as they shared memories of attending first grade with Andrew Jackson.

My room turned out to be a converted broom closet in the dark and dusty basement, one of a dozen such low-rent rabbit warrens. It was furnished with a single half-bed and a tiny scarred table hardly big enough for my portable typewriter. Period. I had to growl at management for three days before being awarded a rickety straight-backed chair. My single window afforded a view of a brick wall some fifteen feet away, and a number of overflowing trash cans where bums and derelicts gathered to warm themselves by impromptu fires and pass around their bottles of cheap wine or worse. I shared a bath with an aging, croopy pensioner who lived on the other side in a tiny cubicle a twin to my own. Through the thin plywood bathroom door I was treated each morning to the music of his lengthy ablutions accompanied by a deep rattling cough, the hawking and disposal of much mucus, and an astounding amount of sustained noisy flatulence; the old fellow's kidneys assured that I would wake several times each night to thrill anew to the gurgling and groaning of ancient plumbing. I shortly yearned to be back once again amid the happy conveniences of Heartbreak Hotel. Years later, I would learn that the young Lyndon B. Johnson, as a fresh-off-the-farm congressional aide in 1931, had lived in one of those Dodge House basement cubbyholes—perhaps even my own—but I doubt whether knowledge of that bit of historical trivia would have cheered me at the time of my occupancy.

The one thing I liked about my dim, dank dungeon was its price: $75 per month. Money, or the lack of it, was becoming a critical problem. I practiced economy by buying milk, orange juice, cheese and lunch meats, which I placed on the ledge outside my single window and allowed the winter air to refrigerate. I had to remain alert, however, as hungry winos waking from their naps in the alley soon discovered where to find breakfast. Often I would look up from a slow-forming page of *The One-Eyed Man* to see one or more derelicts creeping up on my store of foodstuffs, and would raise my window to threaten them, poking at them with a broom handle. They would retreat with sullen mutters and sit like vultures across the alley, awaiting my mind's flight back to the pages of my book, then try their luck again. Between the bums and the raids of neighborhood pigeons, I rarely could accomplish more than a half-dozen paragraphs before again having to take up the broom handle. One day a big, bold rat—spitting and persisting when I lunged at it with my trusty weapon—made off with half my cheese supply; thereafter, I gave up trying to keep food on the window ledge.

I lived for those noon hours when Rosemarie came down from Capitol Hill bearing gifts of cold beer and delicious sandwiches—roast beef and cheese, meatball, Italian subs—with side feasts of pickles, cole slaw and potato salad. We had reached an accommodation, of sorts, after our battle on the day I had reluctantly moved into the Dodge House. Yes, I said during our subsequent negotiations, I could understand her reluctance to be tied down; indeed, I felt something of that reluctance in my own right. Perhaps we should *each* date other people. I saw her brown eyes widen in surprise, and could hardly suppress a grin: my new tactic showed promise of working. I was careful to date three or four women chosen largely because I knew my ladylove did not care much for them, and as an added spur took care to escort them to places where I figured to encounter Rosemarie and her own dinner dates. Once I knew Rosie was very much aware of my presence, and that I was not dining alone, I danced great attendance on my dates—complete with warm glances, intimate gestures and rapid departures, as if we might have better things to do in a more private place. Though this tactic of courtship seriously depleted my limited finances, only a half-dozen such encounters were required before Rosemarie sued for peace: thereafter, it was agreed, my true love and I would have eyes only for each other. Soon I was spending more leisure hours in Rosemarie's apartment than in my Dodge House quarters, though she insisted that for appearance' sake I should be gone before dawn. Many a morning I groaned at the jangle of the five o'clock alarm and sleepily made my way back to the Dodge House in shivering weather. The process had the virtue of getting me to the typewriter early, however, and my manuscript grew apace.

In early fall I had completed the *Harper's* article; Willie Morris worked his editing magic on it. He was unable to convince his editor-in-chief, Jack Fischer, to pay the promised $500, however. Mr. Fischer, an old Oklahoma and Texas newsman who had never gotten over the Great Depression, figured that writers should be grateful to appear in his magazine for nickels and dimes; he wanted to offer me $250. Willie hectored and bargained until the price got to $400, with Fischer finally and reluctantly agreeing. (Though Mr. Fischer was flattering about my early work, there was no end to his parsimony. Once he asked me to fly to New York from Washington to discuss a writing assignment. He took me to a rundown old restaurant in the East 30s where the prices were cheap and the food reflected it. When the bill came he carefully added it, quibbled with the waiter over fifteen cents, wrote in a small tip and then—after more pencil work—said to me, peering over his glasses, "Your share will be eight thirty-two." Since it is normal for editors to pay for lunch when they confer with writers, I laughed at his little joke. But Mr. Fischer was not joking; I had to come up with my share. Perhaps it was my punishment for refusing the writing assignment he had offered: "We'll pay four hundred dollars plus a hundred toward your airline ticket," he had said of a story that would require my going to Texas. "Christ, Mr. Fischer," I had answered, "my round-trip ticket would cost more than that! What am I supposed to do when I get there, live in an open field and eat bush berries?" Mr. Fischer's lips pursed as if he had just sampled a green persimmon and he said, shortly, that that was his best offer. I declined it. Later, when I billed *Harper's* for my expenses to New York for that discussion, Jack Fischer refused to pay because I had rejected the assignment. Only with Willie Morris going to bat for me once again was the expense money extracted.

I literally was down to pocket change by the time Willie got approval of the $400 payment for that first *Harper's* piece, and despite working occasional odd jobs—unloading boxes and crates for a large department store, delivery "boy" for a messenger service, pinch-hit night counterman for a chain of cheap hamburger joints—could not keep pace with my child support obligations or the monthly note on my 1962 racy red-and-white coupé hardtop. Rosemarie for a time assumed the full burden of my child support payments. One night I realized I had to surrender my car to the bank holding mortgage papers on it: a repossession expert had been nosing around Capitol

Hill trying to find me or, better still, my car. Rosie trailed me in her car while I drove to the bank's deserted parking lot around midnight, abandoned my car and left a note on the windshield saying the financiers were welcome to it. I was careful not to leave a clue as to where I might be contacted for fear a Conspiracy of Merchants might result in my being hounded by everyone from a dairy company to department stores to a furrier, all looking to collect their share of more than $16,000; three years or more would be required to retire those debts.

Another struggling, impecunious writer, an old Texas friend, Jay Milner, then was wrestling with his own Muse in a sorry hotel a few blocks from the Dodge House. Jay's digs were so scabby that when I stayed at Rosemarie's place or traveled to New York, he temporarily moved into my more "posh" quarters.

Milner was the author of a novel, *Incident at Ashton*, published in 1961; like most first novels, it had been received with great critical indifference and matching sales. He was attempting to craft a second novel. A former reporter and editor for the *New York Herald Tribune* and for Hodding Carter's *Delta Democrat-Times* in Mississippi, Jay also had suffered a recent divorce and was living hand-to-mouth while chasing his writer's dream. His only earnings came from writing occasional feature articles and political pieces for the *Fort Worth Star-Telegram*, which paid in small coin. We gave each other such aid and comfort as two broke writers could. Rosemarie often invited Jay to join us in her apartment for a home-cooked meal, and occasionally treated her two impoverished aspiring Artists to a night on the town.

One night as we drank wine in Rosemarie's apartment, Jay gloomed that he was $300 in arrears to his innkeeper and didn't know where the urgent sum might be found. He had been ordering his meals and cigarettes from room service, for fear that should he go into the lobby or the adjoining restaurant he might fall under the eye of the hotel manager and be dunned for his debt. "He caught me today," Jay sighed, "and demanded his money. I told him I'm expecting a big check from my publisher by Thursday. I ain't, of course. I don't know what I'll do when Thursday comes." As one who was being hunted by more hostile folks than tried to track down John Dillinger, I could certainly empathize.

A day or so before Jay's fateful Thursday—the deadline to settle his bill—I dropped by his hotel to offer condolences and buy him a consolation beer. As I reached the top of the creaky stairs leading to Milner's digs, I heard an alarming amount of noise issuing from behind his door: cowboy whoops, tent-preacher screams, Rebel yells. I first thought the hotel manager was torturing Milner on the rack, but soon realized they were *happy* sounds. After much door-pounding on my part, Jay heard me; he ceased his wild whooping and opened up. The instant he recognized me he whooped again, grabbed me in a bear hug and danced me around his small room. Then he jumped about like a kangaroo, still whooping, waving a piece of paper that looked suspiciously like a check. I snatched it from Jay and saw with astonishment that it *was* a check: in Milner's favor, for the unheard-of sum of $1,200, from *Sports Illustrated*. Then I began whooping and dancing Jay around the room.

When we calmed down, Jay told an improbable yarn. "I had been asking for mail at the front desk a couple times each day lately," he said, "trying to reinforce my story that I was expecting a big check. Never was anything there, of course, but each time I would groan and complain and assure the manager or desk clerk that *surely* my check would arrive in the next mail." An hour before I happened by Jay's hotel room, the desk clerk had telephoned to tell Milner his long-awaited check had arrived. "Hell, I just *knew* he was trying to trick me," Jay laughed. "I figured they were getting me out of my room by a ruse, see, and then some flunky would padlock my door. So I stammered a little and finally told the clerk, 'Well, I'm working real well just now. I'll pick it up later.' "

A bit later, trying to sneak across the lobby to get cigarettes—his room-service privileges having been rescinded—and while wondering whether he should hastily pack and hope to slip out some unguarded back entrance, Milner was spotted by the alert hotel clerk. The clerk called Jay's name, waving an envelope with a window in it. Though Milner remained certain he was being victimized by an elaborate ruse, he felt he had no choice but to meet his fate. "I couldn't believe it when I saw the envelope *was* for me and *did* look like a check." He ripped it open to find a king's ransom: twelve hundred beautiful, unbelievable dollars. "The hardest thing I ever did," Milner said, "was control my urge to shout and scream like you just heard me doing."

The sudden gift from the gods requires explanation. Some months earlier, perhaps a year earlier, Milner had written a piece about his experiences as a high school football player in Texas and had submitted it to *Sports Illustrated*. Jay's football story in itself was as improbable as his receiving the *SI* check when he had: Milner and his young Lubbock High teammates had lost their first four games of the 1939 football season and then, following the sudden death of their coach, had vowed over his casket to go on to win the state championship—which they had miraculously done, earning a legendary spot in Texas schoolboy football history and the nickname the "Cinderella Kids."

As so often happens when a writer desperately needs quick money, the Cinderella Kids piece bounced back from *Sports Illustrated* editors with a request for rewrites; then it would be considered again. Jay rewrote the thing three or four times but couldn't satisfy the editors; his final rewrite had occurred so long ago he had all but forgotten about the piece and had concluded it never would be sold. Then, like the answer to a last-ditch prayer, came the surprise check when Jay needed it most. . . .

Jay grandly settled his hotel bill, treated Rosemarie and her broke-writer boyfriend to a fine dinner at the new Monocle restaurant, and then handled his remaining $800 as judiciously as I might have: he flew to New York, put up in the swank Plaza Hotel, squired a beautiful lady about Manhattan for three days and nights, tipped lavishly . . . and returned to his dismal Washington digs with a total of $12 and change. You can't beat Class.

Days later, on borrowed money, Milner bought an airline ticket to Texas to take a newspaper job. Rosemarie invited him for dinner his last night in town and gave him a milk bottle full of pennies amid much merriment about Jay's having gone from rags to riches to rags again in less than a week. The pennies amounted to enough cigarette, beer and hamburger money to see Jay to Texas and a fresh start. He went on to report, columnize and edit for newspapers in Fort Worth, Lufkin and Dallas; he founded a country-music magazine, free-lanced for other magazines, anchored a PBS-TV news program, served as a promotional and idea man for singer Willie Nelson (and just look where Willie Nelson is now!) and became a truly outstanding journalism teacher at Texas Christian and Southern Methodist universities. It is such camaraderie as I shared with Jay Milner in the lean, hard-scratching days that I miss, and find increasingly precious, as an older and fatter fellow.

By early 1965 I had accomplished two-thirds of my own novel; I had sold another piece to *Harper's* for a fresh $400 (Jack Fischer still holding the line against ruinous inflation); one each to *The Progressive* for $125 and to *The New Republic* for $150; a number of book reviews to *The Nation* and articles to the *Texas Observer* for their minor sums. I also had written, edited, designed and laid out the first few issues of an ill-fated monthly magazine, *Capitol Hill;* for this, I believe I received a total of $300 and the promise of 10 percent of future profits, of which there proved to be none. On January 20, 1965, I worked a twelve-hour day for CBS Radio, standing in the cold on Capitol Hill and periodically telephoning in my observations of Lyndon Johnson's inauguration and the attendant parade. For this, the rich network paid a princely $50. All told, my writing earnings in my first year—including the $1,500 advance on my novel— had provided, as best I can reconstruct it, about $3,500 or less. Strangely, I was not discouraged. By God, I *could* sell my prose, I was proving it, and I felt it was a matter of just keeping on.

In mid-February 1965, Rosemarie Coumaris Kline and I were married in a ceremony we had ordered to contain just enough traditional words to satisfy the Commissioners of the District of Columbia and never mind about God. I practiced no religion; though Rosemarie had been raised in the Greek Orthodox faith she long since had left it. Indeed, we had intended to be married in chambers by a judge in a purely civil ceremony but discovered at the last moment no judge willing to don his working robes on the Saturday selected. A sympathetic legal secretary recommended a certain Reverend West, pastor of a small church I recall as being of some offshoot denomination far from the theological mainstream. I had settled the time, place and simple meat-and-potatoes ceremony with Reverend West by telephone.

My planning, however, reckoned without the fertile brain and mischievous instincts of my designated best man, lawyer Warren Burnett, who flew up from Texas. ("I helped you out of one marriage and I'm helping you into another," he said on arrival. "Now we are even.") Learning that I wished no religious rigmarole, Burnett secretly decided I must have all he could provide. Four of us—Ella Ward standing up for Rosemarie—drank champagne and vodka toasts in Rosie's apartment for the better part of Saturday morning, and then attempted to drive to our rendezvouz with destiny and Reverend West. I had lost the address of the minister who had agreed to the quick, painless ceremony, but I assured my bride I perfectly recalled it from memory. Following a certain amount of to-and-fro in a most unfashionable section of Southeast Washington, we stopped where I designated, knocked on the door of a modest house and in due course exchanged greetings with a smiling houselady who asked us in.

"Is the Reverend West here?" I inquired.

"No," the good lady said.

"Would you mind if we waited for him?"

"No. Please be seated." We sat in a small alcove off a pleasant living room, chatting about the cold weather and other inconsequentials. The lady excused herself and repaired to the rear of the house. We soon heard her making kitchen bustle.

After perhaps ten minutes Warren Burnett said, "I have a feeling our charming hostess may not even know the good Reverend West."

"Oh, horseshit," I said. "Why would she have permitted us to wait for him?"

"My feeling is strong and persistent," Burnett insisted. He visited the kitchen to there discover that our hostess indeed did not know Reverend West and therefore could not tell us when, or even if, he might somehow turn up. We departed in a flurry of giggles, puzzled then—and now—at the nice woman's conduct; after perhaps only forty minutes more of circling hither and yon we came upon a small, faded old church where a little man dressed in a shiny suit paraded nervously while intently peering at traffic.

My best man asked to use the restroom and with Reverend West as his guide was marched through the church basement, where—as Burnett later would tell it—reposed stacks of old shoes and old clothes the church had collected for rehabilitation for the community's poorest. I stood fidgeting in the church while Rosemarie retouched her makeup (Ella Ward flitting about helping her do it), remarking on the plain unpainted wooden benches so much like those I had suffered as a reluctant child of God in Texas. Soon my best man and the parson returned; we lined up in the empty church for the simple quick ceremony.

Reverend West opened with a long, pious prayer from a standing start. He next lectured at length on the holiness of matrimony. Then he ordered that we kneel; once we were so disadvantaged, he ripped off yet another wordy prayer: we were to be bountifully blessed with children raised firmly in the Faith, praythee, and so on and on and on. I was getting angry and began muttering that I wasn't a damn Catholic, what was all this kneeling about—my bride elbowing me and attempting to shush me—when I flashed a look at Warren Burnett and saw on his face a wide and happy grin.

My best man, while ostensibly gone to the restroom, had informed Reverend West that—while I might have ordered otherwise—my parents had insisted that he, Burnett, old family friend that he was, see to it that my marriage should be conducted with enough religious content to completely satisfy God and His entire heavenly court. "It would break his sweet old mother's heart should I have to tell her it happened otherwise," Burnett said piously, as he flashed a hundred-dollar bill before pressing it into the poor parson's hand. "I have given the dear old Christian soul my sworn word," my personal Judas unctuously purred on. "Surely God will bless you for carrying out that aging old angel's wish."

Say for the Reverend West that when he sold out he sold *out*. I had never before witnessed, and have not since witnessed, so long and pious a marriage ceremony or, short of a British coronation, so much kneeling and bowing and scraping. I am sure the good reverend would have tossed in much impressive Latin had he but known any.

Lack of money prevented a traveling honeymoon, though after a night in town and notifying Rosemarie's relatives of her fatal step the next morning, we repaired to the cold, docked *Prez* for the remainder of the weekend. There were traces of snow on the ground and icy fingers in the wind, but with the aid of a small portable heater and our love to keep us warm we managed quite satisfactorily.

Quite suddenly, one day, Bob Gutwillig flew in from New York with startling and frightening information: he was leaving McGraw-Hill for a bigger job with another publishing house, New American Library. And soon. I began wailing and wondering what would happen to me, certain that Gutwillig's change of houses would doom my novel; no one had told me that the editor who bought one's precious book might just *quit*, might walk off and leave it abandoned like an unwanted child to be ignored or cast out by some new . . . goddam wicked *step*-editor or something! Goddammit, he couldn't do this to me! *Sumbitch and shitfar!* And so on and so forth. Bob made a few soothing, clucking sounds of reassurance—though, I later would realize, not forcefully enough to calm my fears. Just when I was on the edge of hysterics, claiming I loved him more than life itself, and would throw myself in the Potomac although unable to swim a lick, Gutwillig cleared his throat and said, "Of course, there is a solution. It's up to you."

Whut? Dammit, *whut*?

"Well, you could go with me."

What the hell you mean?

"You could ask McGraw-Hill to release you from your contract. I can't ethically take your book with me. But *you* might be able to persuade McGraw-Hill that this being your first book and as you and I have developed a working relationship you depend on, and la-di-da and so forth, you'd come artistically unglued and all that song and dance. You know the number."

By God, I did! Hell, this was just like politics! But wait . . . what about the fifteen hundred bucks McGraw-Hill had in my novel?

"Well, naturally, at best they'd want that money back," Gutwillig said.

Shit, Bob, I ain't got $75!

"Arrangements can be made, if that's the only obstacle."

Like what?

"Well, my new publisher would give you fifteen hundred dollars. Then you would give the money to McGraw-Hill."

Wait a minute, Gutwillig. You said *at best* McGraw-Hill would want its money back. What *at worst* might happen?

"They could say, 'Sorry, you have a contract. Go shit in your hat.' Happens all the time. You may have to be very persistent, very forceful. If you want to go with me."

If I *want* to go with you? Look, Bob, it's a Ruth-and-Naomi deal!

Whither thou goest I goest also, and all that good stuff.

"I'll help you frame the letter," Gutwillig said. We shook hands, grinning.

Rosemarie, who'd looked on in silence, suddenly said, "Sweeten the pot?"

I stared at her in amazement. Why in hell was she butting in on the genius, career-saving deal I'd just made?

Gutwillig laughed. "I might be able to do that, provided Larry can get his release quickly."

How much? my bride asked.

Gutwillig said, oh, that would have to be negotiated. He was in no position to do that now, it wouldn't be proper, but maybe we could hope for another fresh, oh, two thousand bucks or so, should I promptly extricate myself. I sat stunned at this prospect of new riches, *found* money, money jumping off the ground into my pocket. In that moment, I think, I strongly suspected for the first time that I might truly need a literary agent to look after my interests in the market-place.

I told Gutwillig let's have a beer or three and draft that damn set-me-free letter. He smiled, opened his briefcase and produced "a few notes" he'd jotted down; they amounted to a first draft. The letter told how I was scared, brokenhearted, couldn't write or sleep or keep my food down, and might shoot myself if McGraw-Hill didn't do the honorable thing by giving me my freedom.

McGraw-Hill stalled for about six weeks upon receipt of my letter, then sent an emissary to Washington to attempt to persuade me to remain in place. I remained adamant, however, making it clear they would have an unhappy, loud and reluctant writer in their stable. Finally, grumbling a bit about loose ethics, McGraw-Hill pooh-bahs consented to my release. New American Library paid back the $1,500 advance and gave me an additional $3,500 in fresh money. I applied $1,000 to debts, sent a like amount to my children for clothes and still had more money remaining in my pocket than at any time since before I quit Congress.

Do not, please, go away thinking that my friend and editor, Bob Gutwillig, was guilty of sharp or unusual practices. What he did happens in the literary business all the time, has for years, and will be happening long after this book and its author have returned to ashes and dust. You'd be surprised, neighbors, how often the Literary Life imitates Real Life when money is on the line. Damn few people in publishing, politics or poker are in the game primarily to make friends.

Of course, about four years later, when I broke a contract with New American Library to switch to Viking, Bob Gutwillig wasn't half as pleased with the fit of the shoe. But, as they say, that's another story and shall be told in its turn. . . .

My published pieces had attracted the attention of other magazine editors, who began to solicit my work. The time had come to secure an agent. Editors buy writers as cheaply as they can; the writer needs a hard-nosed, experienced advocate who understands the worth of his work, subsidiary rights, contracts and other business mysteries.

I had asked Gutwillig, Willie Morris and such few writers as I knew to name the "three best" literary agents in New York. The names most frequently mentioned were Robert Lescher of Brandt and Brandt, Don Congdon of the William Morris Agency and an independent, Sterling Lord. I wrote each of them for an appointment, sending along copies of my published stuff and ideas for future work. A few days later, Rosemarie and I flew to New York.

Mr. Congdon seemed distant and preoccupied; he opened by reciting at great length what a busy man was he and how he never solicited clients; in general he made me feel the intruder or as if I had come to beg charity. I did not tarry long before crossing Mr. Congdon off my list. Bob Lescher and I hit it off over lunch. I found him down-to-earth, the type of fellow a country boy might quickly take to, and was on the verge of telling him he was hired—simply scratching off that Lord fellow—when Lescher volunteered, "I don't like your written humor much. Maybe humor isn't your thing." I was more than slightly taken aback; hell, I thought humor was my strongest point. I didn't have much to say after that, and rushed through dessert. (Years later I encountered Bob Lescher at a book party for one of his clients. He grinned and had the grace to say, "I've been dining out for years on the story of how I advised Larry L. King to avoid humor in his writing.")

Sterling Lord came from rural Iowa, despite having a rich name going for him at both ends. He was, however, as far from the hayseed as one might imagine. He ate in the flossy East Side restaurants and wore coats with fur or velvet collars, rakish Russian fur hats, ascots and the like; he had a ruddy face and a merry twinkle. I found him businesslike, yet friendly. After a forty-minute chat I left to join Rosemarie at our hotel and talk over the relative merits of Lord *v.* Lescher. I had little more than arrived before a telegram was delivered to my door: I HOPE THE VOTE GOES TO THE GENTLEMAN FROM IOWA. STERLING LORD. That impressed me. He wasn't too big to solicit my trade, and he had cleverly couched his bid in political terms while addressing a political animal. I figured if he could sell himself so well, he was probably capable of selling me. I picked up the telephone, called Sterling Lord and hired him.

Some weeks earlier, noting in the Washington newspapers that former middleweight boxing champion Sugar Ray Robinson would soon fight a nobody at old Uline Arena, I had decided it might be interesting to chronicle a former ring great now operating on his last legs. On impulse, I called the hotel where Robinson was reportedly staying and, passing myself off as a writer for *Sports Illustrated,* wormed my way into his camp. The deception didn't bother me; at least it wasn't against the law, as I had broken the law while a young Texas newsman in flashing a dime-store badge, representing myself as an FBI agent, in order to learn the identities of crooked sheriff's deputies who had been shaking down whores for money and sex.

I spent a week with Sugar Ray Robinson, his wife, Millie, his manager and a few remaining hangers-on; after he had decisioned somebody named Young Joe Walcott—a fighter of limited talents who, I had discovered, Sugar Ray was frequently beating up for money in different towns—I wrote the story and mailed it to my writer friend Edwin (Bud) Shrake at *Sports Illustrated.* I did not know he was in Mexico writing a novel; his secretary tossed it in the "slush pile," where repose great stacks of uninvited, unsolicited "over-the-transom" offerings. I had not queried the editors, or made other professional arrangements. Very, very few stories so submitted are purchased anywhere.

Shortly after I had hired Sterling Lord that day, Rosemarie suggested I call *Sports Illustrated* to see if anything had developed with my Robinson story. I was reluctant; by then I had concluded I had wasted my time and that *SI* would not be interested in the piece. How unprofessional to have mailed it in over the transom! But Rosie persisted, and hectoring wives often attain results.

After due confusion among *SI* operators about whom I might speak with, I was connected with the office of a senior editor, Ray Cave. "I've been trying to reach you in Washington for a couple of days," he said. I wondered briefly if it was to chew me out for having misrepresented myself to Robinson's camp as one of his staffers. "We rarely buy anything over the transom," he said—and I braced myself for the rejection—"but in this case we've got the right piece at the right time. We had talked at an editorial meeting about assigning someone to do a Sugar Ray Robinson piece and the next day or so yours came in. We like it, and we'd pay you one thousand dollars for it. Will that do?"

Would that *do*? Jesus, man, it was more than twice what Willie Morris had been able to tug from Jack Fischer for me on two occasions! I stammered that yes, $1,000 would do nicely.

Mr. Cave told me at what generous length he would run the piece and that it would be the issue's cover article. *My first cover article! Hot damn!*

I hung up, war-whooped, and danced a raindance with Rosie. "Call your new agent and tell him about it," she enthused. I did, feeling very proud of myself.

"Gee, Larry," Sterling Lord said when I had finished my brags, "I wish you'd had the man call me. I don't think that's enough money for a piece of that length. Especially for a cover piece. Would you mind if I call Ray Cave?" Well, uh, I guessed not; but I had sort of given my word I'd take $1,000. Not to worry—my new agent said—because Ray Cave was a pro and knew how these things worked. I shuffled around the hotel room, fretting that Mr. Cave might get his back up and cancel our deal.

Fifteen or twenty minutes later, Sterling Lord called to say that—sure enough—I would not be getting $1,000 after all. I would be getting $1,750. This bit of news immediately sold me on the agenting business. Rosemarie and I danced another happy jig, then grabbed our hats and hit the nearest bar to begin an all-night celebration.

I had begun to take to the New York literary scene. With Willie Morris as my guide, I had been steered to a new bar-restaurant—a long, narrow place near the intersection of 88th Street and Second Avenue, which I recall as then having sawdust on the floor—opened in 1963 by a lady named Elaine Kaufman. The proprietress was a friend of numerous writers, including George Plimpton, who had in-

troduced Willie Morris to her joint; Willie, in turn, took me in for
drinks one night, saying, "It's a writer's hangout. You'll meet guys
you've been reading for years." Sure enough, that first night I got
to chat with Plimpton, playwright Jack Richardson, the great Norman Mailer and other of my literary betters; my Texas pals at *Sports
Illustrated*, Dan Jenkins and Bud Shrake, soon became regulars.
Norman Podhoretz of *Commentary* (in that time when Pod still associated with commoners and did not yet suspect everybody of being
half-Communist) came in often, as did Pete Hamill, Jules Feiffer,
Tom Wicker, Jimmy Breslin, David Halberstam, Gay Talese, Tommy
Thompson and many others of the craft. My quick acceptance by
such writers astonished me and probably is accounted for by Willie's
credentials as a hot young editor at *Harper's*. Morris was careful,
always, to describe me as "a writer you'll be hearing about."

This was long before the Beautiful People had discovered Elaine's,
before one encountered there famous Broadway or Hollywood faces,
TV biggies or Madison Avenue ad men wearing on their arms
hungry-looking, hollow-cheeked young models. Elaine's then was more
a private club for working writers. One could pound the typewriter
all day, then stop by for a bite to eat and a few drinks to talk shop
or general bullshit, or play midnight poker with one's writing contemporaries. I learned early on to shy away from the poker game
should Jack Richardson be holding cards: Jack was a good gambler
with a gambler's instincts, knowledge of the odds, and flair, and the
rest of us were shoemakers. I grew fond of Elaine Kaufman in short
order. Despite her sometimes gruff exterior—especially with strangers
or anyone who pushed her—she had a true warm spot for writers
and spoiled us silly. As she prospered, her private loans and chari-
ties to out-at-elbows novelists or playwrights and down-at-heel journalists bordered on the legendary. Many a writer, proudly showing
visiting relatives or pals the town he allegedly was conquering, or
impressing a new girlfriend, might have had to settle for the Auto-
mat had he not reached a private understanding with Elaine.

I must admit the aging kid from Texas loved hobnobbing with the
New York literati, reveled in his membership at the three "family"
tables—reserved for Elaine's best writing buddies—and enjoyed the
occasional invitation to private bashes at Mailer's Brooklyn Heights
home, with its unparalleled view of the Manhattan skyline across the
river, or gathering at Plimpton's spacious digs on East 72nd Street.

Willie Morris and his bright and lovely wife, Celia, often hosted writers and editors in their apartment on the Upper West Side. I most enjoyed those small gatherings, where over leisurely dinner one might hear the witticisms and observations of the literary world as remarked by my writing betters. I was beginning a decade of what I look back on as the most exciting period of my professional life. I still had some innocence then; both mystery and promise awaited in the future: beckoning, smiling, inviting me to soar to impossible heights. I felt all I had to do was reach for the world and it would be mine. . . .

On an unseasonably blustery and cool May day in 1965, I wrote the concluding words of *The One-Eyed Man*, some twenty-one months after my original tappings. It had not come easily. I had sometimes been blocked, seemingly unable to complete one more paragraph, or got lost in the backroads of plot without a clue as to where next to go. In the late fall of 1964, Bob Gutwillig had virtually kidnapped me and had delivered me, under protest, to his country place outside Stonington, Connecticut, with curt orders to "pull yourself together and finish your goddam book." Abandoned during weekdays as Gutwillig worked in New York, I fought with his rawboned Swedish *au pair* girl, who bitched constantly about my cigarette smoke and the country-western music station I had discovered on the radio. Gutwillig each weekend brought to Connecticut a sprightly bunch of editors and their spouses, the old house ringing with merrymaking not helpful to a writer's concentration.

I had been kidnapped to Connecticut on short rations, and damn near starved. Not that the Gutwilligs prepared a stingy table. They specialized, however, in lobster, oysters, squid, smoked salmon and other saltwater inedibles; my code permitted the consumption of little grown in water save catfish, of which Connecticut seemed in short supply. Neither did I take to feasts of artichokes, asparagus, broccoli and cauliflower, which Gutwillig offered in monopoly portions; I pined for okra, collards, yams and red beans. After poking desultorily at my official meals, I repaired to my lonely third-floor digs and listened to my gut rumbles. Each evening, once the household had settled, I crept out to shiver my way by shank's mare the two miles to town and there fell with glad cries upon a single cheeseburger; I was then too broke to eat my fill. Unfortunately, the energy expended in walking back to *chez* Gutwillig left me hungrier than before. I wrote hardly a line, but slept and read the clock around.

Of course, with the natural perversity of writers, I would not admit to my editor that little work was being accomplished. When he inquired, I waved a thick clot of pages to show my progress. Only the top two or three pages constituted actual work; the others were as blank as when they came from the stationery store. When I refused to let my editor read what I had allegedly written, he became suspicious and found me out. His reaction was a cross between a heart attack, a running fit and a boiler exploding. Gutwillig returned me to New York in a sullen silence broken only by occasional diatribes about a whole month's having been wasted and passionate orations about the craziness of writers in general and his in particular. I flew home to Washington, where Rosemarie's earthy laugh greeted my tales of misadventures among the weird Yankee fish-eating tribe. Appropriately attended there, I sweated my book to conclusion by trial, error and much rewriting.

I went into a terrible depression on finishing *The One-Eyed Man.* Letting go of it seemed to leave me without purpose; I was restless, glum, irritable. I have since learned that a certain amount of those old postcreative glums are inevitable and normal. After one has lived with a writing project for months or years, finishing it brings one quick burst of elation and then that unnerving feeling of being at loose ends. A deep-blue funky melancholy soon follows.

I soon learned there was also a physiological reason for my morose catatonia and deep fatigue. For months I had been taking "diet pills," then easily available across the counter or loosely prescribed by many physicians. They were amphetamines or, in street jargon, plain old "speed." I honestly did not know that or the long-range consequences of popping speed; all I knew was the pills made work easier. Each morning, on waking, I would take a diet pill with my coffee; soon would come this incredible burst of energy. I wrote, fingers flying, hour after hour, while sipping beer. When my energies flagged, I simply popped another pill. Invariably, there came a time each day when I was too energized to stay at a desk and so I fled into bars or the streets, rattling to strangers like a machine gun. Sometimes they looked at me funny.

Each morning, however, I woke to increasing fatigue and depression. I remember saying to Rosie, "I feel as if I want to cry, but I don't know why." "Take a pill," she said. The magic pills, sure enough, quickly restored my energy; I kept repeating the cycle and increasing the dose. My weight, normally around 200, slipped to 170 and then below. I ignored food for days and then devoured great masses of pizza or fried shrimp or cheeseburgers—usually to find that my body quickly rejected them. So I would pop another pill.

Shortly after finishing my novel—gaunt and sleepless, alternately jangling with energy and totally fatigued, breaking out in ugly rashes—I consulted a physician. He discovered that I was on the verge of amphetamine poisoning. I was ordered to quit the pills cold turkey. The withdrawal symptoms included cold sweats, the shakes, dry mouth and tongue, leg pains and a fatigue so complete I hardly stirred. I stuck it out and kicked the amphetamine habit in about a month, though it would be weeks more before I felt anything like normal.

I began a new novel, *The God Business*, about a television evangelist with Elmer Gantry qualities; after a few weeks of struggle I saw it was going nowhere and scrapped it. I decided to concentrate on magazine work until I felt another book building. I took assignments from *Holiday*, *Harper's*, *True*, *Cosmopolitan* and *Saturday Evening Post*. Except for *Harper's*, where Jack Fischer continued to offer coolie wages, my work was fetching $1,000 to $2,500 per article as editors learned I would turn in good copy by deadline time; it helped to have an agent who knew the marketplace and what my work should bring in. I didn't get rich, but I took care of my obligations to my children and slowly chipped away at the debts I had inherited in my divorce settlement.

One morning the mail brought a letter from the personnel director of *Time* magazine, asking me to drop by to discuss doing work for his publication. On my next trip to New York I marched to the Time-Life Building at Sixth Avenue and 50th Street, letter in hand, and was directed by a crisp receptionist in the lobby to a room high in that steel-and-glass tower. There I found a roomful of well-scrubbed young men and women filling out long forms; before I could produce my letter from the personnel manager, a receptionist handed me such a form; it proved to be an application for employment. She began directing me to one of many cubicles where I could fill it out, and to tell me where next to take the application in the cattlelike process. I was insulted. Hell, here I was with a letter soliciting *me* and being treated as if I'd come in hat in hand fresh from a college campus. I flashed my letter quite haughtily, and demanded to see Mr. Jones or whatever his name was.

The receptionist ran off and came back with a nice lady of mature years, who took me into a little office and made chitchat. Where was Mr. Jones? I inquired. The lady excused herself. Ten or fifteen minutes later she returned with a gentleman—not Mr. Jones—who took me into another office, and *we* had a go at chitchat. After so long a time I said this was very pleasant, but didn't seem to be going anywhere: may I now, please, see Mr. Jones? The gentleman excused himself and departed the room. I had another fifteen minutes of solitude and the opportunity to wonder what in hell might be going on. Ultimately, the fellow returned and led me through many mazes and corridors to the office of Mr. Jones himself. There followed a great deal more chitchat. I began to feel I might be on *Candid Camera*. Finally I took a deep breath and said, "Look, Mr. Jones, you asked me to come see you about writing for you and here I am, but no one seems to want to talk about it. What's going on?"

Mr. Jones looked faintly agonized. He squirmed. "Well, this is a bit embarrassing. We've been mailing those letters for years to writers when their names turn up in other publications a certain number of times, and well, frankly, you're the first person who has responded. I've spent the past hour trying to find out what we had in mind when we began sending those letters. Nobody remembers."

I stared at Mr. Jones down to his bones. Then I began laughing. And laughing and laughing. Couldn't stop. The absurdity of it—my naiveté leading me to do in quick-step what no other writer apparently *ever* had troubled to do, *Time* having lost its memory of why it mailed out such random invitations—well, I was simply in hysterics and unable to control my mirth. Mr. Jones originally looked alarmed. As he began to consider the absurdities he, too, started chuckling, and the chuckling turned to chortles and then graduated to a belly laugh. Soon we were both wiping our eyes and trying to recover from merriment. When we were straight, Mr. Jones said, "I feel as if I owe you something. Do you have any suggestions? Anything in particular you'd like to do for us?"

"Sure," I said. "I'd like to review books, if the money's right."

"Fine. Let's go see Jess Birnbaum. He's our books editor."

Through the mazes and corridors we weaved, into an elevator and up to a still-higher floor, occasionally grinning and shaking our heads. Mr. Jones kept a straight face in relating to Mr. Birnbaum that he had written to inquire whether I might be interested in writing for *Time* and that I was disposed to review books.

Mr. Birnbaum, who claimed to have read some of my articles, thought something might be worked out. We soon agreed that I would be sent books on a regular basis and would receive $300 per review accepted: damn good money for the working time required. Mr. Birnbaum assigned me a John Hersey novel on the spot; I left the building with the book under my arm, happy the deal had worked out after its rocky beginning and musing on an old preachment of Coach Nooncaster, my high school football mentor: *You make your own breaks*.

Time's critics were not then permitted to sign their reviews, but I was more interested in the steady money flow. Soon Jess Birnbaum was sending me a book almost every week. I accomplished much of the work in hotel or motel rooms, while on other writing assignments, when I otherwise might have been ogling bad television. The convenient arrangement lasted about eighteen months before I managed to screw it up.

I had reviewed a football novel by Robert Daley, *Only a Game*, had liked it well enough and had said so. When my review of Daley's book appeared, I was in New York; returning to *Harper's* offices at 2 Park Avenue after a long lunch with Willie Morris, I bought a copy of *Time* at a newsstand. On reading my review I was astonished: though the words were largely my own, some anonymous pencil-and-paste man had switched the prose around and edited it so that instead of being mildly favorable to *Only a Game*, the review was distinctly unfavorable. This angered me. I got Jess Birnbaum on the line and gave him hell. He seemed puzzled by my reaction: my name wasn't signed to the review, so why did I care? If Willie and I hadn't so doggedly celebrated lunch that day, I might have been more articulate in my objections. Instead, I settled for some rather indiscriminate cussing.

Shortly after returning to Washington, I found a letter from Jess Birnbaum asking whether I would like to come aboard as a full-time

Time staffer. I scrawled a note declining the offer, saying I was content to review books under the present arrangement so long as anonymous *Time* editors didn't again turn my reviews around by 180 degrees. Two or three weeks passed and I received no books to review. When I called New York to check the situation, Mr. Birnbaum was not available. Soon I received a stiff note saying that *Time* had adopted a new policy: thereafter, no books would be assigned for review to other than "potential staffers"; since my recent note had removed me from that category, it had been nice knowing me.

I wrote Jess Birnbaum to say I didn't see the need for such bureaucratic bullshit: if he had been offended by my rebellion, why hadn't he dismissed me out of hand rather than indulge in the gamesmanship of our recent exchanges? To this Mr. Birnbaum sayeth not. I have not heard from him since, although I have often wondered whether that letter accounts for *Time*'s reviewing none of my own books until sixteen years had passed.

One night in October—less than eight months after we had been married—Rosemarie placed my hand on one of her breasts and said, "Feel that." My original instinct was to make a ribald joke; then I distinctly felt a small, hard lump. "My God, baby," I said, "how long has that been there?" Rosie shrugged, muttered, "For a while," and attempted to change the subject. I insisted she see her physician the next day. She did, and he immediately made her an appointment with a specialist.

I was at the typewriter when Rosie returned from that examination to say she would be undergoing exploratory surgery within the week. "There's definitely something there," she said. "They'll perform a biopsy to see if it's benign or . . ."

We assured each other everything would be fine; each of us, however, surely thought dark thoughts we left unuttered. "Get your hat," I said. "Let's go to Harrigan's and hear some jazz."

Harrigan's was a waterfront joint on the Potomac, only a couple of blocks from our apartment, where we often repaired for drinks, pizza and the music of a small jazz combo featuring several musicians who had played in bands with Rosie's late husband, Paul Kline. We did a little desperate merrymaking that night, talking loudly and cracking jokes, though I felt the dark cloud hovering, as I'm sure

Rosie did. As we left Harrigan's to walk home, she clutched my hand and said, simply, "King, I'm scared." I squeezed her hand but said nothing. What could I say? I was scared, too.

We had been told that a short operation—say, forty-five minutes to an hour—would signal good news. If, on the other hand, a malignancy should be found, then Rosie might be in the operating room as long as four hours. I gathered at Georgetown Hospital with Rosemarie's three brothers and three sisters and their spouses; the women told each other the odds would be much in favor of someone only thirty-five years old; the men smoked and paced. We had not told Rosie's siblings what a long stay in the operating room might portend. When more than an hour passed, I felt fearful. At the end of two hours, I strongly suspected the worst; after three hours, I knew in my heart that my young wife had cancer. I took a long, solitary walk around the hospital grounds, smoking, cursing and blinking back tears.

Not long after I returned to Rosemarie's waiting family, the operating surgeon called for me. He took one of my hands in both of his and said, "I'm sorry. It proved to be malignant. We had to perform a radical mastectomy."

I related the bad news to Rosemarie's relatives, the women sending up wails of grief and the men shuffling about uncertainly. As soon as Rosie had been removed to a recovery room, I visited her bedside.

She opened her eyes, looking frightened, and said, "What time is it?"

"You're going to be all right, baby," I said, my throat full and my chest bursting.

"What time is it?" she repeated.

"Don't worry about it," I said. "Try to rest."

It would develop that Rosie did not remember that conversation. Much later she awoke in great pain to discover what had happened to her. I held her in my arms while she sobbed and raged. I was worried about the image she might have of herself after disfiguring surgery: she was as physical a woman as I have ever known, one who put great stock in her appearance and took a great pride in it.

Rosemarie's physician shared my fear. "It might be good therapy to take her south for the sunshine," he said. "She often mentions that she would love to recuperate on the beach." I knew of no way to raise money for that purpose; Rosie's surgery and attendant medical costs, plus future treatments, would not all be covered by insurance; there were also my ongoing child support payments, old debts and daily living costs. I did the best I could to cheer Rosie, and she tried to show a happy countenance. But often, in unguarded moments, I would find her staring into space with a terrible sad expression in her eyes, and more than once I came upon her quietly weeping.

The One-Eyed Man was to have been published earlier in the fall, but when New York newspapers went out on strike my publisher decided to postpone publication: "There's no sense in bringing the book out in a vacuum." I argued that newspapers were published elsewhere, that we had television and radio for promotional purposes, but to no avail. My frustration ran deep. The delay, as it turned out, probably benefited me. For, quite tardily in the game, a major book club got interested in my novel. I was unaware until Sterling Lord called late one November afternoon and said, "Are you sitting down?" "No," I said. "Then sit down," my agent ordered. I did so, my mind flashing on dark thoughts: *What the hell else had gone wrong?* Then he said, "Literary Guild, the second largest of the book clubs, had just bought your novel as an alternate selection. You'll be getting ten thousand dollars in front money. Congratulations!"

Wellsir, I whooped and bellowed until possibly they heard me over in Baltimore.

My agent, knowing I needed it to aid my wife's recovery, said he would push to have the money in hand within thirty days. I spoke happy babble, hung up and telephoned the hospital where Rosie had been returned following complications from her surgery. "We're gonna take the whole damn wad and blow it wintering in Florida," I told my wife. Her glad cries indicated she had no problem with that notion. "Call some friends and celebrate," she said. "I will," I answered. "I wish you could be with us." I rounded up old pals from my days on Capitol Hill—Ralph Hutto, Fritz Kessinger, Bob Miller, Sid Yudain, a fledgling young comedian named Mark Russell—and we pub-crawled into the wee hours.

About a week before Christmas, with Rosemarie stronger, we packed our car and pointed it south. We went to Sarasota, on the Florida west coast, because—conveniently—New College there had just asked me to consider a teaching job. The job didn't pan out, but we loved Sarasota with its unhurried pace, white beaches and palm trees and decided to stay there rather than spend the winter in Miami. We took a small motel room until we located a glass house on Siesta Key, where Gulf waters lapped at our back door and we had our own private beach. I plunked down a handsome sum covering rent through April—more than four months—and we happily settled in.

Sarasota had its own colony of writers and artists; I had the temerity to telephone McKinley Kantor, who had won the Pulitzer Prize for his novel *Andersonville*, and introduce myself; he was kind enough to ask me to his home for drinks. Mack Kantor was at that stage a caustic-tongued old curmudgeon whose right-wing politics I found abominable; I grew fond of him despite that handicap. However, we got off to a bad start. When I reported to his spacious waterside home that first afternoon, Kantor greeted me with a glare and a short comment: "You're ten minutes early." Well, I said, I guess I could go drive around the block awhile. "No, no," he grumbled. "You've already interrupted me. Come on in." Had I not been so curious about the man who had written *Andersonville, Spirit Lake, Glory for Me* (made into the movie *The Best Years of Our Lives*) and fifty-odd other books, I might have departed in a huff. Instead, I entered to be led to a huge, well-appointed writing room with a view of water and palm trees where a large red-white-and-blue sign over a purely decorative fireplace instructed me to "Fuck Communism!"

While Mack Kantor poured drinks, I studied the framed dust jackets of his books covering the walls and fantasized of someday having my own rich digs full of career baubles and honors. When he returned with my Scotch, Kantor said, with an expression close to a sneer, "And I suppose *you* are one of those tortured and tormented young writers who go in for symbolism and find themselves the darling of the critics?" "No such fucking thing," I said. "I'm just a goddam storyteller like you, that's all." He laughed with delight; in that moment a friendship was born.

Mack Kantor was the dean of a sizable Sarasota writing colony; he headed up an informal club that lunched each Friday, from noon until dark at the Plaza Restaurant downtown. "I'll invite you to the luncheon once," he told me bluntly, "and then we'll secretly vote on whether we want you again. If I invite you a second time, you automatically become a member." It sounded a little high-handed, though I liked the challenge and the notion of a group bold enough to make its selections without fear.

The group included the best-selling author John D. MacDonald (best known for his Travis McGee private-eye series); Borden Deal (*The Tobacco Men, A Joyful Noise,* many others); David Weiss (novels, a Broadway play, screenplays); Joe Hayes *(The Desperate Hours)*; biographer Alden Hatch (he had just finished one on Mountbatten); historian Carl Corimer; folksinger-actor Burl Ives; several painters and old Nick Kenny, a retired New York newspaperman who wrote absolutely the sorriest poetry in the world and thought it the equal of Shakespeare. Those were the regulars, though almost every week one or more writers or artists passing through Sarasota would attend as guests.

The drinking was serious, the storytelling raucous and the bouts of liar's poker deadly and expensive. Survivors repaired after dark to the home of McKinley Kantor or Borden Deal to be joined by their ladies—including one novelist, Babs Deal *(The Grail; It's Always Three O'Clock)*—and partied into the wee hours. I rarely missed one of those late sessions. Kantor and Borden Deal played bad guitar; I soon became the group's most persistent soloist so long as the musical fare remained strictly country-western. During what was left of the tattered weekend—or during the week—those writers or artists who wished company flew large "drinking flags" outside their homes. In the absence of such a banner, each homesteader was to be left to work in peace until the Friday luncheon. By midweek I usually went cruising in the hope of spotting one or more welcoming flags; only a couple of the older fellows, and John D. MacDonald, failed to occasionally fly their flags during the week; I later concluded this perhaps had something to do with MacDonald and Kantor having published fifty-odd novels each to that point.

In the morning hours through the week, Rosie generally lolled at the water's edge while I wrote. After a lunch break we took a short drive or visited our private beach before I again returned to the typewriter. I was doing the book reviews for *Time* and several magazine pieces—one, for *True,* on a little-known congressman from Michigan named Gerald Ford; a *Harper's* piece on the gore and glory of World War II movies; others I no longer recall—while waiting to be smitten by a new notion for a second novel.

Bob Gutwillig flew in from New York, bringing galley proofs of *The One-Eyed Man*, so that we might cut out a huge hunk—I believe it was something like 25,000 words—in order to comply with the length desired by the Literary Guild Book Club. I found the cuts painful, as writers usually do, and screamed more than a little. Gutwillig kept assuring me the novel needed trimming anyhow, and reminded that I could ill afford to blow the book club deal. I grumbled, but acquiesced. New York was in the middle of an icy winter, complicated by a subway strike, and I'm afraid we took excess pleasure in watching the miseries of our Yankee friends on television while we took the sunshine, smoked grass, drank tropical concoctions and indulged ourselves in Sarasota restaurants.

A couple of incidents—call them misunderstandings, and blame my contributions to same on my inexperience in the trade—marred what was otherwise a fine season in the sun. Sometime in January, Sterling Lord called with exciting news: the Literary Guild soon would choose my book or another—*Indian Summer*, by John Knowles—to become the club's primary monthly selection rather than a mere alternate. The difference in front money was significant: $40,000 as opposed to $10,000, I believe. The final decision, Mr. Lord said, would be made by the Literary Guild board on the upcoming Friday. Elated, I gave my agent the telephone number of the restaurant where I would be dining with the Sarasota writers and artists. On the target day I chewed my knuckles the afternoon long and, naturally, foolishly told my companions of new high expectations. No call came in. I sweated and stewed through the weekend, but could not reach my agent for an explanation.

On Monday, Mr. Lord called to say the Literary Guild board had been unable to decide. The contest was still on; I should again stand by on the upcoming Friday. Again, on the target day, my innards ate on themselves. And, again, no decision was forthcoming. This frustrating, nerve-wracking scenario was played out a third week, possibly a fourth week—and, I believe, even a fifth. Perhaps it only seemed that long. When the decision finally came in, John Knowles and I both had lost. Unable to choose between our books, the Literary Guild folk had compromised and tossed the big money to Gwyn Griffin for *A Last Lamp Burning*.

Wellsir, I threw a shit fit. Not because of losing—I foolishly told myself and others—but because I had been dragged through worry, sweat and pain for nothing. Human nature being what it is, I had become dissatisfied with writing a mere book club alternate, where, before new riches had been dangled and my expectations raised, I had been content and proud. I yelled at Sterling Lord for having unnecessarily put me through tough times; his apology failed to appease, as did his defense: he had simply been eager to bring potential good news to a new client. I fired him by telephone. Bob Gutwillig soon called to say he thought I had made a mistake. At his behest, I patched up the quarrel and Mr. Lord resumed representing me.

Not long after that contretemps, an old Texas friend, Dan Blocker (best remembered as Hoss Cartwright of the *Bonanza* television series), got in touch to say Paramount Pictures was looking for a movie to star him; he was interested in *The One-Eyed Man:* would it be possible to get galley proofs before the book was released to the public? Sure, Dan, I'll see they go in the mail immediately. We chatted about the character Blocker was interested in playing, Governor Cullie Blanton, and I telephoned New York in great excitement.

To my astonishment, I found that neither my agent nor Bob Gutwillig agreed with my plan. I had overstepped my bounds—they said—in promising the galley proofs to Dan Blocker. They planned, at the proper time, to send galleys to any number of motion-picture companies, and they were reluctant to favor one over another. I found that dumb reasoning—then and now. If a big-name star is interested in your book, what can you lose by getting a copy in his or her hands at the earliest moment? Much yelling. I several times flatly ordered the galley proofs dispatched to Blocker, but my associates stalled and didn't comply.

The moment I laid hands on a copy of *The One-Eyed Man*—before its official release date, but long after I had wanted galleys sent—I mailed it to Dan Blocker. He responded enthusiastically after a quick reading, saying he had sent the book to John Huston, whom he hoped to persuade to direct the movie. After that, nothing. Nothing at all. I now know that much talk and little or no action by Hollywood folk is common when one publishes a book, but, alas, I did not then possess such wisdom. A bit later, Paul Newman and his people got all hot to star him as Cullie Blanton. There again was a brief flurry of excitement before contact was cut off as abruptly as if I suddenly had died. Hooray for Hollywood.

(Small-world department: a decade after the Blocker incident, my friend and TV newsman Sander Vanocur visited John Huston's home in Mexico. In the director's library he found a copy of *The One-Eyed Man*, autographed by me to Dan Blocker—who was by then tragically and prematurely dead. When Sander returned to New York, he inquired as to the chain of circumstances permitting Dan Blocker's personal copy of my book to end up in John Huston's library. Vanocur already had asked Mr. Huston, who, by that time, had absolutely no recollection or explanation and said he didn't believe he had ever read the book.)

Although I failed to come up with an idea for a second novel while wintering in Florida, I accomplished a bit of magazine work and had the satisfaction of seeing my wife's spirits rise as she tanned, rested and regained her infectious laugh. We were near to broke again when we headed north to Washington in late April, but I never for a moment regretted spending that book club money exactly as we had. Had I any way of then knowing the painful future awaiting Rosemarie, and how relatively short it would prove, I am certain I would have borrowed money to prolong our holiday in the sun—and the devil take the hindmost.

Chapter Two

LEARNING THE ROPES

*** Our hopes for my first book remained foolishly high as we re-settled in our Washington apartment, in late April, to await its June publication. Though I was cautious about predicting a runaway success to others, my secret parts counted on a surefire best-seller. And perhaps—a little voice whispered—just *perhaps* I might favorably astonish the critics. Rosemarie, who knew even less than did I of the literary realities, openly planned a new wardrobe, a big house, world travel and a large seagoing yacht. I alternated between ordering her and begging her not to publicly put out so many bright flags.

All the signs, as we privately read them, portended Great Things: the sale to the book club, Hollywood interest, optimistic predictions from Bob Gutwillig at New American Library and Irv Goodman at the Literary Guild. Generous prepublication quotes had been gathered from writers whom we didn't personally know—Richard Condon, Vance Bourjaily, Gerald Kersh, John Kenneth Galbraith—and who presumably, therefore, were speaking their true minds. High marks were given by the Virginia Kirkus reviewer ("Written with a social satirist's skill, *The One-Eyed Man* has our vote") and *Publishers Weekly* ("The writing is vivid, the insight into Southern politics is remarkable, and Governor Cullie Blanton is a great character"). *Library Journal* offered a cheer. All that left little room for doubt in the mind of a brash fellow who, by nature, perhaps excessively cherished himself. In retrospect, it's clear we set outselves up for a great fall; nothing short of *Gone With the Wind* sales figures, complemented by the sort of critical adulation Malcolm Cowley visited on Faulkner, could have satisfied our expectations.

In early May we motored up to Putnam County, New York—near

Hyde Park country—where Willie and Celia Morris had purchased a fine 130-year-old farmhouse of many rustic charms; it was perched on a hill overlooking a picture-book valley full of old barns, church spires and frequent misty hazes. The weekend had been billed as a "Southern Dogwood Party," Willie bragging that he owned the largest dogwood tree above the Mason-Dixon line; alas, the Yankee hills and trees still wore their skimpy winter coverings; of blooms there were none. We took up the slack by eating a purely Southern dinner: ham, black-eyed peas, candied yams, green salad, pecan or apple pie; there was good wine and fine cigars; smooth brandy and spirited shop talk followed.

I was atwitter because the guest list included several acclaimed writers, and it would be my first personal encounter with them: Robert Penn Warren, William Styron and the historian C. Vann Woodward. (Later, reading a piece I wrote about that evening for the *Texas Observer*, Celia Morris would point out my male chauvinism: the guests *also* included the novelist Eleanor Clark, who happened to be married to Robert Penn Warren; Rose Styron, in her own right, was an author of children's books and a poet. For that matter, Celia herself harbored latent literary instincts; as Celia Morris Eckhardt, she went on to write a fine book on the nineteenth-century feminist and social reformer Fanny Wright, published in 1984 by Harvard University Press.)

Mr. Warren, then one of my hero-of-heroes for *All the King's Men*, *World Enough and Time*, *The Night Riders*, *Flood* and other novels, looked his role as professor and country squire. He also struck me as a gentlemanly, formal man slightly on guard against vague dangers. Perhaps he was on guard for good reason: I sailed in asking personal questions and begging his trade secrets almost before he had his hat off. He proved courtly and affable, however, kindly claiming to agree with me when I took the liberty of brashly ranking a half-dozen of his novels. Mr. Warren modestly confessed to not having much luck writing the short story in volunteering that Eudora Welty was perhaps the only natural or masterful short-story writer then working in America.

He asked my background, an embarrassment when it became necessary to offer my *curriculum vitae* as both a high school and college dropout. I was, after all, speaking to a Yale professor—and an original member of the intellectually revered old Fugitives group at Vanderbilt University—as well as a distinguished man of letters. Defensively, perhaps, I blurted that there were many books I would like to write, "But I have such little formal education, I'm just so goddam absymally *ignorant*, there's so much I don't understand or even suspect, that I'll never be able to come close to doing what I truly aspire to do."

Mr. Warren said, "Well, if you thought you understood very much about anything I doubt whether you'd be successful at the creative process. I've always found that I write to learn, as much as I write to tell or to instruct. I don't believe a writer is having a creative experience when he merely tells. There should be in the writer's work a great seeking." Since I had a couple of days earlier jotted in my notebook the observation that "writing is largely an act of discovery: the writer may, indeed, be a first cousin to the explorer," I was ready at that point to kiss the Great Man's feet; anyone agreeing with my theories is demonstrably smart.

Things were going swimmingly well for the rookie writer, so Rosemarie mysteriously decided to let a certain sharp-clawed cat out of the bag. Some weeks earlier, Bob Gutwillig had mailed Mr. Warren galley proofs of my novel and shortly received this terse response: "It looks as though your new writer is writing in my sleep." Gutwillig and I had laughed; there was much truth in the charge. The similarities between *All the King's Men* and my own groping novelistic effort were all too obvious, except as pertained to quality. Each had a former newspaperman, in the hire of a nutcracking Southern politician, as its narrator; the stories were unreeled across the same Southern terrain. Not yet having found my own writer's voice, I spoke too often in one perilously close to Mr. Warren's—a mistake and gaucherie for which some critics soon would punish me.

Anyhow, around Willie and Celia's dinner table that night, Rosemarie let it escape that I was the new writer about whom Mr. Warren had penned the "writing in my sleep" line. Robert Penn Warren flushed red, though not a split second before I did. Probably each wished to hide under the table. "Oh my, how ungenerous of me!" Mr. Warren began—his reddish complexion splotching and deepening in hue—and he apologized and apologized and apologized. I hastened to assure the man of letters that no harm had been done me; that I considered his comment a compliment; I bumbled on through other lame utterances. All the while, I flashed dark killer looks toward my bride; she quickly slipped from sight in the vain hope she might soon pass from mind. I am afraid I yelled at Rosie in our bedroom around three in the morning when I staggered upstairs from fireside, where I had tarried exchanging yarns over grog with Styron and Morris long after those with better judgment had gone home or to bed.

Styron's *Lie Down in Darkness*, perhaps more than any single novel, had given me the resolve to become a novelist. It was a beautiful book when I read it in 1952 as a young man, and a recent re-reading persuades me it remains so. What is amazing is that Styron wrote it before reaching the age of twenty-five. During that wee-hours session in Willie's country home, back there in 1966, Styron spoke of a book he then was writing about a Virginia slave who had led a revolt against his white masters in the 1830s. I fear I paid scant attention and now recall little of his report. A few years later that work in progress would win a Pulitzer as *The Confessions of Nat Turner*.

I was delighted to find Bill Styron full of good tales, laughter and a general affability; I soon wrote my cousin Lanvil Gilbert—not all tongue in cheek—that "Styron is a great deal like me except for being handsome, rich and of proven talent." I meant that he had proved an easier companion, much more old-shoe, than I somehow had expected; that he had entered into tale-telling, boyhood memories, the whiskey-bawling of old country church hymns and a back-and-forth quoting of lurid Scriptures as if it all came naturally. In short, he had not played the remote god as I somehow anticipated he might. At some point, the evening's surviving whiskey soldiers voted Styron a mock literary prize—I think it was the Bull Connor Brotherhood Award for the Best Dog Story, or some such nonsense—and I made a drunken oration as Willie Morris presented the winner with a pair of Boss Walloper work gloves, a tin of snuff, a Mexican fuck book and a theoretical two-weeks-on-a-desert-island with his companion of choice to be selected between Alfred Kazin and Susan Sontag.

Styron soon wrote me that he had just read galley proofs of *The One-Eyed Man;* he was full of praise for the book's vitality and plot and its depiction of the Southern boondocks. I leaped to the phone to share this exciting news with Bob Gutwillig. My editor was ecstatic: "Jesus, call Styron and ask his permission to lift a line or two from that letter! A quote from him could really help!"

I telephoned "Styron's Acres" in Roxbury, Connecticut, several days' running but received no answer. I then wrote a letter. Silence. Days later, I received Styron's apologetic note: he was just back from Russia and was sorry not to have responded more promptly; yes, he had meant every word he said of my novel—took nothing back—but please understand he was so plagued by writers begging quotes he had, in self-defense, established a policy of giving *no* quotes; it was the only way to avoid constant harassment, mountains of required reading, serious intrusions on his own work time. I understood, though not as well as I now do. Nonetheless, I was sick with disappointment. (These years later, more ringwise, like an old boxer who has seen all the tricks, I conclude that Bill Styron originally wrote a kind letter to a new acquaintance he had enjoyed drinking with and momentarily got carried away; faced with having to go public with comments intended only as a friendly, personal encouragement, he then had to choose between accommodating me or sticking to his literary standards.)

Then much worse news arrived: Warren Miller (who had first called me to Bob Gutwillig's attention, and who had been kind enough to hire me as a book reviewer for *The Nation* when I had been penniless and totally unknown) was dead of lung cancer at age forty-four. The news stunned me. I had known that Warren was ill, that he had undergone surgery a year earlier, but had no notion his situation was critical. Miller's wife, Jimmy, and his friend Gutwillig had kept Warren's true condition a secret even from him. The last time I had seen the man, perhaps six months earlier, he had looked good and had shown his usual wry humor and courtesy. As Rosemarie and I babbled on about my upcoming book—as if no other book would be published in that year or, perhaps, within the decade—Warren had grinned at his wife and said, "What does this remind you of?" She smiled and said, "Us. Fifteen years ago."

Miller took me aside to warn against boundless optimism. "First novels go a hard route. Most critics ignore them. If good things should happen, wonderful. But don't expect the moon. If you don't get everything you hope for, well, remember it's the long haul that counts. Keep writing honest books, true books, and it will happen for you one day." I knew his words were well-meaning, though I must confess I permitted them to pass in one ear and out the other. Like the soldier who has not yet come under fire, I didn't know enough about the horrors to fear combat.

The last thing Warren Miller said to me was that he looked forward to receiving my galley proofs and that he took pride in having helped me get started. We shook hands and parted, I having no notion I never would see him again. Gutwillig got galley proofs to Miller shortly before his death, but he was too ill to read them. The man's death brought more than the pain of losing a friend and mentor: it brought fresh fear tied to Rosemarie's own battle with cancer. Rosie cried on hearing of Warren Miller's death; while I am certain her grief for him was real, I also believe she may have been crying, in part, for her own uncertain future.

Despite preoccupations with the fate of my novel, I continued to work steadily in the magazines for better pay. *Saturday Evening Post* paid $1,500 for a front-of-the-book "Speaking Out" essay on the failure of Congress to discipline its erring members; *True* paid $2,000 for an article on those ruses employed by young men intent on dodging the draft and avoiding service in Vietnam. Neither of those projects brought much personal satisfaction, though the Congress piece was my idea and not the notion of some editor assigning space to fill. I considered most such pieces to be "work work" and to contain no poetry.

My best work was being done for Willie Morris at *Harper's*. This was because of the way he nurtured and edited me. Morris had a way of engaging writers in conversation on diverse subjects; when the writer began to glow and verbally roll, he would simply say, "Write about that for me." A discussion of the roots of home and America's rapid urbanization led Willie to send me back to my birthplace to write "Requiem for a West Texas Town"; a chat about Fundamentalist parsons prompted him to send me to Bob Jones University in South Carolina, a severe preacher-boy school, to write "The Buckle on the Bible Belt." When he learned I had spent part of my military service playing bit roles in Army training films, Willie suggested I combine those experiences with an essay on the gore and glory of Hollywood's propagandizing World War II movies; this resulted in "The Battle of Popcorn Bay." Morris had managed to creep my fee up to $750 at *Harper's*, despite reflex opposition from John Fischer—

a miracle almost equal to making bricks without straw.

There were disappointments. *Sports Illustrated* commissioned for $1,200 a medium-length piece on my youthful experiences as a small-town sportswriter; the editors rejected the piece as unsatisfactory, and I settled for a 20 percent kill fee. (A kill fee, usually ranging from 20 to 50 percent, depending on the reputation of the writer— or how tough his agent is—is negotiated to compensate the writer for time and effort expended should the editors decide against an article's publication.) I salvaged a little more money, if no pride, by selling the rejected piece for $250 to the *Detroit Athletic Club News*. No good-pay magazine proved interested in "Making the Scene at Mailer's," a fun piece about an overflow party of gate crashers (of which I was one) at the famous writer's home following the opening of his play *The Deer Park*. I let it go to the *Texas Observer* for $35 because I wanted it in print. A short story, "The Clutch Hitter," failed to sell to *Atlantic Monthly* and several lesser sources; that experience did little to reassure me about my fictional talents.

The Reporter commissioned an article about Texas governor John B. Connally with the notion of showing how close Connally was to LBJ. They had once been close, it's true, but my article stressed they were moving farther apart because of Connally's disaffection with President Johnson's "Great Society." The piece was not exactly flattering to either Connally or LBJ, which meant trouble: the editor-publisher of *The Reporter*, Max Ascoli, was much enamored of Johnson and was hawkish about the Vietnam War. He edited the piece with such a heavy hand I screamed "censorship." After much heated wrangling and backing-and-filling (I would restore most of Mr. Ascoli's cuts and he, in turn, would again cut what I had restored), I withdrew the piece and declined his $750 fee. Since the idea for the piece had originated with the magazine, I did not feel at liberty to sell it elsewhere. Now, wiser, I would peddle it in a trice.

Human beings do not require long to become spoiled or dissatisfied with the status quo. A couple of years earlier, I would have been delighted with my magazine opportunities. Now, however, I fretted that such small piecework might be wasting time better spent weaving the fabric of a big new novel. I had not yet recognized the obvious: that I was stronger and more accomplished writing nonfiction.

New American Library planned a bigger promotional effort than normally is associated with a first novel. I thought it would be exciting to preen on television, submit to newspaper interviews, sign autographs in bookstores, host a big promotional party and otherwise push my wares. This was before I realized how grinding the road can become when one goes from airport to interview to bookstore to motel—and wakes, not remembering if he is in Cincinnati or Pittsburg, only to repeat the cycle. It is sheer drudgery. It is shitwork without joy. Nor did I know, back then, how ill prepared many would be to receive me. My assumption was that interviewers would have done their homework—else why would they have invited me on their shows or knocked on my hotel door? The reality proved to be something else. I offer as a general rule of thumb this observation: newspaper people almost always will have read the book under discussion, and perhaps even other books by the same author; radio interviewers may or may not be prepared, while television folk—well, I am tempted to offer a cash prize to the person able to prove to my satisfaction that any television interviewer anywhere in America has read any book whatever. That is an exaggeration, of course, but in my time I have issued many larger ones.

I have had television folk get my name wrong, the name of the book being promoted wrong, and incorrectly announce my novel as a book of nonfiction or vice versa. I have had them stare at me with their bright, false, fixed smiles and say, "Tell me all about your book!" No book in the world is best presented by a summary monologue from its author. Unless there is give and take in an interview, with both parties knowing something of what is being discussed, the exercise is stillborn. Studio audiences cough and restlessly shuffle; the poor doomed author can hear TV sets being switched to livelier channels all over America, and knows that once again he is wasting precious time and energies. Yet, so firm is the belief in the power of television to advance the cause of books—among publishers' publicity people and salesmen—that Sin or the notion of it shall pass from this earth before promotional tours do. Many authors hardly agree, though a refusal to submit to promotional tortures may create ill-will in the author's publishing house and provide a handy dart for throwing should the author's book fail: "Well, hell, King! What do you expect? You wouldn't allow us to give you public exposure! You seemed to want the book brought out in secret!"

As with so much in the publishing game, I was originally innocent of the promotional pitfalls and pratfalls. You could not then have persuaded me that a writer could appear in a bookstore, which weeks earlier had agreed to host an autographing session, to discover that its on-duty personnel not only had never heard of the author but had not a single copy of his book. Or that one might sit in a bookstore for two hours or more, gamely grinning behind a huge stack of his new book, while customers galoomped in to buy murder mysteries, cookbooks and how-to books, throwing a covert look toward the author and his stacked books and then scuttling away sideways like so many crabs escaping the firepot.

New American Library planned a promotion party for *The One-Eyed Man* in Washington on June 10: publication day. The event would conveniently coincide with an American Booksellers Association convention in the city, where I would autograph books and smile at, and chat with, bookstore owners and operators in the hope of signing them up for orders. Select bookstore folk would be invited to my party, as would media types and key politicians. Bob Gutwillig asked me to find, "at a reasonable rate," a hall capable of holding about 150 revelers. Food and drink would be laid on.

I found a good hall for free, by persuading my former boss, Congressman Jim Wright, and another good friend, Congressman Morris (Mo) Udall of Arizona, to cohost the party at the National Democratic Club in the Sheraton-Carlton Hotel. As members of that club, they were entitled to reserve its party room free. I assured them NAL would pay food, drink and entertainment costs to the last dime. Rosemarie arranged for several jazz-musician friends to play for the party, while wearing eyepatches and billing themselves for the evening as "The One-Eyed Men." NAL officials appeared delighted: what better place to launch a political novel than from a noted political base in the most political of cities? The participation of two congressmen as cohosts, and other congressmen and senators as guests, seemed a surefire way to obtain much free ink and TV coverage.

It was one big lovefest—until we mailed our guest list to New York. Then NAL factotums discovered the 150 guests they had authorized had magically swelled to 300 or more. Eruptions were heard up and down the Atlantic Seaboard. Bob Gutwillig ordered the guest list pared: he had a party budget of $1,200 and it would cost more than twice that to accommodate our larger list. "Who *are* all these damn people?" he demanded.

Many of the invitees were, indeed, difficult to explain on a strictly business basis. Rosemarie, a true democrat at heart, had invited her cleaning lady, handyman, paperboy, the fifteen or twenty women who worked in the House Office Building cafeteria, her favorite waitresses and bartenders, assorted taxi drivers, at-liberty jazz musicians, and the old gang from high school—to say nothing of twenty-three adult blood relatives. As her best friend, Ella Ward, then was dating cohost Congressman Udall (and later would marry him), Rosie thought it only fair that Mo and Ella should invite some of *their* cronies. I, myself, had invited more than a few affable strangers in bars late at night. I dunno, sir, the list kept growing and next thing you know it got plumb outta hand. . . .

Bob Gutwillig listened to my lame explanations with a stony face and a heart to match: off with their heads. Rosie, told of this hard decision, buckled on her battle gear and vowed not to surrender a single guest. Guess who got caught between Scylla and Charybdis? I bounced back and forth, attempting to appease first my editor and then my wife, having absolutely no luck in showing either of them the other's point of view. Each only grew more intransigent, and each increasingly threatened to have the messenger's head.

One night, well stoked, I took typewriter in hand to fire a shot across Editor Gutwillig's bow:

I have about decided to hell with any promotion party. I'm just tired of the hassle. I don't have it in me to fuss with you anymore over the guest list. The game's not worth the candle, and is turning what should be a pleasant experience into a burden.

To trim the guest list from my standpoint would force me either to eliminate (1) many personal friends and relatives or (2) the Washington officials and publicity outlets that would get us in the papers, on radio and TV. I can't do the former because of personal considerations and the feelings of old friends and relatives. To do the second would make the party without purpose. So rather than have a half-assed thing that isn't personally satisfying, I think I'd rather forget it.

At the hazard of repeating information you already know, let me point out that I've busted my ass to get this book off the ground. You said get a hall for the party at a reasonable rate: I got the best, free. You said come up with a gimmick: I got us up to our asses in cooperative prominent politicians and a national political club to promote a political book. And how about those eyepatch-wearing dudes blowing their horns for free? Did you say *gimmick*, sir? I *gave* you gimmicks! I've met with your sales people and agreed to visit every bookstore in Washington to seek window displays—this at my own initiative. I've told your people I would go anywhere, sing any song or dance any step to sell books. I wrote the dust-jacket blurb, furnished free pictures for the dust jacket and the ads, and went over the book line by line with you in the editing process. All this was based on the assumption that NAL is as interested as I am in selling the book in which we are partners. If we have to squabble over a hundred people at a party, however, then apparently I was mistaken. I therefore withdraw from the field. So advertise or don't advertise, as you please. I'm not disposed to knock myself out and wind up on the short end or have to continually fight and scrap for goals meant to benefit us all. The book apparently will be lost among the hundreds to spew forth this season, so I am planning to get a full-time gig and write only in my spare time. It's the only way I can make it. And at the very least it shouldn't be any more aggravating than this useless shit.

Sort of a fuck-you-strong-letter-follows approach, gang. But if I expected Editor Gutwillig to quail in a corner, I soon found he could deliver firepower of his own. His answering letter seemed, at the time, to accuse me of everything that had gone wrong since Adam ate the apple:

I write you out of what I hope you know is very real friendship and affection, although the words that follow are hard to write and probably harder to receive.

You're way off the track in your [recent] letter and you have been way off the track for many, many months now. Sterling Lord and I have discussed this on several occasions and we thought that since you were under very considerable personal tensions, which we quite appreciate, we would not meet issues head-on that you were raising, and so we have made what now appears to have been a very large mistake.

Now about this party. The facts of the case are these: You were the one who wanted the party in the first place. I agreed to please you. These parties rarely, if ever, help do anything except enlarge the author's ego. Still, publishers are partially in the business of enlarging authors' egos and so we do give parties when we see no alternative.

Unfortunately, you lost your head over a period of time and made commitments that you could not possibly fulfill as far as the invitation list was concerned, unless you are planning to give the party yourself. I don't know where you got the idea that a business party is a party to which one invites one's friends and relatives. The purpose of this party is basically promotion and promotion is business. If it can also be fun, OK. If it can't, tough. Now until you ill-advisedly blew apart, we were willing to accommodate some of these friends and relatives. Why? Because we are good people and because I carry a certain amount of weight around here.

Now there are two kinds of authors. There are those authors who write their books to the best of their ability and leave all the rest of the business to the business people, and there are those authors who write their books, sometimes to the best of their ability, sometimes not, and become involved, sometimes to the benefit of the book, sometimes not, with all of the business details. You, apparently, are one of the latter. In my opinion this is a mistake both for you now and in the future, but that is your business, not mine. By extensive personal promotion you may well sell an extra 200 to 2,000 copies, but on an hourly rate it will work out to something like fifteen cents an hour with no time-and-a-half for overtime.

You mention that you "agreed to visit every bookstore in Washington at my own initiative." This is certainly true. You will remember that no one asked you to do this, and that I mentioned to you that booksellers quiver and quake under this kind of treatment. Still, I acquiesced with a certain muted enthusiasm because you seemed to want to do it.

It is true that you wrote excellent jacket copy, better copy than anybody else here would have written. You are a writer. One of these days, unless you spring the kind of antics you have been exhibiting in the last few months, you may even become a most important and successful writer. You went over your book by line-editing with me because that is your job and mine. You learned a great deal while you wrote this book and you learned a great deal during the editing process. You are one of the few writers I know that can learn and absorb and go on to better things.

As far as the book being lost among all the hundreds of other books, that is nonsense. We have made a special offer on the book to booksellers and the advance sale is going very well. The book is a book-club alternate, as you know, and that is extremely unusual for a first novel. Let's remember that this *is* a first novel! We shall do our very best for it, and that will be substantial. I hope you will simmer down and do your very best for it, too.

I very much hope that you will not give up writing full-time and take a job, particularly out of pique, for that would violate the spirit of all our agreements including all the money I have been laying out to you over all these years.* If you do so out of financial urgency, of course, that is something that I regret but that I understand. In summary I have only three words to offer: Take it easy!

Rosemarie, on reading Bob's letter, wanted me to fire him.

"Goddammit, Rosie, a writer can't fire his editor! It doesn't work that way."

"He says he won't let my friends and relatives come to the party," she pressed.

"Well," I said, "the stick didn't work. Now leave us try the carrot."

"What do you mean?"

"Suppose," I said, "we find out who at NAL is in physical possession of the engraved party invitations. Suppose I then call that person and say, 'Look, I know you're as busy as coal shovelers in hell and we have some nice volunteers who have agreed to address the party invitations for you. We'll take that load off your back.' So they send us the invitations."

"But just a hundred and fifty," Rosie reminded.

"Sure." I grinned. "We go to a printer here locally and get *another* hundred and fifty duplicated. That won't cost us much. Then we'll send invitations to NAL's official hundred and fifty *and* to our hundred and fifty folks."

"They're only ordering drinks and food for a hundred and fifty people," she objected.

"We know who the caterer is. A couple or three days before the party, I'll telephone the caterer and instruct him to double the rations."

"Lar . . . are you sure this is right or legal?"

"No," I said. "But do you want your friends and relatives to at-

---

* I had at one point drawn an additional $2,000 from NAL against future royalties, later had borrowed $1,500 from Bob Gutwillig personally in three increments and also had signed a second-novel contract for a $22,000 advance, $12,500 of which was paid on signing and the remainder due on completion.

tend the party, or do you want to debate legality and integrity and whatnot?"

It worked. Not a peep, ever, out of NAL. I don't believe they even noticed.

Reality arrived about 12:20 a.m., Sunday, May 29, 1966, a couple of weeks before the party. We had just polished off a post-midnight snack of apples and cheese and were readying for bed when the telephone rang. I answered, to hear Rosemarie's excited sister Christine: "Got your Sunday paper yet?" No, not yet. "Your book is reviewed!" Christine trilled. "Let me read it to you!" My heart turned flipflops. I grinned, fired up a cigarette and settled back to await poetry and praise.

"Who wrote the review?" I asked.

"R. Z. Sheppard. Assistant editor of *Book Week*."

"Okay, Chrissie. Go!"

She began reading: "Mr. King is, among other things, a contributing editor of the *Texas Observer*, a liberal periodical which is often a burr under the saddles of high-riding Texas politicians. Perhaps the best-known writer of what has loosely been called the *Texas Observer* crowd—"

I thought, *Thank you, R. Z.! Thank you, Jesus!*

"—is Bill Brammer—"

I thought, *Oh!*

"—a former Lyndon Johnson aide who turned his political experiences into a first-rate *roman à clef* called *The Gay Place*. It starred Governor Arthur (Goddamn) Fenstemaker, a sympathetic mixture of shrewd intelligence, cornpone, and pragmatic goodwill—"

I thought, *Goddammit, R. Z., get to my book!*

"—qualities so recognizable as belonging to The Man Himself that Brammer hasn't been seen at an LBJ barbecue since his book was published in 1961. . . ."

I thought, *So what else is new? Get on with it!*

"Now Mr. King, who has been an administrative assistant to two Texas congressmen and plumped for Lyndon Johnson's presidential nomination in 1960—"

I thought, *Okay, kiddies, here we go!*

"—attempts to turn the lead of political experience into the gold of fiction. The result is something less than ten-karat—"

I thought, *Whaaaaat?*

"—a static, often pretentious, and derivative assemblage of clichés which at times reads as if Mr. King were parodying Robert Penn Warren and even Brammer himself. . . ."

I thought, *Oh, shit! Oh, dear! Oh, fuck!*

"But mostly it reads like imitation James M. Cain—"

I thought, *Jesus Christ! This can't be happening!*

"Ah, Larry," Christine said. "Why don't you wait until morning and read it yourself?"

"No, Christine! Finish it!"

"Well, see, I didn't read it before I called you. I didn't know, uh. Why don't you wait and—"

"No, goddammit, Christine! You *started* it! *Finish* it!"

Rosemarie was standing by looking agonized, massaging my shoulders, shifting uncertainly. I irritably shrugged off her attentions.

"Okay," Christine sighed, and reluctantly resumed reading. "—like imitation James M. Cain: 'The old wheel of fortune keeps spinning in worn grooves and the X of chance falls wantonly on the squares, and about all any mother's son can do is ride with the play. . . . Only the historians don't dig it. . . . So before they rip it up and go labeling it pure grade-A History, and wrap it in the clear cellophane of hindsight, I want to tell it like it was.' "

I thought, *Christ, that's terribly embarrassing shit! Why didn't Gutwillig edit that out?*

Christine, stammering and stuttering, continued doing her penitence: "That's from the lips of the narrator, the familiar shopworn ex-newspaperman turned political press agent and hatchetman. His yarn has to do with the efforts of Governor Cullie Blanton to convince his Southern state (unidentified) that the North won the Civil War and it is necessary to accede to a federal order to integrate the state university. . . ."

I thought, *At least the bastard got the plot right.*

"Blanton, too, is a sympathetic mixture of shrewd intelligence, cornpone, and pragmatic goodwill—"

I thought, *Well, thanks for small favors, R. Z.*

"—although he is too composite and exaggerated to resemble the living."

I thought, *Fuck you, R. Z.! Just fuck you!*

"The high point of the book—"

I thought, *Oh, you admit there is one?*

"—is Blanton's politically suicidal speech in which he attempts to awaken his legislature to the realities of the twentieth century. But to get to this tough, moving message the reader must be prepared to wade through far too many swamps of local color, hoked-up dialogue and bargain sentiment."

I thought, *Ouch! I'm dead in the water. Goddam!*

"That's all," Christine said hurriedly. " 'Bye." I sat listening to the growling dial tone, a man in shock.

"You look pale," Rosie said. I rushed to the bathroom and gagged, but could not bring up the bile I felt. I ran cold water over my head, groaned, sighed, cussed, kicked a wall. Nothing helped. Mainly I felt mortified, just embarrassed beyond description. "Oh, shit," I moaned. "Goddam *Book Week* not only appears in the *Washington Post* but the *New York Herald Tribune* and I think Chicago and San Francisco and maybe even goddam Japan! I'm ruined! Gutted! Oh, shit shit shit!"

"Come to bed, baby," Rosie said.

"Not for a goddam week. Maybe not for a goddam month."

"Was it . . . really *that* bad, Lar?"

"Rosie," I said, "it's the ugliest thing to appear in print since my ex-wife's divorce deposition."

I suddenly insisted that we run out to buy a paper: maybe the review wouldn't *look* as bad as it had sounded. Rosie didn't think it a good idea; I insisted. We found an all-night drugstore. I was almost to its door when I wheeled, marched back to the car and said, "Rosie, you go buy the paper. I don't want anybody to recognize me. They might laugh." Rosie said I was being silly. I persisted. My wife sighed, climbed out and went off on her strange errand of alleged mercy. I sat in the dark car peering around furtively, like a fugitive from a bounty hunter, silently vowing not to appear in public for at least thirty days.

The book party! Oh, shit! The goddam book party was less than a dozen days away! Well, fuck the book party! I wouldn't go! Maybe Bob Gutwillig would be pleased his goddam guest list had been reduced by one. Shit on everybody! Shit on the United States! Shit on the world!

R. Z. Sheppard's review looked every bit as bad as it had sounded.

I prowled and cursed for hours, tossing down a fresh beer about every three minutes, alternately smoking dope and nicotine. Periodically I issued long, wailing moans like some poor wretch on the rack being pulled apart a rib and a tendon at a time. Rosie rolled joint after joint and comforted herself with a parade of vodka martinis.

I made long, loud speeches to R. Z. Sheppard. "Clichés, you say, you silly little prick? Too many 'swamps of local color, hoked-up dialogue and bargain sentiment'? Well, mothafucka, politics in the South *is* a matter of clichés, local color, hoked-up dialogue, bargain sentiment. Witness Pappy O'Daniel, Lurleen Wallace, Maw and Paw Ferguson! You probably haven't even heard of them, you snotty Yankee popcorn fart!"

"Tell him, Lar," Rosie said.

"And you say the governor is 'too exaggerated to resemble the living'? How about LBJ saying to a reporter, 'Why do you come to me, the Leader of the Western World, with a chickenshit question like that'? How about crazy old Uncle Earl Long cursing on the House floor when he was in Congress, and then as governor of Louisiana going on that demented car trip across Texas and New Mexico, wearing pillowcases over his head, shaking his dong at reporters and photographers in an El Paso hotel? How about the nut buster, Huey Long? Alfalfa Bill Murray, who as governor of Oklahoma called out the state guard and threatened to invade Texas over some minor dispute about river water? How about George Wallace bumping bellies with a federal marshal in a schoolroom door down in Alabama? Or General Walker rousing the rabble at Ole Miss when James Meredith enrolled? I guess all that was too goddam 'exaggerated' to resemble real life—huh?—you ignorant pile of dogshit!"

"You got him, Lar," Rosie said, laughing and applauding.

"Yeah, sure I have. Here in this room. But how to tell the people who read his goddam review? No way I can reach 'em!"

With the aid of chemicals and utter fatigue, we got to sleep about 5:30 a.m. Probably I jerked and cried out in the dark for my mother. Before nine o'clock I woke with ground glass in my eyes, carpet fuzz on my tongue and people pounding my head with croquet mallets. After choking down a couple of bloody Marys I telephoned Bob Gutwillig to ask whether he'd had the pleasure of perusing that Sunday's *Book Week*.

"I don't read in my sleep," he grumbled.

"Well, drop your cock and grab your socks," I said. "And brace yourself." I read him the ruinous review. My editor groaned, moaned and cursed almost as passionately as had the author. When I finished Gutwillig said, "Fucking catastrophic! We're dead everywhere that review runs."

"Goddammit," I said, "I called you for *comfort!* I thought maybe, I dunno, maybe you could think of something."

"I can think of suicide," my editor said.

I can vouch, these years later, for the accuracy of my thoughts, words and actions that miserable night because I wrote it all down in the form of a letter to Lanvil Gilbert before Sunday was through. My cousin, a good and kind man, shot back this supportive response:

> Of course, my name and my book have not been slandered—so I can sit here as cool as a British killer and consider the matter of one R. Z. Sheppard.
>
> I am not using hindsight to say that simply on the basis of statistical chance—not to mention certain logical factors—such a review by *some*one was almost inevitable. It never occurred to me, though, that such a review would be the *first* one; it never occurred to me there would be a "first" review. Looking back, I can see that I harbored a vision of a shotgun start, with all the horses coming out of the starting gate at once; and that you would find general acceptance from multiple reviews, with considerable variation between the reviews simply as a result of the considerable variation between the specific reviewers. It was single-cellular of me not to consider that the reviews would come out not as a race begins but as it ends: first, second, third and so on.
>
> So the first one is out. And not like a horse but like a bomb. You were ill-prepared for it. Your Clarkship* of expecting the worst had been lulled into expecting the best; and not without reason. You had worked hard and written truly on a subject you truly knew (which lent confidence) and you had met uniformly favorable comment from several regal sources (which lent encouragement). So how could you possibly have been prepared for R. Z. Sheppard? Furthermore, as an author you were too emo-

---

*Our mothers, identical twins, were two of nine Clark sisters born to a natural pessimism and dreadfully fearful outlooks; a darker-minded brood never lived.

tionally involved to give proper weight to certain logical factors.

There is a large field of endeavor called Literary Criticism. *Criticism.* That's an unfortunate choice of words but our culture is stuck with it. College catalogs carry no courses in Literary Analysis or Literary Judgment but simply in Literary Criticism. Now, in an earlier day the word "criticism" was a kinder word: it mean simply judgment, with an equal opportunity for beauty and fault. But not today. "Criticism" means criticism in its harshest sense. For proof look at Webster, who defines it as "the art of criticizing, especially unfavorably."

So the gun is loaded. The majority of reviewers lean toward unfavorable reviews, and they don't even know it. They are not aware that they can't seem to let a good book be. They have to pick at it. How many times have I seen critics write favorably of a book, all down the line, and then earn their spurs at the end of the review: "One wishes, however, that helpful maps (or an index or a more attractive format) had been presented."

Thus the professional pique of the critic creeps in. And not a minor consideration is that Freudian matter of "Here is another book *I* didn't write. I hate it! I hate it! I hate it !" So, faced with a deadline and a professional challenge and Freud, R. Z. Sheppard came through. In fairness to R.Z. (Cola, anyone?), we'll have to concede that he honestly didn't like the book. Surely certain other individuals won't: somewhere a delicate nun, and somewhere a delicate President. But most people will like it. . . .

Brother Sheppard has no sense of humor. He really hasn't. Some of the funniest stuff I ever read is in your book, and if I didn't respect the characters on one hand I would laugh at them on the other. And, alas, my condolences that you met a reviewer who is local-color-blind. Well, the swamps are there and they are many and they are good. But most of all, they are justified! Our South happens to be the way it is, credible or not. I wonder, really, if R. Z. Sheppard knows what a real Southerner looks or sounds like? Not just a sleepy, drawlin' one but an *activist* Southerner—Cullie Blanton, Long & Long, Ferguson & Ferguson, Wallace & Wallace, and the old ex-champ Pappy O'Daniel—the kind that's born runnin' and never stops till a "nigger" digs his grave. . . .

My spirits were further lifted by the appearance in the *Washington Evening Star* of a rave review by Carter Brooke Jones, followed quickly by good words from critics doing business for the *Boston Traveler*, *Houston Chronicle*, *Cleveland Plain Dealer* and *Miami*

Sun. I thus approached the big promotional party at the National Democratic Club feeling less gut-shot than formerly, and without wearing a mask. That event went off pleasantly enough and inspired a good column by Dick Schaap in—of all damn places—*Book Week*; we also received a goodly amount of publicity in Washington and Texas quarters. According to Bob Gutwillig, my appearance at the autograph booth during the American Booksellers Association convention—and contacts made with other booksellers at the promotional party—led to a sizable flurry of new orders for *The One-Eyed Man.* NAL's people went home happy.

Since I have made so much of that damning first review, the curious may wonder about the overall critical reception accorded *The One-Eyed Man.* It was a mixed and disappointing bag. The novel received eleven truly "bad" reviews, about ten indifferent ones, thirty-two "good" ones and five "raves." Unfortunately, the better ones appeared in places like Wheeling, West Virginia, and Casper, Wyoming. Where it counted most—in the big, influential publications many book buyers consult for guidance—my book was either ignored or carved on. *The New Yorker* couldn't abide it; the *New York Review of Books* couldn't be bothered; the daily *New York Times* did not review it or mention it, while the critic for the Sunday *Times* devoted exactly twenty-four lines to my thirty months of labor and waiting; I here wish again to thank him for his brevity.

In retrospect, I judge that my flawed and inexpert first novel received roughly what it critically deserved—with the possible exception of R. Z. Sheppard's early-bird overkill.

I toured the country for a month, touting my crippled book, in the process learning that not all television folk majored in American literature and that bookstore visits could provide unexpected hazards. I returned home tired, blue and knowing in my heart *The One-Eyed Man* was clearly doomed. "Looks like you'll have to wait for your seagoing yacht," I told Rosie. "Right now it's more a matter of providing beans." I jumped back on the magazine treadmill.

Saturday Evening Post paid $3,000 and expenses for a story on an aging former football superstar—Ollie Matson—who had been benched by the Philadelphia Eagles and seemed in danger of losing his place on the squad. This required three weeks at the Eagles' summer camp in Hershey, Pennsylvania, and weekend flying trips to Atlanta, Chicago and New Orleans for preseason games. I didn't mind the trips, but found Hershey not an ideal place to spend long, hot summer days. My hotel room, cramped and dim, was directly across the street from the city's famed chocolate factory; some broiling mornings the overpoweringly sweet, cloying odor from the factory failed to assist the health of one who had spent much of the night boozing with rugged old pro-footballers.

From Hershey I wrote Willie Morris a desperate letter begging for a raise and predicting that in the absence of more money I soon would be required to shave my chin whiskers and seek a job in the straight world. I then was writing a long cover piece for *Harper's*, ultimately published as "My Hero LBJ" (to inspire in President Johnson a sense of outrage toward me that didn't die until he did), and urged Willie to try to push Jack Fischer up to $1,000 or even $1,200 for that piece. I had little confidence in his being able to attain such sums, however, for I had just received a sharply worded note from Mr. Fischer professing to be "shocked" by my $105 expense statement submitted in connection with an article I had written for him on William F. Buckley, Jr.; Mr. Fischer said he had "assumed" that my "generous $850 fee" had included expenses. I don't see why he so assumed; no editor had before or has since. Much to our mutual astonishment, Willie Morris ultimately managed to extract $1,000 for the LBJ piece. "I feel like I've broken the sound barrier," I told Willie. "You have," he said.

On receipt of my desperate letter from Hershey, Willie called. His voice carried that hushed quality I imagine spies use while transmitting war-winning secrets. "Larry, I can't tell you any more than this: hang on. Just hang on, that's all. Don't take a job. Before long I think I'll be able to pay you much more than *Harper's* pays you now. I'm not at liberty to say more, and you must promise you'll keep even that much strictly confidential."

I immediately promised and in the same breath demanded more details. No, Willie said, he wasn't free to say more. Something big was in the wind, something that must be closely held, something that could benefit me hugely if only I would be patient and provided I kept my mouth shut. I hung up semi-encouraged, but without knowing why.

One morning in Hershey I got up at five-thirty and motored to Harrisburg, catching a train for New York to confront Bob Gutwillig over advertising—or what I thought was the shameful lack of it—for my novel.

"Jesus!" Gutwillig said. "I've already spent eighty-eight hundred dollars, and that's unheard-of for a first novel. The book's got to take off before I can pump more money into it."

"Well, hell, how's it gonna take off if you don't give it a push?"

"We're pushing, we're pushing," he assured me. "The problem is, we haven't received one good major review. They love you in the sticks, sure, but they don't buy books out there."

I was offended. "Goddammit, I got a really fine review in the *Chicago Tribune* last week. And, uh, Louisville, Kentucky, and St. Petersburg, Florida, and uh . . ."

"Yes?" Gutwillig said.

"Oh, shit, Bob! I'm just sick over the failure of this goddam book!"

"It's not a flat failure," he assured soothingly.

"Bullshit. We both know it's a failure."

"No, now, look here." Gutwillig rummaged in his desk and came up with a sheet of paper. It was a list of NAL's current hardbacked offerings to the book-buying public, known to laborers in the publishing trade as a "hot sheet." It showed *The One-Eyed Man* running fifth in a field of twenty-two, far behind the two front-runners, Ian Fleming's *Octopussy* and Maud Shaw's *White House Nanny*. The rest of the books were anything but hot.

I studied the mournful numbers and said, "Well, I guess I didn't exactly expect to keep up with James Bond. But shit, it's depressing in the extreme to be outsold three to one by Maud Shaw."

"Come on," Gutwillig laughed. "A book by the lady who nannied Caroline and John-John? You know how Kennedy stuff sells!"

"Yeah. Much better than King stuff."

I begged for an ad in *Harper's:* "Most of my fan mail comes from that magazine's readers. And that audience buys books." Gutwillig said he couldn't promise, though he would check the possibilities. I asked if he could think of the tiniest smidgen of Good News; if so, I would like to have it now, please; I need it.

"Look," my editor said, "quit acting like your mother died." He waved the NAL sales sheet. "You're second only to Ian Fleming on this list in fiction—or soon will be, if my projections are accurate—and for a first novel that's, well, that's really tremendous."

"But we didn't grab the big brass ring, did we, Bob?"

Well, no.

"And we thought we would, didn't we?"

Well, to be honest, yes.

"Shit," I said. "You ain't worth a flip at cheering a fellow up. I'm going back to Hershey."

In late August, Gutwillig wrote an obviously "stroking" letter as part of his duties coming under the heading "The Care and Feeding of Authors":

> More jolly news. I can't—after all—put the ad in *Harper's* because that little spot costs $400 and we simply can't afford to do it. In fact, I have been unable even to recommend such an ad to my colleagues because they have been giving me such a hard time since I last saw you about the amount of money [$8,800] we have spent to date on *The One-Eyed Man*. I tell them that it was more than worth it—not only to help to sell the hardcover and paperback editions of this book, but to publicize an author (who has done more than his share to publicize the book) whom we are going to be publishing successfully for years and years to come. All I get in return for such propaganda are grunts.
>
> I do not think by any means that the book is done. Just quite the opposite. I think that we will have continuing sales—mostly to libraries now—for the next couple of months. On the other hand, I do think that the bookstore sale is probably about over, because of the adverse reviews.
>
> I do think I should put on paper my feelings about all that has happened and that has not happened to *The One-Eyed Man*. I think it is a terrific novel, and I think the reviewers who have either vilified or ignored it are clearly wrong. I think you have done a tremendous job in writing and rewriting and rewriting and rewriting, and I know that you are going on to become the writer I have felt you could become since I first met you and read the first chapter. . . .
>
> It seems to me that—partly through your own publicity efforts and partly through our publicity and advertising efforts—*The One-Eyed Man* has sold remarkably well in the face of critical inattention. . . . What I'm trying to say is that, after all, *The One-*

Eyed Man is, among other things, a first novel. First novels are tough to sell (if you think first novels are tough, wait till you see what happens to the second!).

I hope to spend an evening with you and Rosie in Washington in a week or two. Meanwhile, I don't want you to be depressed or distressed about *The One-Eyed Man*. I am—on the whole—pleased and encouraged. Be of good cheer.

Though the stroking was transparent, I appreciated the gesture. When Gutwillig came to town a week or so later he said over wine—mainly to please Rosie, I think—that he expected the book to top out at about 14,000 hardback sales. It did not, of course. It topped out at 9,884 (according to the last royalty report I find in my ancient files) and died unmourned save by a tiny handful of friends and the man who made it.

Disappointment with the fate of my first novel probably had a great deal to do with being unable to write a second. Though I started not one but three new novels, each fizzled after forty pages or sixty pages or eighty pages. Having faith in none of the stories, and shrinking confidence in myself as a novelist, I retreated to nonfiction. Magazine pieces did not fill my need to accomplish another book, however.

Bob Gutwillig was enthusiastically apathetic when I approached him with the notion of making a book of my magazine articles.

"Collections don't sell for shit," he judged.

"But there will be new material, bridging material, some pretty funny stuff. I've thought about the project and I know I can pull it off. Dammit, Bob, I need to get back in hardcover before people forget me—if they haven't already, and provided anybody ever heard of me in the first place."

"I don't give a damn if it proves that Martin Bormann is an Israeli jet pilot," Gutwillig said. "If the information is in a damn collection, that news will never get around."

I began the book anyway. By God, I was determined to have it published and thought I knew a way. When I had completed about one hundred pages, in October of 1966, I wrote Willie Morris to ask whether Harper & Row—a publishing house with historic ties to *Harper's* magazine—might be interested in the collection. Willie spoke with Evan Thomas of that publishing house and found that he was, indeed, interested. I flew to New York to announce this news to Bob Gutwillig and had as evidence a letter from Mr. Thomas saying he was "keen" to publish the book.

My editor was predictably livid. He waved my NAL contract in my face, threatened to sue, lectured on the damnable ingratitude of writers in general and myself in particular, and came close to dunning me for money I personally owed him. The fight lasted most of a heated afternoon, but ended with Gutwillig's consenting to publish my nonfiction collection "against my better judgment." Frankly, that was how I had figured it would turn out: not for nothing had I spent ten years in political manipulations on Capitol Hill. Within days I signed a contract for a small advance ($4,000) while Gutwillig grumbled that even such a modest sum probably would not be earned back.

Just then my *Harper's* piece on LBJ hit the newsstands, exciting more mail, comment in columns, newspaper editorials and invitations to talk shows than I had formerly received. It also caused other magazine editors to contact me with offers of assignments at their better rates. A dissenting vote or two was heard from Washington. Jack Fischer and his wife attended a White House dinner where, he reported, staff man Jack Valenti raked him over for publishing my piece and said unflattering things of its author. The Prez himself, according to what another White House staffer confided, put out word that "I don't want that lying, bearded son of a bitch down here eating my groceries anymore." (I had on a single occasion, at the invitation of a White House staff friend, been asked to lunch at the White House mess. Perhaps my friend had tardy second thoughts, for when I arrived all starched and combed he mumbled about the White House mess being booked solid that day; we retreated to Harvey's restaurant for lunch—where I got stuck with the check when the aide received a telephone call requiring his return to duty halfway through the meal. So, for the record, I ate none of LBJ's groceries.)

Frankly, I never understood the big flap. The piece wasn't all that tough or unkind. It did trace my evolution from a starry-eyed farmboy who idolized Lyndon Johnson to a more percipient adult who, as a congressional assistant, observed that our President had a fierce temper and often cussed behind closed doors. Everyone knows all that—and worse—of Lyndon Johnson by now; I think my special crime was that the *Harper's* piece appeared while LBJ still was benefiting from a generally good press. Also, because I had worked for Texas congressmen, and in Johnson's own abortive campaign for the presidency in 1960, he saw me as a turncoat telling tales out of school.

The LBJ piece, and the William Buckley piece soon to follow in *Harper's*, got me tagged as "controversial" but neither article hurt business. I had great fun researching the Buckley piece, which included interviews with such writers as Murray Kempton, James Wechsler, Michael Harrington, Irving Howe, Norman Mailer and (by telephone) my old benefactor John Kenneth Galbraith. And I enjoyed, too, the sprightly verbal show toward which Mr. Buckley is inclined. He also treated me to a scary ride up Park Avenue at rush hour, from downtown to midtown Manhattan, perched behind him on a motor scooter while I hugged him for dear life. In matters of politics and the world's realities, however, I suppose my piece judged the conservative iconoclast as a bit blockheaded. Mr. Buckley naturally was not taken with that evaluation, and refused an ad in his own *National Review* which Willie Morris hoped to place there to advertise my *Harper's* piece; I later learned that on encountering Murray Kempton, shortly after my article appeared, Mr. Buckley said, "Murray, your friend Larry King has serious deficiencies as a gentleman." A year or so later, however, Bill Buckley apparently reevaluated: he sent a friendly postcard after I had praised his book *The Jeweler's Eye* in the *New York Times*. Writers have a way of reacting at the gut level to other writers reacting to them or their work.

In early 1967, Willie Morris again called with conspiracy in his voice and asked me to fly to New York on a given evening: "I can't say what it's all about. Don't come to the office. Go straight to the Such-and-So restaurant and be damn sure you're sober when you get there." The last order gave me pause: Willie never before had seemed to worry over whether I might lack timing and balance. I also wondered why we were to meet at a strange restaurant miles off our beaten path. Willie adamantly refused information.

He was waiting when I arrived at the chosen restaurant. He suspiciously sniffed my breath, then gave permission to order a Scotch and water. "We've got fifteen minutes until John Cowles, Jr., joins us," he said. "Do you know who he is?" I did not. "He and his father own the Minneapolis newspapers. And they're related to the Cowles people who own *Look* magazine." I nodded, wondering if Willie was readying to leave *Harper's* for *Look* or some newspaper.

Morris lowered his voice almost to a whisper and looked around for the Gestapo. "Cowles is buying *Harper's*. He wants to make me editor-in-chief. And I want to bring you and David Halberstam aboard as my first two staff writers. Now, Larry, all you hear tonight has gotta be as secretive as . . . well, you just can't mention it. You've got to dummy up like Allen Dulles. If you leak any of this to anybody . . . well, just *don't. Just don't!* Promise me you won't." I swore on a stack of absent Bibles and a handy basket of French bread.

Morris confided that he wanted to get John Corry from the *New York Times* and another free lance, Marshall Frady, for his *Harper's* staff. He thought he might be able to pay me $2,000 per article, and he hoped I could do at least six, preferably eight, pieces a year for him. This calibrated well: for all my scrabbling, I had earned only about $15,000 from magazines in 1966; I quickly estimated that I might earn $16,000 from *Harper's* alone under Willie, and add another $6,000 to $8,000 from other magazines.

"Does Jack Fischer know about all this?" I asked.

"Well, yes and no," Willie said, his eyes darting nervously around the restaurant. "He knows Cowles is interested in buying, but he doesn't know about . . . well, Cowles jumping me to the top job and bringing in you guys. See, the problem is to get Mr. Fischer to quit. Cowles doesn't want to run his old ass off. On the other hand, Cowles wants me in the top slot. We've talked a lot and he likes my plans for the magazine. Now here he comes, Larry! Stay sober and answer his questions, but don't go volunteering a lot of crazy shit."

Willie put on a hearty welcoming smile and stood to shake hands with a tall, slim, youthful-looking man whose clothes and bearing screamed *rich boy, right schools, right clubs, tennis* . . . ! I had always been ill at ease in the company of such people; perhaps by way of compensation, I would sometimes rudely ask were they getting any or whether they'd ever roughnecked in the oilfields. Willie flashed me one of his don't-you-dare looks, however; I knew enough to play it straight. Hell, it could be suicidal if I didn't: Willie in the big chair could help my writing career more than a little.

Morris and young John Cowles talked of what was wrong with the magazine and what might correct it. "It's gotten so dull," Cowles said. "It seems to publish too many long, dry, thumb-sucking pieces by State Department retirees. It seems not to have much vigor."

Cowles said he was mindful of the many years of loyal service Jack Fischer had given *Harper's*. "He's got to go in a way he can live with. I'd like to ask him to continue to write the 'Easy Chair' column every month. Though that's usually a prerogative of the editor-in-chief, Willie has agreed. I'd also like to offer Mr. Fischer a sort of editor emeritus role, the opportunity to continue to contribute ideas to the magazine and a desk in the office if he wants it." Willie Morris said he owed Mr. Fischer a great deal, that Fischer had brought him to New York from Texas and had treated him as the fair-haired comer who might one day succeed to the top post. He, too, would insist on Mr. Fischer's being comfortable with the new arrangements. I said, well, Mr. Fischer had been nice to me . . . though maybe he held the purse strings a bit too tightly.

"That's a problem," John Cowles agreed. "*Harper's* isn't attracting many top writers because of its pay scale. I'd like to get Styron, Mailer, Philip Roth—those people—in the magazine regularly. It once published Mark Twain, William Dean Howells . . . the best writers of their times. We should be able to do that again."

Cowles gave me a look and said, "You used to be in politics. How do we arrange the transition so that we get what we want but we don't step on Jack Fischer?"

I knew, from earlier talks with Willie Morris, that about twice each year Mr. Fischer drafted a letter announcing that six months later he would retire. After showing the letter around the office, he always placed it in his desk drawer and there it reposed—unmailed, unsigned—until he felt the need to draft another. I knew, too, he frequently told the owners of *Harper's* his retirement was imminent. Then went on working.

"The next time Mr. Fischer drafts such a letter, or says anything to you about retiring," I said to Mr. Cowles, "then *you* must act. Grab his hand, wring it and express your regret that he's leaving. But don't let it end there. Write him or call him or both—I mean, really keep *pressing* him—about the new role you envision for him on his retirement: he'll keep writing 'Easy Chair,' he'll be editor emeritus, he'll continue to have input and so on. You'll have to stay on top of him, make him understand that his threat to retire has been accepted as a reality and is inevitable."

Cowles grinned and said, "You know, it might work."

That meeting occurred, I believe, in February. In mid-May the public announcement was made of Willie's takeover effective July 1; Mr. Fischer would remain in an advisory role and write the 'Easy Chair' column, but largely would devote his time to the writing of books. Senior editor Robert Kotlowitz would replace old-timer Russell Lynes as managing editor (and, though it was not then announced, Midge Decter soon would join as executive editor). *Newsweek* remarked on the hiring of two new "contributing editors": "Already, Morris has hired Pulitzer Prize winner David Halberstam, late of the *New York Times* [as a foreign correspondent], to make a three-month trip to Vietnam for a progress report, and Larry L. King, a Texan with a Mencken touch, to take up residence in [political] Washington."

Willie Morris issued a statement promising the new *Harper's* would be lively and relevant to the times (if sometimes irreverent in attitude) and would have "a stronger appeal for younger readers—young in age, young at heart." Indeed, most stories about the big shake-up remarked on the "youth movement" at *Harper's:* At forty-two, Bob Kotlowitz was the old graybeard; I was the runner-up in the wizened department at thirty-eight—a year older than new owner John Cowles, Jr.—and Halberstam was just thirty-three. The new top dog, Willie Morris, was only thirty-two. "The boy editor," I joshed my friend as we celebrated in New York shortly after the official announcement had been made of Willie's elevation. That night, in a cab returning to our hotel, I hugged Rosemarie and made her a promise: "We're on the way now, baby. For sure, ain't nothin' gonna stop us now."

Chapter Three

A PERIOD OF ADJUSTMENT

*** No huzzahs or street parades greeted the completion of my nonfiction collection in the summer of 1967; I was bucking an in-house, perhaps industry-wide prejudice against short pieces gathered between hard covers. Such books are reputed in editorial rooms to sell on a par with shit-flavored chewing gum. Though there are writers who thumb their noses at this marketplace rule—Kurt Vonnegut, Nora Ephron, John Updike, Erma Bombeck, Russell Baker, Art Buchwald—I fear the commercial bad rap against most short, recycled material is not without historic foundation. Though I had selected my best stuff from *Harper's* and a half-dozen other magazines, and thought I had put together a readable collection, certainly my publisher had little reason to believe such a book carrying my byline would cause his stock to split.

I also bore the handicap of having disappointed in my maiden effort despite a more generous advertising budget than usually was accorded newcomers. Writers, like field-goal kickers or pinch hitters, are most often recalled in the front office for their recent failures. New American Library honchos probably looked on me as a sports franchise might consider a "bonus baby" rookie who signs for kidnapper's sums and then is discovered to have difficulties tying his shoelaces. The mere sight of such a maladroit practitioner reminds the scout who found him and the executive who signed him—and their superiors—of certain embarrassing old errors of judgment. Bob Gutwillig's cause had not been helped when he signed me to a second novel for that $22,000 advance, a novel which I had been unable to produce despite having no trouble spending the $12,500 I had received in exchange for my signature; I had been unable to get past a few pages, though changing subjects and titles three times. As a young editor not long in the trade, I'm sure Gutwillig felt keen anxiety when coldly eyed by NAL brass. By the time I delivered my nonfiction manuscript, Bob understandably had lost a great deal of his original enthusiasm for his "hot property."

He briefly thumbed through my manuscript pages (idly, as if riffling a deck of cards) and immediately began trying to persuade me to write a novel about professional football. "Pro football is on the verge of exploding as the next big fad. Take us behind the scenes in a novel full of the violence, the pressures, the gambling, the deals, the sex. There's a damn big book in that." I demurred; it simply wasn't a book calling out to me. My editor thumped my fresh manuscript, regarding it as he might a transcript of obscene phone calls made to an orphans' home. "I once thought you would be a big-money writer. Now here's *this!*" We waved our arms, raised our voices, issued hot disputations over the relative merits of Art vs. Greed. I departed Gutwillig's presence like a rookie being ushered out from a butt-chewing by his head coach, wondering how long I might be able to remain on the NAL team.

The pressures eased slightly when *The One-Eyed Man* blossomed as a paperback in drugstores, bus stations and airports, enjoying a brisk sale through three printings. This may be because the lurid paperback cover depicted a couple lolling on a mattress in the altogether; the imaginative artwork, quite bold for the times, was backed up by a quote from some obscure critic claiming the book was "calculated to shock with sex." In truth, unless one judged by my old hymn-singing mother's standards, that political novel contained barely enough sex to get by. I had burst into laughter on first seeing the paperback cover and had mildly protested that it was inappropriate. Gutwillig said, "You want to sell books or not?" So I said no more. Such are the small deceptions of the literary marketplace.

I spent a month in Atlantic City that summer with Louis Armstrong for yet another *Harper's* piece. The old musician was playing a tough, draining three-shows-daily gig at the Steel Pier, but was amazingly energetic and adventurous for a man pushing seventy. Following his late shows we partied from midnights until many dawns in his hotel room: eating soul food, drinking, smoking what he called "Mexican

boo smoke" or "ganj," spinning yarns, making music. I had asked to
sing onstage with the famous trumpet man—purportedly to write
how it felt to sing with a legend, though really because I thought
doing it would be a hoot—but his manager had recoiled in alarm and
nixed the notion. In the privacy of Armstrong's suite, however, I
got to sing along with Satchmo. "You know this one, Pops," he would
say, and start blowing "Hello Dolly" or "Blueberry Hill." And we
would be off, my off-key bellow mixing with Armstrong's fog-and-
gravel voice. It was a blast. I called Rosemarie, the jazz fan incar-
nate, and she drove from Washington to join the fun. I had such a
wonderful time that Willie Morris was forced to order me off the
road in the interest of economy and my approaching deadline.

I never met any musician so aware of sounds, all sounds, as Louis
Armstrong. The man heard music in all things. One night after he
had showered and toweled we stood at the end of the darkened Steel
Pier, smoking in silence. I later would write, "For long moments he
looked up at the full moon, and watched the surf come and go. The
glow from his cigarette faintly illuminated the dark old face in repose
and I thought of some ancient tribal chieftain musing by his campfire, majestic and mystical. There was only the rush of water, gently
roaring and boasting at the shore. 'Listen to it, Pops,' he said in his
low, chesty rumble. 'Whole world's turned on. Don't you dig its pretty
sounds?' "

When Louis Armstrong died a few years later, the piece I'd written for *Harper's* was chosen to be reprinted in the official program
issued at Pops' memorial service. I flew to New York for that service
and shed a tear or two as Peggy Lee (about whom I had earlier
written for *Cosmopolitan*) sang a medley of songs the old man would
have enjoyed or, indeed, have been delighted to join in.

If Louis Armstrong was the most open of subjects, the most closed
and uptight was New York's Governor Nelson Rockefeller. He feared
anyone's getting an inward glimpse of him. I don't know whether he
had something to hide or was so basically insecure he privately judged
himself a fraud and thus feared exposure. Probably it was no more
than that he was powerful, arrogant and determined to play all games
by his rules. Usually, he got away with it.

I was not enchanted when Willie Morris originally asked me to write about Rocky for *Harper's*. Rockefeller had been interviewed thousands of times; he had heard the elephant and seen the owl. I sensed he would be a difficult subject. Sly old politicians generally are. Like veteran boxers, they're able to slip punches while exposing little of their chins.

"Rocky might be the only man capable of keeping Nixon out of the White House," Willie said. "He has some attractive qualities, and he's a legitimate subject to profile."

"True," I said, "but I don't think he's my type. Why don't you give the piece to Halberstam or Corry?"

"Well," Willie said, "John Cowles wants you to write the piece. He's a friend of Rocky's, you know, and he's supporting him over Nixon."

"Oh shit, Willie," I said, "are you telling me I wouldn't be a free agent? To pull my punches?"

"No no no," Willie assured me. "Not that at all. Cowles just thinks you could do a piece that might be funny and perceptive and show Rockefeller's human qualities. This is the first thing Cowles has asked me for. I'd appreciate your taking the assignment."

Willie had done so much for me I couldn't refuse. But I didn't feel good about it; I felt intimidated and a bit hog-tied.

Rockefeller was affable enough as I followed him while he campaigned for new bonds to finance New York subway improvements, flew with him to Syracuse and Buffalo for routine speeches and met his wife, "Happy," and banker brother David. Though he talked a lot he didn't say a goddam thing outside of generalities about loving people and thirsting to solve unspecified "problems." And though he came on like Mr. Congeniality—winking and grinning and slapping backs—I got the notion his staff people lived in terror of the man. After a few days of this dog-and-pony show I came down hard on Les Slote, Rocky's press secretary, demanding a private audience with the governor. If I did not get it, I said, then I would quit the piece. It took all of Slote's persuasive powers to get his boss to grant a tête-à-tête. When I appeared for it, I found stringent ground rules: no direct quotes might be attributed, and most subjects we discussed couldn't even be *indirectly* attributed. Rocky explained that a man in his position, trying to do public good, couldn't be too careful. Any misquotation or misunderstanding might impair his effectiveness. He had at his side a functionary with one of those machines court reporters use to transcribe every word, sigh or cough. When I objected to the fellow's presence, on the grounds it might impede a true one-on-one exchange, Rocky squirmed a bit and finally asked his man to leave the room. Not five minutes passed, however, until Rocky excused himself and shortly returned with the functionary and the machine. "I just must have a record of this," the governor said.

Much of what Rockefeller said that November day in 1967 in his office might have turned up on the front page of the *New York Times* had he uttered it outside the ground rules I had foolishly agreed to. Should he be elected President, he told me, he would negotiate face to face with Ho Chi Minh to end the Vietnam War. Though he was just "too goddam tired" to actively seek the GOP nomination for President again, he thought—should it appear that Dick Nixon might be nominated—the party might turn to him because Nixon was a "born loser" and Republicans had learned their lesson in the crushing of Barry Goldwater in 1964. He thought that Nixon might offer him the Secretary of State post in exchange for his endorsement; no, he wouldn't make that trade because he felt Nixon's mischief-making potential couldn't be risked. In fact, the only Cabinet position Rocky might accept in any administration was one not even in existence: a "Super-Cabinet" post, something like "Minister of the Cabinet," the holder of it being the boss of all other Cabinet members. ("The problem is, I'm the only man I know who as President might create that job.") No, should he become President he definitely would *not* offer Dick Nixon the Secretary of State job: "I love foreign policy and would be my own Secretary of State. And Dick has that 'used-car salesman' image that wouldn't serve a Secretary of State well." Yes, it was true he held no love for New York Mayor John Lindsay: Lindsay wasn't very bright or serious, merely a young man on the make.*

Governor Rockefeller prattled on for a couple of hours, taking swipes at all whose names got mentioned. I see from my old notes he wasn't exactly fond of one Ronald Reagan: "He's a disaster. Reagan thinks he's clever. He's not. He has the instinct to do the wrong thing, the insincere thing. He thinks politics is all a big game. He

---

*Later, when I wrote a piece about Lindsay for *Harper's*, the mayor said that Rockefeller felt threatened by any other "strong" politician and that accounted for the coolness between them.

has no idea what is at risk. The fella has no class."

I hurried to my hotel room, feeling full of hot stuff, and typed a six-page, single-spaced memo to Willie Morris. Early the next morning I rushed with it to *Harper's*—though for what purpose, since I had agreed to Rocky's off-the-record demands, I cannot now even guess. Morris got excited: "Larry, you've simply got to persuade Rocky to let us use some of this!"

When I tried to recant my off-the-record agreement, Rockefeller exploded: first at his staff for persuading him to grant a private audience, and then at me for attempting to welch on the ground rules. Frustrated and angry at myself, I promised to kick my own ass should I ever again permit any source to go off the record. My original thought had been that perhaps a candid interview, even off the record, might bring clues and insights I otherwise would not receive. In a certain way that proved true: I concluded that Rockefeller was an arrogant prick, and that much of what he had said—after making certain I couldn't use it—had been self-serving bilge telling me what he thought I wanted to hear. Hindsight is wonderful, but I regret having written that powder-puff piece to this moment.

Reporters all too often, I think, permit their sources—especially if they are powerful government officials—to go off the record or on "backgrounder." They excuse themselves, as I did, by rationalizing that they may learn something helpful to their work. That may occasionally be justified, but I think not. Too often politicians use the "backgrounder" or nonattributable ploy to conceal or propagandize. Any journalist offered an interview under those terms should probably pick up his hat, if he has one, and leave. Maybe if we would all do that the politicians would finally learn they can't use us for their own purposes.

The Rockefeller failure aside, my *Harper's* pieces were attracting the attention of magazine editors who claimed to palpitate for my work. My natural appreciation of myself, certain to flower when sprinkled with even the slightest drops of success, gave me a growing sense of my literary worth (everywhere evident, it seemed, except at NAL) and led me sometimes to demand fees perhaps more appropriate to my literary betters. More than one editor screamed, "Good Christ, I wouldn't pay Mailer"—or Talese or Breslin or Tom

Wolfe—"that much money!" If I have learned anything as a free-lance writer, it is that many magazines pay about a decade behind the prevailing wages in other industries and resent surrendering even that much. I suppose this is the natural by-product of their being besieged by supplicants willing to work for coolie wages in exchange for the honor of being published. While I once would have exchanged my own byline for very small coin—and sometimes did—you would be surprised how quickly that arrangement becomes unsatisfactory.

Jim Bellows, then the top editor at *West* (the Sunday supplement of the *Los Angeles Times*), came up with a scheme to get my work more regularly—with more money for me and at less cost to him. Bellows offered a package deal to sister Sunday supplements around the country. Each of them would have the option of printing the same story on a given Sunday and pay according to their individual circulation figures. *West* would charge each of the other supplements a fee for packaging the deal, for choosing the subjects and for fronting my expense money. In this way I might get paid two to eight times per article and *West*, in effect, cleverly would get my pieces free. The happy arrangement lasted through seven or eight articles (on such diverse subjects as oil billionaire H. L. Hunt, then-senator and former Hollywood hoofer George Murphy, and how President Johnson was turning the Texas hill country into a living memorial to himself by the romantic refurbishing of LBJ birthplaces (he sometimes claimed two!), LBJ boyhood homes and LBJ country schoolhouses—before somehow petering out; I suspect this was because Bellows kept choosing California subjects, I kept choosing Texas subjects and this didn't suit editors in Chicago, Miami, et al. While it lasted, the arrangement brought me from $4,000 to $8,000 per article—by far the most impressive magazine money then to have shown itself in my presence.

My favorite of the packaged yarns was called "How to Succeed in Texas Without Really." It was about a shrewd woman, a practical nurse from Tennessee, and her semiliterate shadetree-mechanic husband, who convinced a lot of people who should have known better that the couple had a rightful claim on a vast, disputed oil fortune then slowly being threshed out in the courts. They hocus-pocused millions away from a Catholic order, big Texas banks, Neiman-Marcus and many other embarrassed institutions or individuals hoping to cash in when the "heirs" received their billions.

Meanwhile, the couple visited Lyndon and Lady Bird in the White House, flew on Air Force One, broke bread with the Speaker of the U.S. House of Representatives, and received in their Texas mansion hat-in-hand visits from Governor John Connally and other politicians who instinctively courted the Big Rich. They bustled about in private railway cars and chartered Lear jets, hired Guy Lombardo and his orchestra to play a private dance at their ranch, bought furs or sports cars or diamonds or blooded cattle as casually as you or I might buy a paperback book or a popsicle and, in general, lived a fantasy set to soft lights, rich food and free music. When the scheme ultimately exploded, the couple having no more rightful claim on the oil fortune than you did, a lot of prominent people got very expensive egg on their faces. It was my kind of rascals-win story and I loved doing it. The crowning irony and delight was that Margaret and Ernest Medders, though indicted on many serious charges, never served a day in jail. After one long, costly trial ended in a hung jury—and the public embarrassment of many big shots—the prosecution lost heart. The Medders' lawyer arranged suspended sentences in exchange for their pleading guilty to the relatively minor charge of selling mortgaged cattle. Under the Texas Homestead Act, they were even permitted to retain their big farm, mansion, sleek Cadillac—it qualified, under the old law, as "the family carriage"— and other vital furnishings or equipment. Those of you worried about the morality of the thing may take comfort in this news: the couple eventually had to sell everything to make token restitutions (promised as part of the plea-bargaining process) and to pay their astronomical legal fees. Still, Margaret and Ernest had enjoyed a long free ride that no doubt beat emptying bedpans or replacing leaky gaskets.

Hollywood dickered about buying that story, but, as so often happens when Tinsel Town gets involved, nothing happened except a lot of meetings and big talk. Still, with *Harper's* paying much better, with the package deal in effect, and by working regularly for *True*, *Saturday Evening Post*, *Holiday* and *Cosmopolitan*, among others, I began at last to retire ancient debts and even to harbor visions of higher living.

Now and again I paused to ask myself where all the scrambling about to produce magazine pieces might be taking me as a writer. I felt the need to have a plan, some grand design or purpose. Faulkner had invented his own small world, had mined its ore for a lifetime, and yet dealt in universal themes. John D. MacDonald had settled on the limited private-eye genre, but managed to get in social commentary and his view of the world in a particular time and place. Mailer's theme, running through all his books, seemed to be man's vulnerability and sheeplike conduct in a world increasingly ordered by institutional greed and evil technology. Where was *my* theme? What was I trying to say? Wouldn't it be better to slow down, figure it out and then single-mindedly pursue my goal? But there never seemed to be time. There was always rent to pay, and just one more assignment and then another and another after that. *Tomorrow*, I would promise myself. *I'll do it tomorrow*. But tomorrow, when it came, would find me rushing through another airport on yet another assignment to put meat on the table.

In putting together my nonfiction collection, I had added a great deal of new material: opening stuff, bridging stuff, afterword stuff updating the articles; hell, you've got to dress up retread goods as best you can. In a hurry to produce that second book, I had too hastily written much of the new stuff but assumed my excesses would be pruned by a loving editorial hand. When my galley proofs arrived, it became painfully evident my manuscript had hardly been touched. I took the proofs to Willie Morris, so that he might read them before writing a foreword to the book. "Larry," he said, "there's some good new material here but it sure needs editing. Somebody has to cut it and shape it."

I telephoned Bob Gutwillig to pass on that comment. You might have thought I had begged to spend a private weekend with his wife: "Goddammit, that's bullshit! If Willie Morris isn't satisfied with the editing of your goddam book, then let him do it!" *Bang! Bzzzzzzzzzzzz.* I gallomped back to Morris and begged him to do it. Sorry, he was simply too busy with *Harper's*, and besides, he was writing his own book, *North Toward Home*. I swallowed my pride, called Bob Gutwillig again, kissed his ass, told him jokes and was just about to sidle up against begging more editorial assistance when he interrupted: "Look, buddy, I've given your damned collection all the time I can. It may surprise you to hear this, but I have other books to edit and other crazy writers to appease. If you aren't satisfied with our editing job, do it yourself."

Furious, I shouted that I goddam well *would* edit the book myself and banged the phone in my editor's ear before he could again bang it in mine. My editing and rewriting, accomplished between magazine assignments, occupied three or four months. When I finished, there was a big fight with NAL management over whether I or the publishing house should pay for the considerable cost of resetting much type. Much blame-placing and howling occurred. Eventually Bob Gutwillig (perhaps because he felt twinges of guilt over hardly having touched the manuscript, or perhaps merely to rid himself of my angry midnight calls) persuaded his superiors that the publishing house should pay. "Your book is a little tighter and better now," he grudgingly admitted.

Next we fought over the title. I wanted to call my collection *Something Old, Something New.* Everyone from the editor-in-chief to the lowest NAL traveling salesman said nix: it was a nothing title, a blah title. Worse, according to Gutwillig, it tipped off prospective buyers we were trying to pawn off a collection. I then suggested *Not a Collection,* only to receive a lecture on the need to be serious and do everything possible to encourage sales. Okay, then, how about *Uncle Larry's Fuck Book?*

We settled on *My Hero LBJ & Other Dirty Stories,* a title inspired when a friendly Texas congressman passed word that President Johnson had branded my *Harper's* article "a damn dirty story." Everyone seemed happy. A dust jacket bearing that title was designed, approved and whisked off to production. Then guess who suddenly announced he wouldn't run for President again?

The morning following LBJ's abdication, Gutwillig called to say the dust jacket was being changed and we must find a new title: "Now that the old boy's quitting, it might look like we're pissing on the corpse." I argued that six months remained until my book would be published, and by then nobody would care. Gutwillig and his colleagues did not agree. Since we had little time to procrastinate, the title was truncated to . . . *And Other Dirty Stories.* This decision later caused reviewers not knowing a certain history to grumble about a nonsensical title, and old ladies who ran bookstores to hide my book under the counter with their soft porn.

LBJ's abdication caused me other grief. Only days before he quit, I published in *Harper's* a tough, heated—if not precisely reasoned—"Easy Chair" column, "Epitaph for LBJ," asking him to quit. Though that column had not a thing to do with the President's decision (he obviously had been motivated by Senator Eugene McCarthy's strong showing against him in the New Hampshire primary, Robert Kennedy's jumping into the race and citizens rioting in the streets against the Vietnam War), many of LBJ's more avid supporters blamed and cursed me; his detractors, on the other hand, congratulated me on my power and perspicacity. I might have been able to accept plaudits for having chased a President out of office more gracefully had I not so authoritatively told the Canadian Broadcasting Company, only hours before LBJ gave the nation his notice, that his pride and macho personality would *never* permit him to quit. The next morning, distressingly early, the CBC folks knocked on my door with their cameras again in hand to give the seer a chance to say why he had been so spectacularly wrong. I am afraid I spent most of that airtime blushing and tugging my forelock.

The book-title problem more or less resolved, our next war was over the size of the first print run of *Dirty Stories*. "You're gonna scream," Gutwillig predicted, "but the first printing will be six thousand copies." I screamed. Why, hell, unless the run was at least *twice* that, why bother? Shit, you couldn't sell a mere 6,000 of anything at $5.50 and show a decent profit! "We couldn't sell ten thousand of your highly publicized, overly advertised novel," Gutwillig countered. "What makes you think a little collection will fare better?" I argued that my magazine work had created new fans. "All of whom will have read eighty percent of the stuff in your collection," my editor counterpunched, "and who won't be tempted to lay out five-fifty to read it again."

Secretly, I figured him right. I had no choice but to fight for a larger press run, however, because of that damnable thing publishers call the Formula. The Formula—may it be forever cursed and one day soon become extinct—largely determines the size of the advertising budget for a given book. The Formula is worshiped in publishing houses at least three times each day, and invoked anytime an author makes so bold as to question why miserly advertising sums have been attached to his Art: "Well, we've already spent all we can under the Formula. . . ." People's peckers fall off, you see, the minute the Formula is violated, and earthquakes occur in Times Square.

One ingredient in the Formula is the size of the advance royalty paid to the author; another is the size of the first printing. The more a publisher has paid for a book, and the more copies he publishes, the better for the author when the Formula is invoked at ad-campaign time. Conversely . . . well, you immediately understand why I felt compelled to fight. Considering I had received only a $4,000 advance for *Dirty Stories*, and that NAL planned a mere 6,000 first run, one could easily discern that one's advertising budget was likely to be exhausted by cab fares to a half-dozen Manhattan radio talk shows.*

I failed to persuade them to increase that first printing. The best I got was a loose promise that should my book show an unexpected "early leg"—i.e., initial good sales—then a second printing, of indeterminate size, would be "immediately considered." As I left Bob Gutwillig's office, I decided that was not enough of a commitment.

I went straight to my agent to say that the New American Library romance was over: my publishing house obviously had lost confidence in me, and I was rapidly losing confidence in it. I wanted out of my contract there quickly as it could be arranged; by dark, if possible. Sterling Lord, a cautious man, said he thought that might be a shade abrupt. However, given time, he thought we could gain my release. Several publishing houses had quietly let it be known that I would be welcome in their rooms anytime I needed shelter; my agent would discreetly probe to determine the degree of their interest. Perhaps, however, we should not make a binding decision until after my collection was published four or five months in the future: should my book receive good critical treatment, I might become a more valuable property. He would begin careful probings, but I should meantime remain close-mouthed, rock no boats, burn no bridges. I knew that would be difficult in my case, but agreed to try.

---

*It perhaps should be said the Formula is occasionally relaxed, as in the case of my first book. My current editor, Chuck Verrill, claims I have overly simplified the Formula and its applications, but that is an *editor* talking.

On a mid-May morning in 1968, my wife's doctor telephoned from the National Institutes of Health hospital with disturbing news. Rosemarie's most recent X-rays had revealed what might be abnormalities; the doctors thought she should immediately check into NIH for extended tests. Did I want to tell my wife, or should the doctor? I said I would handle it, and called Rosie for lunch; she had returned to part-time work, perhaps six months earlier, for a House subcommittee chaired by Congressman Hugh Carey of Brooklyn.

I had been confident that Rosie was doing well physically. She had not complained of pain or fatigue and—except for a bout of depression at the time of Dr. Martin Luther King's assassination in April—had seemed of good cheer. Indeed, her doctors recently had indicated that should she make another three months without regressing then she might be home free. God, I hated to bear the bad tidings! Showering and dressing for our luncheon date, I tried to find words that might break the news gently or offer comfort. I found no magic in my head.

I had suggested that we go "somewhere off the beaten path" for lunch, claiming to be tired of the Democratic Club, the Filibuster Room and other Capitol Hill spots we frequented. Actually, I had wanted to be in a quiet, private place should Rosie have an emotional reaction to the bad news; somewhere she wouldn't be seen or heard by friends and coworkers. I should have known she would not be so easily fooled. When I picked her up outside the Longworth House Office Building, Rosie hardly had settled in the car before shooting a quick glance and saying, "Something's wrong, Lar. What is it?"

I told her, haltingly, trying to sound much more casual than I felt or than the circumstances perhaps warranted. Her face tightened, she nodded and she said, "Goddammit, I've sensed something was wrong since last October." Then why hadn't she told me? She shrugged and asked what good would that have done. We rode in silence until she said, "How drunk can I get at lunch?" Well, I said, actually the doctors wanted her to check into NIH that same night to begin tests the following morning. "No," she said. "I'll go in tomorrow night. Today and tonight we'll party."

Rosie asked to go to the New Market Inn, not far from our apartment, where they served large, strong drinks and featured a big

piano bar famed for loud, rinkety-tink music and old songs the customers joined in bawling. I thought it a curious choice, given our
mood and the fact that Rosie cared not at all for such alleged music.
But it seemed not the time to quibble. Once we'd ordered drinks,
Rosie called Congressman Carey to say she wouldn't be back for a
while and to confide why; Hugh Carey had been our friend long before becoming Rosemarie's boss, so he was kind and understanding.
I telephoned NIH to arrange for my wife's admission in accordance
with her wishes. Then we began hours of a desperate, forced merrymaking while an assemblage of drunks murdered "Sweet Adeline,"
"My Buddy" and the like. Never had I had such little fun getting
drunk.

Rosemarie's tests required two weeks. At their conclusion, her
doctors recommended new major surgery. She then would remain in
the hospital for observation and treatment for several weeks. Trying
to put a good face on it, I guess, the young NIH doctor said we were
lucky: the tests had revealed difficulties which might not have appeared on X-rays for six months or a year, so we were getting a
jump on the problem. This was not the kind of luck we felt inclined
to celebrate. Rosie was particularly upset that a trip we had planned—
to New Orleans and then to the white beaches of coastal Mississippi
and the rocky bay of Galveston, while I wrote a *Holiday* piece to be
titled "The Gumbo Riviera"—had to be canceled. I told her it was
just a postponement, not a cancellation.

My wife did not recover well. She was in much pain, had post-
surgical complications and fell into a deep mental depression. Visiting her every day, my depression soon matched hers. That was the
beginning of a periodic despair afflicting each of us, times when we
found it difficult to communicate beyond the most shallow chitchat.
We tried, but the shadow was too big. Fearful things lurked in that
shadow we couldn't yet bring ourselves to talk about, though we
were all too aware they were there. I now know this was almost
classically "normal"—the first painful step each partner takes in a
doomed relationship, even if subconsciously, to begin to disengage
from it. The first internal recognition that all is lost. . . .

When not visiting the hospital, I tried to blot out reality with hard
work and whiskey. I wrote book reviews and pieces I already had
researched or that did not require much research or interviewing: a
frothy thing for *Cosmopolitan* about the differences between North-

ern women and Southern women, some others I can't recall. When I got too drunk to write, I tumbled into bed to sleep a dark and dreamless sleep.

Every writer in America—except me—seemed to be writing stories about Senator Robert Kennedy. Sometime in late spring or early summer, as it became increasingly clear Senator Kennedy just might gain the Democratic nomination for President, I proposed to Ronnie Dugger that I write an article for the *Texas Observer* looking into a crystal ball: how might Kennedy II differ from Kennedy I in the White House? Though I was supporting Senator Eugene McCarthy, and rather resented Bobby Kennedy's jumping into the presidential race after McCarthy had proved LBJ vulnerable in the New Hampshire primary, the Kennedy vs. Kennedy comparisons excited my imagination. I was perhaps halfway through a rough first draft of the piece—having worked on it one night into the wee hours after watching Senator Kennedy claim victory in California—when it became sadly moot. Moments after I'd turned off my TV set, Sirhan Sirhan fatally shot the young senator in a passageway off the kitchen of a Los Angeles hotel. Only when I woke at midmorning did I discover that Robert Kennedy had been dying during the hours I shaped an article trying to predict what he might do as President of the United States.

I morosely watched television with Rosemarie in her hospital room as the train bearing Senator Kennedy's body brought him from New York to Washington for burial in Arlington National Cemetery beside his older brother. In a bizarre accident, the funeral train killed spectators who had overflowed onto the track. Rosie and I talked little on that dismal day. Death, its grim jests and sterile accouterments, seemed all around us; seemed to lurk in every corner of the room as we stared, numb and speechless, at the television set in that strangely sunny and airy cancer ward. . . .

Shortly after my Rockefeller piece appeared in *Harper's* that spring I received a call from the governor's irrepressible press secretary, Les Slote, saying Rocky had liked it. "He should have," I blurted. "It was a goddam candy-ass job and you know it." Slote laughed, then got down to business: confidentially, the governor—after months of waffling—had privately decided to make a last-ditch run for the GOP presidential nomination to keep Dick Nixon from getting it, and he wanted to hire me as a speechwriter. I was momentarily startled, then laughed and declined: I had done the political staff bit when younger and simply wasn't interested. "When a Rockefeller wants something he usually gets it," Slote said. "Why don't you catch the next flight up so we can settle the specifics? We don't have time to waste haggling. Name your price." I remained adamant. Slote warned I had not heard the last of it.

Within an hour John Emmett Hughes called; he once had been the head speechwriter for President Eisenhower and now was in that capacity for Governor Rockefeller. Hughes made warm, welcome-aboard sounds in asking how soon I could report for duty. I said I had really meant it when I declined the job to Les Slote. Hughes pumped me up about how much help he needed, how much Rocky wanted me and all the power to be delegated my way. It all sounded nice and friendly, I told Mr. Hughes, but I was unwilling to interrupt my writing career and had a crawful of working in politics. He asked me to think on it and said he would be back in touch. Almost immediately Les Slote again called: "Listen, you goddam fool, don't you want to make some money and help to make a President? We're serious about this!"

Well, face it, *I* had begun getting a little serious. After all—I rationalized—I had never risen above the spear carrier's role in a presidential campaign; it might be heady to whiff the gases of real power. And even should Rockefeller fail in his last-gasp grab for the presidency (and I could not imagine the GOP nominating him) I might get a decent book out of it. One of those "inside" jobs that sold better than hula hoops. And there was that tempting Rockefeller bankroll to be dipped into. I didn't know how long Rosemarie might be ill, or how costly her treatments might become. I knew that no matter how hard I worked for the magazines, if worst came to worst I wouldn't be able to earn enough to pay for her treatment and care; free-lance writers have difficulty getting group insurance rates.

I called Willie Morris to solicit his advice. "Larry, you would be making a big mistake," he said. "You write a lot of politics, and it won't help for you to become known as 'Rockefeller's man' or anybody else's man. Please don't do it." I said I was not inclined to do it, but wanted to think a bit more. My friend Warren Burnett thought I should do it: "Get your hands on that big money. Store it away like a squirrel storing nuts. It can make you more independent. And have you ever heard of a man being hurt by associating with Rockefellers?" Hardly had this advice been delivered than Willie Morris called back to say he could not too strongly recommend that I resist temptation: "I don't think Rocky's really got a shot now, and you could lose momentum in your writing career." I cogitated but briefly, decided Willie was exactly right, then telephoned both Les Slote and John Emmett Hughes to say thanks but no thanks.

Perhaps fifteen minutes later a honey-voiced young lady told me to hold on for Governor Rockefeller. I grinned. Damn Willie Morris! Morris, you see, could drop all the Southern mush from his voice and successfully imitate almost anyone on the telephone: Russian generals, British fops, Ivy League clench-jaws, various celebrities or our mutual friends; he several times had victimized me with such ruses. Well, this time I was ready.

"Governor Rockefeller" came on the wire, burbling about how he needed me in his campaign, about how America needed me, how we would reach for the stars together and such foolishness. He just wouldn't take no for an answer, now, so he would look forward to receiving me at three o'clock tomorrow in his Manhattan office.

"Sure you will," I said. "Then right after that you can go piss up a stump."

Silence. Then: "I beg your pardon?" I laughed. "Come off it, Willie." Another silence. Then the voice said, "Who *is* this?"

It dawned that I was, indeed, speaking to Governor Rockefeller. I spluttered, stuttered and burped a speech about what a high honor he had offered, how I was flattered beyond any singing of it, but really couldn't take the job for many reasons, including my wife's health problems. But Rocky said, "Come to my office tomorrow and we'll talk. I'm confident we can work it out. Problem-solving is my business."

Well, hell. What now?

I called Sterling Lord and brought him up to date: "What I want is some way out. I have a notion Willie's right. I also suspect the big promises being made will evaporate into thin air. Other politicians have promised me the moon, and I didn't even get a piece of green cheese." We decided to demand an outrageous price and conditions to match: I wanted $1,000 per day, Sundays included; I could not travel to New York or beyond except sparsely, because of my wife's illness. I would insist on doing most of my speechwriting at home. Anyone wanting to confer with me would have to settle for the telephone or fly to Washington. We laughed about how quickly our demands would be rejected; I went back to the typewriter.

A few minutes later Sterling Lord was back on the phone: "What do we do now? They want to know how quickly you can start."

Well, *Jesus*! A thousand bucks *a day*? Seven thousand bucks *a week*? And hardly have to leave the house? Hell, even if Rocky fell on his face I might grab a quick $75,000 before he hit the ground! "It's something to think about," my agent said. He had the sound of a man who had been computing his 10 percent.

Willie Morris was as stunned as I had been: "There ain't that much money in the world!" The old Mississippi boy then said, well, hell, he couldn't tell a friend not to jump in a honey bucket—but he did think his initial reaction had been right; he hoped I would at least sleep on it before consenting to become Rocky's man. "What poor boys forget," he laughed, "is that it ain't easy to price a Rockefeller out of the market."

I went to the hospital to tell Rosie. Her jaw dropped. "Lar, are you *crazy*? Take it! Call Rockefeller's office right now!"

I had trouble finding sleep. The next morning, after warning Rosie what I was about to do, and gaining her grudging consent, I telephoned Les Slote and leveled with him. He, too, thought it amusing that I had tried to price a Rockefeller out of something he wanted. We laughed together, though my laughter may have been a little hollow as I saw $1,000 bills winging away on the wind. I recommended for the job a fellow Texan living in Connecticut—David Niven, then a staff writer for *Life*—and quickly called Niven, before Slote could reach him, to recommend he not sell himself cheaply.

Governor Rockefeller, of course, got the squat beat out of himself in that final, ill-considered grab for the presidency; the GOP machinery and Dick Nixon quickly steamrolled him and again humiliated him. Still, for a time I wondered whether I had made a giant mistake in turning down all that money. One day I got a note from David Niven indicating I had not: he had quit after only a couple of weeks because working conditions had proved impossible and, sure enough, all the big promises made him had not been kept.

I tried to use Niven's experience to get off the hook with Rosemarie: "If mild-mannered, patient David Niven couldn't last but a couple of weeks, then you know damn well I would have lasted only about half of that."

"True," she said. "But at least we'd have seven thousand dollars."

Willie Morris was obsessed with *Harper's* having the best political convention coverage of any national magazine in 1968; he spoke of devoting an entire issue to making history with "the most detailed, analytical, insightful look at the American political processes ever."

David Halberstam was to draw the choice assignment—the warring Democrats in Chicago—while I had to be content with invading Miami to spy on and reveal the Republicans in their expected coronation of Richard Nixon. Naturally, I bitched over this unfair division of labor. The expected bloody fratricides in the Democratic camp constituted a real story; the Republican convention looked so cut and dried it hardly qualified as a story at all: even the official prayers would probably be on the TelePrompTer. Besides, how many Republicans do you know who are any fun? Would you look forward to spending a couple of weeks with a whole damn arenaful of them? Halberstam had been on the road with the Democratic candidates to the last in number, however, and was presumed to have developed alliances and sources superior to my own. I think, too, he was perceived as a more serious-minded man and thus more likely to interpret the bloodlettings in a rational, acceptable way. Perhaps Willie feared I would give him too much of Hunter Thompson if inflamed in Chicago; Miami presumably would lull me to a less dangerous state.

For months I spent all possible spare moments reading and talking about Nixon and the Republican supporting players—haunting my Capitol Hill sources—and the drill was about as exciting as watching fat men play croquet. Much time was consumed in filling out the many forms and résumés necessary to gain proper convention credentials. Morris was required to accomplish tedious paperwork vouching for me; for all his talents as a near-genius editor, he fell short of brilliance in administrative matters. I stayed on his ass to the point of mutual irritation. The closer the GOP convention loomed, the more vague and shifty Willie seemed in response to my inquiries about credentials, quarters, legmen and logistics. One night it dawned that Willie had not told me everything, that I possibly was being counted out without having seen the punch. The next morning I flew to New York to face him.

We repaired for lunch to Greenstreet's, in the East 30s near our magazine offices. "Okay, Willie," I said, "what is it you ain't told me about that goddam Republican convention?"

Morris shifted in his seat and gazed into his martini. "Well, Larry, you know I love you and ol' Halberstam like brothers. You are two of the best, most sensitive writers working in American letters." After he'd compared us favorably to the Rock of Gibraltar, good grass and sweet rain, I said, "Cut the poetic bullshit, Willie, and just tell me the damn deal."

"Well, see, sorta at the last minute Norman Mailer has become available to cover both conventions for us. And I just couldn't turn that down! John Cowles, you know, he's been eager to get some of the best big names in the magazine on a regular basis, and, well, anytime you can get *Norman Mailer*, why, you *get* him."

"Goddammit, Willie! Why couldn't you at least have told me so I could have tried to line up another magazine? Hell, I might have been able to find one that would have assigned me the Democrats! Shit, man, now all that work getting ready has gone to waste and I've been associating with goddam Republicans for nothing!"

Willie murmured soothing sounds, vaguely promising to make it up to me. I sat stewing, sputtering and pouting. I knew Morris historically had a tough time breaking bad news to writers; he would procrastinate forever rather than pipe unpleasant music. While I sympathized with his reluctance to drop bricks on people working in a most uncertain business, I felt that in his efforts to be kind Willie sometimes complicated lives by not quickly facing problems that wouldn't go away.

Morris bought a batch of drinks by way of making up. I drank them, of course, though they did little to cool my red ass. "What are you paying Mailer?" I challenged after a long silence.

"Larry, now, you know I can't tell you another writer's price!"

"Oh, bullshit! This is *me* you're talking to! Not some damn *Times* reporter."

"Well . . . you gotta promise to keep it strictly to yourself." I nodded. Willie's eyes swept the room, searching for hidden microphones. "Ten thousand dollars," he whispered.

"Ten thousand dollars! Jesus Christ!" Willie, flushing red, frantically shushed me as restaurant patrons turned to stare. "Dammit, Willie, I have to write *five* pieces for you to earn that much!" Morris said, well, dammit, Mailer would fill an entire issue with his prose, he would be at the conventions for weeks, a lot of work was involved, and, after all, Mailer was *Mailer*.

I sulked awhile and said, "This is the second assignment Mailer has cost me this summer."

Willie sat up straighter, his interest evident. "How's that?"

"Well, *Holiday* offered me three thousand bucks—a fortune to them and to me—to do a long piece on Mailer. Hang out, observe him, interview him. Rhyme him with his work. I'd love that. So I called Mailer and he said he couldn't give me any time until after the conventions. I now know why." Willie hid in his martini glass. "When I tried to pin him down to a date, Mailer said he felt 'overexposed.' He wasn't sure he wanted a big piece written about him just now. The best I got was a promise we'd have dinner in October or November and talk it over."

"I guess ol' Norman's pretty busy," Willie said.

"That's fucking self-evident," I snapped. We finished lunch in a cracking tension.

Sure enough, all magazines my agent contacted had earlier hired their convention writers. I settled for writing a short piece on network television coverage of the conventions ("Goodnight Chet, Goodnight David, Goodnight Rosemarie") which was lost in the same *Harper's* issue dominated almost cover-to-cover by Mailer's double-convention piece.

Mailer, of course, did a superb job of reporting those conventions. Columnists, feature writers, talk-show hosts and editorials took notice of his good work. This naturally reflected well on *Harper's*. When Mailer's work came out as a book, *Miami and the Siege of Chicago*, it won critical acclaim and was a commercial success. I had to admit that no matter how much Willie's decision had irritated and pained me, he had made the correct one for his magazine.

Weeks later, I dined with Mailer to discuss the *Holiday* piece. At that point where liquor aided candor, he frankly said he hoped I would not insist on writing the piece. True, he felt overexposed at the moment, but beyond that he feared the piece might somehow cause hard feelings between us; it was difficult, he said, for one writer to write about another and for both of them to end up feeling good about it. He named another writer he had thought a good fellow, but the man had written such an evil, envious piece—the devil had been in it—that Mailer would forever after think of that writer as a bad man. He thought there were enough feuds and backbitings in the literary world: Why should we risk adding another? On reflection I agreed. I knew all too well how sensitive writers could be when they, or their work, came under the critical eye of a fellow scrivener. And I had learned it the hard way.

My first lesson came when *The New Republic* asked me to write a long essay on the then-existing literature about Lyndon B. Johnson. My piece treated perhaps a dozen books. One veteran writer, whom we shall here call Freddie Barfmore, took exception to my comment that his was a book offering LBJ not the slightest benefit of a single doubt; the writer's anti-LBJ prejudices, I said, were flagrantly paraded and sometimes bordered on the vicious. Almost immediately I received a love note from Mr. Barfmore. Because the copyright laws reserve publication rights of letters for the person who writes them, not the person who receives them, I am unable to directly quote Mr. Barfmore without his permission; my gut instinct is that he would not accommodate my permissions request even these many years later. I *can* say, however, that Mr. Barfmore's note guessed that I might be a young faggot who knew no history; he also accused me of knowing that LBJ, Bobby Baker's aide, was involved in crooked deals and of having done nothing about it, and of supporting Lyndon notwithstanding his war. His concluding paragraph compared my character to maggots and garbage.

There were several errors in Mr. Barfmore's letter. For one thing, I was not all that young and have a history of appreciating girls. I had *not* risen to the defense of LBJ—indeed, because of what I had earlier written about him, I was on the President's shit list. I had not cheered his Vietnam War but had quarreled with it in print and had demonstrated and spoken against it. I had made no claims of being cognizant of Bobby Baker's specific improprieties, having referred only to a general knowledge on Capitol Hill that Baker was a high-flying wheeler-dealer in the corridors of power. I should have responded—if at all—by correcting Mr. Barfmore's accusations. Early on in my writing career, however, I had determined that should I receive rude, abusive letters I would respond in kind and, if possible, return more vitriol than I had received; this possibly stemmed from frustrations when I worked in Congress and, in responding to abusive mail sent to my bosses, had been under orders to turn the other cheek or respond with that soft answer which allegedly turneth away wrath. Mr. Barfmore's insults triggered the following response:

> Dear Mr. Barfmore:
> You apparently are a man of two no-talents: not only can you not write, you cannot read.
> Thanks for giving me your candid opinion of what I am like. On the basis of your book and your letter, my candid opinion is that you are a dry-balled, humorless, self-righteous, spoiled old shit.

Mr. Barfmore, pulse obviously pounding, raced to the typewriter to say he had reproduced my letter and mailed copies to various magazines and public figures, including my "hero" LBJ. He snidely offered to enlarge the mailing list if I thought it might help my career, provided I sent him the names.

I spent the better part of an afternoon typing the names and addresses of perhaps 300 good Americans and dispatched them to Mr. Barfmore with a scrawled note saying (1) I hoped he would strive to circulate my letter in a timely fashion, (2) I trusted he was feeling better and (3) might one day be able to get his pecker up. This response somehow excited Mr. Barfmore's wife. She wrote me a postcard marked "personal"—rather funny in itself—containing such tender mercies as wishing I could be forced to spend the rest of my life in a military hospital where I would be required to gaze in perpetuity on those good American boys Lyndon and I had crippled in our war.

I decided it was getting a bit sticky, and that I didn't know the lady well enough to respond in kind; besides, a loyal spouse rising to the defense of a presumably fouled partner should be given room enough to caper just short of lethal weapons. The Barfmore correspondence makes the point, I believe, that writers other than myself sometimes react dramatically to the critical word.

As time passed and I increasingly reviewed books, I received other cutting letters from wounded authors (though none so spirited as the Barfmore Letters) or saw my alleged victims turn their backs at social affairs. I also learned that should one review a book by a friend—

or, sometimes, even by a casual acquaintance—and fail to give the author a clear nod over Shakespeare, George B. Shaw and either Hemingway or Faulkner, then he likely had made an enemy who would teach his descendants to hate all Kings through the seventh generation. I have often fretted over the wisdom of passing literary judgments: *someone* must review books, of course, and isn't it better for those of us who know something of what goes into the making of them to do the job rather than leave it to theorists, specialists, dry academicians or other dwarfs? On the other hand, why should one let oneself in for grief and insults from other writers when neither the money nor the thrill is worth it? At times I pondered the quitting of reviews, but like all addicts had difficulties with my resolve.

Years after the Barfmore incident, the book editor of the *Chicago Sun-Times*, Henry Kisor, asked me to review *Authority*, by one Richard Sennett. Lord knows I tried. Ultimately, however, I wrote Mr. Kisor the following letter:

Dear Mr. Book Editor:

I wouldn't blame you if you poked me in the eye with a sharp stick. For three weeks past the agreed deadline I have been trying to muster the nerve to say I simply cannot review *Authority*, by Richard Sennett. It may be my fault more than Mr. Sennett's, but anytime I read more than three consecutive lines of his prose, my eyes glass over and my mind goes black and I fall plumb smack-dab to sleep if I am lucky. This is especially true should Mr. Sennett cite more than five historical or philosophical or mythical references in that short span. Which he usually does.

It appears to me that Mr. Sennett goes round and about the bush to make very long affirmations of the obvious. In doing so he exhibits a marvelous vocabulary, and evidence of having went to good schools. But this leads to thinking on the respective worths of the game and the candle. For example, I read two whole pages of fancy footwork that said to me, when I boiled it down, "If somebody pinches you likely you will hurt, and if somebody tickles you likely you will laugh."

I already knew this without consulting academicians, though I certainly hope that is not against the rules. Possibly Mr. Sennett meant to say more, though I am not wholly satisfied that he did. Whatever he said, he was most solemn in the saying of it.

And that, Mr. Editor, is my problem in a capsule: Mr. Sennett is a solemn fellow, and I am not. He writes solemn books, and I do not—at least on purpose. So we have the case of the wrong critic being handed the wrong book. Mr. Sennett is reputed to be a high-domed thinker; on the basis of such little as I have read, I am willing to accept that he is. I require no further proof.

Mark Twain once said he might be able to read Jane Austen on a salary, but I regret to say I cannot read Mr. Sennett even under those conditions—though I hear he has won medals and awards and much praise for works I have not read. I am willing to let him keep them provided I do not have to read the things he won them for. I will go so far as to say Mr. Sennett is hereby relieved of any obligation to read my stuff. Fair is fair.

Originally, when I saw that I had been very poorly matched with *Authority*, I thought to write a smart-ass review poking much fun. But that would be unfair, Mr. Sennett apparently taking his work with utmost seriousness. It would seem poor sport for me to be so publicly amused where no fun was intended. Additionally, such a course of action would have required me to wade through the remainder of Mr. Sennett's book. And that I have neither the constitution nor the willpower to do.

So, while I much regret the inconvenience caused to you and the *Sun-Times*, I here resign from that particular job of work. I may be mean and small-minded, but in an effort to improve my image I here volunteer to review any other book of your choosing. I just hope you will have the kindness to choose some work that does not put such literary responsibility on me. Surely there is a middle ground between Mr. Sennett's Art and cookbooks; it is that ground I encourage you to seek.

May I suggest you assign the review of *Authority* to Mr. Norman Podhoretz of *Commentary* magazine? I cannot, of course, guarantee whether Mr. Podhoretz will love it or hate it, though generally it is safe to say he looks down on prose other than his own. Mr. Podhoretz will match Mr. Sennett in solemnity, that much I do guarantee, and he will wade joyously into thickets of prose and forests of footnotes likely to intimidate those of us who prefer to find air on the page and know where we are at.

Wishing the very best to you, the *Sun-Times*, and Mr. Sennett, I beg to remain . . .

I was not entirely surprised when Mr. Kisor shortly wrote to suggest that he publish my letter; he would get some critic more in tune with serious matters to have a go at *Authority*, but how about using my remarks as a sidebar? Well, hell, why not? The letter perfectly described my reaction to the book, and besides, I will sell any letter I have ever written for the $150 Mr. Kisor offered. None of that only-one-to-a-customer stuff will be invoked, either. You bring that sum per letter and I'll sell you a gunnysack full of letters, many of them foolish and personal in the extreme.

But when the *Sun-Times* published my letter, Lord-dee mercy, much fit hit the shan! Not from Mr. Sennett, no; to this day I don't know whether he personally suffered the slice of my blade. But soon I heard that one Studs Terkel was having conniptions. Mr. Terkel reportedly told the book editor I was irresponsible for having written—and that the book editor was equally irresponsible for having published—such silly and immature blatherings about a Great Book. For the next few months, anytime I encountered a covey of writers one or more would report that Studs Terkel was steaming and blowing like a malfunctioning calliope. I regretted that. Truly did. I had long admired Terkel's books, particularly *Hard Times* and *Working*; I had been impressed by his thorough preparations and intelligent questions when I appeared on his Chicago radio show; I had enjoyed one memorable night lifting libations with Studs and his old writing buddy, the fiercely talented Nelson Algren, and I generally thought Studs a good heart and a bright fellow. Still do. Why he took such personal exception to a review of a book not his own is a mystery, unless he found me wanting in the intellectual-integrity department. In which case I would remind that in the instant case I am as honest as he is: Studs loved the book; I hated the pretentious thing; we each reacted according to our opinion of its worth.

Once again, however—given the highly emotional reactions of writers when their pet cats are clawed—I was given pause as to the wisdom of continuing to utter candid appraisals of other people's books. I still review a few, but only infrequently and on the sneak, like a kid smoking forbidden cigarettes behind the barn. And, honest, I'm really trying to quit.

I was sleeping in on a late-August midmorning in 1968, having worked until near dawn, when the telephone jarred me awake. Bob Gutwillig's unaccountably cheery greeting caused me to respond, "Ah, a voice out of my past." I had not heard from my book editor in weeks, perhaps months; not since we had quarreled over the small first printing of . . . *And Other Dirty Stories*. Now Gutwillig was gushing about my being "the man of the hour" and joking—I guess—that it looked as if he might have to start treating me better.

"I'm still half-asleep, Bob. What are you babbling about?"

"Better hop up and get the *New York Times*. There's a simply glowing review of *Dirty Stories* in there today."

"Well, I'm a son of a bitch," I said.

"Not as much as you were before Mitch Levitas' review today," he laughed. "Levitas seems to think you can write a bit. Your stock has risen here in the home office." Gutwillig read the review to me, considerably brightening the day, and rang off after cheerfully inviting me to New York to discuss our next book together. I did not tell him there would be no next book together: my agent had been reporting progress in seeking a new publishing home, and I was determined to find one. The *Times* review certainly would not impede the search.

Rosemarie soon telephoned from New York (where she had gone for shopping, hoping to combat her postoperative depression) and was full of hot excitement. She had bought the *Times* as her breakfast companion; while thumbing through it she ran upon the review and my picture. "Jesus, I was so excited I spilled coffee all over the place. The poor waitress had to think I was tilted. While she tried to mop up I kept sticking the review in her face and bragging that you're my husband." It was good to hear Rosie laugh again, to hear new life in her voice. She sounded like the Rosemarie I knew for the first time since surgery.

Uniformly good reviews popped up all over: from Geoffrey Wolff in the *Washington Post*, Herman Kogan in *Book Week*, Jack Conroy in the *Kansas City Star*, Robert Cromie in the *Chicago Tribune*, Lon Tinkle in the *Dallas Morning News*; on and on. Only Bill Buckley's *National Review* was full of scorn; a citizen doing mischief under the name of P. P. Witonski wrote, "Larry King is one of those tedious 'in' journalists whose glossy prose clogs the pages of pretentiously imperative literary magazines like *Harper's*. Like the rest of his all-too-slick breed, he is at his best when dealing with the non-event, the vapid individual, or the blatantly boring. . . . Perhaps if King devoted more time to being intelligent rather than clever, he might develop into a first-rate essayist. As things stand now, he is one of the better pop-journalists, a fact which may serve to remind us of the low state of contemporary American letters." That was the worst shot I took; ol' P.P., shit, he couldn't hold R. Z.'s tar pot. Tougher and wiser than when *The One-Eyed Man* took its early clobbering, I might have fielded slings and arrows with more equanimity the second time around; happily, I was not put to that test.

I have discovered over the years that good reviews strangely fail to make the author feel as good as bad reviews make him feel bad. I don't know why; I believe, however, the observation holds for many writers. I have heard more writers damn a critic for what he did *to* them than praise a critic for what he did *for* them. I also have heard any number of writers claim they "never" or "seldom" read reviews of their work. Horseshit. The author who seriously offers that malarkey shows such talents for mendacity he should quit his typewriter and run for public office. I hold with the view of playwright Arthur Miller: "If the world blew up while a playwright was opening his newspaper, he'd be looking for his review on his way up through the stars."

Writers are curious folk by nature, else they would not poke and pry and torment the mysteries while trying to solve or describe them. One willing to shed the sweat and suffer the miseries of shaping and delivering a book or play, I am convinced, is bound to harbor enough leftover curiosity to seek out critical reactions. Many times I have heard those who claim to pay scant attention to their reviews say— after a few more drinks—what a lousy bastard is So-and-So for the judgment he passed on their Art, and then quote him. Verbatim. Writers can, of course, pay excessive attention to critics—many of whom couldn't find their asses with both hands and a helper, or who may possess literary sensibility equal to that of a moss-covered rock— but I believe we all find it difficult to ignore them. If someone says your nose is too big or your feet stink, you are likely for a while to stand in poses shielding your nose from close inspection or to compulsively wash your feet. Never mind *you* don't think your nose is all that outsized or your feet particularly malodorous: your critic, temporarily at least, will have put a certain poison in your mind. That is the main reason working writers find critics so detestable a breed. It is when the writer begins to write *for* the critics, however—rather than follow his own instincts—that he likely is on the way to doom. Class dismissed.

Early soundings by New American Library found that *Dirty Stories* was moving well in the stores for a mere collection. A second printing of 2,000 was ordered—not nearly enough to satisfy the author, who, of course, became momentarily convinced his little masterpiece soon would zoom by the offerings of Jacqueline Susann and all the Irvings—Wallace, Stone, et al.—to establish itself atop the best-seller lists. We had the small consolation of selling all copies printed—a limited honor, to be sure, but one is comforted by the knowledge that small gains are better than large losses. The original numerical scarcity of *Dirty Stories* accounts for its now costing $40 to $50 (depending on whether the dust jacket has survived, and its general condition) if a rare one can be found in dusty used-book stores. I know this because what with getting drunk and mailing them to old friends, or pushing copies on outstanding airline hostesses I hoped to know better, I ultimately wound up with absolutely no copies— and had to pay those outrageous prices to replenish the family archives.

Sneaking around in soft shoes, Sterling Lord talked with a dozen publishing houses about prospects of my escaping to their tender care. Only five threw up their hands in horror when Lord said he intended to put me on the auction block winner-take-all—and, oh yes, there would be a little matter of $12,500 the auction winner would be required to pony up to satisfy the advance I had drawn from NAL for my purely theoretical second novel. My agent wanted me to talk personally with pooh-bahs of the seven houses interested in bidding, but first we had to officially win our freedom. He called Bob Gutwillig in late October to make an appointment: "So the three of us may sit down to discuss Larry's publishing future." Gutwillig, no fool, had to know we were not crossing Fifth Avenue to say everything was peachy-keen at NAL and could we please hug everybody's necks. He would, no doubt, be well armed against the invading barbarians.

On the target morning I had a severe case of nervous stomach. I truly liked Bob Gutwillig; we'd had some laughs together, he had accommodated me in tough times and had given me a start in the book business. Yet I felt Bob was under such in-house pressures because I had not lived up to expectations (however foolishly high they may have been) that other NAL authors would forever after receive the big money, the big advertising budgets and the big hellos while I scrambled for table crumbs; one who has been ardently courted is not satisfied with mere handshakes once the kissing and cooing stops. *Try to act like a cold-blooded oilman,* I told myself. *Hailfar, boy, ain't no room for sentiment when a buck is on the line. Just stick the knife in, twist it, grin and walk away.*

The three of us wore serious faces when we met in Gutwillig's office; there were formal handshakes, stiff greetings and a careful assigning of seats as if we might be representatives of warring nations maneuvering at the peace table. Meaningless chitchat. Time came for the nut-cutting. Mr. Lord launched into his set speech in my behalf about love, respect and gratitude as applied to Bob Gutwillig personally. But—he said sadly, and with much regret—it now appeared my publishing house had lost confidence in me, leading to a general disinterest and neglect. This, in turn, had caused me to lose faith in my publisher, spend much time in weeping, et cetera and so on and la-di-da. It was, therefore, time for sad goodbyes—though, of course, we would hand back all money owed New American Library almost as soon as we cleared the door.

Bob Gutwillig received Mr. Lord's speech with artful gasps of astonishment and theatrical grabs at his heart. For reply he put on a funereal expression and sadly shook his head: why, he just couldn't imagine what in the world we were talking about; not a night passed but what he, personally, and New American Library editors, collectively, got down on their knees and humbly thanked a merciful God for giving them Larry L. King; they intended to spend more money advertising my second novel than the Ford Motor Company had committed to pushing the Edsel; while he was personally cut to the quick by this unprovoked surprise attack by an old friend—which doubtless would go down in infamy along with Pearl Harbor—he was willing to be big enough and forgiving enough so that our purely imagined differences might be worked out over a cup of coffee. Cream and sugar?

It was my turn. I said Damon and Pythias were knife-wielding leaders of rival street gangs when compared to myself and Mr. Gutwillig; that the thought of having anyone else as my editor caused me heartburn and to consider taking poison; that a thousand years after the sun had died, leaving a cold void upon the earth, our spinning ball of mud would remain at least lukewarm due to the white heat of my personal affection for Gutwillig. And now that we've got all that on the record, I said, leave us cut the fiddle music and get down to the dirty bidness at hand: I had been treated like a stepchild here for the past two years, I want out, I want out *now*, and I hope we can accomplish the leavetaking without being reduced to calling one another horse's asses and chickenshits.

Gutwillig's mouth tightened. He said he had presumed there was such a thing as loyalty. I said loyalty worked both ways, and from the time *The One-Eyed Man* failed to win the Nobel Prize or chase Irving Wallace off the best-seller list I'd had trouble getting NAL to answer my phone calls. Gutwillig grabbed a thick document from a suspiciously convenient spot on his desk, wildly waved it in the air and reminded me I had a goddam *contract*. I said, speaking of loyalty and contracts, how about the time you coached me to flummox McGraw-Hill and follow you to a new publisher? Gutwillig said he didn't remember it happening that way, and besides, I was certain to get a bad reputation if I kept running out on contracts and taking money for books I didn't write. I said at least a half-dozen publishing houses thought my reputation good enough to risk offering me contracts as soon as I had shed my NAL chains. He said, oh, so you've been sneaking around for months setting up this chickenshit deal, have you? I said if he called me a chickenshit again I was gonna forget our gentleman's agreement and call him a horse's ass. Very much fist-clenching and bellowing followed: shouts of rage, shouts of pure pain, as both of the adversaries claimed to have been foully gored.

After the young bulls had worn themselves out locking horns, Sterling Lord stepped in to make a soothing little speech: These matters always were painful, especially when it involved two wonderfully close friends such as Gutwillig and myself; regrettably, however, he felt that our differences—and even our conflicting perceptions of those differences—had been made abundantly clear within the past hour. He therefore saw no hope of reconciliation or a realistic solution. We would soon send NAL its $12,500 and ask in writing for my release; he was certain we would be able to work it out as gentlemen without having to resort to invectives or lawsuits. There followed a quick flurry of perfunctory handshakes and awkward mumbles; suddenly my agent and I were in the hall and headed for the elevator.

"Are we free?" I asked.

"I think it's all a mere formality now," my agent said. I felt relieved the big hassle was behind us, though some considerable hunk of me wanted to go back, hug Bob Gutwillig, invite him out for drinks and share the old laughter once again.

Shortly before Christmas I hied to New York and nervously prowled my agent's office waiting for four o'clock to arrive. Beginning at that time, for one hour, representatives of seven potential new publishing homes would telephone to bid on a new book I had proposed.

The book was to be nonfiction; my working title was *The Lost Places*. I would travel small-town and rural America for a year, perhaps more, sometimes taking odd jobs in the communities the better to know more people quickly. My purpose would be to record what was happening to towns being bypassed by the network of new superhighways, and to the people in them. I had worked in Congress when the National Defense Highway Act passed in 1957 (in those Cold War days you could pass almost any bill by adding "National Defense" to its title) and the landscape of America began to be radically altered. By the early 1960s, in my drives between Washington and Texas, I found that for all the efficiency of the new super roads I missed passing through the small towns and villages now bypassed. Several times I quit the superhighways to briefly visit the abandoned places (that's when I began thinking of them as "lost" places) and found them dying on the vine. Tourists no longer brought the visiting dollar, each one being recirculated in the economy seven times according to local Chamber of Commerce lore; even longtime residents drove to the nearest super road and blatted to larger cities to shop; old businesses floundered or closed.

I had personally visited with editors and publishers of the seven houses due to bid on my services, pitching them verbal sales spiels about the book but not submitting anything in writing, as I recall; this allowed great leeway in adjusting my patter to fit their interests and questions. All said they wanted the book.

We had, however, been forced to amend the ground rules before the actual bidding; no house seemed willing to directly pay $12,500 to New American Library to gain my release. Some said it was against their policy to "raid" other houses or to kidnap writers already under contract; they wouldn't feel comfortable paying what amounted to ransom money. We found a way to satisfy the fastidious: okay, forget the direct payment, but remember that we must somehow pay back that money. Consider that when you bid. In other words, should the winning bid be $35,000 (the figure my agent and I privately hoped for), we simply would lop off the first $12,500 and dispatch it to NAL. My agent then would subtract his 10-percent fee from the remaining $22,500; I would pocket $20,450 for my end. Okay money, but far from a fortune when one considered that I would pay travel expenses out of it for a prolonged period. (We had asked $5,000 expense money for this purpose, over and above my advance money, but all seven houses were fearful of establishing a dangerous precedent. Or so they said. I have a tough time believing it had never been done by any of the seven.)

Strangely, as if perverse gods wished to toy with my emotions, the bids came in exactly in reverse order of their acceptability: low bids first. This served the dual purpose of at once depressing me and yet offering momentary encouragement with each new raise in the gambling game. Houghton Mifflin came in early at a paltry $15,000. "Oh, shit!" I said, casting my agent a worried look. Not to worry, he said: HM Co. was a conservative Boston-based outfit normally pretty cautious with its purse; things would get better. I thought, *They damn well better, or after paying back NAL and my agent's cut I'll be writing a book for less than $2,000. No way!* I feared that what Sterling Lord had said of Houghton Mifflin was propaganda to calm me in a nervous moment. My God, what if *everybody* bid as if buying a bus ticket?

Simon & Schuster raised the ante, but only to $17,000. I went to the men's room, gagged, washed my face, cursed, smoked another in a series of cigarettes and returned to the torment. Harcourt Brace came in at $20,000. Better, yes, but still not in the ballpark. W. W. Norton, as if reading Harcourt Brace's mail, raised by a single chip—to $21,000. *Jesus!* My instant calculation revealed that sum could mean only $7,650 for me. Mighty short rations.

Random House came in at $25,000, and I smiled for the first time. I could live with that figure if forced to the wall. Not happily, no, but . . . well, at least it would provide a new beginning, and I liked the Random House people I'd met. Still, I preferred Knopf and its young whiz-kid editor, Bob Gottlieb, or Viking Press and its gentlemanly veteran editor-in-chief, the puckish Alan D. Williams. Yet, neither of those houses had been heard from. I found this surprising, since Knopf and Viking had given the impression of being more eager than the others. Had they changed their corporate minds? Was yet another damnable conspiracy of New York Editors at work against me?

Only about fifteen minutes remained on the bidding clock when Knopf called to bid $30,000—though much of the charm fled when I heard my agent say, "Oh, but for *two* books?" I shook my head vigorously, muttered curses, and flashed a stiff middle finger; Mr. Lord rightly interpreted this sign language and told Knopf he believed not. Just when it looked as if I might be Random House–bound— and with about four bidding minutes remaining—the Viking folks called to offer $30,600; I grinned, nodded yes, and relaxed for the first time all day.

Though we had fallen almost $5,000 short of our hopes, and my personal end of the money would be $16,290—less than I'd fantasized putting in my poke—I felt good enough to telephone Rosemarie in Washington and ask her to fly up for a celebration: "Sixteen Gs won't buy you that seagoing yacht, baby, but it'll do wonders toward a steady supply of vodka martinis."

Chapter Four

GOOD TIMES
AND BAD

✳✳✳ By early 1969 Willie Morris's *Harper's* had become what the trade called "the hottest book" around. News magazines, trade publications and the daily press wrote glowing reports; *Harper's* was gaining a reputation as a showcase for lively, excellent writing. Morris had landed many of the accomplished "big name" writers coveted by owner John Cowles, had unearthed and published a number of talented unknowns and was coaxing fine work from his contributing editors. On campus tours I heard again and again from students, "We can hardly wait for each new issue."

I rejoiced in being a part of that good and heady time. Even so, the magazine treadmill was wearing me out. I felt great pressures as I met my *Harper's* quota and scrambled about for other periodicals. Life seemed to have become nothing but deadlines and travel. Some days I felt incapable of producing even one more piece. I felt, too, that almost before the ink was dry my work disappeared into a bottomless maw. Perhaps much of that hurried work fully deserved to be forgotten quickly, but that knowledge was less than comforting to the author of such perishable goods.

As time approached to hit the road to gather material for my book on America's "lost places," I felt dread rather than a proper sense of excitement. Having just passed my fortieth birthday (an event, in itself, traditionally bringing bursts of melancholy and disappointing inventories), I did not look forward to grunt jobs and hand-to-mouth living on the road for more than a year as I researched the book.

"I haven't a thing but fatigue to show for all those magazine pieces," I said gloomily to Willie Morris, "and now I've got to go off and grub stumps while writing a book that'll be lucky to sell five thousand copies." Willie commiserated about the grind of gears indigenous to the free-lance life and buttered me up about how valuable a cog I was becoming in America's literary machine.

"Willie," I blurted, "I've got to have a year off from *Harper's* with full pay." My editor blinked and said he doubted that ideal situation could be arranged; *Harper's* simply hadn't the resources to become a charitable foundation even in the good cause of resting burned-out wordmen. "It's the only way out," I insisted. "My *bones* are tired. I need to go off with Rosie, sit in the shade and study my navel. I've got to decide where I'm going as a writer. I can't keep up this mad scramble to no purpose."

"Wait a minute," Willie said. "There just might be a way." He told of the Nieman Fellowship program at Harvard, providing mid-career pauses for working journalists. They were paid a stipend—he didn't know how much—and could study courses of their choice in Cambridge for a full academic year. "It's very competitive," Willie warned. "If we *can* get you a Nieman slot, I might convince John Cowles that *Harper's* would benefit in the long run by giving you some support money." Far from greeting this generous offer with enthusiasm, I grumbled that it seemed a long shot and recalled my historic apathy toward classroom disciplines. "I'll check it out," Willie insisted. "It might be the answer."

Willie soon called to say the Nieman stipend was $534 per month, most of which would probably be required for housing in Cambridge; if I elected to try for a Nieman slot, I would be competing with about 300 American and foreign applicants. He warned that the selection committee usually favored newspaper journalists over magazine writers or free-lances. "They only take about a dozen Americans and three foreigners each year," he said. "Also, there's a tradition that no Nieman may have passed his fortieth birthday by the time he reports for classes." Hell, I said, that eliminated me: I would be going on forty-one by that time. Besides, I couldn't scrape along on $500 per month. "Hold on," Morris said. "I've talked to Cowles and he's agreed to go along with a $12,000 subsidy for you—if you're willing to write just two or three articles for us in the nine or ten months you'd be at Harvard. As to the age limitation, it seems they waived it during World War II. Perhaps you could cite that as a precedent." I decided to try. My publisher, Viking, consented to postponing the "lost places" book should I get lucky.

My letter of application stressed that I was "old, ignorant and uneducated" in pleading that my last chance at refurbishing rested in Harvard's hands. I invoked the World War II relaxation of the age standard. Required to furnish letters from three writers or editors who knew my work, I enlisted Willie Morris, David Halberstam and John Kenneth Galbraith. I was required to sign a pledge not to write for publication while at Harvard, the institution's idea being that Nieman Fellows should take a break from professional pressures so as to fully sample Harvard's offerings. But how would that pledge square with my promise to *Harper's*? Willie Morris said not to worry: if he knew me I'd find it impossible not to accomplish a certain amount of writing and he doubted whether Harvard would search my mailbox for contraband manuscripts or expel me if they found them; just sign the damned pledge. So everything was in order. All I needed was to be selected.

In due course I was asked to report to the Mayflower Hotel in Washington on a given Saturday morning for a half-hour interview with the selection committee: three working newspaper editors, three Harvard faculty members and the Nieman curator, Dwight Emerson Sargent. For two or three days before my "orals" I memorized poetry, studied the dictionary and otherwise schemed to impress with my keen intelligence and poetic soul. When I arrived for my appointment (wearing my only suit, a rumpled tie and atypically polished shoes) I waited in a Mayflower hallway while hearing through a half-open door the voice of a young applicant who, in a Southern accent, haltingly tried to explain why he throbbed to quit his weekly newspaper in Arkansas for Harvard. I thought he made a mediocre case and sent him a mental message: *Too bad, kid! Now get your fumbling ass out of there and let an old pro go to work on those stuffed shirts.*

I opened with a short rehash of my written plea (that Harvard somehow owed the world my rehabilitation) and answered a perfunctory inquiry or two. Then someone—noting from my application that I once had worked in Congress and was a Texan—asked what LBJ was *really* like. Though far from an intimate of Lyndon Johnson's, I failed to admit it and forthwith set about telling colorful LBJ yarns one after another; a few of them may even have been true. My audience laughed and hooted as if I were a nightclub comedian on a hot roll.

Then, all too abruptly, Nieman curator Dwight Sargent said my half-hour had expired and steered me toward the door. I was dumbfounded. Hell, I hadn't yet had the opportunity to invoke Shakespeare or employ any of the impressive new dictionary words I had cribbed. I felt an impulse to shout, "Wait a sec! Alfred Bernhard Nobel invented dynamite! The Battle of Hastings was fought in 1066! Side-angle-side equals side-angle-side!" But before I could parade these bits and pieces of knowledge, I ran belly to belly with a fresh-faced Nieman applicant coming through the door. Probably he wondered why that old, bearded codger shot him such a murderous look.

I repaired downstairs to the Mayflower bar, angrily tossed down a couple of quick drinks and telephoned Rosemarie. "I blew it," I said. "Goddammit, I got to bullshitting and telling LBJ stories and forgot where I was or my purpose. Just simply made an *ass* of myself!" Rosemarie chuckled and said it wasn't the first time. "No way we're going to Harvard," I said. "Start packing. We're heading out to the sticks to write that damned book about the lost places."

An old Army buddy, Dag, had suggested the small North Carolina town where he lived as ideal for my "lost places" book. His was a one-industry town—tobacco—where a major company owned and controlled everything but the city water tower. The new interstate highway system had passed his town by; it was going through an economic readjustment; locals were frightened and circulated rumors the largest tobacco company might move away.

Dag's wife, Trisha, worked in the personnel office of the big tobacco company and thought she could help me find temporary employment there to assist my book research. Dag himself, retired from the Army after twenty-odd years of service, had a good way with the bottle, yarns and a fishing rod; I knew he would be a good companion and that he might provide valuable insights, as a native of the little town, that I would be a long time acquiring on my own.

Rosie and I approached the town on an old, little-used highway flanked by fading signs advertising bargain prices on popular cigarettes. I had an initial flush of enthusiasm in reuniting with Dag, but somehow couldn't get with the writing project. Dag and I spent several days drinking and jabbering, roaming the countryside and going fishing. Rosie and I made a few perfunctory sallies from our motel to inspect rental houses but found them so old, decrepit and depressing we quickly retreated to our motel to repair our heads.

I visited the reigning tobacco company, where, with Trisha's influence, I was offered a vague job as a "trainee." I don't know what I had expected: to sit around in the shade smoking menthols while writing press releases assuring the public cigarettes cured cancer, perhaps. Instead, I was led through dusty warehouses, factory assembly lines, old sheds stinking of tobacco dust and harsh residues where some mysterious grading of tobacco leaves occurred. Ironically, "No Smoking" signs prevailed.

The foreman in charge of trainees, a redneck in a short-sleeved wash-and-wear shirt and an antique necktie, seemed less than friendly; he answered my questions with perfunctory grunts or mumbles. All he specified was that (1) I would be a general trainee, (2) trainees worked for low wages, (3) he would keep his eye on me and (4) I would be required to shave off my beard. To the last I said, "No, I don't believe I want to do that." The foreman reddened and said, "We'll see about that."

I was given a date and an hour to report for work—my God, 7:00 a.m.!—but still had no clear idea what my job might be. The night before I was to begin, I couldn't sleep for dreading the mystery work. The factory, warehouses and grading sheds had depressed me more than any place of employment I had known since, in 1949, I had worked for three days in a lead and zinc mine near Joplin, Missouri, before deciding I wasn't meant to tunnel underground like some damn blind mole. I sat up most of the night in that North Carolina motel, drinking beer and smoking, attempting to shame myself into getting into the spirit of my book. What I really wanted, however, was to be in Manhattan partying at Elaine's with my writer buddies. For damn sure I didn't want to be sweating under the hard eye of a hostile redneck foreman.

Came work time. I was stoned out of my mind and deep into beer. So I called in sick. The redneck foreman said, "You have them whiskers cut off afore you git here tomorrow mornin'." The following morning, still bearded, I telephoned to report my delicate health unimproved. And the third morning. The foreman said, "Lissen, bub, I wouldn'ta hired you no way if Personnel hadn't twisted mah arm. Either you come in slick-shaved tomorrow mornin' or I'm markin' you down on my shit list." I said, "Why don't you put me on your shit list now, you cretinous cocksucker?" Rosemarie sat up in bed, cackled and closed her eyes. Sensing a limited future in tobacco, I officially resigned and told Rosie to pack: we would find a more hospitable "lost place" to record for posterity. We stopped by Dag and Trisha's house to apologize for conduct unbecoming one who had been assisted by well-meaning friends, but they laughed and said not to worry.

We bummed around North Carolina for a couple of weeks. After one day or two days or only a few hours in one or another prospective target town I would mumble, "Naw, this ain't the place," and we would repack and move on. The truth was dawning hard and bright: while my "lost places" book had sounded romantic on paper, I found myself unwilling or unable to live through it. What I had forgotten was that the reason I so enjoyed visiting the old farms and towns of my youth was the fresh opportunity to celebrate having escaped them.

One night in some scabby outback greasy-spoon café, as we gnawed undercooked ribs, Rosemarie said, "Lar, you don't have your heart in this book. Even if you did, I don't think a city girl could face a year of these hick towns. Let's find a beach place on the coast while you think of another book to write." Within the hour we were on our way, lighthearted and laughing in relief of the lifted burden. "I don't know what the Viking folks will say about my abandoning the project," I warned. Rosie said don't tell them about it right now; wait until I had thought of a substitute book. That problem settled, we blithely motored on as if we knew what we were doing.

We found a small, little-populated island reached by a short causeway outside Atlantic Beach and arranged to rent a three-bedroom waterfront cabin—so two of my three children might visit—for most of the upcoming summer; the cabin would not be available for several weeks, however. We leisurely drove back to Washington, stopping in a number of old Virginia country inns and lingering in blissful idleness. My bones and my spirits began to feel rested and lighter. I did worry a bit that no money was being earned while my "lost places" book advance was being rapidly spent, but not enough to stir off my comfortable duff to do anything that might reverse the trend.

Back in our Washington apartment I dug into the stack of accumulated mail and was astonished to find a short note from Harvard accepting me as a Nieman Fellow come September. I whooped and yelled, "Saved by the school bell!" Now it would not be necessary to confess to Viking that I couldn't perform the "lost places" book; now I could conjure a substitute book at my leisure under cover of Harvard's refurbishings. I immediately decided to use the summer writing magazine articles at the beach, in order to edge a bit ahead of the game financially; the knowledge that I would soon be off the magazine treadmill for a spell seemed to fill me with new energy.

Some months earlier I had discussed with Willie Morris writing a long piece about black militancy and the resulting nervousness and abrasiveness between the races in America. I had been hurt and angered by what seemed, to me, unnecessarily rude treatment. I proposed an article to be called "How I Became Whitey"; it would take an injured tone: here was I, a decent white liberal who wished blacks well, and now I couldn't pick up a newspaper or magazine or turn on the radio or television (or encounter blacks on the street or at social gatherings) without hearing myself referred to as "whitey" or "honky" and similar pejoratives. My piece would stress how unfair it was to lump "enlightened" or "good" whites with overt bigots and flaming white racists.

I sat down to compile evidence supporting my theory: I would list all the many, many things I had done for blacks. It soon developed that list was so short as to be embarrassing. What *had* I done, really? Marched in a couple of brotherhood parades. Picketed a couple of restaurants. Argued with a few bigoted cab drivers. Hired the first black staffer in the Texas congressional delegation—and then, yes, had assigned him to a back-office desk where he was not highly visible. Jesus, was that *it*? 'Fraid so, old scout.

This was painful information requiring rethinking. I soon realized I had approached the typewriter to write a lie and the truth got in the way. Some fellow once said he had found writing to be "an act of discovery"; it certainly was in the case of my "Whitey" piece. I spent most of the summer reading the history of racism in America and jotting notes of my own experiences in what I increasingly admitted was, indeed, a racist society in many more mean little ways than I had previously taken into account. About the time I left for Harvard I sent my article to *Harper's* bearing the title "Confessions of a White Racist." It had required so much research and rethinking that I accomplished no work other than that one piece all summer.

Thus my "lost places" advance had been greatly depleted.

Hunting housing in Cambridge proved to be a frustrating experience. Rosemarie's health was deteriorating—she was requiring more and more treatment at the National Institutes of Health—so it became imperative that we locate near Harvard Yard if she was to participate in the part of the Nieman program involving spouses. She also had difficulty climbing stairs, thus requiring a building with an elevator. We found only one apartment house fitting the bill hard by Harvard, but rejected it on first inspection because the rent for a one-bedroom unit was more than the $534 monthly stipend Harvard would pay. The building superintendent shrugged and said, "You'll be back." I haughtily advised him not to count on it.

Three days later we were back literally begging for billeting; our experiences had made his modern building on Concord Street, fronting Cambridge Commons and just around the corner from Harvard Square, appear to rate with palaces. High-rises along the Charles River had demanded an arm, a leg and steep security deposits despite being long hikes from the Harvard complex. We had dispiritedly paraded through creaky old row houses, smelly walk-ups, cold-water flats: places I wouldn't have kept pigs. I was reminded of small towns suddenly blessed by burgeoning military bases during World War II, where landlords charged ransom sums for converted chicken coops. The same flinty greed prevailed in Cambridge. Landlords didn't care whether prospective tenants signed up; someone more desperate, they knew, would soon be along, hat in hand.

Dwight Sargent's secretary, in the Nieman curator's office, helpfully suggested we might obtain better value in the suburbs. Unable to reveal that Rosie's condition made this impossible (due to Rosie's personal wishes), I cracked, "No, I plan on being much too drunk to drive on a regular basis." This earned a cold, disapproving New England sniff. After appropriate groveling, and promising not to keep pets or play loud music, we settled into the Continental Gardens Apartments under the watchful eye of the building super who had correctly predicted that, like General MacArthur, we would return. For a mere $550 per month we had a small living room, a smaller bedroom, a kitchen Rosie and I had difficulty visiting in tandem—and absolutely no garden; there was a communal laundromat, requiring coins for its machines, in the basement. Its most distinguishing feature was a huge sign prohibiting its use past 7:30 p.m. What management considered a dining table was a glorified end table; I claimed it for my typewriter and other tools of my sullen craft. We ate buffet-style, off our laps. But at least we had an elevator for Rosie, and I could almost have thrown a rock to Harvard Yard.

Rosie refused to permit our Nieman colleagues to know she had cancer: "I don't want everybody fawning over me or acting as if I'm some kind of freak." Required to fly back to the National Institutes of Health, outside Washington, for periodic treatments, she told people that she absented herself to visit a sick sister.

Invariably, on returning from chemotherapy treatments, Rosie would be ill with chills, fevers and vomiting. In such terrible times we shut ourselves away, avoiding the numerous "Nieman Family" outings and parties. This resulted in our earning a reputation as standoffish snobs, whispers of which got back. I was made uncomfortable and quarreled with Rosie about her attitude. She remained adamant, however: "One of the things I like about being away from Washington is that here no one calls to ask, 'How do you feel?' and nobody treats me like I'm dying." I felt duty-bound to honor Rosie's secret no matter how much I disliked the tactic. We ultimately did confide in the Nieman couple closest to us—Wally Terry, a *Time* correspondent just back from Vietnam, and his wife, Janice. No man— or woman—being an island, it helped immensely to have them to talk to.

The early days in Cambridge were carefree and leisurely. I enjoyed the absence of deadline pressures even if, at first, this strange new freedom left me feeling vaguely guilty and a little disoriented. I paid pop calls on classes in ancient history, American history, economics, theology; whatever struck my fancy. As always, however, I quickly tired of lecturing voices and classroom confinements. Soon I spent most days reading in the stacks of Widener Library or at home, deserting my books only to attend afternoon or evening Nieman seminars three or four times weekly. Here we heard, and questioned, academicians, publishers, journalists, novelists, government officials, military men and industry captains. I spent more than a little time with a few choice Nieman colleagues—Jim Standard of the *Daily Oklahoman*, Cliff Terry of the *Chicago Sun-Times*, Barlow Herget of the Paragould, Arkansas, *Daily Press*, Joe Zelnik of the Delaware County, Pennsylvania, *Daily Times*, *Time*'s Wally Terry— drinking and yarning in Harvard Square bars. We were at Harvard to relax, were we not? The writer Dan Wakefield sometimes joined us; other visiting writers—Michael Herr, Norman Mailer, Willie Morris, Larry Goodwyn—joined the pack when in town.

But I most clearly remember the early, endless dark of those icy New England winter months and the feeling of being isolated from the real world while racial and social revolutions were occurring at home and Asia shook with bombs. It had been years since I had stayed on the sidelines, far removed from current events. As a congressional aide I had participated in events, and as a journalist had reported and interpreted them. Now as a mere long-range observer I felt lost, impotent, powerless, excluded. These emotions were magnified during Rosemarie's painful periodic bouts of illness. Often I sat alone getting rather desperately, stupidly drunk while trying not to think of what might be in store for us—and having little luck at it. I fear I often failed to conduct myself with valor in the face of my wife's adversity. Too often I quarreled with her, or sulked, or got raging drunk when she didn't need a madman to cope with. Hearing her groan from the bedroom in her restless sleep, I would take another drink and hiss at the darkness, *Goddammit, what is the purpose of all this shit? What is life's goddam purpose?* Nothing, or nobody, answered.

One day I learned that Jimmy Breslin would visit Cambridge to promote his funny new novel of the Mafia, *The Gang That Couldn't Shoot Straight*. I called at the Harvard bookstore to find a long line of kids queued up to obtain autographed copies of Breslin's book. Almost any writer I knew—myself included—might have killed for the opportunity to wallow in adulation while making satisfactory sales. Jimmy, however, was horrified: "Get me outta heah. Let's go drink in a goddam bahr."

I demurred: Viking was Breslin's publisher as well as my own; I didn't want word reaching the front office that I had purloined away a Viking author faced by a sizable crowd with money in hand. "Then come back in thutty minutes," Breslin begged in his Queens accent. No way, Jimmy. "An hour, huh? Come get me in an hour!" I made vague promises, drifted away and judged the line would keep Breslin busy a good two hours.

When I returned, Breslin was still signing books. On sighting me, however, he bolted from the table to abandon his remaining fans. "Let's find a workingman's bahr," he growled. "Get away from these damn college kids so we can talk private." When we found such a bar just off Harvard Square, however, Breslin's appearance excited much comment from blue-collar types taking their midday "balls and shots." It dawned that perhaps Breslin, no stranger to television appearances, had known where to find fans other than Harvard types; he seemed happy among the workmen and gave them as much attention as he paid me, or more.

I noted a young man eavesdropping a few feet away and writing in a notebook.

"Who you with, kid?" I asked.

"*Harvard Crimson*," he said. I had the notion he had struggled not to add "sir."

"Yeah? You know Frank Rich?"

The kid looked stunned. "Well, *I'm* Frank Rich."

I shook his hand and said, "I'll be goddamned. I've read your stuff in the *Crimson*. You're the best they've got over there." This did not, of course, make the kid mad. On impulse, I invited him to my apartment for dinner that evening; it began a friendship that continues. Frank Rich went on to become the film critic for *New Times* magazine a year after graduating from Harvard, then worked in the same capacity for the *New York Post*, *Esquire* and *Time* before joining the *New York Times*. Now he is chief drama critic for that important newspaper, and in a position to pee on my Broadway offerings should he feel like it. Small world, right.

As the new year, 1970, approached, I found myself once again restive in the classroom or library; my mind wandered like a hobo. When I found myself writing stories or screenplays in my head, oblivious to the drone of professors, I knew it was time to start typing again. One evening at dinner in the home of Ken Galbraith I confided my new itch to write, but said I'd signed a pledge promising Harvard I would not. Professor Galbraith issued an oath not common to Ivy League gentry at table. Then he said, "It is a writer's duty to write. Go home, write and forget that silly pledge."

I was vastly relieved to have Galbraith recommend that which I probably would have done anyway. *Harper's* had just published

"Confessions of a White Racist"; the article had created a favorable stir. Three publishing houses (Indiana University Press, Grossman Publishers, Harper & Row) had contacted my agent to say they would pay money should I be inclined to expand it to book length. I was eager to accept, but first offered the book to Viking because of my contractual obligations there. Viking officials agreed to accept the book; soon I had a contract and monthly payments of $1,700 against a $15,000 advance.

My final semester at Harvard I attended a few classes and Nieman functions, but spent most of my time writing the book on racism as well as three articles for *Harper's* to satisfy the terms of that magazine's endowment of Nieman support money. There was, as is indigenous to my nature, a certain amount of guilt attached to not being a full-time scholastic. Still, I felt the Nieman year had served me well. The announced purpose of the Nieman program was to refurbish us a bit and reenergize us; that it had done.

Some three weeks before the Nieman year was to be officially over, Rosie said one night at dinner: "Hey, Lar, I talked to my sister Christine today and she said spring is busting out all over in Washington." I took one look at the still-wintry New England landscape—muddy from slow-melting snows; trees and bushes still bare—and said, "By the powers vested in me by the Harvard Board of Overseers, I hereby declare school out. Goddam, baby, *let's pack!*" The next day we slipped away to reclaim our apartment on the banks of the Potomac from a week-to-week subleasing tenant, singing and laughing all the way.

My *White Racist* manuscript was warmly received at Viking Press in late June. Editor Alan Williams suggested a final short chapter updating acts of racial violence on both sides of the color line and a stronger closing summary. I agreed to have that material ready within a month or six weeks. Meanwhile, I was concluding a *Harper's* piece about a controversial right-wing, flipped-out Southern comedian billed as "Brother Dave" Gardner and beginning a second piece for the magazine reporting on life at Harvard during a tumultuous campus year.

Willie Morris came down from New York for the July Fourth holiday; we philosophized into the wee hours in bars from Capitol Hill to Georgetown. One night Willie said he had just caught hell from the ownership at *Harper's* for having exceeded the editorial budget by $90,000. "They called me out to Minneapolis and attacked me without warning," Morris complained. "Months ago I told John Cowles we couldn't help but break the budget if he expected me to get the hot, big-name writers we agreed we wanted. John more or less said we'd cross that bridge when we came to it. Didn't show the slightest concern. Just sort of shrugged. Then, without warning, he called me to Minneapolis and he and his business managers read the riot act. I was stunned." Morris said he was toying with the notion of resigning, but I knew he so loved his job he might be difficult to chase off at gunpoint. Consequently, I didn't take his complaints seriously. Before a year passed, my careless indifference would prove a huge mistake.

In mid-July Rosie and I motored to Ocean City, Maryland, and rented a small beach cottage, where I hoped to finish the Harvard article and write the concluding chapter of my book before going to Texas for a month's visit on Padre Island with my children. Mo and Ella Udall visited for a great week of fun, sun and surf; my work went well; all seemed right with the world. Then, one late afternoon, Rosemarie had a frightening experience.

We had returned from market, burdened with sacks of foodstuffs and beer. As Rosie preceded me up the cabin's back stairs she suddenly fell as if shot; the sack she was carrying fell through the outdoor stairs, its contents spilling on the sand below. I did a precarious balancing act so as not to fall over her and shouted, "Are you hurt?"

She gave me a strange, unbelieving look and said, "Lar, I can't get up. My legs are numb." I attempted to help her. "I can't move," she said. "I have no legs. What's wrong with me?"

I lifted her, took her inside the cabin and placed her on a couch. She tried to stand, but couldn't. Looking puzzled and dazed, Rosie said, "My legs just quit on me. I don't feel any pain. I don't feel anything." I was, of course, scared. I started for the telephone to call her doctor at the National Institutes of Health, but Rosie insisted on waiting a bit against the hope she might recover as suddenly as she had been stricken. I massaged her legs, to no avail. Over her strong protests I then called her doctor. "Get her to NIH emergency room right away," he instructed. "I'll meet you there."

Rosie, dressed in casual beach attire—shorts and halter—madden-

ingly insisted on dressing more formally for the trip. "Good God," I
said. "First things first! You're not entering a fashion show." But
she persisted. I tugged off her beach clothes, struggling to get her
into a summer frock and a certain pair of shoes she proclaimed vital.
Then she insisted on making up her face. I paced, scowled and shot
impatient looks at my watch: how could she remain so goddam *se-
rene*? By the time I carried Rosie to our car and stretched her out
in the backseat amid a sea of pillows, it was well past dark. During
the two hours I sped toward NIH, just outside Washington, her condition remained unchanged. Her only complaint was that she felt silly.

Doctors could find no medical reason for Rosie's paralysis. One of
them privately suggested her condition might be a form of hysteria.
I was angry: "Hell, man, she fell as if poleaxed. Don't tell me that
crap!" I was not soothed when he responded that the human brain is
a complex and powerful mechanism. I wanted to tell him *his* certainly was not, but held my tongue.

By morning Rosie had regained some feeling in her legs; in the
afternoon she walked around the hospital room with assistance. Several days of tests failed to solve the mystery; Rosie began walking
and moving normally. We returned to the Maryland shore, but within
a few days my wife began suffering sharp pains in her lower back. I
closed the cabin and returned her to the hospital. After additional
tests and X-rays the doctors concluded Rosie's problem had not been
one of "hysteria" after all: strange new growths had been found.
Rosie was scheduled for surgery on August 3. I telephoned my children to say I would be forced by circumstances to postpone our Padre
Island seashore holiday indefinitely. Being children, they reacted with
sharp disappointment and wails.

Rosemarie was in much pain following surgery; the first two times
I saw her she quite abruptly asked me to leave: she simply didn't
feel like suffering conversation. She required periodic sedation to sleep.
Within a week, however, she was stronger and in good spirits. She
insisted that I go to Texas to be with my children before their school
year started: "I'm getting good care in this hospital. My brothers
and sisters can keep me company."

Rosemarie also knew that I several times had promised my aging
father to take him to see the Alamo in San Antonio and the state
capitol in Austin; he had wanted to see those shrines since childhood,
he once confessed, but—short of money or free time and slavishly

devoted to work—had never made the trip on his own. I had vowed to make that dream a reality but for one reason and another had procrastinated. "He won't live forever," Rosie warned that summer. "Take care of that trip as you promised."

I flew to Texas, rented a car and persuaded my eighty-two-year-old father to accompany me and two of his grandchildren on the long-awaited trip. He would consent only if my mother (not agreeable to "wasting time" sightseeing) promised to spend a few days with her twin sister in my father's absence. The old man delighted in his rare trip, seeming to shed years and regaining old vigor. Long before returning to Washington and Rosie—now home from the hospital—I was grateful beyond words for her having pushed me to keep my promise to Dad.

I returned to my typewriter in Washington, finishing the Harvard piece and the final chapter of *White Racist*. Rosie, feeling well for the first time in weeks, wanted to go to New York in early October to see a few shows and to shop. We stayed there almost a week, returning after midnight—in the early hours of October 12—to our Washington apartment. We had hardly attained sleep, it seemed, before the telephone jangled me awake.

I grumpily answered to hear my brother say, with a catch in his voice, "Well, we lost our old daddy a few hours ago." My father had worked in his yard all day, eaten a hearty meal and then collapsed in great pain. He died before my brother had been able to contact me. Even in shock and grief my first thought was *Thank God I took him on that trip*.

Two days later, an hour or so after my father's funeral, Willie Morris telephoned Texas to extend condolences. He often had urged me to write an essay about fathers and sons, using my relationship with my father to personalize it; though I had several times attempted the piece I had never been able to go beyond four or five pages. "I'm intimidated by it," I had told Morris. "I guess I envision his reading it and disagreeing with my judgments, or maybe being somehow hurt by it." After Willie and I talked awhile on the day of Dad's funeral, I heard myself blurt, "Willie, I can write that piece now." I felt a *need* to write it. Flying home for the funeral I had dwelled on the up-and-down relationship I had known with my father; on the good times and bad, on that peculiar mixture of love and resentment, of pride and shame, of tenderness and gruffness, and the other complex emotions we—like many fathers and sons—had experienced. It was a story demanding to spill out. I wrote and rewrote for thirty emotional days. The resulting piece, "The Old Man," was published in *Harper's* in April 1971. It drew the most and the best mail I have received in my writing life, has been anthologized more times and in more nations than anything I have written. It won no awards except the best one imaginable: my mother's comment, "Every time I read that piece, it brings him back to me for a while."

Shortly after Dad's death, Rosemarie suffered another setback; once more it was back to the hospital, where radium treatments were begun. This caused her hair to fall out and brought new lows of spirit. Rosie obtained several hairpieces and instructed me I was never—ever—to enter her bedroom-dressing room unannounced: "I couldn't stand to have you see me bald."

Rosemarie's doctors confided that they considered her condition irreversible, that her death was only a matter of time. This was something I already knew in my bones, but the official stating of it was hard to take. I asked the doctors to keep the dark news from my wife, and they agreed. Driving home from the hospital that day, I pulled into a scenic overlook on George Washington Parkway, where I had a stunning view of the city and the river below, to chart in my mind—as best as I could—what I must do in the future. I concluded that I couldn't, or wouldn't, do much traveling for purposes of writing until whatever would happen had happened. I soon told Willie Morris this, and also my Viking editors. Any work assignments must keep me close to home.

Suddenly one night, shortly after returning from her hospitalization, Rosie said, "Lar, I know you won't like this, but we've got to have a talk." She was right: I didn't like it; I knew the talk would be of the inevitable—of death—no matter the euphemisms we might employ. I muttered a weak protest. "We've got to face it," she said. "I'm not likely ever to be well again. I don't want you to feel trapped and start hating me because of it. No, don't interrupt—I've talked with the shrink at NIH and he says no matter how hard we try not to, I'm gonna resent you for living and you're gonna resent me for dying." I visibly flinched; it was the first time we had used the word, the first time we had brought it out in the open. "He thinks," she continued, "and I agree, that you should live as normal a life as possible. Your career must go ahead. You've got to travel or do whatever is necessary. I'll only feel worse if you don't, and I'm in enough trouble as it is."

I couldn't look at her or answer. Finally Rosie said, "Well?" I turned away and muttered gruffly, "Aw hell, baby, all this low talk is way too premature. It won't serve either of us to hear it. I'd rather hear music." I walked to the hi-fi and put on a stack of Louis Armstrong records. I suppose it may have been an ungracious response—if it *was* a response—but I couldn't face what had to be faced. Not yet. And already, yes, I felt guilty because the NIH shrink had me perfectly pegged: I did feel occasional flashes of anger and resentment; I did feel trapped in a web of hard and unfair circumstances; I did feel as if we might be living a nightmare out of Kafka. Such feelings made me ashamed, but they were there.

Despite Rosie's admonition, I quietly canceled writing assignments that would have taken me long distances for appreciable lengths of time: a profile for *Life* on Colonel Sanders of fried-chicken fame; a *Playboy* piece on West Coast evangelists; a week with the writer of potboiler Mike Hammer detective yarns, Mickey Spillane, for *True*. I also stopped planning a nonfiction book Viking editors liked the notion of: a run for a seat in Congress, in 1972; not to win, that expectation was unrealistic, but to show how impossible it might be to run a wholly truthful, honest campaign while eschewing big money from special-interest sources. I thought such a book—provided I seriously campaigned and gave the experiment an honest shot—would dramatically speak to the deceptions, compromises and sellouts all too prevalent in American politics. But the scheme required my returning to Texas to establish full-time residence so as to qualify for the race, and at least a full year of hard campaigning. My wife's condition simply eliminated such possibilities.

In November of 1970 I began a stay-at-home project for *Harper's*. Old friend Mo Udall had announced he would seek election as Majority Leader of the U.S. House of Representatives; I saw a chance to write a behind-the-scenes story revealing how in-house political fights for institutional power were won or lost. The race would be the most meaningful and open struggle for congressional leadership in many years. Generally, when the Speaker of the House retired (as old John McCormack was doing) or died, the handful of men on the "leadership ladder" automatically stepped up one rung each and business went on as usual. But Udall was challenging the old seniority system. Though he had served a shade less than a decade in the House—a small speck of time indeed, given the glacial pace and customs of the place—he was openly seeking power against his elders. This challenged institutional ground rules and habits; the old bulls were furious and a bitter fight, pitting reformers against stand-patters and have-nots against haves, was assured. I knew, too, that some who ideologically should have favored the liberal Udall would not—because, by their lights, he was attempting to leapfrog over them into a tall chair of power. I couldn't leave such marvelous story material alone.

Udall and his staff subordinates pledged to let me in on all strategy and developments without exception, and to instruct the dozen congressmen acting as his lieutenants to do likewise. But unless I received similar pledges from the other four candidates—Hale Boggs of Louisiana, in line for the job because of his position on the "leadership ladder"; Jim O'Hara of Michigan; Bernie Sisk of California; Wayne Hayes of Ohio—I feared I could not get the complete picture. I called on each of them to say that while Mo Udall was my close personal friend, I was motivated to make a serious study of a major American institution in its internal threshings and I could not adequately do so unless they, too, made me privy to the secrets of their respective camps. I would not pass anything along to Udall, I pledged, or to any other source. My piece would not be published until well after the winner had been chosen, so what did they have to fear?

Boggs and Hayes looked at me as if I might be an escapee from the bug house—which did not surprise me—though Sisk and O'Hara promised to cooperate. I took their pledges with a grain of salt, knowing that no politician shares his secrets with anyone outside his camp. But by candidly admitting my Udall friendship, I hoped to disarm them enough to get something. And I did extract pledges from all that once the race was over, they would bare their hearts, minds and records about what had actually gone on.

The piece required more old-fashioned journalistic legwork and ditch-digging than anything I had done in years, but I felt the efforts would be worth it. The job required about three months of interviewing and observation before I wrote a line of "The Road to Power in Congress." The piece came in at a lengthy 16,000 words and was published virtually untouched. I was well pleased with the work. A good job was possible because the candidates and their supporters *had* been amazingly candid once the campaign was over, telling their secrets and permitting me to reveal each camp's strategies, mistakes, intrigues and calculations so that the piece read like a crackling mystery yarn. (Hale Boggs won, Udall finishing second.) Though I had no way of knowing it at the time, that piece—my twenty-sixth for *Harper's*—was also my last for that magazine and would not be published until shortly after I had departed it.

Willie Morris increasingly had grumbled of difficulties with the *Harper's* ownership: John Cowles, Jr., and what Willie called the "money men and hatchet men" in Minneapolis. Morris reported their complaints of costs, their unhappiness at the magazine's running in the red—which it had done for years before Willie took over—and gripes about "strong language" in the book. Morris had pioneered in permitting magazine writers to use the language, warts and all, as it is spoken; while this tactic pleased writers and many readers, it was disturbing to the old-line Midwestern sensibilities in control of *Harper's*. Soon we heard of some ill-defined direction the owner wanted his magazine to go, but was apparently unable to articulate. Reports reached us that Jack Fischer, our editor emeritus, was openly expressing distaste, throughout the publishing industry, at the operation and direction of the magazine he long had edited. I originally discounted these as the normal carpings of an aging, ousted king pained by the decrees and changes of his successor and onetime protégé. Normal enough, I thought. An old story. A predictable one. I did not then know that Jack Fischer's complaints were being taken seriously in Minneapolis.

Soon after buying *Harper's*, Cowles had dispatched to the magazine's offices at 2 Park Avenue a veteran of the Madison Avenue advertising wars, one William S. Blair, and installed him as business manager. Willie Morris was stunned when informed that Blair would be considered his superior. "I had not been given a hint the move was being contemplated," he said. Those of us editing and writing for the magazine stiffened our necks and protested to Cowles that we would brook no interference from the business side on matters of editorial content, policy or practices; Cowles backed off, assuring us that such interference had not been intended and saying that Morris and Blair would be on "an equal footing." We should have known that wouldn't work, that a ship can't operate with two captains, but we chose to make a benign interpretation of Cowles' statement.

Morris and Blair coexisted uneasily at best. Willie soon came to believe that Blair was poisoning the well against him in the home office and undercutting his authority. (Indeed, Blair once referred to himself, when talking with me, as "the boss." "You're not *my* boss," I told him. "I'm not a goddam accountant. I'm a writer. Willie Morris is *my* boss.") But perhaps because Willie sometimes tended toward dramatic narratives, and because we writers were caught up in our own work both for and outside *Harper's* magazine, we did not trouble to sit down with Morris, or Junior Cowles, to learn the particulars or the degree of the widening split. This neglect would prove fatal.

On Monday, March 1, 1971, I flew to New York, my piece on the congressional leadership fight in hand, to find gloom and despair in the *Harper's* offices. Editors Bob Kotlowitz and Midge Decter told me that Willie Morris had returned over the weekend from Minneapolis, where a no-holds-barred fight had occurred with Cowles, Blair et al., and that the enraged Morris had that very morning drafted a letter of resignation. "It's a tough letter, leaving no room for compromise," Kotlowitz said. "If Willie mails it, he's through."

I located Morris; we went to Greenstreet's, our favorite restaurant in close proximity to the *Harper's* offices. Willie handed me his letter of resignation. After reading it, I said, "Willie, this letter is irrevocable. It leaves no room for maneuvering. You musn't mail this. I'll work with you on a firm letter, but one that doesn't grab Blair and Cowles by the throat." (I had, by then, talked with several coworkers and we had agreed on a strategy of getting Willie to tone down his letter, if we could not dissuade him from sending one. None of us wanted to break up what we had going at *Harper's*.) But Willie was weary, angry and unwilling to change a word. "You guys haven't been out in Minneapolis eating shit like I have," he said. "I won't be a figurehead editor like they want. Larry, dammit, those bastards are talking about making *Harper's* a goddam specialty magazine! 'Like *Ski*,' that asshole Bill Blair said. Can you *imagine*? The oldest magazine in America, the magazine with the proudest history, and they want to scrap all that without a backward glance! Well, by God, Willie Morris ain't about to hang around to take part in that desecration." I calmed and soothed and clucked, all being against my nature, and got Morris to agree not to mail the letter until at least the following day.

Then I went to Bill Blair, whom Morris had heatedly told he was resigning, to say that I thought Willie and Cowles should talk before irrevocable steps were taken. Blair said he already had called Cowles to tell him of Willie's intent to resign and that Cowles had said, "Let's wait and see what his letter says before we stir things up." Once Cowles had read Morris's letter—Blair said—he then would call Morris. I objected: why wait until Willie sent such a letter? Why not begin negotiations immediately and head off troubles at the pass? Blair said Cowles was on grand jury duty and might not have time to call. I lost my temper: "Goddammit, grand juries don't meet all night! Have Cowles call late this afternoon or early evening!" Blair said he would give Cowles that suggestion; an hour later he told me he had reached Cowles and "he'll call tonight or early tomorrow." I said tomorrow might be too late. I stayed in the office late, along with David Halberstam, Bob Kotlowitz and others, awaiting Cowles' call. It did not come.

By noon the following day—Tuesday—Cowles still had not called. (He later would claim to have called the *Harper's* office "about 9:00 p.m." on Monday night. Several of us had remained at *Harper's* until well past 9:00 p.m.). I again went to lunch with Willie and groused that I couldn't understand Cowles' indifference. Willie gave a half-smile and said, "He'll call before this day is over. I guarantee it." I studied him and said, softly, "Goddam you, Willie. You mailed that letter anyway." He nodded. "Yes. I couldn't leave matters hanging. That letter perfectly said what I feel and it will bring events to a head." He had mailed his resignation airmail, special delivery; there was no calling it back. I ordered a new round of drinks and told the waitress to make mine a double.

When we returned to *Harper's*, Bill Blair's secretary met us in the reception room—as if waiting in ambush—and said, "Oh, Mr. Morris! I'm so sorry you're leaving us!" Willie and I traded quick glances. I thought, *What a shitty way to break it to him! Sending a minor functionary!* Morris mumbled the appropriate amenities, then plunged toward his office. "My God!" he said, as we rushed down a deserted hall. "They've accepted my resignation!"

"Didn't you think they would?"

"No," he said.

Willie asked to be alone; I went to consult my colleagues about what we should do next. Sometime during this, Junior Cowles called Willie to read him a statement announcing Willie's departure; Morris objected because the statement made it appear that he had been fired. After a few minutes of back-and-forth, Cowles said—Willie later would reveal—"Well, just issue whatever statement *you* wish to make. I'm going with what I read to you." Morris, angry, banged down the phone and disappeared from the office.

Within the hour the *New York Times* and other publications began calling for the comments of *Harper's* survivors. The contributing editors had a heated shouting match with Bill Blair because he and Junior Cowles had released the statement without apprising us of what had happened or what was in the statement. Blair professed not to understand: Cowles had merely accepted Willie's resignation, that was all. What were we so worked up about? Somebody called him a shitass. We stomped out to regroup. By day's end we had reached no consensus and agreed to meet the following morning.

I had accepted an invitation, days earlier, to attend a dinner party that night at the home of Willie's friend Muriel Oxenberg Murphy; Norman Mailer was there, along with Bill Moyers and then–pro basketball player Bill Bradley of the New York Knicks; all but Bradley had written for Willie and *Harper's*. Morris, in breaking the news of his resignation and its acceptance, told Mailer that his long piece "The Prisoner of Sex"—just published in the magazine—had been a factor in bringing to a head the recent tumultuous events. Mailer, shocked, gave a long, low whistle. He turned to me: "What are you *Harper's* writers going to do?" I said we had not yet decided; probably we would seek a meeting with Junior Cowles. Our goals would be the reinstatement of Willie Morris as editor-in-chief or, if that failed, the installation of managing editor Bob Kotlowitz as top man with Morris becoming a roving editor-writer. This might work, because it would free Willie from administrative worries—which he hated, and where he was not particularly strong. Mailer's eyes flashed: "You guys owe Willie your loyalty. You've got to quit." I much admired Mailer as a writer, and liked him as a person, but his remark infuriated me. "Goddammit, Mailer, you don't know half the facts or ramifications. Fuck your rush to judgment!" We raised our voices in hot dispute. Frustrated, I delivered a swift kick to an antique chair—so as not to physically attack Mailer—and it shattered into very expensive debris. Nobody mentioned the cost damage, however, because I was ranting like a wild man—sobbing and cussing—and it probably didn't appear an appropriate time to negotiate restitution. (By the next night, Mailer had learned more facts and apologized to me; I apologized to him for going crazy on short notice. No permanent damage was done to any save the antique chair.)

On the morning of the third day, Bill Blair sought me out to ask whether I might be willing to talk with Junior Cowles about what might be salvaged. I agreed, assuming my role to be that of intermediary on behalf of the entire *Harper's* staff of writers and editors. Blair said he would have Cowles call me. Within the hour, however, John Corry and Marshall Frady came into my office looking hard-eyed. "What's this we heard about your going over to the other side?" Corry demanded. Blair, it turned out, had told my colleagues that I had agreed to stay on at the magazine no matter what, and was working out a deal for myself with Cowles. I was furious. Grabbing Corry and Frady by the elbows, I propelled them into Blair's office, called him a son of a bitch and demanded he admit to having lied. All Blair would admit was "a misunderstanding." I roundly cursed him, said I would have nothing to do with him the rest of my life and forbade him ever to speak to me again. Later in the day David Halberstam cursed Blair and threatened to whip his ass for having told the *New York Times* that the contributing editors were overpaid and had not produced the number of pieces called for in their contracts. Only one of the several contributing editors was guilty of such a shortfall; two of us had produced more pieces than our contracts required. As for money, all were paid higher rates by other magazines than we received at *Harper's*. I was never paid more than $2,000 for a piece in that magazine. *Life, Playboy, True, Cosmopolitan, West* and *Saturday Evening Post*, among others, paid me considerably more.

On Friday—five full days after the *Harper's* uproar started—Junior Cowles agreed to meet with the writers and editors at the St. Regis Hotel that evening. We met first at Halberstam's apartment to define our goals and plot strategy, agreeing that we would act as a unit. We told Lewis Lapham, who had become a contributing editor only scant weeks earlier, that we would not bind him to the unit rule; he had freshly quit another magazine to join *Harper's* and could have had no notion he was signing aboard the *Titanic*. Lapham, however, made a brave speech about loyalty to the group and the need for unity: he would go along with the rest of us. We shook his hand and welcomed him to the brotherhood. Lapham would remain a revered member for about three hours.

Junior Cowles immediately made it clear he was not seeking give-and-take negotiations. He whipped out a 1,700-word statement and read it aloud. Boiled down, it said that (1) William Blair would be promoted to publisher, effective immediately; (2) Blair would choose the new editor and be that editor's superior; (3) *Harper's* editorially would go in unspecified "new directions" and (4) Willie Morris was gone for good and all. David Halberstam later would remark, "It was as if from a distant headquarters the commander had arrived on post to shore up the authority of his colonel." Indeed, we were treated as buck privates in the rear ranks—lucky to escape court-martials. Stunned, we gaped first at each other and then at Junior Cowles.

Halberstam, our designated spokesman, asked Cowles to define the "new directions" his magazine would take. Cowles offered only generalities but would not, or could not, be specific. Halberstam next attempted to learn what Cowles objected to in the *Harper's* maga-zine we were producing, pointing out it was reputed to be "the hot-test book in the trade." Junior snapped, "A magazine can't live on favorable press notices and dinner party chitchat," ultimately blurt-ing, "much of the magazine bores me." Maddeningly, he would not be specific, and the brotherhood began to growl.

Cowles alluded to a reader survey poll showing "we should try something else" but was unable, or unwilling, to define the some-thing else. This led to a general braying against the insanity of per-mitting opinion polls to dictate editorial content, but Junior only shrugged and mumbled that changes were necessary. Halberstam reminded Cowles that he had promised us five years in which to turn the magazine around—saying that in reader response we certainly had done so—and now Cowles was pulling the rug more than a year early. Cowles said he just couldn't give it more time, that the mag-azine had become a cross to bear and that his father had urged him to sell it or padlock it "because it simply isn't worth the trouble." This cavalier dismissal of a magazine we loved, and that had an hon-ored history and tradition in American letters, infuriated the broth-erhood. We began to shout of money *Harper's* management had wasted in redesigning the magazine's binding, in remodeling Bill Blair's offices, in commissioning useless readership surveys, in buying *The Reporter*'s circulation for huge sums when that magazine folded and then doing nothing to keep that circulation. Junior Cowles was offended that a scruffy bunch of writers would presume to question his business acumen, and the air grew chillier within the St. Regis.

We urged that Robert Kotlowitz, who had performed superbly as managing editor, be given a fair shot at replacing Morris in the top job. Cowles replied only that it was "quite possible" Kotlowitz was on a list from which Bill Blair would choose the new editor-in-chief but refused any commitment. Invoking Blair as the ultimate authority was like throwing gasoline on a fire. I whispered to Frady, "The bastard wants us *all* to leave. Let's accommodate him."

John Corry said, "All right, John, are you telling us the magazine will change but you won't say in what direction, and that Bill Blair will remain in power or become even more powerful?"

"That's pretty much the case," Cowles said.

That was enough for me. I stood up and said, "Then fuck it, there's no reason to stay here. I resign." I left the room. One by one the others walked out—Halberstam, Corry, Frady, Kotlowitz. Cowles called out, "Wait! Stay and talk!" Somebody shouted, "Of what?" There was no answer. In the hotel lobby we counted noses and realized Lewis Lapham had stayed behind. We waited a few minutes and then went on without him, wondering what he was up to.

We headed for Elaine's, where Willie Morris waited to be apprised of the evening's events. When Lewis Lapham entered the restaurant perhaps an hour later, he blithely announced he was the new managing editor, replacing Bob Kotlowitz. I was at once flabbergasted and furious. Lapham had made his "one for all" speech and then had recanted at the first opportunity. A rich boy—his father held a seat on the New York Stock Exchange—Lapham was not hard up for money or a job. "They will never say of you," I hissed to Lapham, "what they said of Roosevelt—that he was a traitor to his class. You saw the opportunity to cozy up to power and to embrace another spoiled rich man's son and went to 'em like a goddam homing pigeon." Halberstam hotly told Lapham he would never write for *Harper's* as long as "you, Cowles or Bill Blair have any connection with that magazine." Each of us who had quit took that vow, as did Norman Mailer and Bill Styron.* The next morning, executive editor Midge Decter and poetry editor John Thompson also handed in their resignations.

The mass walkout was big news in the literary world. Said *Saturday Review,* "In issue after issue *Harper's* writers put their own lives on the line in passages of personal revealment and commitment [and] provided pieces of penetrating journalism." Wrote George Frazier in the *Boston Globe,* "In four years Willie Morris converted a moribund, stuffy, utterly humorless *Harper's* into one of the very best magazines ever published in America." Norman Mailer was quoted in the *New York Times:* "[This is] the most depressing event in American letters in many a year because *Harper's,* under Willie Morris, had become the most adventurous of all magazines. Morris is a great editor. I never saw him take a backward step on a piece." Bill Moyers (who turned down an invitation to replace Willie Morris) said of him, "He knew how to feed writers' egos, to make them want to write their best. And he handled their copy in a cool, professional and loving way." Almost everywhere we won the battle of the media, but that didn't change the fact that we had lost a magazine, and professional associations, that we valued highly. I now look back on those *Harper's* days as the most exciting and fruitful of my writing life.

Jack Fischer came back as temporary editor-in-chief until a permanent one could be found, and forthwith issued a graceless statement that I interpreted as a slam against Willie Morris and all his writers: "We don't need articles about dead people. We don't need reminiscences of childhood. We don't need articles about defeated politicians. We need material about people who are on the way up, not on the way down." I found that as antiliterary a statement as I had heard: go only with winners! A shoddy literary measuring stick, indeed. And I felt that Fischer had singled me out for criticism in particular. "The Old Man" had been about "dead people" and "The Road to Power in Congress" might have been considered, by a narrow interpretation, to be about a defeated politician. I cursed, crumpled the newspaper containing Jack Fischer's statement and threw it in the wastebasket. Not ten days later I received a letter from

---

*These years later, we all have kept that promise, though several of us have been solicited.

Mr. Fischer asking me—incredibly—to continue writing for *Harper's*. It, too, went straight into the wastebasket.

In retrospect, *Harper's* as we knew it was doomed early on. The Nixon recession of 1970–71 caused losses larger than had been anticipated, and Bill Blair was a bottom-line business type who cared no more for literary standards than a billygoat. Willie Morris, with only a small appreciation for office politics, had neglected to stroke Cowles and Blair when it might have been helpful. We contributing editors were so wrapped up in our work we didn't pay adequate attention to business problems or deteriorating relations with management. Management considered us no more than troublesome hired hands, making no attempts to let us know of growing problems until it was too late. When the crunch came, as Willie Morris said, "It was the literary men against the money men. And, as always, the money men won."

Harper's ultimately would try a number of editors-in-chief, the opportunistic Lewis Lapham holding the job twice. But if Junior Cowles ever found his "new directions," before ultimately selling out to a nonprofit foundation with right-wing tendencies, I was never able to discern it. Today's *Harper's* is a thin, pale ghost compared to the magazine in its glory days under such talented editors as William Dean Howells, Bernard DeVoto and Willie Morris.

Shortly after the *Harper's* debacle, Rosemarie went to the hospital for another operation. Doctors, in an effort to ease her pain, used wicked-looking needles to block or freeze nerve centers near the spine. The operation was not noticeably effective. We talked and decided I had no choice but to hit the road out of economic necessity. I went to Tennessee for *Today's Health* to report the trial of Jesse Hill Ford, a writer charged with the murder of a black man that had resulted from a tragic misunderstanding; I traveled with the Baltimore Colts football team for an *Atlantic Monthly* article on the violence of the pro game. Meanwhile, I batted out book reviews and short political pieces for the *Texas Observer*. The review pieces brought in $125–$200; Ronnie Dugger had raised me to a whole $50 to write for his shoestring operation.

Congressman Paul McCloskey of California, an opponent of the Vietnam War, had announced he would oppose President Nixon in the 1972 Republican primaries. It seemed a suicide mission, but Simon & Schuster signed McCloskey to write a book about his political experiences, beliefs and philosophy. In the fall of '71 I was contacted by Chuck Daly, a McCloskey associate, who asked me to bring form and order to the congressman's undisciplined manuscript. Simon & Schuster editors agreed to pay me $5,000 for this book-doctoring; I would also receive 15 percent of future sales royalties. In order for the book to be published to coincide with the '72 New Hampshire primary, I had to accomplish the work within thirty days. After signing, I learned that Congressman McCloskey had turned in only 35,000 words—rather than the 70,000 he had contracted for—and I would be expected to flesh it out. I then insisted on more money, asking that my fee be doubled to $10,000, but managed to extract only $2,000 more in a side agreement with McCloskey.

I flew with Congressman McCloskey to peace rallies, political fund raisers and dinners, attempting to understand the man and his ideas. For all his energy, affable personality and reputation for brains, McCloskey proved to have an attention span that peaked out at about forty seconds on any given subject. It was maddening: he would veer off in mid-answer to my questions to tell a joke having absolutely no relation to the subject matter, or dig in his briefcase for something to read or abruptly go to sleep. Ultimately, I had his staff furnish me with his complete voting record and all his speeches, newsletters and other writings; these, along with the manuscript he had turned in to Simon & Schuster, constituted my raw working materials. Working almost night and day, I managed to meet the length requirements of the book and the deadline.

I had high hopes of good sales, since McCloskey was receiving a great deal of favorable press. His publisher announced big plans to issue simultaneous large printings in hardback and paperback, and did. But on the day McCloskey's book was officially released, he suffered such a sound thumping in the New Hampshire primary—Nixon winning 72 percent to 28 percent—that he immediately announced his withdrawal from the presidential race. This gave his book a shelf life of about forty-five minutes; I never saw a nickel other than my original fee.

The day following the New Hampshire primary and the resulting collapse of McCloskey's book, I got solitary drunk while thinking dark thoughts about sinking to the level of hack work as a book doctor. What had happened to my grand, innocent dreams of producing memorable literature?

Then, suddenly, fortune seemed to smile. My old friend David Halberstam persuaded his publisher, Random House, that I was perfectly situated to write the definitive cradle-to-the-grave biography of Lyndon B. Johnson. Halberstam, in selling me, invoked my Texas background, my years on Capitol Hill when LBJ and Sam Rayburn had controlled the two houses of Congress, my work in Senator Johnson's preconvention swipe at the Democratic nomination in 1960, my spear carrier's role in the Kennedy-Johnson campaign against Nixon, my general political connections and specific contacts among Johnson's political friends and enemies. He did such a persuasive job Random House offered an $80,000 advance; a second publishing house, Lippincott, heard rumors of the book and asked to bid. Sterling Lord talked with Viking, and that house offered a $100,000 advance to keep the Johnson book and its author in their house.

I signed a contract for $15,000 in immediate front money, to be followed by thirty monthly payments of $2,500 each and a final $10,000 on completion of the book—plus a goodly percentage in sales royalties. My spirits rose immensely. I made plans to begin the book in early 1972 and told Rosemarie, "This book can be the making of me. It can put me over the hump. No more cheeseburgers and motel rooms after this one."

I then had no way of knowing that the Johnson book would plague me for years and bring me to my lowest career point.

Confessions of a White Racist, in hardback, was greeted in mid-1971 by the kind of gee-whiz reviews inspiring front-office handsprings and visions of riches. Viking launched me on a twenty-eight-day, thirty-three-city drumbeating tour we felt certain would culminate in spectacular sales. Before I had reached the tour's midpoint, I knew that hope to be a vain one. During television interviews conducted before live studio audiences, people began coughing, sighing and shifting in their seats the moment I started to talk of racism in America; after years of racial turmoil and upheavals, they simply didn't want to hear it anymore. From the reaction of those studio audiences, I figured TV sets were clicking to other channels all across

America. Sales figures confirmed my fears; spot checks showed my book to be lumpishly reposing, undisturbed, in bookstores. *White Racist* sold a pitiable 5,329 copies in hardback despite hard hucktering and great reviews in *Life, Newsweek,* the *Washington Post,* the *Los Angeles Times,* the *National Observer*—just about everywhere but the *New York Review of Books,* which again indicated that perhaps I should learn a tradesman's skills, and the Sunday book supplement of the *New York Times,* where Walker Percy curiously faulted me for not offering "solutions" to the nation's race problems. Later, in a Viking Compass quality paperback edition, the book sold about 24,000 copies, largely because it was used on many campuses in black studies courses. Commercially, however, that book was one of the biggest bombs since the Edsel car. It died unmourned, leaving a red-ink legacy of about $20,000.

On the last stop of my wayward promotion tour, the free-lance publicity woman in charge of my schedule proved to be a serious alcoholic. She was so drunk I almost jumped out of her car between the airport and my hotel. For three days she was late to all appointments; this irritated media people we had hoped might write or say nice things of the touring author and his book. In the city's largest bookstore, my escort repeatedly introduced me as "Mr. Green" and, when corrected, said, "King, Schming, it's all the same to me." At our next stop she asked the bookstore manager whether he had copies of *Confessions of a White Racist;* when he said yes, he had a sizable order on hand, my tub-thumper said, "And I'll bet you haven't sold a goddam one!" I telephoned Viking's publicity people in New York to complain, and they in turn ordered the lady to straighten up. Fat lot of good it did. When I left her city for the airport, I refused to ride with her—she was stumbling drunk—and chose a cab. She followed the cab through the streets, honking and shaking her fist while shouting that I was depriving her of her livelihood. The last I saw of the poor lady, her car was being forced to the curb by a police car wailing at full siren.

When my homecoming flight landed at Dulles Airport, in the Virginia countryside outside Washington, I saw Mo and Ella Udall awaiting me. My first reaction was an uplifting surge of spirits, a wave and grin. Then I thought, *Oh, shit, something bad has happened to Rosie!* Ella saw the alarm in my eyes and called out, "She's okay! She just had a little accident."

Rosie had walked outside our apartment on some small errand; a neighbor's bad-tempered German shepherd had leaped out of its restraining pen and charged her, barking and growling. Rosemarie quickly turned to hurry back indoors; a hipbone, weakened and brittled by cancer, snapped. She took a wicked fall, tumbling down a short flight of stairs. As it was the middle of the day and our neighbors were at work, no one answered her shouts for help. Somehow, she struggled to her car a few yards outside our front door and drove herself to the hospital. She would remain there for days, and when released she had to use crutches. Never again would she walk without them.

Mo and Ella drove me to the hospital from Dulles Airport. I hugged my wife and commiserated with her. She shrugged and said, "Breaks of the game." But I knew (because her doctors had told Ella, who passed the word to me), and Rosemarie may have suspected, that this new misfortune likely would hasten her end.

During the remainder of 1971 I worked for *Playboy*, *Life*, *Atlantic Monthly* and others while starting to read and research for the Lyndon Johnson book. Rosemarie was in and out of the hospital and required much chemotherapy. Chemotherapy sometimes works in strange ways. The recipient of such treatment appears to fairly glow with health at a given point, though this stage lasts only a few weeks, causing the unknowing to presume improvement where improvement is not. Rosie went through that cruel stage. People complimented her on her vibrant appearance and told me how great she looked. We accepted the compliments with nods and smiles, though knowing the truth to be something else.

In November, just before Thanksgiving, I went to NIH once again to check my wife out of the hospital. Her doctors had me intercepted before I reached her room. They wore gloomy faces. One of them said, "She keeps talking of a trip to Greece. If such a trip is planned, you'd better go immediately. We think she'll be bedridden by February." One is never prepared for the end, or even the beginning of the end. I managed to say, "How long has she got?" The doctors looked at each other; one said, "Less than a year. Probably six months." I said, "About this Greece thing. Her parents came from there, and she's always wanted to go. Is it possible there's time?"

Very risky, they told me. They would advise against it. She really wasn't strong enough for the trip. It might kill her.

I don't remember much about checking Rosie out of the hospital that day. As a surprise, I had earlier booked a table for lunch at a grand old inn in the Maryland countryside. Deep snow was on the ground, presenting a beautiful sight, and large snowflakes fell as we drove toward the isolated inn. Rosemarie—in high spirits—talked, as I feared, of visiting Greece. We took a table near a fireplace where logs crackled merrily in an orange blaze. I attempted to match my wife's high mood, but wasn't actor enough to fool her. Midway through our first drink, she said, "Okay, it's show-and-tell time. What's wrong, Lar?" I looked at her, opened my mouth and couldn't force out a word. She saw my distress, squeezed my hand and said, "Take your time." I managed to say, "Baby, about that trip to Greece . . ." I could say no more. We held hands in silence until Rosie said, "Do they say I'm not up to the trip?" I nodded. She said, "Tell me the truth. How long have I got?" Well, I began, they're never entirely sure about these things. . . . But Rosemarie interrupted. "Don't bullshit me. I want to know, Lar. All of it." So I told her. She gripped my hand so hard it hurt. Little twin rivers of tears started down her cheeks. "Goddammit," she said, softly. "Goddammit, all I wanted was one good year."

She didn't get it. By January Rosemarie's pain was such that her doctors taught me to shoot her with morphine, every four hours, around the clock. Though I incessantly practiced by shooting oranges with injections of water, I was clumsy at the job and hated piercing that poor violated flesh; I knew, however, my wife couldn't stand her pain without those shots. Her dosage was increased several times; still, she often woke me in pain. Soon I slept little more than she did, and almost as restlessly.

I had to forget working. Nothing occupied my mind but my wife's agony, my own confusions and resentments, the nightmare we shared. I dreaded giving each shot from the moment one was finished to the next; sometimes I botched the job, bringing blood and causing Rosie more pain and anger. I fear we were not always gentle with each other. Life became a blur of catnaps, cries in the dark, those accursed morphine shots. We hardly touched the inexpert meals I prepared. We saw virtually no one, rarely answered the telephone. When Rosie was alert enough to talk, we found conversation tougher than walking across boggy ground. There seemed nothing left to say that we could bring ourselves to say. We stared, mindlessly, at television; I couldn't concentrate enough to read. When Rosie slept fitfully, I drank as much as I dared without becoming unable to perform my nursing duties. In that hard time I grew a new appreciation for the true meaning of the word "misery."

One morning in February, Rosie said, "Lar, call my doctors. Have them make arrangements to admit me to the hospital. I think I need to be there." I knew her concern was as much for me as for herself, and so protested. My wife gave me a crooked grin and said, "Okay, you're on the record. But there's no use in both of us being miserable every moment. Call my doctors." We talked little en route to the hospital; privately, I figured Rosie might never come home again and wondered if she had those thoughts. I think she did. She asked to be driven on George Washington Parkway, through the Virginia countryside along the Potomac River she loved, and I had the notion she was telling it goodbye. Weeks later, she would ask me to have her body cremated and her ashes scattered at a given point in the woods near that river.

I visited the hospital daily. The remainder of the time—night and day—I partied and drank and waited for the end while trying not to think about it. Though I told my friends I was working on the big LBJ book, I actually worked on nothing. All I managed was a few private letters. My life seemed in limbo; nothing was real; there would be no tomorrow. I was alternately manic and stoic, crazily euphoric and darkly depressed; I picked quarrels with strangers in bars and had a few fistfights. Late at night, when alone, I placed stacks of records on the turntable—Willie Nelson, Merle Haggard, Linda Ronstadt, Jerry Jeff Walker, Waylon Jennings—turned the volume up to full roar, turned off my mind and drank until I attained oblivion.

Twice, in April, Rosie's doctors thought she was dying. We gathered—relatives and friends—for the death watch. Each time, she came back and briefly appeared stronger. Ella Udall and Jenny Battista, two old friends, took her for drives, shopping and to lunch on a few good days; I took Rosie out, when she felt able, for lunch or early dinner. By then she was confined to a wheelchair.

Late in that cruel month, I went to the hospital one morning with rare good news: *Confessions of a White Racist* had been nominated for a National Book Award against books by such prominent writers as Norman Mailer, Tom Wolfe, Mike Royko, Victor Navasky and five others. Rosie rallied to show keen interest in external events for the first time in months. "I'm going to those awards ceremonies in New York," she announced. When they occurred two weeks later she was not, of course, physically able to make the trip. But her doctors said my book's nomination had so rasied her spirits, "She's in better shape than in weeks and weeks."

I wired my wife a dozen red roses from New York on the day of the awards ceremonies. We both were hopeful that I might win. One of the three judges, Digby Diehl, book editor of the *Los Angeles Times*, had written a laudatory column about my book and was, additionally, an old friend of many party wars and barroom skirmishes. I cautioned Rosie that Mailer's controversial *The Prisoner of Sex* or Navasky's biting *Kennedy Justice* probably would win. Not until I had lost—to the goddam *Whole Earth Catalog*, for Pete's sake—did I realize how strongly my heart had counted on winning.

The awards ceremonies, where I was concerned, proved to be a comic opera. Too nervous to attend the afternoon press conference where winners would be announced, I waited in a bar with friends and treated my condition with whiskey. Several Viking editors and publicity types had been instructed to call me there with the news of the winners. Everybody thought somebody else would call, so nobody called. I may have been the only writer in the city—certainly the only nominee—to remain ignorant of the winners hours after the official announcements. When I appeared for the awards ceremonies that evening, trying to show I was a good loser, it developed I had lost my invitation; I almost had to force my way in. (Probably I had mistakenly thrown away my invitation when discarding the acceptance speech I had learned I would not need.) At the cocktail party for NBA nominees following the awards ceremony, an officious young woman guarding the door refused to believe I was an honoree; I was admitted only after a considerable ruckus. Sometime that night my hotel room was burgled: I lost a new coat-and-slacks outfit, about $60 in cash and three ounces of good grass. The next day, as Digby

Diehl and I shared a cab in midtown—he apologetically explaining why I hadn't won, though strongly indicating he had been in my corner—he bounded out at a red light to buy a *New York Times* that blew his cover story. "Of all the books nominated this year," my good friend Digby Diehl was quoted as saying in the nation's newspaper of record, "only *The Whole Earth Catalog* will be remembered fifty or a hundred years from now."

I salvaged what I could by selling to *New York* magazine for $1,000 a short article called "Confessions of a Black-hearted Loser," recounting my NBA misadventures and exploring how one's foolish hopes and fancies, unbridled, can build up to provide a crash of dreams. *New York* published it in early May. Rosie chuckled and chortled while reading it. That would be the last time I would hear her laughter.

At midmorning on June 8, 1972, one of Rosemarie's sisters called to say I should not visit the hospital that day. "Take a day off from the routine" was the message my wife had sent. Since for two or three days Rosie had been sinking—and only minutes earlier I had called her doctor to learn she wasn't expected to last through the night—I immediately suspected she thought to spare me a deathbed scene, or possibly she wanted to be spared my morose, awkward company. I drove to the hospital with much dread. Though I am far from a praying man, I thought, *Lord, let it be easy for her.*

Heavily sedated at her own request ("I don't want to know when it happens"), Rosie slept through much of the day. She stirred in midafternoon and wanted water. As I gave her a drink she whispered, "Go home"; then she again went to sleep.

Rosie's relatives had gathered. About three o'clock I suggested they go home to rest and eat, because we expected to keep a night vigil. For more than an hour, alone, I fitfully tried to read a new novel by Joe McGinnis while Rosie slept. About four-thirty she roused herself, and pantomimed that she wanted to be sedated. I rang the nurse. After her shot, Rosie apparently drifted away again. A few minutes later I heard her whisper my name and looked up from the McGinnis book. "Up," she whispered, making a cranking motion to indicate I should elevate her hospital bed. When I had done so, she pointed to my chair and whispered, "Over there." I hesitated, puzzled. "Go there," she whispered, again pointing to my chair. I obeyed, not knowing what to make of it. Propped on a pillow, she looked at me with astonishingly clear eyes, more alert than I had seen her in days. I thought, *My God, she's making another of those miraculous recoveries!* I opened my mouth to ask if she wanted anything, but she cut me off with a shush and a fluttery motion of a hand. For what seemed two or three minutes she stared at me—as if memorizing something—and I held her eyes with my own. Amazingly, she suddenly winked at me. I winked back. She motioned that I should crank her bed to its normal position and whispered something; I think it was "Down, baby," or perhaps "Damn, baby." As I cranked down the bed, Rosie turned her head to the right, away from me, issued a little soft sigh—*Aahhh!*—and in that moment she died.

Chapter Five

MUDDLING THROUGH

*** In the fall of 1973 I began teaching at Princeton, partly against my better judgment. Though harboring serious reservations about my worth in the classroom, and knowing I never had prospered there, I was tempted by the $26,000 salary. I hoped, too, given the serenity of a small-town campus, that I might again find that writing discipline, drive and sense of purpose I had lost during Rosemarie's final year and had not been able to recapture.

Since Rosie's death I had wandered the country like a gypsy minstrel, singing sad songs, pointlessly roaring, creating havoc, carrying my own chaos along. There was anger in it and self-pity and real grief and not a little guilt. Though I wrote the occasional magazine article, and claimed to my editors and friends to be progressing with my Lyndon Johnson biography, I mainly got drunk and became involved in witless, fruitless personal entanglements. Surely I became a trial to friends, a burden to editors and a crazy puzzle to several women. My income had dropped sharply, despite the monthly Viking checks, and yet my wasteful whoopee spending reached an all-time high. I couldn't seem to tolerate Washington or my apartment there, and so often split in something close to panic for New York, Austin, Chicago, Nantucket, New Orleans: pit stops on an aimless race to nowhere.

The Princeton job sounded ideal for my rehabilitation. I saw the opportunity to hibernate and heal, regain decent writing habits. Except for the two days each week I would teach—a creative writing course one day, a political science class the next—I would be free to visit among former LBJ associates, now scattered to the winds, for purposes of my biography. Between the Viking and Princeton checks my income would approximate $5,000 per month; three or four magazine pieces per year should raise that to $6,000 monthly on average.

Assuming new personal disciplines, that should see me through. I should have ample time to make headway on the Johnson book. On paper it had the look of a grand plan.

It didn't work out. I had reckoned without writing comments on 35,000 student words each week, office hours required by my students, the interruptions of random campus poets, the arranging of transportation, quarters and entertainment on behalf of visiting writers and editors to speak to my classes. I had two weekly lectures to prepare, writing assignments to make, papers to grade; reporters from every daily newspaper in New Jersey, in or near Philadelphia, and some from Texas visited with photographers to observe the "cowboy professor" or "the high school dropout professor" accommodating to the Ivy League, and vice versa. Despite all efforts to dodge involvement in faculty affairs, I couldn't escape them all. It soon became apparent the soft "part-time" job I had envisioned required much of my energies and time. I had not reckoned, either, on my inability to accept such serenity as occasionally presented itself. I stared at blank paper, at the walls, television; grew bored and restive. Princeton was a pretty little town, yes, but as the old geezer told a young man smitten by a beautiful woman, "Son, purty don't last long enough to *be* enough." As at Harvard, I felt isolated from the world and the mainstream: the Watergate scandal, the largest story in years, was being revealed piecemeal and I was on the sidelines.

By the time the second semester started, in the early snows of 1974, I was admitting to myself that the Princeton experiment had proved a disaster; to others, not on the scene to witness my disorganized scramblings, I claimed to be happy and fulfilled in the campus life. I had signed on at Princeton for two years and felt obligated to muddle through. And I gave the job as much as I could drag from my innards, though privately admitting it was far from my best.

February brought the publication of a nonfiction collection I had managed to get together, *The Old Man and Lesser Mortals*. My mood was much improved by excellent reviews, but received a severe setback when sales figures proved embarrassing. It was the same old story: good press, bad business. I was unwilling to go on the road to hustle my book; Viking, perhaps burned by the expensive, nonproductive tour on behalf of *Confessions of a White Racist*, didn't insist. My publisher ran a few token ads touting my collection, I did nothing, and as a result it sold a zinging 2,794 copies in hardback and a magnificent 1,648 in a paperback edition that Dell's Delta released and promptly forgot. Mario Puzo sells that many books while out to lunch. To date that collection—my best, I think—represents my all-time low in the marketplace. Grant it, dear Lord, that I will be able to make that statement through the rest of my days.

I dismissed my classes at Princeton a month before other professors quit theirs, because I didn't believe in final examinations and because I was eager to escape. My immediate goal was never to live in Princeton again; I would commute, thereafter, to my classrooms from New York City.

In June I moved into a fourth-floor, two-bedroom apartment in a high-rise building at 32nd Street and Second Avenue. The blattings of trucks and the gibberings of street crazies replaced the chirpings of crickets and academicians suffered in Princeton. Manhattan always having the ability to promise high adventures, I settled in happily and with great expectations. I hummed and whistled in converting one of the bedrooms into a book-lined writing room. Surely, amid the roars and sirens and howlings of the great energetic city, my Lyndon Johnson book would almost write itself.

I had selected the Kip's Bay area, bordering Murray Hill, because it was handy to the offices of a new magazine, *New Times*, where I had earlier signed on as a contributing editor. It was to be a muck-raking journal, lively and hard-hitting, a formula that appealed. And there was a small personal bonus: *New Times* had located at 1 Park Avenue, directly across the street from my old *Harper's* digs; I envisioned thumbing my nose at Lewis Lapham and Bill Blair daily.

George Hirsch, founder of *New Times*, also had signed as contributing editors Jimmy Breslin, Pete Hamill, Murray Kempton, Mike Royko, Dick Schaap, Joe McGinnis, Nicholas von Hoffman and others—a dazzling bundle of talent. He brought aboard two competent former *Life* editors with whom I had worked, Steve Gelman and Berry Stainback, as his executive and managing editors; on my recommendation he hired Frank Rich, only a year out of Harvard and not prospering on a small weekly newspaper in Richmond, as his movie critic.

To help raise money to found *New Times* George Hirsch had persuaded me, and other contributing editors, to parade in front of bankers and financiers. There we preened and promised our best loyalties to the new enterprise and our intent to bring our best work to it. Those who so performed were promised an opportunity to invest in the magazine. My financial condition being on a par with that of New York City—then tottering on the brink of bankruptcy—with a credit rating that equated me with bank robbers, I was unable to invest. When it finally got down to contract-signing and nut-cutting, others decided the deal wasn't as good as Mr. Hirsch had made it sound. Soon, for one reason or another, most of the heralded contributing editors had moved on; Breslin, I believe, wrote only one article before storming out the door; Hamill almost immediately followed. One by one, my colleagues trickled away. I still had high hopes, however, and stayed on to write more full-length articles than any other writer in *New Times'* short history and, for about two years, also wrote for each issue a column called "Fulminations." I was paid $2,000 to $2,500 per article—depending on length and what each piece entailed—plus $900 each for the columns. Though the magazine originally had trouble finding its special voice, and would never be entirely successful, the potential seemed to be there. I was content enough, and prepared to dig in at *New Times* while getting serious about my Lyndon Johnson book. I also had agreed to become a contributing editor to a new magazine in Austin, *Texas Monthly*, where my work fetched their top rate of $3,000 per article. All this in addition to my Princeton duties. It would prove too much to chew.

When classes resumed in the fall of 1974 I found the commute to Princeton exhausting and irritating. Each Monday I rose in the dark to shiver or splash to the New York Port Authority terminal, there to shove for seating space on packed and uncomfortable buses; they seemed to stop at every village and crossroad; the one-way jouncings required more than two hours. The alternative was to take a train to Trenton, then cab from Trenton to Princeton; though this was easier on the nerves and the tailbone, it was also prohibitively expensive. Perhaps these minor hardships would not have loomed in my mind as major ones had I been happier in my work.

I taught both my classes on Mondays, overnighted in the Princeton Inn with a bottle as my companion—drinking pal Geoffrey Wolff having quit his Princeton teaching post to move to rural Vermont, and old sidekick Joe McGinnis having disappeared from his New Jersey farm to research a book on American heroes—and held office hours Tuesday mornings. After lunch at the faculty club I prepared the upcoming week's writing assignments for my kids, posted them on the bulletin board outside my office and returned to New York in the dark aboard those gas-fumy old buses.

Working conditions had changed at Princeton. Walt Litz, the gentlemanly scholar who headed Humanities, and who was my boss, had departed to England for a year's sabbatical to continue Shakespearean studies. Another faculty member would "nominally" oversee my endowed-chair operation, Dr. Litz told me. But my new straw boss had Simon Legree qualities; we clashed almost immediately. Where Walt Litz had given his professors free rein, the new man issued no more rope than might be needed for a snubbing post. I abhor short leashes, so we were doomed from the start.

My first day back on campus I found tacked to my office door an order to report to the new acting chief. We clanged swords like two generals each demanding the other's surrender. The new man said I had violated my contract by moving from Princeton, and must immediately return from my New York abode. No, I said, my agreement to live in Princeton had been limited to the first academic year; where I now lived was not his business. But, he countered, he required me to participate in faculty functions and *that* would require my presence as a resident. No, I said, Walt Litz didn't require that faculty bullshit and I felt no need to participate. Also, he added, I was to be the new faculty adviser to the school newspaper, the *Daily Princetonian*, and that job required my ongoing presence. No, I said, that advisory bit wasn't in my original agreement and I wouldn't permit it to be added now; when I signed on, I said, I had told Litz and the entire selection committee that I must be free to pursue my own writing or I wouldn't take the job; they had agreed; no other source had authority to countermand that agreement. Back and forth, back and forth. Each week when I came to Princeton the new Simon Legree had appended another of his damnable notes to my office door. We haggled for six weeks, the only "progress" being that he ultimately said he would settle for my presence on campus a full three days per week rather than the two I gave. I refused his compromise.

The last time we met—at lunch on a Monday—the new dude said, "If you aren't willing to satisfy my standards by the end of this week,

I'll be forced to make other arrangements." I flipped out. "You can't fire me," I said, "because you didn't have a goddam thing to do with hiring me. I have an appointment for two years to an endowed chair *you* did not endow and do not control. I'm not bucking for tenure, so I don't give a shit if I get along with you. I don't have to kiss your ass. On the other hand, you should feel perfectly free to kiss mine. And I shall not be seeing you again, no matter how many notes you tack on my office door. Enjoy your wine." Whereupon I left behind a very purse-mouthed luncheon companion.

Before the week was out, I concluded that both Princeton and its reluctant visiting professor might benefit from my resignation. I met with two members of the original selection committee, told them I would finish out the semester but please have someone ready to replace me at its conclusion. I then telephoned the *Daily Princetonian* to announce my upcoming resignation. On Thursday, shortly after the campus newspaper was published, I received a call in New York from my agitated straw boss. He said he was catching flak from on high, and that I had ruined him. I said if I had, I wanted to assure him that act had not been accidental. I never saw the straw boss again during my remaining weeks at Princeton, which was one of the nicest things that happened to me there.

Now I was totally free to write the big Lyndon Johnson book, the book that would be the professional making of me. Who, or what, could stop me?

Well, among others, I could. By constantly writing for *New Times*, *Texas Monthly*, *True*, *Cosmopolitan* or any magazine whose editor approached me rattling coins. By starting, one after another, sure-fire novels that petered out forty or eighty or somesuch pages down the line. By spending my nights drinking and my days nursing hangovers. I was, by then, sore afraid of the Johnson book and felt incapable of crafting it. But having drawn, and spent, the majority of the advance money, I saw no way to confess failure and survive it.

Though I don't want this to come off as blame-placing, I had a little help in attaining failure. One of LBJ's former intimates originally had promised me access to his private journals, kept during Mr. Johnson's final years in the Senate, in the vice-presidency and the White House. One night at dinner, years earlier, he had said, "I'll never write a book about the man. I was too close to him and it makes for not being able to see the forest for the trees. But I can help you. I think you'd be the perfect writer for that book." This promise, in turn, related to Viking, had helped me land that $100,000 contract. But as time moved on, I found the old Johnson crony increasingly vague and elusive. He was "too busy" to submit to interviews; he wanted to review his journals before passing them on; he could not talk until Johnson died; when Johnson did die, he was "too full of grief" to consider the matter immediately or objectively. Ultimately, he confessed that he had decided to do his own book. Goodbye, journals.

Other LBJ associates refused interviews because I was not exactly in good odor with the Johnson crowd; many remembered LBJ's anger at my *Harper's* pieces and critical comments I had written of their old hero elsewhere as the Vietnam War escalated. Some knew, too, of my support of Senator Eugene McCarthy against President Johnson. LBJ himself, while in retirement at his Texas ranch, never answered my two letters asking to see him.

One particularly vitriolic Texas congressman, a man I have always considered so chickenshit by nature I never have understood why he works so hard at chickenshitery, labeled me a "mad dog" in warning his colleagues against granting me interviews. "That bastard will ask you for a match and then burn your ass with it," he was quoted to me by a friendlier Texas congressman. (I had, indeed, burned the congressman in question in *Saturday Evening Post* and *Progressive* articles, though not—I think—unfairly.)

I told those congressmen who had known LBJ well they owed it to history to talk to me candidly; most, however, were not persuaded. Some, inside and outside Congress, though friendly, confessed they didn't feel free to talk candidly so long as Lyndon Johnson—or his wife, Lady Bird—remained alive. "If they read I had said anything about him that wasn't high praise," one Texan said, "I would become a nonperson in their eyes. Especially hers. She's tougher and more unforgiving than he is."

I didn't want to write a book containing only that which already was known and part of the public record—mine was to be the *definitive* book—so I found those comments and cool receptions discouraging and intimidating. They helped dry me up, along with my own lassitude and, yes, fear of failure. Johnson was such a complex man, often play-acting and showing so many faces—changing his accounts of events to suit the moment or his audience or immediate purposes—that one could never be certain what was real or what was mock show. I doubted whether any writer could capture or define the man in the absence of cooperation from many sources that were proving to be closed to me; I was petrified at thoughts of producing an inferior book, and so produced none. I now see, in retrospect, that my alcoholism caused me to turn and run. Had I been clear-headed and hungrier, I might have pushed on. There were ample sources to interview, as David Halberstam proved in writing his brilliant *The Best and the Brightest*. But I didn't have—couldn't then muster—Halberstam's will and determination. Ironically, after Halberstam got the publishing world interested in my writing the big Lyndon Johnson book—and I failed to exploit the opportunity—he went on to write the best one of the period.

I did make numerous false starts toward the Johnson biography, but after fifty or one hundred pages I would groan at the pedestrian results and hasten to destroy them. Once I actully turned in about sixty good pages to my Viking editors, beginning with LBJ's funeral and then flashing back to his childhood on the land he was buried in, but it was all I had save for pages and pages of disorganized notes. I claimed to my editors that I had much more in rough draft—100 pages, 120 pages, 150 pages, 200 pages; whatever I thought they might believe—and told the same to inquiring or concerned friends. I don't believe anybody was truly fooled except a few gullible newspaper journalists from Texas, who came to interview me about the big work in progress and reported as gospel my claims of crafting an exciting work that each day brought me to the typewriter early, eager and keen-eyed. Nothing was further from the truth—not even Richard Nixon's many calculated and transparent Watergate lies.

Articles, however, spewed from my typewriter: about Watergate, rodeo cowboys, the American redneck, Vietnam, professional gamblers, horse traders, the eternal battle of the sexes, sexual hypocrisy, Congress, country-western music and musicians, the unexpected rise of Jimmy Carter, the drive for success in America, lingering scars of the Great Depression on my generation, vocational role-playing, the bribery trial of John Connally, what rejection at the polls does to politicians, the closing down of a famous Texas whorehouse—even two or three articles about my old nemesis Lyndon B. Johnson. I had the ability to pull myself together to accomplish short work, even if I couldn't sustain long projects, and much of that work was—strangely—among the best I have done. Still, I fretted because it amounted to no more than literary piecework and I felt much the failure. (Perhaps I could write short stuff because I *had* to if I hoped to survive, and in my heart I knew I couldn't write the kind of LBJ book I had sold. Writer's block is difficult to explain.) Though the magazine money was as good as or better than most writers were able to command, I blew it as fast as it came in, going ever deeper in debt and falling behind in taxes.

In 1976 an actor-director I did not know, Peter Masterson, and a composer-musician I did know, Carol Hall, approached me about adapting for the stage a piece I had published in *Playboy* two years earlier, "The Best Little Whorehouse in Texas." They thought they saw a musical comedy in it; listening to them, I thought I saw two crazy people. None of us had ever written a musical show; what I knew of the theater could be stuffed in a thimble and rattle around. They were persistent, however; I agreed to work on the project as I could find spare time—but I didn't take it seriously, expected nothing to come of it, and for a long time worked only when Peter Masterson badgered me.

Also in mid-1976, Bobby Baker telephoned to ask whether I might be interested in ghosting his book about his days of power (and subsequent fall from grace) as a Lyndon Johnson intimate and powerful Capitol Hill wheeler-dealer. As secretary to the Senate Majority, Baker had in the 1950s and early 1960s made a reputation as the Capitol Hill connection—a man not only talented at counting votes and helping LBJ in the persuasions of senators, but also the Mr. Fixit you sought out hat in hand or money in hand if you wanted to do quick business in Washington. Baker had prospered far beyond his government salary. But a disgruntled partner in a vending machine business, claiming Bobby Baker had double-crossed him and forced him out of profitable contracts with government agencies, blew the whistle and filed a lawsuit. Baker resigned under pressure; congressional investigations and grand jurys began exploring his activities. Baker ultimately was convicted of numerous felony counts, including tax evasion and fraudulent misappropriation of $100,000 he extracted from savings-and-loan lobbyists—allegedly to guarantee the vote of a powerful senator—and then was accused of applying that money to his own uses. After years of legal wranglings, and unsuccessful appeals all the way to the Supreme Court of the United States, Baker had served about eighteen months of a three-to-five-year sentence in federal prison.

There had been a time, when Baker's problems and legal moves made headlines almost daily, that I might have fought a gorilla to write his book. We had met a couple of times in those days to explore the possibility. Then Baker's lawyer, the famed Edward Bennett Williams, had decreed that no book would be written until all charges against his client had been resolved, all trials completed, all appeals disposed of. I saw riches go aglimmering; at that time, Baker's book doubtless would have fetched top dollar.

By 1976, however, I doubted whether many Americans remembered Bobby Baker or gave a hoot about his story if they did. Most of the famed characters in his drama were dead, defanged or had themselves been forgotten. Consequently, I couldn't see much profit in writing Baker's book. So I told him no, I was not interested in being his ghost. He then asked whether I would recommend another writer. I suggested he take that problem to my agent, Sterling Lord, who likely would accommodate him for a percentage of any contract resulting. Soon Mr. Lord called me to say he had talked for several hours with Baker, had read a number of documents Baker had provided, and he believed I had made a mistake in turning down the project. "I think there's money in it," Mr. Lord said. The Lord in heaven, as well as the Lord on Madison Avenue, knew that if I then needed anything it was money. I agreed to fly to Washington to talk to Baker, tape him and decide whether I thought his story would reveal enough for a book, provided my agent paid me for my time and expenses; if a book resulted I would repay him; if none did, my agent would have gambled and lost a couple of thousand dollars.

The problem was that Bobby Baker wanted to use his book to vindicate himself—to claim he had been a victim of partisan politics and a sacrificial goat abandoned by politicians as guilty as he, or guiltier—while I needed to extract enough confessions and out-of-school tales on the mighty to interest (1) publishing houses and (2) the book-buying public. Eventually Baker agreed to level with me (though he insists, to this day, he did not steal the $100,000 bribe money, but gave it to the late Senator Robert Kerr of Oklahoma) and I became convinced a passable, salable book might be written.

I submitted to about fifteen publishing houses a lengthy prospectus revealing roughly what the Baker book would tell; they were invited to bid a week later. I urged my Viking editors to bid strongly, believing the book—properly promoted—had the potential for excellent sales and that Viking might at long last recover its investment in me. But a quirk of life caused Viking not to bid at all: Mrs. Jacqueline Kennedy Onassis had newly signed aboard as a Viking editor; she was a longtime friend of Tom Guinzburg, then the chief officer of that publishing house. He, and others at Viking, feared that Mrs. Kennedy Onassis would be egregiously offended should they publish a book containing passages about JFK's womanizing, his love of sexual gossip involving the famous and powerful and his worldly cynicisms. Though these qualities were only a part of the John F. Kennedy mix, they were considerably outside that image and legend preferred by the flame keepers. "Jackie would have a fit if we bid on that book," I was told.

I figured the Baker book to require two years' work. I must read thousands of pages of court proceedings, appeals briefs, judicial decisions, lengthy congressional committee hearings and reports; I felt an obligation to reread stacks of old newspapers and magazines to recapture the mood of the pertinent period. I wanted to talk to Baker's defense attorneys and a few surviving role players in his old drama, by way of checking his claims and veracity. I knew, too, that I would be required to spend months with Baker, quizzing him and taping him for hundreds of hours, and that often we would be working at cross-purposes: he to gild his lily, and I to prevent it. I also knew that Baker's personality, like my own, was erratic and sometimes bombastic and that he loved whiskey almost as dearly as I did; these factors led me to presume (correctly) that we would not always work smoothly in harness. And after all the personal tuggings and reading and interviewing preliminaries, I still must get the words right on paper. I took the job only after being assured a generous piece of sales royalties, so that if a killing was to be made I would get as fat as or fatter than anyone else.

The advantage was Baker's as to advance money, 55 percent to 45 percent; that being the case, I told Lord and Baker, I couldn't afford to write the book unless it produced a minimum of $100,000 in front because my $45,000, after taxes and agent's fee, would not average out exceptionally well over two years. My agent perfectly understood this; Bobby Baker did not. He scoffed that his book—including the TV miniseries and Hollywood movie he counted on as certainties—would reap at least $1 million or perhaps $2 million up front. He could not be persuaded that his story was worth a dime less than it had been a dozen years earlier, and he otherwise knew absolutely nothing of the market realities. Despite all my agent and I could do to adjust Baker's high expectations downward, he constantly built himself up for a big letdown. "I won't take less than a million," Baker boasted. "Yes you will," I always countered. "You'll have to."

On the afternoon of the telephone bids I went to a long, liquid lunch in Washington, at Duke Zeibert's restaurant, with Baker and his live-in girlfriend, Doris Meyers. Bobby loudly toasted us as soon-to-be millionaires, telling all whom he could detain that New York, Hollywood, the TV networks—and perhaps Zanzibar—in that moment were bidding for his big book-movie-TV series. I wanted to hide under the table, listening to that unrealistic bullshit, but hid instead in many Scotch-and-waters.

We repaired to the modest Baker-Meyers apartment to await our agent's report. He called about dusk. "It's disappointing," he said without preamble. "Several houses didn't bid at all. The top is sixty thousand. And that's for hardback *and* paperback rights." I said, "No goddam way. I can't even think of working for my cut of that money." Across the room, Bobby Baker literally paled. I put down the phone and recited the mournful numbers; Baker appeared in shock. Suddenly, he dropped to his knees and turned his back; his shoulders shook; I wondered at his appreciation of the absurdities until I heard his sobs. "That was all I had left," he choked out as Doris comforted him. We drank and cursed the fates into the wee hours; I crashed on a couch dangerously near dawn.

Doris Meyers left for work the next morning long before King or Baker stirred. I was brewing instant coffee, and a wan Baker was toweling after his shower, when I answered the telephone's ring. Sterling Lord's chipper "Good morning!" seemed inappropriate to the circumstances. "In a pig's ass," I muttered. "No," he said, "hear me out." Lord said he'd just received a call from an executive of a publishing house that had intended to bid but had been unable, the previous day, to contact its chief executive, then in Europe, to establish a maximum bid ceiling. Contact now had been made: was it too late to bid?

"I trust you're not calling to say you turned him down," I said, holding my breath and daring to hope for a $100,000 bid offer.

Mr. Lord chuckled. "I told the man we'd permit him to bid late if he'd keep it to himself. He offered us one hundred and fifty-five thousand in advance monies."

I whooped, threw the telephone in the air and shouted the good news to Bobby Baker; his appreciation of the realities of the literary marketplace having markedly improved overnight, Bobby gave an answering whoop and performed a naked dance.

While covering the trial of John Connally for *Atlantic Monthly* in the winter of 1974 I had met, and quickly become friends with, a fellow Texan and lawyer named Lynn Coleman. Coleman then headed the Washington offices of the huge Texas-based Vinson, Elkins law firm—in which John Connally was a senior partner—and after the trial I began to drop by those offices to visit Coleman when down from New York. In the summer of 1976 he invited me to a weekend at his country place (which he shared with California Congressman Peter Stark) on the Maryland Eastern Shore. There I was introduced to another Vinson, Elkins lawyer—a young lady from Texas, one Barbara S. Blaine; she was a close friend of Coleman's fiancée (now his wife), Sylvia de Leon.

"We met at Yale," Miss Blaine said during the introductions.

"I beg your pardon," I said, "but I have been to Yale only once in my life and I can hardly remember it."

"I am not surprised," she countered.

That got my attention. I began searching my mind for old Yale details. I had been invited from Harvard to appear in connection with a symposium on Texas politics at Yale's Silliman College. On the train ride from Cambridge to New Haven I had fully enjoyed club car hospitalities. Arriving, I was greeted by Willie Morris, Bill Styron and a group of Texans that included State Senator Don Kennard, State Representative Malcolm McGregor and lawyer Warren Burnett. We feverishly celebrated in New Haven bars and hotel rooms throughout the afternoon. I was not, therefore, overly alert when our group repaired to a Silliman College reception and dinner in our honor.

Barbara Blaine, newly transferred from Mount Holyoke College as one of Yale's "pioneer women" in the first year it had accepted female undergraduates, had been assigned to Silliman College there; she was one of a handful of Texans the headmaster had dragooned into appearing to "honor" us. By luck of the draw, she claims to have been seated next to me; I am in no position to argue the point.

Those several years later, at the Maryland shore, I required Miss Blaine to refresh my memory: what had we talked about at Yale? "On learning I was from Texas," she said, "you immediately offered a long lecture about how it was my duty to return home after Yale because 'Texas always exports its best brains and that is what is wrong down there.' I then asked how long since you had lived in Texas. I believe you confessed to something like twenty years. I suppose it now would be about twenty-seven years you have deprived Texas of your brains, wouldn't it?"

I tugged my forelock, mumbled that it was good to have seen her again and sidled away from Miss Blaine's lovely claws. On subsequent trips to Washington, when visiting Lynn Coleman in his law offices, I sought out Miss Blaine to exchange pleasantries. She showered on me the full attentions she might have visited on a doorknob. Nonetheless, being a good fellow, I telephoned to ask her to dinner, in early 1977, shortly after renting a tiny apartment in Washington to work on the Baker book. Miss Blaine reported herself earlier booked for that evening.

How about tomorrow night?

Sorry. Busy again.

The night after?

Still busy, I'm afraid.

Uh. The night following the night after that?

So *very* sorry. Same story.

I don't suppose there's a chance in the world the *next* night is—

She feared that was correct.

Thank you very much, I said, the perfect gentleman; I replaced the phone and shouted, "Miss Blaine, you can go suck a goddam lemon! I have been humiliated at your hands for the last time!"

Miss Blaine, too, apparently sensed that she had humiliated me for the last time unless she amended her position; soon she called back to say that perhaps she could cancel one of her engagements three or four nights hence, it not amounting to as much as her others, if I still insisted on buying her dinner. Nowadays I am still paying for her dinners and those of the two children we have produced.

When in the capital city, I worked on the Baker book, signed on as a thrice-weekly columnist for the *Washington Star* and regularly bought Miss Blaine's breakfast, lunch and dinner; when in New York I worked on the *Whorehouse* play and my *New Times* pieces and columns. I'm uncertain why I have always compulsively heaped on my writing plate more than I can comfortably eat; perhaps it is the reluctance of a child of the Great Depression to turn down a dollar; maybe I assume that added pressures force me to produce more work; it could be that I am betting the numbers: the more opportunities one has to showcase one's wares, that reasoning runs, the more likely one's ship to come in. In truth that heaping-plate policy generally leads to a mad scramble to keep up with all projects, and invariably means that some of the prose one sends to the marketplace will arrive there not quite ripe. For almost a year I commuted between New York and Washington, scrambling to meet first this deadline and then that one. I would not want to do it again, but, somehow, it all worked out.

In 1977 Peter Masterson wangled $10,000 out of the famed Actors' Studio in New York to present there a showcase production of *The Best Little Whorehouse in Texas*. A showcase production is one designed to attract potential producers and investors. No immediate money accrues to playwrights during showcase productions; they are betting that some producer will see the potential for a profitable commercial production and will option or buy the property. It's something like betting on hog futures.

We opened at Actors' Studio in late October for fifteen performances scattered over three weeks. Writers, actors and others who saw the production gave it wonderful word-of-mouth; we received a good press in theatrical trade papers. Still, I doubted whether I would ever see a dollar. The odds seemed too long, and I barely knew the difference between a libretto and a pirouette. There was both agony and ecstasy in the work. I found the theater fascinating and exciting, but working in collaboration with others—melding song and story and dealing with the whims of actors—drove me up yonder wall. Nor was my participation in the *Whorehouse* project popular with my associates in life: my agent groused that I was wasting my time in a speculative venture, Bobby Baker was pissed that I didn't give his book 100 percent priority and Barbara Blaine in a fit of anger once said, "I hate this goddam show! You don't have time for *anything* but this goddam show! All you talk about is this goddam show!"

In truth, that goddam show was fast sending me to the poorhouse. I gave it an incredible amount of time—writing and rewriting for months and then again through long weeks of rehearsals, conferring with Pete Masterson and Carol Hall, haggling with actors over their parts and stage bits—and, consequently, lost money I might have earned for magazine work. It also held up payments for the Baker book. Some intelligent executive at the publishing house had decreed that the King-Baker partnership would be paid in increments released only as each new chapter was turned in. No new chapter, no new money. Fiddling with *Whorehouse*, I fell behind in the delivery of chapters.

Midway of the Actors' Studio run we were approached by Stephanie Phillips, an executive with Universal Pictures, who professed interest in developing our show for an off-Broadway production—then going on to Broadway and Hollywood, assuming the show worked. I originally figured Ms. Phillips would drop huge advance money on us, but quickly learned the theater business does not work that way. The playwright is allowed to take risks along with the producer, receiving only a nominal fee up front—I believe Masterson, Hall and I shared $5,000 front money—and makes big money, if at all, by getting a percentage of the play's gross box-office receipts. I also learned that when one begins to slick up a show with an eye on Broadway, the repairs are not minor. Our Actors' Studio production took pains to develop the play's characters and contained generous amounts of dialogue; we had no dancing; songs, while plentiful, were not stuffed in willy-nilly at the expense of the book.

Universal Pictures, however, wanted a big musical musical and began to slick and trick and fluff it up. This is because as a rule musicals, should they become hits, make much more money than do nonmusical theater offerings. We began ripping the play to shreds and pasting it together again. Tommy Tune was brought in to co-direct with Pete Masterson, and to be choreographer; Carol Hall wrote new songs. Each time a song or dance number was added, I lost precious dialogue and pieces of my mind. Scenes I loved and pre-sumed untouchable were tossed in the trash can or pared to the bone. I began to think of my book portion of the production as a mere skeleton on which to hang greatcoats of song and dance. Naturally, I howled and hooted—loudly accusing all hands of ruining my play, and predicting just as loudly that the "cartoon version" emerging would close quicker than a switchblade.

And, of course, the thing took off like a rocket and burst through the roof. We played to sellout houses off-Broadway from April of 1978 to June and then moved to Broadway for a run lasting more than four years: 1,639 performances, which landed *Whorehouse* among the top twenty of Broadway's all-time long-running productions. Al-exis Smith toured the nation's major theaters with it for seventeen months; June Terry starred in a Houston-based company for more than a year, then toured with the show for almost two more. Bus and truck companies toured for years; if *Whorehouse* did not play your town, likely you do not have sidewalks and traffic lights. The show ran in Australia for a year, in South Africa almost as long and in London for six months. Now seven years later—eight, should you count Actors' Studio—summer-stock, community-theater and college-theater revenues provide me six-figure sums annually. A costly, terrible movie was made and released in 1982; you may have to dodge it on television until you die. As dreadful as it was, and is, that movie continues to produce revenue from TV airings, cassette sales and rentals, and sound-track albums. If anybody ever gives you a choice between a hit musical and going partners in oil with a rich Arab, take the musical.

There was even a bit of artistic satisfaction. Carlin Glynn, the original leading lady as Miss Mona, won a Broadway Tony, its Brit-ish equivalent and a Theatre World Award from critics; Henderson Forsythe, the original leading man as crusty old Sheriff Ed Earl Dodd, also won a Broadway Tony. Joan Ellis, a supporting actress, was nominated for one; so were Tommy Tune, Peter Masterson and your present hero. The show itself won a Tony nomination as Best

Musical, losing out to *Sweeney Todd*. But our softball team beat theirs, 8–7, for the championship of the Broadway League that year. So there.

Barbara Blaine became my wife at the Washington home of Lynn Coleman and Sylvia de Leon on May 6, 1978, during the off-Broadway run. She also became my lawyer and agent. The dumbest thing I ever did was to fail to make her my agent *before* signing all those *Whorehouse* contracts; then she, not someone else, could have bought a yacht with the 10 percent agent's cut. This is still mentioned at our house occasionally, though I am rarely the one to bring it up.

When we returned from our honeymoon in England, France and Ireland we discovered that my good buddies at the Internal Revenue Service had given us a unique wedding gift; them playful boogers had garnisheed all my box-office money, save $50 per week, to satisfy back taxes of more than $13,000. Fortunately, *Whorehouse* was doing such good business my embarrassment lasted only four weeks.

The Baker book *(Wheeling and Dealing: Confessions of a Capitol Hill Operator)* was published in the fall of 1978 to fair-to-middling reviews. It made several best-seller lists: *Time, Washington Post, Publishers Weekly*, a few others. No way to know whether it might have edged onto the big "official" best-seller list—that of the lordly *New York Times*—because, in one of those quirks of life devised to drive writers crazy, that vital newspaper was closed down by a strike just as the Baker book came from the bindery. Though *Wheeling and Dealing* neither ran James Michener out of town nor put Robert Ludlum on the welfare dole, it sold a respectable 30,593 copies; perhaps you need to knock about the literary marketplace for a spell to truly appreciate those numbers; you would be surprised how many books sell no more than 1,000 to 1,500 copies no matter how much time, love, attention and sweat the poor authors invested in them. There was no movie or TV miniseries as Bobby Baker had counted on. Ironically, after years of lusting for decent book sales, I hardly noticed—or cared—how the Baker book sold because of the huge *Whorehouse* success. In this crazy business something you do for fun or almost by accident may go through the roof, while the project counted on to deliver you from the poorhouse may not pay for the paper it is printed on.

My friend Joe Goulden once divided time writing two books, one of which was a biography of labor leader George Meany and the other about Washington law firms. Goulden told his friends the Meany book would deliver him from creditors, but that the lawyer book was just a little thing he was dashing off to satisfy an old contractual obligation. And, of course, the Meany book did not sell well even among labor unionists—while the "dashed-off" book, *The Super Lawyers*, stayed on the *New York Times* best-seller list for twenty-four weeks.

When the *Whorehouse* musical was running practically everywhere, I greeted the mailman one morning and discovered a check for more than $46,000 as my take for a mere one week. "Godamighty," I said aloud as I stared at it, "how long would it take to earn that at Ronnie Dugger's *Texas Observer* rates? How long would my old daddy have worked for that money at a dollar an hour, or for the three dollars per day he got during the Depression as a cotton-gin hand?" I tried to develop a decent sense of shame but it just wouldn't come, even though I reminded myself of starving little children in China and such. No, by God, I had paid my dues: taking odd jobs as a delivery boy and a busboy when almost forty years old, in order to practice the writing craft, while my calendar contemporaries had become senior partners in law firms or bank executives and had been establishing generous retirement benefits. I had gone far out on a thin limb to survive—or perhaps perish—as a writer. So I said, again aloud, "By God, I ain't about to apologize if a great deal of good luck has finally come my way."

But if I didn't feel the need to apologize, why did I so insist I wasn't required to?

In 1979 I coauthored with an old Texas friend, Ben Z. Grant, a one-man play about the late Louisiana politico Huey Long. Barbara Blaine produced a showcase production (at a cost of $10,000) of *The Kingfish*, running twenty-odd performances at New Playwrights' Theatre in Washington, and starring the lawyer-thespian John Daniel Reaves.

Our goal was eventually to turn *The Kingfish* into a big musical. We had what appeared to be a serious nibble from Mike Nichols and his partner, Lewis Allen, but they got involved in other things and our talks went nowhere. I still harbor hopes for such a musical in the future after the fate of another musical of mine—now in the hands of New York producers—is determined. The idea of hitting the big-money jackpot again appeals, yes, but I truly am beguiled by the theater for other reasons. I like writing dialogue, I like seeing my work actually come alive and there is that thrill of tossing the dice with a great deal at stake and not knowing how the spots will come up. I'm working now on a straight dramatic play I feel strongly about and know I will be rewarded, in a corner of my soul, should it attain a good production and not make a dime. Dr. Samuel Johnson and my wife-lawyer-agent might be made uncomfortable by such profitless talk, but it's true.

Viking published another of my nonfiction collections *(Of Outlaws, Con Men, Whores, Politicians & Other Artists)* in 1980, to generally outstanding reviews and to a surprisingly brisk sale, for a collection, of 11,143 in hardback and 9,736 in quality Penguin paperback. The book made a little money and was pleasant work. Not so kind was the fate of *The Whorehouse Papers*, the 1982 saga of how a hit show accidentally came into being. My publisher apparently was experimenting with subliminal advertising in that case. Actually, the durn fools blew the entire pitiable $6,000 advertising budget on radio. I do not believe folks thirsting to read great books, or even semigood ones, take their recommendations from radio blurbs. Somebody at Viking apparently thought differently, though I promise Viking an interesting season if they try that radio crap with this book. Anyhow, *The Whorehouse Papers* sold only 4,318 copies in hardback; we have not been able to give away the paperback rights, despite good reviews and the use of that work in several college drama courses. Bah humbug.

You will note I have not mentioned how much advance monies I received for my last three books, including this one. That is because there was none. Barbara Blaine worked it out so that Viking would get these books, at no immediate cost, in payment toward the $100,000 I took for not writing the Lyndon Johnson book and another $30,000 for not writing the "lost places" book. Be sure your sins will find you out. The only thing wrong with that arrangement is that Viking has invoked—as I'm sure any publishing house would invoke—its god-durn advertising Formula, earlier mentioned. That is the Formula based on how much the author got in front money and the number of copies published, these largely dictating how much advertising money will be spent. Since I have received no front money, the Formula grants me advertising sums you could earn in a week selling pencils given decent weather, a good corner and a bright cup.

In 1981, the Encino Press, in Texas, published a limited edition of about 3,000 copies of my Christmas story *That Terrible Night Santa Got Lost in the Woods*. It has sold perhaps 1,500 copies—about half of which Barbara and I have bought for cheap Christmas gifts—though people keep telling me it would make a wonderful TV movie for the entire family, tugging at heartstrings and making little old ladies cry and such. I wish they would go tell that to the goddurn TV networks; we have tried to foist it off on all of them whose addresses we know. At first the TV folks get all excited and compare the story to Truman Capote's *A Christmas Memory*—which seasonally reappears on TV almost as often as the Superbowl—and then after a while they hum and haw and say the story does not contain enough "action." By "action" they mean "violence." Nobody gets raped or shot or whomped with tire tools or overdoses on drugs in this story of a dead-broke daddy faced with providing Santa Claus for his young son during the Great Depression and a freak winter blizzard. The moment those TV biggies start suggesting hoking up my story with packs of wolves and wild dogs and hurricanes and robbers and such— yes, they actually have suggested all that—I snatch it back and say, "No deal." One outfit wanted to "modernize" the story; it would be set not in 1930s rural Texas but in Houston, last Christmas or next, and there would be in it an unemployed daddy and a working mommy and adultery and a hurricane—honest—and a big robbery and fist-fights and a car wreck. The problem is, it wouldn't be the story I wrote. So why don't they just go ahead and make *that* damned movie and leave me and my story alone? Television loonies, take it from me, are first cousins to Hollywood loonies. You will read more about Hollywood loonies in the upcoming section.

I suppose that here and now I should drop to my knees, cast my eyes skyward and thank all who have had a hand in bringing me ample magazine work and the *Whorehouse* play; otherwise, my Loved Ones would have long ago perished with their ribs showing while I, myself, would be petitioning heartless officials for release from debtors' prison. I don't believe God wants my books to sell well. The best I can figure it, all my books—in hardback, and in paperback where applicable—have sold a grand total of only about 150,000 copies. Lee Iacocca, the big automobile executive you see strutting himself on TV while bragging on his rolling stock, in 1984 sold *one million hardbacks* of the only book he has written in his life, and that with the help of a ghost; I hate even to think of how many paperbacks he'll ring up on the cash registers.

If he don't cut that shit out, I'm going into the car bidness.

Should I find myself standing tonight at St. Peter's gate, and the gatekeeper required me to justify my time as a writer, I suppose I would have to tell him something like this:

I am better now than when I started, and on my best days I feel the need to apologize to few—though, like all but the worst hack writers, I don't feel I have worked to my potential or attained, artistically, anything like my early hopes or goals. I have accomplished a fair amount of work I'm proud of, much I would like to do better, and some I wish I had not done at all. By and large I have been my own man while avoiding bosses and boring sweat work. Though I have sometimes despaired as a writer, I have known high moments and had some great laughs. I have also been lucky in my associations and opportunities: without that luck, whatever I amount to as a writer would be considerably less. Had I my life to live over, I would again choose to become a wordsmith. Mine is a craft where there remains, always, the hope and promise of creating work that pleases the writer and others. Any flaw in my old dream of becoming a first-rate writer has been the fault of the dreamer, not of the dream.

Part Two

RANDOM JOTTINGS FROM A WRITER'S NOTEBOOK

ORIGINS OF MATERIAL

Many writers keep notebooks or diaries to record observations, emotions or experiences fresh in their minds. Mine has been loosely kept; weeks or months may pass without my touching it. Nor is it a neat, bound thing with a rich leather cover and stylish penmanship. I carelessly type my sporadic entries and toss them into wayward cubbyholes, replete with bad grammar, misspellings and exotic punctuation. Those offered here have been touched up for publication, though I have taken pains to change neither the tone nor the substance. I wanted to show the convolutions and inconsistencies of the writing mind in varied times and circumstances.

A few entries are highly personal laments never intended for publication, and originally meant to allow steam to escape; when I couldn't tell someone else I told my journal. I have permitted a few such steam-blowers in this book because they say something of the writer's ongoing struggle to produce and persevere. Perhaps the darker passages may encourage others by proving that, no matter one's degree of temporary despair, it is possible to keep typing and come out on the other side.

Some entries were made with the notion of someday publishing them. The compiling of such future materials permits the writer to believe he is not lying fallow when he probably is. To that extent the writer's notebook sometimes amounts to a necessary survival trick.

"Other than telling a story"—one of my students said as a group of youngsters drank beer with me in the Rusty Scupper—"what is writing all about? What is, you know, the writer trying to do?"

Good question. But, God, I flinch inwardly and get uptight when bright kids ask stuff like that! For one thing, I fear sounding pompous or pretentious; for another, I fear they'll discover I don't know what the shit I'm talking about. And, certainly, I fear telling them something that is wrong or that might promote harmful misconceptions. But one has no choice other than to take a deep breath and wade in: I am, after all, a *professor*, and professors must profess; that is what they pay us for.

I told the kids roughly as follows: the writer attempts to reflect what he has learned of his world and what he thinks of it. A particular point of view—or "voice"—distinguishes one writer from others. Good writers are in the business of leaving signposts saying, *Tour my world, see and feel it through my eyes; I am your guide.* The reader may or may not accept the writer's viewpoint, but that isn't as important as the writer's remaining true to his own visions. Remember, I told them, Mr. Hemingway's line: "Write the truest sentence you know."

Then I shuffled my feet under the table, hid my face in a beer flagon and hoped I hadn't disgraced myself.

Soon I found it necessary to defend humor in writing; the kids seemed to think that to permit humor meant the writing wasn't "serious." I invoked Twain, of course, and a number of others in preaching that the kids should not be afraid of fun or laughter in writing. Too many people, I said, become stiff, formal and artificial when they write. They become so conscious of the writing *act* they can't tell their stories. Looking at the absurdities may loosen the writer, permitting him to shed artifice.

"You write autobiographical stuff a lot," one kid said. "Why is what has happened to you so, um, important? Why should, uh, other people care enough to read it?" ("When," my mind completed the unspoken part of his sentence, "you ain't no prime minister, movie star or even Norman Mailer?")

Floundering, I said maybe in truth what happens to me isn't all that important to others; perhaps I'm excessively vain. But I would like to believe there is a larger purpose. Most of my first-person stuff moves from the specific (my own experience) to the general (the experiences of others) in a commonly shared time. Should you read what I say of growing up in the Great Depression, or of observing racism in America or even practicing it without really being aware of it, then that wasn't my story alone but represented what had happened to many others. I was relating history as a small participant in that history, maybe. Suddenly, I had the good fortune to recall a quotation from George Bernard Shaw: "The man who writes about himself and his own time is the only man who writes about all people and all time." Once Shaw had been enlisted on my side, sage nods occurred around the table. The kindly old professor, it appeared, had passed his pop quiz.

I looked at my watch, burbled about being late to some vital appointment, hastily drank up and got the hell out of there—while I still might be marginally ahead, and before the kids could decide I was just another old fart bumbling his way through the snow.

Washington
June 1984

Last night I attended one of those dreadful mill-around-and-grin cocktail parties and buffet dinners, there encountering *nine* times the question I most hate: "What are you working on now?" Perhaps I should have stood on a chair early on, whistled for attention, cupped my hands and delivered my spiel to the assembled. The tactic might have startled some, but would have had the virtue of getting the drill over with quickly.

People don't seem to inquire socially of surgeons the next body part they will cut up, or ask lawyers to relate the specifics of their ongoing cases, so why do they bedevil writers about work in progress? It might not be so vexing if they would settle for the short answer; if one could just say "A novel," "A play," "A nonfiction book," "A musical comedy"—and then be rewarded by a mute nod—life might be easier. But such answers only beget more questions: "What's the title? Where did you take that title from? What's it about? Where is it set? What time period? How many characters? Who's writing the music? Whom would you like to see play the lead in the movie (or onstage)? When and where will it open?"

There are practical reasons why I detest such inquisitions. (1) A writer risks talking any project to death. The more one babbles of the particulars, the less mystery and discovery left in the work—and the quicker the writer is likely to tire of it. At best, most writers grow sick of work requiring dogged pursuit for months or years. Anything likely to agitate that condition is dangerous and to be avoided. (2) The writer, having been closeted with his Muse all day, generally is eager to escape it come recreation time. Being forced to talk of the ongoing project is like being robbed of one's day off. (3) I simply don't like to share with any but a handful of intimates what is currently grinding in the mill. It seems an invasion of privacy when strangers presume the right to ask personal questions about what is, at that point, a purely private pursuit. (4) Much of the stuff a writer is asked *can't* be answered in the moment. The work in progress may still be taking shape; even if well along in it, and knowing fairly well where it is going, the writer won't have the slightest idea who may be in the movie or stage play or if there will be a movie or stage play. These things don't announce themselves full-blown, with a cast of thousands. (5) It is damned stone boring to cover the same ground repeatedly. No inquisitor stops to think that the writer surely has been asked those same questions countless times. They are forcing him to suffer what amounts to a press conference that will produce for him no ink.

I have sometimes claimed not to be permitted, contractually, to discuss the particulars of a given project. This may pacify the inquisitor and leave him with a satisfactory feeling of having gleaned inside information. More likely it won't: the response is more likely to inspire a dozen questions as to *why* that is so.

I understand "writing" questions if they come from students or those making serious efforts themselves to write. But I'll be hanged if I understand why nonwriting laymen so persist about picayune details or why they suffer the illusion it makes stimulating party chitchat. If they are so damned interested, why don't they buy more books? I have often tested my inquisitors by asking what book they currently are reading or the title of the book most recently read. A high percentage appear not to have read anything since they last cracked the Bobbsey Twins.

I think, hereafter, I may smile and say in response to "What are you working on now?" something like this: "A treatise on dynamics of thermonuclear osmosis as it affects high-tech synthesis." Perhaps, should one issue that nonsensical utterance and keep moving, he might put a safe distance behind him before the inquisitor recovers.

Washington
September 1979

An aspiring young writer cornered me in the lobby of New Playwrights' Theatre last week to ask whether he needs a literary agent and how to go about getting one. On campus tours I'm probably asked that two-part question more than any other.

There is a sort of Catch-22 factor involved. Most established agents are reluctant to take on writers with little or no track record. Agents working on commission (usually 10 percent) aren't eager to sign unpublished unknowns unlikely to make decent money until well into the future, if ever. They know that green and uncertain writers—in need of periodic strokings and full of basic questions—may make heavy demands on their time. "Signing new writers who know nothing of the business," I once heard an agent say, "is almost like adopting children. You have to baby-sit them. They can wear you out with demands for attention."

Many established agents will sign unknowns only should a veteran editor or writer recommend them—if at all. But when such truths are recited to aspiring writers they wail, "But *how* can I make a track record if nobody will open doors to me?" It is, admittedly, something of a chicken-or-egg situation.

Most magazines and book-publishing houses have either stopped or severely curtailed the reading of unsolicited manuscripts coming in unannounced "over the transom." Not one in a trainload being purchased, it makes no economic sense to pay readers for searching the "slush pile." Where unsolicited manuscripts are read, the potential Flannery O'Connor or Ross Thomas may be judged by a low-level reader fresh out of Bennington or Southwest Texas State; such inexperienced people know little of marketable prose, and may be of the notion that any manuscript not qualifying as a classic should never see print.

I recommend that agentless or unpublished writers *not* mail their manuscripts in the blind, but write a letter of inquiry giving precise details—in two pages or less—of the project they have written, are writing or propose to write. Then ask whether the editor is interested in seeing the work. Assuming the writer's letter is concisely composed, not replete with bad grammar or otherwise betrayed by marks of the hopeless amateur, a yes or no response generally may be expected.

Beware, neophyte writers, those ads in newspapers or magazines offering for a fee to read or critique your manuscripts or set your song lyrics to music. These are exploitive operations; the so-called agents operating in that manner probably have few contacts among legitimate publishers; they make their piles off your innocence while offering little or nothing in return.

There is no guarantee you will find the perfect, blue-ribbon, all-services agent even among legitimate pros. Some agents are strong in the magazine and book fields but know little of Hollywood, Broadway or television. And the converse is true. Some agents aggressively seek to originate work for their clients, while others sit on their asses content to peddle what their clients conceive in blood and then execute in sweat or tears. Some agents may lend money against future earnings to their producing—if penurious—writers, while others may be as close-fisted as flinty Republican bankers. Some agents are careful with their writers' contracts; others permit them to sign absolutely horrible documents when complex subsidiary rights are at stake. A couple of horror tales here:

One of my friends, a novelist of some repute, tardily discovered that his agent had sold all *future* rights to certain of his characters in making a movie deal; my friend wrote a new book using some of those same characters before learning this; he had to buy back his own characters. Another friend, upon completing a sequel to his best-selling novel of a dozen years earlier, learned that his agent had foolishly permitted him to sign away screen rights to any sequel (when the agent sold the original book to Hollywood) for a mere pittance. As the writer had become a much bigger "name" in the interim, and his market value was much greater than formerly, the careless act may have cost my friend $300,000 or $500,000 or more. At this writing he is seeking a legal way out of the impasse—including thoughts of suing his agent.

You may ask why writers, themselves, sign careless contracts. Pardon me while I laugh. No writer I know is capable of wading through those convoluted and unreadable legal paragraphs indigenous to contracts; they are not written in conventional English. Lawyers are specialists in making certain that laymen cannot follow their jargon; they are highly paid for their sly mendacities designed to confuse and screw the person doing business with the lawyer's client. Faced with some 300 pages of obtuse legal complications when I appeared to sign away the stage and screen rights to *Whorehouse*, I could only shrug and hope to hell my agent knew what he was doing. I couldn't have made sense of those contracts given a year to read them at a handsome salary.

I have come to believe that a writer may be better off when represented by a lawyer competent in contractual matters, entertainment law and copyright law than by an agent untrained in the legal niceties. Some agents retain lawyers to attend their more complex contracts—generally passing the cost on to the writing client—but I prefer to be represented by a lawyer I personally know; perhaps that is among the reasons I ultimately married a lawyer. For the *established* writer, then, I recommend lawyers over agents. The neophyte, however, is probably better off with an agent because of the agent's contacts in the literary marketplace and because the writer's early contracts will probably be fairly standard ones. Don't permit agents to sign you to long-term contracts: insist on a simple agreement you may break by giving thirty days' written notice. Once the writer has his own friends and contacts in the business, and a bit of a reputation, he might want to consider dumping the agent for a good lawyer. Cold-blooded? Listen, chum, we ain't talking pattycake games here. Careers, money and futures are at stake.

Washington
May 1981

Saw one of those advertisements the other day announcing that "a representative of a New York publishing firm" would soon be in the city and implying much eagerness to meet with writers in possession of unpublished manuscripts. The ad was, no doubt, the handiwork of one of those "vanity" houses offering to publish manuscripts for a fee or "subsidy." Take note, inexperienced wordsmiths: any legitimate publisher will *give* you advance money, not *take* it from you, to publish your work. Should a "publisher's representative," or anyone else, ask you to help with the cost of publication then you should rapidly seek the door.

Here a cautionary tale. Perhaps twenty-five years ago an old Texas friend mailed me the manuscript of a novel. Though I was not yet published, he knew of my interest in writing and asked me to help sell his work. One reading convinced me my friend's manuscript had little to recommend it and, by conventional judgments, was simply unpublishable; I tried to tell him so in a gentle way. This earned his enmity and a hot letter telling me I didn't know shit from shoe polish.

A few months later my friend called to announce, in great triumph, that a "New York publisher" had agreed to publish his book. When my friend named the publishing house, I recognized it as a notorious "vanity" operation; though I knew little of publishing, Bill Brammer had warned me against vanity houses. I tried to persuade Joe—we shall call him—he was about to be taken to the cleaners. Only made him madder, of course. He told me I was jealous because he was soon to be published and I was not.

Joe said he had been promised ads in major publications, reviews and placement of his book in bookstores. I tried to convince him that no legitimate publisher could promise any writer a single review, and that the promises about ads and bookstore placements were so vague as to be legally satisfied by only minimal actions. Joe did not want to hear it: he was on the verge of reaching the Promised Land.

My friend coughed up $3,000, as I recall. Sure enough, he got his "ad" in a major publication: the vanity house listed his book, along with a dozen others, in microscopic print in a big-city newspaper. One time. You might have seen it, had you a magnifying glass and known the day to look. As my friend had been a gung-ho Marine during World War II, and had written a novel of his combat experiences, the vanity publisher did obtain unreadable reviews in a few tiny military-post newspapers. The publisher placed a few dozen copies of his book in small bookstores and military libraries. The publisher also sent a press release to my friend's hometown weekly newspaper. That was all Joe received for his money—except for about 1,000 unsold books that long gathered dust in his garage.

One might have assumed Joe had learned a hard lesson. I did, until he called one night in high excitement to say he had just received a small "royalty check"—for less than $100—with a note from the publisher saying his book had "started to move." It was doing so well, Joe said, the publisher wanted to bring out a second printing! I couldn't believe my friend was about to swallow the same bait and hook twice.

"How much more money do they want?" I asked. Well, Joe said, because the publisher had wisely retained the original plates, he would be required to put up only $1,500 this time. *Jesus!* I said, "Joe, tell you what you do: wrap the remaindered copies of the first printing and mail them, C.O.D., to your publisher. Tell him you don't feel right about selfishly keeping them in your garage while there is such a public clamor for them, and he has your permission to sell them forthwith." Joe finally got the picture and held on to his $1,500. Think he was grateful? Hell no. When I began to publish he took it with ill grace.

I have read defenses by "vanity" publishers claiming they serve a vital, humanitarian function in publishing writers who otherwise would not attain print; if they want to spend their money that way—say the vanity folk—and derive satisfaction from it, why not? That won't wash. I think it criminal (though vanity presses are careful to stay within the letter of the law) that they exploit the hunger of would-be writers to see their stuff in print. Their victims are usually no-talent, unsophisticated people who probably can't afford their financial losses without sacrifice. Like all of us, however, these writing hopefuls have dreams; they may fancy themselves the next Hemingway or the next Whoever, and the vanity houses in "choosing" them affirm those gross miscalculations. The authors are cruelly crushed when they figure out the con game. Vanity presses apparently have little difficulty finding suckers, as many have been in business for years. They wouldn't stay in business unless they showed profits—a thing their writers almost never show.

Princeton
February 1974

I served on one of those writers' discussion panels at the University
of Pittsburgh recently. After the formal dog-and-pony show, during
the whiskey-drinking mixer that followed, an extremely angry young
man hemmed me in a corner to charge that no publisher in America,
and perhaps the world, is willing to give the unpublished writer a
chance. I attempted to dissuade him, remarking that all writers once
were unpublished, so his argument wouldn't hold water *per se*. He
waved his arms and yelled, "Bullshit! Bullshit! Bullshit! They don't
care! None of them cares!" He said he had mailed many wonderful
manuscripts to any number of publishers and the sorry pricks wouldn't
even give him a reading. Writer John Knowles told the kid that any
writer of talent who persists is almost certain to be one day "discovered" if good enough. I thought the kid might choke, and slipped
away under cover of his oratorical bombardment of Knowles, for fear
he might (1) give me several of his wonderful manuscripts and ask
me to prove my theory by getting them published or (2) whip
my ass.

Frankly, I would have much preferred the latter. These Princeton
students (not so much my own, but those wandering poets who trap
me in my office or in the Annex Bar across from the main campus
gate) have gratuitously wished on me so many reams of free verse
or dramatic offerings, with curt instructions to see to their immediate publication or production, that I think I shall weep at the sight
of one more Unrecognized Genius. Or his goddam illegible, wrinkled,
stained, wretched manuscript.

Boy artists are more persistent than girl artists—by a ratio of
about 30 to 1—though one young Princeton lady is driving me bat-
shit with her "stream of consciousness" offerings. I may be forced to
change drinking hangouts to avoid her; I haven't visited my office to
pick up mail or telephone messages for a month, save at three o'clock
in the morning, for fear she will jump from behind a bush with a
gunnysack full of new Joycean nonsense. In the Annex Bar a few
days ago she screamed and performed a stomp-dance when I recommended more form, substance and rewriting. She pithily gave me
to understand that any idiot knows rewriting will only destroy
"spontaneity." I am at that point where I pray the Little Miss will

drop out of school: but what if she then remained in town and became free to haunt and torment me full-time?

There *is* perhaps a little something to what the kid at Pitt charged, though I feared to admit it lest he become my friend for life and immediately transfer to Princeton. The known hack with a certain number of credits—present company excepted, of course—*does* have an easier time getting read, and certainly has better access to editors, than may the more talented unknown. That trend is likely to accelerate; as big-money conglomerates gobble up once-gentlemanly publishing houses, where some obligation to develop new generations of writers has long been a part of the collective sensibility, the bottom line may become immediate profit and immediate profit alone. Publishers are increasingly likely to go with the safe or the popular or pure "schlock" if they find it sells.

I have heard tales, though I don't know how many are apocryphal, of well-known writers mischievously mailing in their manuscripts under *noms de plume*—and having them summarily rejected until the writers' true identities were made known. I've also heard that old best-sellers have been turned down when freshly typed and submitted as new work by disenchanted unknowns bent on embarrassing their tormentors. A couple of editors I've asked mumbled yes, yes, such things occasionally happen; they blamed such goofs on inexperienced "first readers," or added that the random worthy book may somehow "drop between the cracks" when hundreds or thousands of manuscripts are considered by relatively small work forces, or that best-seller tastes change, and so on.

Certainly it helps the unknown to have a friend or two at court; witness my own early "rabbi" twosome, Warren Miller and Willie Morris. They got me shots I might otherwise never have had. I do not hold with the theory that all—or even nearly all—writers capable of good books break into print. Publishing people are fallible; the system is fallible; mistakes are made. Remembering the vital early help I received, I have tried to send what I judge to be deserving manuscripts by unpublished writers to New York for airings. To date, I count three manuscripts that turned into books—of, I'd guess, maybe a dozen to fifteen attempts. I try to send only good ones, but sometimes the pressures are great. If an old friend or some good friend's relative has composed a piece of shit and I can't dodge sending it along, I write a private side note to the editor explaining my circumstances. (The same as my friend Bill Brammer once did in my case; I understand better, now, why he felt compelled to do that.) I once had a romantic complication because I was cool to the notion of sending forth my ladylove's sprawling saga of whatever the hell it was. Later she became chummy in the sheets with a couple of other writers who dispatched her saga to many publishing houses; at last report, no sale was in sight.

I have many times refused to pass along hopeless manuscripts; at least one person became angry in each instance: no piece of work, no matter how wretchedly misshapen, is unloved by its creator. But if I routinely sent in obvious junk stuff, my editors or agents might soon decide that anything recommended by King was certain to be of dubious value. And that, in turn, might rob some deserving manuscript and its author of a rare shot—albeit a long one.

> Princeton
> November 1973

I am astounded at how little my writing students read outside their classroom requirements. Their explanation is that their academic loads are so heavy they have little time for "casual" or "recreational" reading. I find it curious that youngsters who profess to want to write professionally do not simply *make* time to read. They seem to find time for beer-drinking and courting and football. Nothing wrong with that—they *are* kids—but the urge to read apparently does not keep them awake nights.

They stutter or look at me as if I'm a Martian when I ask them, "What authors do you read and most admire or enjoy?" or "What writers do you feel may be influences on you?" They seem almost abysmally ignorant of everyone from Dickens to Tolstoy to Styron, though all are juniors or seniors and honors students to the last in number. Mailer? "Uh, yes, I read a book of his about, um, a riot at the Pentagon." Breslin? "Sometimes I read his newspaper columns." Didion? "Not too much, really." Halberstam? "Some of his stuff in, ah, *Harper's*." Larry McMurtry? "I like his movies." Barry Hannah? "Who?" Eudora Welty? "Ah, not lately." Faulkner? "We studied him in a course last year." What makes them think of a *writing* career if they read neither the Old Masters nor contemporary writers? They don't seem to have a decent curiosity, for the most part, about books or literary matters. And where is a writer without curiosity? How do they expect to develop any sense of literary history, movements, experiments, fashions or fads? A rudimentary knowledge of those subjects would seem a requirement of the soul for anyone intending to spend a *lifetime* writing.

I keep telling them, "The writer who won't take pains to rewrite will never improve," and "The writer who fails to read—widely, incessantly, compulsively—is a fool." They nod in agreement. But do they hear?

Princeton
January 1974

"Little men with tiny hammers." That's what some perceptive soul has labeled those literary nit-pickers to be found in academe's blighted groves: those precious bastards incapable of telling coherent stories of their own, and who therefore spend their lives and careers with their noses in the air while passing generally harsh judgments on "real" writers or claiming unusual insights into their private secretions. Perhaps Princeton hasn't a bigger glut of such lit-nits than is its fair share; it only *seems* that way because I'm trapped here among them.

Some few good, down-to-earth working writing men are here. On faculty, I know and like Geoffrey Wolff and Eric Goldman. John McPhee lives in Princeton, as does Fletcher Kneble and Jerry Goodman (who writes books about money under the name Adam Smith); Joe McGinnis is just down the road in a fine old farmhouse. Those guys know something of the everyday salts-and-sours of the real writing world; I'd go nuts without them.

Those precious frauds in the English department and a smattering in Humanities, on the other hand, talk a great game but probably couldn't write themselves into a job on the *Daily Princetonian*. First thing I had to do here was teach my writing students to compose the simple declarative sentence. They confessed, under hostile cross-examinations, that the more convoluted and obtuse their prose—the more footnotes and citations cluttering their pages—the better grades they generally were awarded. Little men with tiny hammers are capable of doing heap big mischief to their charges; you betchum, Red Ryder.

I get frothing mad at the academicians' notion that they make or break literary reputations. Oh, sure, they're an *influence*—more's the pity—but they seem to assume the field is their sole, private property. Not so. Reputations of writers are also shaped by working critics, scholars outside professional lit-nit-pick circles, discerning readers, librarians, good editors and other working writers. But we've still left someone out, gang. Care to guess? *Right:* the writers who actually *wrote* the good stuff! Am I to believe—as some academic fluffs would have me believe—that someone did more for the reputations of, say, Shakespeare and Shaw and Faulkner than they did for themselves through creating in their lonely solitude year after year?

Now, this is no personal sour-grapes complaint; I'm not saying *I* deserve to be ranked with the Hawthornes or Melvilles or Célines or that my writing contemporaries, in general, produce boatloads of prose capable of sitting comfortably on the shelf alongside the works of our honored Old Dead Greats. My beef is that "little men with tiny hammers," sweating and stewing in their stale warrens and dusty carrels, so easily hypnotize themselves—and attempt to persuade others—into believing that what they write or utter *about* the works of writers is more important than the literature itself. A preposterous proposition! If you've had the agony of witnessing a couple of those great pretenders quarrel over sherry that their point of view constitutes the only opinion that counts, you'll understand my ire. Such pygmies largely produce bullshit and busywork; I doubt they could write home to Mama so she'd understand it.

I ran into some of the same foolishness at Harvard. One precious fool tried to convince us that the books, lectures, tortured analytical babblings, rankings and groupings and reevaluations by academicians are all that keeps literary reputations afloat. Well, if that's the case, let them stop their bullshit and permit a few deserved sinkings. I am of the strong notion (and told that silly Harvard toot as much, under the goadings of grog) that more people have been run off from reading more good books and good writers by the boring weighty smothering horseshit blatherings of lit-nit-pick academic dandies than by all other sources.

I dunno, maybe the problem on our campuses is one of architecture: perhaps buildings there should be designed so as to provide more air on the brain.

Washington
August 1982

Published writers are frequently propositioned by well-intended folks wanting their life stories written, or the life of some Loved One set down for the ages. Any writer so honored seldom fails to roll his eyes and groan.

The problems, *never* recognized by the person wanting such a book written, are many and varied: (1) writers generally prefer to work from their own experiences or imaginations; (2) the writer would perform the lion's share, or all, of the work for—the inevitable offer—only "half the profits"; (3) the life story of the average person is so dull and mundane as to be beyond elevating repairs by anyone less talented than Mr. Bill Faulkner; (4) publishers rarely clamor for the biographies of unknown insurance agents, chimney sweeps or computer programmers. But you can't tell people that.

Approached by a stranger, the writer usually is able to sluff the opportunity through pleading the press of other work or contractual complexities; should the person be a friend, however, more imaginative excuses must be paraded. A friendly, persistent small-town police chief bugged me for years to write his memoirs. "Chief Jones" had never been employed in law enforcement outside the little Texas mudflat where he ultimately retired and, for the first fifteen years, had been a specialist in issuing parking tickets; few John Dillingers or Brink's robberies cluttered his background. The old chief many times forced stacks of thick scrapbooks on me and beamed while I glumly noted the headlines: NEW TRAFFIC LIGHT ANNOUNCED BY CHIEF JONES . . . CHIEF SPEAKS TO LIONS CLUB . . . CHIEF JONES ATTENDS OFFICERS' CONVENTION . . . POLICE CHIEF NAMES NEW NIGHT DISPATCHER. Well, what can a book cook make of such thin gruel?

I finally hit on the notion of telling the old chief I first had to write Lyndon Johnson's biography before I would be free to address his own. He so appreciated this pairing with another Great Man that I was left undisturbed while he spent his final years bragging to his companions; he died presumably happy and, for certain, unrecorded.

A year or more ago I heard from a gentle lady wishing me to write the story of her late husband. She enclosed a thick swatch of newspaper clippings. From these I learned that the Loved One had written a great deal of bad poetry faithfully published by his home-town newspaper, that he had been briefly a peace officer, had once soloed in a single-engine private aircraft, had been a civic-minded man who rarely missed a chance to serve on committees, had been a good family man forty-odd years bolted to marriage and had been of a religious bent with a prejudice in favor of Methodists. All well and good, as lives are lived, though I did not read these facts as likely to kick off a spirited auction among New York publishers.

Normally, I would have written the nice lady a sorry-too-busy letter, full of gentle regret for an opportunity missed. But she had gone on at such length about my being the only writer in the world capable of doing full justice to her husband's story—invoking her prayers in my behalf and God's bountiful blessings spilling on me henceforth as if from a bottomless fount—that I knew a routine turn-down would only reap future beseechings. Besides, I was feeling a little frisky and devilish that day.

I wrote the dear lady that—while the information must be held in the *strictest* confidence—I would be unable to take on the job because I was slowly dying of a malady presently beyond the cures of medical science; no way of knowing exactly how much time I had, but she would readily understand the impossibility and impractical-ity of my taking on new major or important work. *There now,* I thought, *let's see her argue with that!* I was about to mail the letter when I noticed a scrawled postscript on the back page of the lady's letter: if, for some compelling reason, I found myself unable to do the work, would I recommend some other writer capable of it? Never mind that for three pages I had been the only writer capable of the honor: the lady was covering her bets.

I added a paragraph noting that due to the lady's obvious religious turn, I could do no better than recommend my good friend the Rev. Dr. Edwin Shrake of Austin, Texas. (This was my way of having a bit of fun with Shrake, who had recently and for $50 become a gen-uine mail-order parson of the Universal Life Church and a "doctor" to boot. Not to brag of my own qualifications, but I, too, had become a minister in that church—Shrake having sent money in my name—although, since I was only a $25 parson, I was not entitled to be known as Dr. King; Shrake claimed this was because I had not done the required reading.) At any rate, I assured the good lady that Dr.

Shrake was a man of much piety and dependability, as good at the typewriter as when presiding over weddings or funerals in his spiritual role.

The good lady dutifully wrote to Dr. Shrake, calling him by high titles and soliciting his writing talents. He, too, found reasons he would be unable to write her book but, being a good fellow, he in turn recommended another writing friend—Dan Jenkins, perhaps, or Peter Gent, I dunno. Before long Texas writers had what amounted to a chain letter going, each new participant recommending yet another writer. My part in the mischief was soon over and I forgot about it.

Just a few days ago Roy Bode, an editor at the *Dallas Times-Herald*, telephoned to hem and haw before finally saying, "Uh, listen, is your health okay?" I said I guessed I was as well as could be expected of a relic. "Not anything bad wrong?" Bode persisted. Bleeding gums and occasional flatulence aside, I said, everything was hunky-dory. Why? "A funny thing happened," Bode said. "Our friend Mike Cochron telephoned, all upset, to say he heard that you're bad sick and dying." We laughed about silly rumors. The next day another friend called to say reports of my doom had reached his ears, from yet another source. A third call of the same type soon arrived.

Now I was angry. I demanded my friends go back to their sources and have their sources' sources contacted until we had discovered the dirty bastard spreading false, malicious rumors of the state of my health. Someone—I had become convinced—was attempting to influence editors not to sign me to new contracts or risk their advance monies because I was sure to die soon. I spent one whole evening making a checklist of people who might be cruel or chickenshit enough—or have grounds enough—to wish me evil and play me foul; depressingly, the list was quite lengthy.

Within a day or so, of course, it developed that the gentle lady whose book I had not written had "confided" to any number of people that poor Mr. King was on his last legs and fast bound for Jesus; the more confidentiality was stressed as the story passed, the more rapidly it traveled. I felt a bit foolish, yes, on learning I had been the original source of those "false, malicious" rumors. It was Twain—wasn't it?—who said, "The reports of my death are greatly exaggerated."

"But why did you lie to that woman?" my wife, Barbara, demanded once the mystery had been solved. Trying to salvage a bit of dignity, I said, "I didn't lie. I *am* afflicted with a slow-acting disease for which there is no known cure. It is called 'aging.' Never once in history has anyone recovered from it; it invariably ends in death."

Washington
October 1983

They say all writers steal from those who have gone before. Well, maybe in terms of style. But to steal another writer's exact words, or near-exact wording and structure, is plagiarism. Plagiarism is against the law. Plagiarism always makes me very angry when I am the victim. I have been the victim on more than one occasion.

About fifteen years ago a young lady in the Midwest began writing me fan letters; each was more effusive than the last. We struck up correspondence. Our letters waxed warmer and more intimate after she sent along a photograph proving her to be the kind of aspiring young talent I would like to know better. So, promoting a book in the young woman's home city, I telephoned to ask her for drinks. Sure enough, she was a knockout. Surely I would have been tempted toward adultery if properly begged. This was made unlikely, however, when the young woman brought along the young man she soon would marry. I found him sullen and unfit, but generously reasoned it was her life to waste.

My young fan told me she aspired to write above all other goals. She had written a number of feature articles published in Midwestern newspapers: would I please read them and—if impressed—pass them on to my *Harper's* editors or elsewhere? She thought she had the talent to go "big-time" but couldn't be certain until real professionals judged her work.

In due course the lady's articles arrived in the mail. I began screaming before progressing past her first lead: the damned little witch had stolen lines from everything she had read of mine! Sometimes whole paragraphs. Well, fuck her, let her go ahead and marry that dippy would-be dentist; they deserved each other and homegrown root canals.

I wrote the aspiring authoress a note significantly lacking in warmth, saying I feared that should I submit her articles to my editors their keen and discerning eyes would quickly recognize many passages as having earlier crossed their desks under my byline. Did she, perchance, have anything to show that *she* had written? That was the last time either of us wrote to the other.

A few years later I met a young Texas newspaper columnist who regaled me with tales of his high appreciation of my Art. Each time I saw him he virtually kissed my feet; naturally, I was impressed by his sagacity and maturity and predicted a great future for him.

One day the mails brought a book the kid had written; he had autographed a copy to me with gooey sentiments of how much he owed my good example. His sentiments were not misplaced, I learned on thumbing through his book: the kid valued my work so highly he had made much of it his own. I counted thirty-odd or more acts of theft—some verbatim, some wearing very thin disguises.

I wrote the young word thief that while Texas was a big place, it was not large enough for both of us to write about it in my language. What he was doing was against the law, I said, and I recommended that should he wish to escape accountings in court he should cease and desist. No response came back.

Three or four years passed. The word thief brought out a collection of his old magazine pieces. He, or his publisher, had the bad judgment to mail me a copy. I thought, *Naw, he wouldn't dare do it again!* Busy with my own work, I placed the word thief's new tome on the shelf, and there it reposed for months. One day I picked it up, started flipping through and—kiss my ass!—once again found my sentences leaping out at me. After counting twenty-odd acts of theft I had a lawyer write on impressive stationery to the culprit and his publisher, threatening the suing of multiple asses. The book publisher rapidly and almost hysterically offered profuse apologies; the word thief himself again chose not to communicate.

Some months ago, visiting Texas, I saw another of the word thief's books displayed under a regional imprint. I couldn't resist buying it for inspection, though I hated to give the copycat even a few coppers in royalties. Wading through about half the new book, I found its author had pilfered from me a mere two times. Since I didn't feel like slogging through the remaining pages, I concluded that perhaps the boy truly was trying to quit stealing and had shown such dramatic improvement in that direction it probably would be unworthy of me to raise a new stink. If I may say so, however, the word thief's books grow duller and duller as he steals from me less and less.

Another careless citizen, from Austin, about ten years ago ripped off one of my *Texas Monthly* articles and made a short movie of it. Bought no rights, received no permission. The movie had been entered in a couple of minor film festivals before I learned of the piracy and threatened legal action. The pirate's lady-friend, an acquaintance of mine, begged me not to sic lawyers on him, claiming he was "just a country kid" who hadn't known any better; I grew up in the country, too, but Mama taught me it was wrong to steal. Nonetheless, I agreed not to haul the young man to court provided he withdrew circulation of the movie. He pledged to do so forthwith. I later learned he had not, and had to pay a lawyer to enforce the agreement. I have since read in the *New York Times* that the simple barefoot country boy has accomplished a full-length movie branding him a film maker of great potential. I predict he has the stuff to become a Big Man among those goddam professional thieves in Hollywood. Probably he'll become the head of a major studio.

A friend sent the following quotes on plagiarists with a note hoping they might give me comfort. From Burton: "They lard their lean books with the fat of others' words." From Colton: "Most plagiarists, like the drone, have neither taste to select, industry to acquire, nor skill to improve—but impudently pilfer the honey ready prepared from the hive."

I ain't all that comforted. The next time somebody steals my stuff, no more Mr. Nice Guy.

Washington
February 1983

"*Where* do you write?" is a question that always surprises me; I can't see it would matter to anyone but the most picayune biographer. Yet, when I visit another writer's home I must confess an abiding curiosity to peek at where my host performs his professional mischief. And when writers visit me, most seem to harbor the same curiosity.

Some writers say they cannot work except in a favored spot during a set period of time each day. I have never been that constipated or, if you prefer, methodical. Assuming I had been, I could not have afforded to indulge such strict whims most of my writing life: I have always written where I had the opportunity and when sober enough. If words insist on coming I can write in cramped, crummy circumstances: should they be reluctant, no help is received from roomy or fancy digs.

I have worked out of scabby rooming houses, beach cottages both dilapidated and commodious, on a boat at anchor and afloat, in rustic cabins and peeling motels and posh hotels, in dusty attics and dark basements, aboard trains, airplanes and buses. I have typed on portable typewriters precariously balanced on my knees, on an old door elevated by bricks and books, on kitchen counters and rickety card tables and on a big, fine "lucky" desk—made available by friends Edward and Sarah Brooks—where other authors earlier had written a number of books, including the best-selling *The Bad Seed*. (And though I then joked about it with Ed and Sarah, who am I to say that desk did not truly possess lucky qualities? I wrote thereon the outline and opening chapter of my first published book.)

Three conditions must be met: I must be able to smoke, have access to habit-forming liquids and be free of random irritating interruptions: I quickly gave up a cozy carrel in the Library of Congress, after waiting for it almost a year, on learning I would be required to plunge down five floors each time a nicotine fit attacked. No deal for a chain-smoker.

I have never hired an office, preferring to work out of whatever house or apartment I occupy. Under certain conditions this is advantageous taxwise. But, more, I like being surrounded by my own books and artifacts. And I dislike traveling to and fro, the wear and tear and wasted time. At home I do not have to take a bath or get out of grungy pajamas to work.

The bane of the writer's life is the wayward interruption. I am not bothered so much by incidental noises: music, others talking in a hallway or adjoining room, passing aircraft or neighbors' lawnmowers. Direct interventions, however, drive me apeshit: telephone calls, people entering my space unbidden to ask questions or chat, the doorbell, screaming children. In short, anything requiring a response. I can work through a small airplane crashing in my yard provided I am not charged with looking for or aiding survivors.

I despise the telephone most, probably because it is the most persistent of offenders. When I lived alone, between marriages or temporary helpmates, the ringing phone bothered me not at all: I rather enjoyed having it shrilly demand attention and choosing not to answer it. The telephone, I am convinced, should be solely controlled by the person who pays for it; it should be an instrument of convenience rather than an instrument through which everyone from idle bores to salespersons to creditors may practice their harassments; if I could find a phone on which I could call out, but no human could call in, I would place my order for six of them before sundown.

For years I relied on an unlisted number; this permits minimal control over the number of maniacs able to telephone one's home, though unlisted secrets somehow are not long kept. Personally, I believe the phone company annually auctions off access to all unlisted numbers. I still maintain one unlisted private line, theoretically available only to intimates and relatives, though evidence indicates the phone company has arranged for all late-night drunks to use that line when practicing the dialing of wrong numbers.

My other line is carefully listed in my wife's name; unfortunately, too many have seen through the subterfuge. My dear wife, additionally, is requested by telephone more times daily, and nightly, than a popular call girl. She has a penchant for serving on committees whether scholastic, political or professional. I, who abhor committees, and would serve on one only if sentenced by a judge—and then sullenly—am forever being requested to provide the particulars of the upcoming School Apple-Bobbing, the seating arrangements at multiple political fund raisers or where the Bar Association's Subcommittee on Double Billing and General Public Flummoxing is next to meet for lunch; my dear wife manages to be in the shower or otherwise indisposed when exactly 94 percent of those committee inquiries come in. I have many times begged that such calls be made *not* to our home but to her law offices, where there are secretaries other than myself. Everybody just laughs.

Our two children, though but toddlers, are caught up in more social activities than the Duchess of Windsor. They are in school groups, play groups, ballet groups, swimming groups, tumbling groups, picnic groups, museum-touring groups, cookie-and-juice groups, finger-painting groups. Such astonishing telephone traffic results that any day now the Pentagon will call, begging us to release one of their communications satellites so they can contact the Russians. Always, when the phone rings, our kiddies' nannie, the cook and housekeeper—each of whom receive so many mysterious personal calls each day I suspect them of belonging to dozens of hyperactive communist cells—are preoccupied in distant crannies and must be fetched by foot. Guess who is the fetcher? Ideally, the writer should strive to grow up an orphan, never marry and live out his days in an all-services hotel with no telephone switchboard.

My scientific observations reveal that 91 percent of all telephone calls bring bad tidings, and that the other 9 percent are wrong numbers. Seriously: How many times have people telephoned to ask you over to make love, to say you have inherited serious money or to brag on you for some outstanding accomplishment? Never, right? Callers always want you to do something you would druther eat a bucket of hairy wigglies than do, berate you for a presumed year-old wrong, dun you with lawyers or announce your mama is dying with a lapsed burial policy clasped to her breast. Piss on Alexander Graham Bell and all his accursed descendants; they have caused more books to go wrong than all the creative writing courses in history.

Washington
October 1984

First David Halberstam. Then A. C. Greene. Now, it seems, all my old writing buddies have lost their hearts and minds to goddam word processors. Beware the writer freshly switched to such infernal machines: he will proselytize you more fanatically than the convert to new religions or fringe political movements.

A couple of summers ago I visted old friend Halberstam on Nantucket Island. He had a beautiful little daughter I had never seen, and a brand-new word processor just off the truck. I was there a week before he showed off the daughter.

Halberstam claimed his magic miracle machine permitted him to do 30 percent more work at the expenditure of only 70 percent of his natural energies. Or maybe it was vice versa. In either case, thanks to his handy-dandy gadget, he could accomplish his work in a scintilla of the time formerly required. I said, "Yes, but look at all the time you waste talking about it." I thought my old friend went a bit grim around the mouth. I said, "Did you have to build this room to accommodate your new giant booger, or did you just lose a bedroom?" Mr. Halberstam has not since insisted that I return to his place of abode.

Arriving home, I found a letter from A. C. Greene from Dallas. Fourteen pages, effusively extolling the virtues of word processors; until I reached the final line I thought perhaps he had quit writing professionally and had taken a job selling the damned machines, so fervent the pitch.

Screw word processors. They do not make satisfying *clackety-clack* noises indicating the writer's progress. You cannot pound them hard when you wish to emphasize the conviction with which you are composing a sentence as true as a mother's love. Watching words pop up on their little gray screens is like reading television. The soulless, antiseptic screen does not show those squiggles, scratch-outs and margin-jottings giving evidence of how diligently the writer has sought perfection or at what cost. Place two word processor "printouts" side by side and you would have difficulty distinguishing between the efforts of Kurt Vonnegut and your Aunt Minnie. What library or private collector will seek the spotless, perfect, juiceless "original manuscript" of one writer over another when none bears distinguishing scars or marks?

If you want to write at the beach, a word processor is the dickens to fold up to fit inside your suitcase; as Mickey Spillane has remarked, you cannot plug it into the sand. You need an airplane hangar or circus tent to house it. Word processors are equipped with excessive knobs, slides, lights, tubes, plastic inserts and other mystifying mechanisms; if I wanted to operate a big, soulless machine I would learn to fly goddam jet planes.

I never even gave in to the electric typewriter when it first came out. Electrics jump and skip when hit with passion. They make smug little purring sounds between pokes and jabs as if to indicate *they* set the pace, not the writer. *(Hmmmmmm. Come on, dummy, I'm waiting. Hmmmmmmmm. What's the matter, stuck again? Hmmmmmmmm.)* Should the writer, in typing, become righteously aroused against the name of some deficient person, place or thing—and smite the keys with vigor to so indicate—electric machines then jam, stutter and refuse to belch the appropriate dirt. I refuse to keep a machine that tampers with my moods or pace or attempts censorship.

I wake in a sweat, periodically, realizing anew that one of these days soon they will quit manufacturing the old trusty manual typewriter. Just flat stop producing them. The typewriters I have so long loved, revered and beaten to death—one every two years, on average—are doomed to fall victim to goddam High Technology. Now and again I rush off to one small, special old office-machine store and buy two to four more manual typewriters against that inevitability. Though I have a stack of such old faithfuls in the basement, the supply may not suffice should I live to ripe years. Any day, I know, that quaint, tiny little office-machine store will go bankrupt or be gobbled up by the evil Word Processor Cartel. Only a handful of us will mourn, or care.

Mark Twain, in 1875, produced in *The Adventures of Tom Sawyer* the first book manuscript typed on a manual typewriter. If I have anything to say about it, I will type the last one.

Princeton
December 1973

Today I received the galley proofs of my upcoming book, *The Old Man and Lesser Mortals*. I am always amazed how much better my prose looks—and seems to read—when in *true* print rather than when in mere typescript. Just as galleys look and read better than original manuscripts with their squiggles, cross-outs and inserts, so, too, do books themselves appear superior to galley proofs. This progression is one of the secret rewards of being a writer, offering private satisfactions and permitting the shaky writer to assure himself anew, "Hey, by damn, I am a writer! This is a real book!"

One may flip through the new tome remembering, with a mixture of sweat and relief, when a particular passage or page or story seemed impossible to accomplish—yet, suddenly, months or years later here it is in one's hand, bright and shining evidence of the writer's having once more typed through his troubles and told his tale. That is what we live for.

Getting one's galley proofs or the first copy of one's new book—before it has been sliced by critics or rejected at the sales counter—is probably the emotional high point of the entire writing process. For a little while, all good things seem possible.

Washington
August 1969

Last year Bud Shrake's novel *Blessed McGill* was published; shortly
afterward, one wet New York afternoon as we solved world problems in P. J. Clarke's saloon, I asked Bud how it was doing. He
produced two tiny clippings—a couple or three paragraphs each—
from small newspapers in, I believe, Ohio and West Virginia. One
raved that *Blessed McGill* deserved to be rated with the all-time
great novels; the other was as disparaging an evaluation as one might
expect to be written by one's meanest and maddest ex-wife. Not
much good happened to *Blessed McGill*; it lost its way among critics
and the public, as most books do. Reviewers who commented generally dismissed it as a tall tale of a buffalo hunter in early Texas; it
was that, yes, but mainly it was an allegory about religious super-
stitions, dogma and rigmarole—and a wildly comic one. I did not
read *one* critic who seemed to tumble to that fact. Recently I wrote
Shrake how astonished I was that they unanimously missed his point.
He responded:

> In my infrequent periods of dejection and despair, about five or
> six per day when I am trying hard, I will read your letter again
> and again and say aloud, "Old Doctor King sure knows what he is
> talking about!" Then I'll swaller a pill and get to typing. It did, in
> fact, amaze me how what I thought that book was really about
> was not what others thought. The movie guy who called me about
> the screenplay last month said, "Of course, we had to take out all
> that religious shit."* Well, what do you say to that? And one re-
> spected friend said he was surprised the book had not a trace of
> humor in it, when I thought much of it humorous and all of it
> ironic.
>
> This fantastic unrelenting nonflagging RIGHTNESS that a
> writer has got to keep up does get me down. It is especially
> outlandish for a drinker-semidoper to maintain, when it is to
> him plain as the nose of an armadillo, that WRITING is the
> FREAKIEST most utterly egotistical endeavor a man can
> undertake. Who could be so sublimely arrogant as to think
> that *anybody* ever would care to use the time and effort neces-
> sary to read an ENTIRE BOOK that this arrogant person wrote,
> to have eyeballs drift across maybe 100,000 words hoping to

---

*There was never a movie of *Blessed McGill*, for all the Hollywood prattle.

transmit ideas? It is probably too much to ask a reader to do all that and then, on top of it, come away with the same notions of what the writer was trying to do that the writer had. Why don't we quit and go in the oil biness? Then everybody could tell what we are trying to do.

Washington
May 1981

I love bookstores. Prowling them. Sampling paragraphs hither and yon. Caressing the books. Enjoying the rainbow of colors flashing from their dust jackets. Making selections for purchase. These simple pleasures can keep me happy for hours on end; in such fine moments I am a miser alone with all the world's gold. Perhaps I have missed almost as many airplane flights or appointments by dallying in bookstores as I have by dallying in bars.

Periodically, however, there comes a time when bookstores can become as depressing as prison dungeons. This time always coincides with the publication of my own books. Then, the larger the bookstore the more acute the pain. One's mind boggles at the sight of such damnable competition: row-on-row, floor-to-ceiling, back-to-front, side-to-side one is assaulted by the hateful view of books competing for the public's fancy, and dollars, with one's own.

Forty thousand titles each year, the gloomy thought flashes. *What chance has my poor little book to live three months? Not only is it in competition with the outpourings of my contemporaries, goddam their souls to the last in number, but it is unfairly matched against the best of all the Old Dead Greats.*

I morosely prowl the aisles—brushing by lavish life-sized cardboard cutouts magnificently calling attention to a hot best-seller—seeking small evidence that my book has, indeed, been published as my editors claim. *Ah, there it is!* Yes. Ain't it, though? Two copies. Two whole copies. At the rear of the store. In a neglected, dusty corner where all lightbulbs are on the fritz. On a bottom shelf in the natural sight line only of nursery school toddlers or midgets. Alone and weeping.

Stealthily, working as carefully as a spy, I stoop to sneak my two orphans from their dark place of concealment. Turn my dust-jacket photo inward, against my outraged body, so no clerk or customer

may match it with my guilty face. Oh-so-casually, innocently whistling, I tippy-toe through the marketplace seeking a more advantageous exhibition of my wares. "New Releases" is not a bad slot, though
if I have the luck to encounter a busy or unwary clerk I may actually
attain the "Current Best-Sellers" table.

Careful, now. Glance all around, eyes darting furtively. Quickly,
I place my pitiful two little books on the desired table, where they
are immediately stunted and surrounded by laughing tall piles of
Mailer and Michener and Andy Rooney and cat books and thirty-six
different diet offerings and twenty-nine titles promising fast riches
in real estate.

Dart away quickly, heart pounding, sweating. Waiting for a heartless clerk to rasp in the voice of the angry Old Testament God, *Hey,
you! What the hell . . . ?*

Out the door at last. On with my appointed rounds.

God, I hate bookstores!

Washington, D.C.
November 1979

Maybe I'm a jinx to magazines. I wrote a half-dozen pieces for *Saturday Evening Post* and then that venerable old institution turned
up its toes and died a decade ago. I was on assignment for the old
Life, seemingly hale and hearty for more than thirty years, when an
editor there tracked me to an Austin beer joint to say his magazine
would fold within two hours and he wanted to tell me the sad news
before television did. I took money to become a contributing editor
for *Audience*, but that show-biz-oriented publication folded even before I could finish an article for it. *Capitol Hill*, of which I was
founding editor, expired of poverty quickly and only one issue after
I quit. *New Times*, from which a chickenshit editor fired me—although I had written more articles for it than any other writer, and
had drawn the most fan mail—staggered on without me awhile but
died within a year or two. *Harper's* has never been the same since
the Willie Morris crew resigned in 1971, though it has several times
changed owners, directions and editors. General-interest magazines
apparently cannot compete with narrow specialized mags, and certainly not with television, for the advertising dollar or the eye seeking entertainment. I feel rather like my late father, who once said,

"The only job I ever had that could hold a candle to farming was blacksmithing. Then the car come along and I was blowed up."

New York
September 1975

American novelists traditionally have hated their Hollywood adventures, excepting only the big money they have earned there. Most of their writings on Hollywood are bitter rather than funny. The funniest, most matter-of-fact comment perhaps was made by Nelson Algren. Algren went to Hollywood (accompanied by appropriate drumrolls and tub-thumps in the press) to help craft the screenplay for his best-selling novel *The Man with the Golden Arm*. Said Algren, "I went out there for a thousand bucks a week, and I worked Monday, and I got fired Wednesday. The guy that hired [and fired] me was out of town Tuesday."

Washington
June 1983

I think I just missed being "Hollywooded" again. By my definition that means "to have been conned out of something for little or no return."

It began with a telephone call from a former newspaperman lately describing himself as an Independent Film Producer. In my youth I would have been terrifically excited over the prospect of speaking to someone with so exalted a title; that was before I learned one may simply declare oneself an Independent Film Producer the same as one might designate oneself a Tent Preacher or a Fortune Teller. No license or proof of prior performance is required. Impressive letterhead stationery and calling cards are optional, though a telephone other than the one in your boardinghouse hall is recommended.

I had once slightly known the self-proclaimed IFP in his newspapering days; our only contacts came from having drinks together in the same bars perhaps a half-dozen times, by happenstance rather than by appointment; we had idly chatted of nothing until more interesting companions came to claim one or the other of us.

When the IFP called me from Hollywood, however, he waxed so

eloquently of Old Times Shared you might have thought us former roommates; he invoked the names of many mutual friends quick or dead. My antennae went *zoom!* and my bullshit detector wildly rotated in four directions, giving off loud beeps. When the IFP rhapsodized on my writing talents over the next five minutes, I knew to hunker in the bunker and go on Condition Red Alert.

"My partner and I have this idea for a great, great movie," the IFP modestly announced. "We totally agree you're the only writer we trust to do the screenplay. You interested?"

Leave us talk about money, I said, then I'll indicate my degree of interest.

"Money, sure," the IFP said. "No problem. Actually, money talk is probably a little premature. We just wanted to kick our idea around with you and check your availability."

I said I would be available if and when proper doses of money became available. And speaking of money: did he have a deal with a major studio, or had he otherwise arranged the picture's financing?

"Money for development we got," he said, airily. "And I guarantee, Old Pal, interest is *extremely* high at every major studio we've contacted." Translation: *We ain't been able to get a foot in the door in two years of trying to peddle this old dog.* I felt my interest rapidly waning; it soon was on a par with Dick Nixon's expressed concern with respect to the condition of the Italian lira.

"What we got," the IFP went on, "is this great plot. X is trying to con Y, see, but in the end *Y* does a clever switch and cons *X*. Got it?" He laughed wildly. I sayeth not. "Maybe," he said, "you could, you know, think about it and write me a few pages—just a letter, nothing formal—of how you might approach that story."

I said that except for occasionally writing to Mama-'n-'em I didn't even write letters free. What he was asking for—I pointed out—was a screen treatment. Any screen treatment from me would cost thousands of dollars and must be part of a step-deal. (A "step-deal," in Hollywood lingo, works like this: the writer is paid to prepare a screen treatment; this is a synopsis of the story line and the structure of the proposed screenplay, including descriptions and interactions of the characters. Then he is paid for a first-draft screenplay, maybe a second draft, then a "shooting" script and perhaps a final polishing. Any number of steps may be agreed upon; the writer is paid for each step as he takes it. The producer may stop the project at any step in the proceedings; when he stops paying the writer stops writing.)

My good buddy the IFP was positively shocked. *Screen treatment?* Oh, mercy no! He had merely meant, you know, a few lines toying with the plot and making certain we were on the same wavelength in our approach to his wonderful story.

I said all he had offered was X and Y plus a mysterious, undefined clever switch. Did he expect me to develop the entire story line as well as all characters, the structure and work out the suitable intricacies of the clever switch?

"Oh, no! We have most of that!"

Fine, said I. Tell you what: mail me what you have. Then I'll know what you need. We then can talk appropriate sums for a step-deal.

The IFP credited me with a wonderful approach; he would immediately mail the details of his marvelous movie. In due course the mail brought this note: "A sports film. Football. X tries to con Y, but in the end *Y* does a clever switch and cons *X*."

I did not feel overly enlightened. The sumbitch *had* no story beyond that terse formula, I was certain, and hoped to con me into fleshing it out. Free. A few days passed. The IFP again telephoned: what did I think of his story line?

I said it was thinner than one-sided pancakes.

The IFP said, oh, sure, what he had *sent* was a little thin. But, after all, he couldn't reveal details until I agreed to write the screenplay. He had to protect his story, see. Two or three unscrupulous sources already had tried to steal his hot idea.

I asked whether he thought I was a damned thief.

Mercy, no! Why, he and his partner fully agreed that Larry L. King was the most honest, most moral writer in all of America! Perhaps in the whole world! But they had to, you know, approach this in a businesslike manner even when dealing with a saint.

I said so did I. I said a screen treatment would cost him $40,000 with the money up front. If he liked my screen treatment, then he could work out a step-deal with my agent. Who, I said, was my lawyer-wife and who, professionally, was meaner than a grave robber's watchdog.

He said, "Hey, baby, we're back to *that* again? Look, I'm just talking about a little proof we're thinking on the same track! All I need is just, you know, a couple pages—a long personal *note*—kinda outlining how you see the story."

I said I would put not one jot on paper until paid. The IFP, sounding less friendly, said he'd get back to me. In time he did. It became immediately apparent he was launching a counteroffensive; where once he had praised me as a major talent flirting with genius, he now implied serious deficiencies.

"You only wrote one screenplay, right? That little whorehouse thing?"

Right.

"That movie didn't do very well, did it, at the box office?"

I said it was hard to tell, since Universal Pictures kept the books and made the interpretations. They showed it had grossed a ton, but claimed losses and expenses almost equal to the cost of World War II. All armies, not just ours.

"The word out here," the IFP said darkly, "is that it was a box-office bomb."

I said I certainly hoped so for two reasons: (1) I would feel a rare surge of confidence in Universal's bookkeeping, and (2) the film had deserved to bomb as a worthless piece of shit. Thanks to the director, with much assistance from the male lead and others too numerous to mention.

"Well, see," the IFP said, "you gotta face it: you don't have much of a track record. My partner's worried about that. *I'm* not worried, you unnerstand. *I* know what you're capable of—but my partner, see, he needs a little evidence you're the right man to do our script."

I said, since the IFP thought so highly of my work, why didn't he just reassure his partner?

He said, "It's not that simple, see. Now if you could just send a little *proof* to persuade him. Like a letter giving, you know, your idea of how to approach our story—"

" 'Bye," I said, and hung up while the IFP was still pitching me. Rude? Maybe so. But I've *been* Hollywooded once or twice, baby, and from here on I'd druther have some watermelon.

Washington
September 1984

A lot of schlocky film felonies and routine cinematic mutants aside, I admit to sometimes being entertained, or even temporarily enthralled, by a fair number of movies. And yet I rarely see one that fails to make me squirm because of its unrealized potential, that gap between what it is and what it might have been. Perhaps the true miracle is that any movie is found meritorious, so many are the divergent hands and factors in its creation. Movies attempt Art-by-Committee, and the odds are against *that* going in.

Of course, I look at movies wrong. I look at them as a writer when, in fact, writing may have comparatively little to do with how a movie turns out. Direction, acting, casting, cutting, photography, pacing, lighting, mood, sound, special effects, technical competence or the lack of it—all may be more important than the writing. Certainly Hollywood thinks so. One of the oldest inside jokes out there is of the starlet so dumb she slept with the screenwriter in hopes of advancing her career. That joke not only defines Hollywood's social pecking order, it says more than I'd like to admit of the writer's influences and shaping of movies.

Such little as I know of screenwriting technique I have been told by successful screenwriters. William Goldman: "Start each scene as late into it as you can." Edwin (Bud) Shrake: "Forget long speeches. It's important to know what to leave out." Dan Jenkins: "Actors like to stare a lot, and most directors don't want twenty words if two will do." William D. Wittliff: "Pare each scene to the bone. Then do it again." So movie-writing is a specialized kind of writing, a sort of shorthand, almost a sign language. It rarely requires, or even tolerates, beautiful prose. Forget your poetic, convoluted meanderings: movies are *blip blip blip*. The writer's main contribution may be made through structuring a movie, and helping to pace it—provided the stars and director will permit—rather than by stunning prose.

My own screenwriting has been limited to the *Whorehouse* abomination, which movie I sincerely believe deserves to rate among the All-Time Turkeys. Hollywood took it away from me and Pete Masterson and applied its own writing genius, much to the detriment—I immodestly insist—of the finished product. It was the worst experience I've had as a writer. Yet, a secret part of me wants to try my hand again—even as wise little voices hysterically shrill, *No, no, you silly ass! It ain't your game!* I have this *feeling* in my gizzard, dammit, that if Hollywood would just trust me we'd all be covered in laurels and greenbacks each time out. That is an egotism never to be tested, because where writers are concerned it never has happened that way in Hollywood history and never will. Still, I occasionally dream. . . .

Perhaps eighteen months ago Dan Jenkins advised me to hire a certain hotshot Hollywood agent. Jenkins said the dude could get me $200,000 a year, in my spare time, "just for doctoring screenplays somebody else has fucked up, or for pounding out screen treatments." Though Jenkins warned that not much of one's labors could be expected to make it to the screen (Hollywood commissioning at least a gallon of work for every thimbleful it actually uses), money talks so loudly I immediately wrote the hotshot agent of my availability. And who knows when lightning might strike? I wouldn't mind the occasional Oscar.

The agent soon telephoned (they never write to you from out there, even when they fire you or mail you money) to express what sounded like genuine enthusiasm; he would begin passing around word of my availability; I should stand by for action. Three months passed without a word. I mailed the hotshot agent a postcard saying only, "Testing, testing, testing." He telephoned to say, "Funny card. Listen, babe, they don't know you out here. They don't read. You should come out here." I said, hell, was I supposed to go out there and read my stuff aloud to them? He said, no, just come out and hang around and socialize with the guys and take a few meetings. I said I didn't think I would thrive on that.

After six months I wrote the silent agent to say he already was $100,000 behind in providing the cash Dan Jenkins had assured me I could earn in my spare time, and here I had went and turned down an Avon franchise. He called to say, "Funny letter. Look, you need to come out here and go to parties. Hang out and let the movie people see you don't have horns. The word out here is that you've put the bad mouth on Burt Reynolds and Universal, so everybody's scared of you. They don't like troublemakers. Come out and shake hands and slap backs and charm everybody." Not having much in common with Dale Carnegie, I did not make the trip. The hotshot agent has never called again.

The more I talk to screenwriters, or read of their more grotesque real-life Hollywood nightmares, the more I sense I am not geared to Tinsel Town or it to me. And the more I learn, the more I realize why it is so difficult for a movie—almost any movie—to turn out as the writer—almost any writer—would like.

Take the very large matter of the "right of script approval." That was virtually unheard-of in the old days when powerful studio big-gies, the Harry Cohns and Jack Warners and Darryl Zanucks, pretty much dictated who would play what role and how. Now "script approval" is almost routinely granted to the bigger box-office stars. Money being the bottom line in Hollywood, any actor or actress who has proved able to lure it in bundles has powers never dreamed of by Hitler. They may name their own directors, fellow players, writers, cameramen, film editors—their every wish or whim. Never mind that their films sometimes might gag a maggot, that their talent may be limited to photogenic qualities or macho swaggers or pretty dimples, or that they may not have sense enough to snap a Kodak. What they want, they get.

Such pampered ladies and gentlemen usually have made it big by playing a given type of movie role; they have long cultivated a tested image. They live in fear that to step outside the narrow confines of their popular standards might suddenly cause their names to disappear from theater marquees and send them back to the farm or the factory. And, really, who can blame them? Actors who have proved they are no box-office world-beaters unless wrecking cars or wrestling alligators would be plumb dumb to try Hamlet. Such stars naturally and immediately go into dancing conniptions of *Sturm und Drang* on sighting any script outside the old, proven stuff that has long worked for them. This factor is the bane of screenwriters.

Say, for example, the screenwriter concocts a scene in which the male lead—being played by the handsome, dimpled big-time box-office star Harry Chesty, in an expensive hairpiece and elevated shoes—is required to fart and belch. Immediately, if not sooner, the poor writer will be excoriated by armies of angry agents, managers, public relations flacks and producers: "You *crazy*? Harry Chesty don't *do* farting and belching! Harry Chesty's fans don't *want* him farting and belching! Harry Chesty's adoring public won't *permit* farting and belching! Harry Chesty don't even know *how* to fart and belch!"

Neither, perhaps, will the persnickety Mr. Chesty or his minions permit a scene in which he is to be seen eating, or permit an actor or actress whom God has made taller to come within a hundred meters of him on the screen for fear of direct comparisons. Neither shall Harry Chesty cry, or be defeated in a fistfight or gun battle, or scorned by a woman or made the object of laughter under any circumstance. There can seem no end to the official no-nos when the poor screenwriter begins matching them against what he feels his story requires.

Come, now, and take an Artistic Meeting in which Harry's worried retainers (by now highly suspicious that the screenwriter's sole purpose is to smash Mr. Chesty's career and send him back to parking cars in Cleveland) sit down to turn the script into a typical "Harry Chesty vehicle." Before they are through, any resemblance between the script they demand and the one already written or being written is purely coincidental. It goes like this:

ZOLLIE: Lookie here, Harry! That fool writer has wrote it down that your character writes goddam *poetry*! Ain't that too sissy-britches?

HARRY CHESTY: Yeth! Whoth got my pocket mirror? Ith it in my purth?

BORIS: Wait, let's think about it. Maybe writing poetry would make Harry look, um, real sensitive.

BIG BERNARD: No, too faggoty! Why don't we just have him go bowling?

(It is decided that Harry Chesty's sensitivity will be displayed, not through composing poetry, but by rolling a perfect-300 game. This will make a beautiful, secretly rich girl—who sets up bowling pins as a hobby—fall slobberingly in love with him.)

MORRIE: Now we got a good romantic angle!

BIG BERNARD: Hold it, schmucks! Harry is *married* in this script. It might hurt Harry Chesty's public image to show him sport-fucking.

HARRY CHESTY: I refuthe to *be* married! Ith bad for my macho rep.

BIG BERNARD: Now, Harry boy, not to worry! We'll kill off the wifey bitch in an early scene so you can romance the rich bitch working at the bowling alley.

(It is decided that wifey-poo shall be dispatched heavenwardly via car crash or airplane accident or runaway horses or maybe by a stray bowling ball—as long as it isn't Harry Chesty who throws it.)

HARRY CHESTY (pouting prettily): Don't expect me to cry at her funeral! I don't *do* crying.

BIG BERNARD (whistling shrilly): Awright, everbuddy, listen up! We kill off the rich bitch after some good steamy sex scenes, see? What's another dead broad when Harry Chesty's image is at stake, right? Harry's on the verge of marrying the bowling-alley twat but then, um, uh, as she's showing off her sparkly diamond engagement ring to a gal friend—no, wait, *Harry* ain't rich, *she* is. So, um, uh. Okay, I got it! Beautiful! A switcheroo! We'll make that a *cheapo* ring Harry gets out of a box of Cracker Jacks at Coney Island, see, and they laugh about it and he puts the ring on her fanger. Just kidding around, and suddenly they give each other warm-pussycat looks, see, and it's violin music time! Moonlight and roses! A cottage with vines and shit!

BORIS: Beautiful! Just . . . beautiful!

BIG BERNARD: Shut the fuck up when I'm talking Story, Boris. So then, see—huh? So, Morrie, who *gives* a shit Coney Island's been closed fifteen years? They don't know that out in the sticks! The next asshole to interrupt me when I'm talking Story can pack for Joisey City! As I was saying: sixteen, seventeen, nineteen street toughs—whatever—come along and rip the ring off the gal's fanger. And rip the *fanger* off too, come to think of it. I mean Bloodsville! Rivers of blood!

HARRY CHESTY: Thweet. I like it.

BIG BERNARD: Then they kill the broad, see? Kill the shit out of her and rape her a little bit. Four, five, six times. Whatever. They're pissed because the ring ain't real diamonds they can hock but is just Cracker Jack shit, ya know? So *now*, see, we got a humdinger story where Harry Chesty can stalk the bad guys down one at a time—through storms and earthquakes and floods and pontoons—

BORIS: Ah, Big Guy, I think you mean *monsoons*.

BIG BERNARD: You're fired, Boris. You're on retainer six months with a limo and two secretaries, which we'll write off to the pitchur, but I don't wanna see your face. Anyhow, Harry schleps through it all, taking his sweet revenge on the badasses. Look at the *variety*! Harry can choke 'em barehanded, drown 'em, slice their asses, beat 'em to jelly. Whatever. See, we're dealing here with um, uh, your *extreme ethnic minority* street thugs. So Harry can kill 'em bloody as he wants, right?

HARRY CHESTY (cooing and blowing kisses): Oh, I juth *adore* it! It maketh me a real stud-horth!

BIG BERNARD: Sure, kiddo! *Action* shit! What's that, Boris? Boris, goddammit, *so what* it maybe sounds a little like Charley Bronson in seven, eight, nine pitchurs? Them pitchurs all grossed a goddam ton, din't they? Say, Boris, din't I just fire you?

BORIS: I thought you meant Morrie. *He* interrupted too.

BIG BERNARD: Oh. Well, then, he's fired too. Lotsa luck to you both, babe.

The poor screenwriter is presented with Harry Chesty's new script requirements. All he must do is fit them to the original story about a sensitive Ivy League Humanities professor who drinks a bit much because of dissatisfaction with the minor poetry he composes in great agony and who, when denied tenure by jealous academic dandies wrongly suspecting him of true—and, therefore, dangerous—talent, farts and belches by way of making a philosophical social commentary.

Somehow the writer magically makes semi-sense of the hybrid confusions, despite his poet's not being allowed to write, read, teach or mention poetry—and frequently having to swish off campus to kill yet another in a long line of extreme ethnic minority street thugs.

Enter, then, one Miss Lovely Longlegs. Miss Longlegs has signed to play opposite Harry Chesty. She, too, has written into her contract the precious "right of script approval." One look at the screenplay now tailored to fit Harry Chesty's demands and she shrieks, faints, cusses, shits and falls in it, cries for three days, flings ashtrays and Diet Pepsi bottles and fires six agents and two road managers—but still shows up with seventeen retainers, including nine Philadelphia lawyers, to announce as follows to producer, director and writer:

(1) She ain't studying playing no low-class dip-shit bitch working in a goddam bowling alley and going gaga-eyed over a cheap-ass Cracker Jacks ring. (2) She most definitely will *not* be raped, mutilated or murdered; she is a Star and Stars Never Die except in corny old World War II movies or in low-budget stinkers hoping to win some dime-store film festival in Poland or some other godforsaken place where they're too dumb to speak English. (3) The picture must be a musical. (4) It must begin in a nunnery in Switzerland or some such snow-and-ice place so she can skate and ski. (5) Somewhere in the screenplay must be a murder she can solve single-handedly. (6) Though she must begin as a nun in love with a priest she selflessly gives up for Jesus, it is understood she also will reign as founder of the only All-Girl Detective Agency in the universe. With offices in Chigaco, Paris, Rome, New York, Madrid and Dothan, Alabama. (Dothan is Miss Longlegs' old hometown, see, and they have promised a plaque and a banquet and a parade the first time she brings a movie production home.) (7) She requires eight solo numbers as to songs, seven as to dances. One of these must be on horseback.

(8) That revolting faggot Harry Chesty is to be the person whose murder she solves in the flick. (9) Other than for these minor changes, everything is hunky-dory and she sure does look forward to working with y'all.

Whereupon Miss Longlegs flashes a brilliant, forty-nine-tooth smile and makes her patented butt-jiggling exit.

These minor changes give the screenwriter pause, and both the need and the excuse to lie drunk for five weeks. When he returns to his word box, pale and trembling, he gets a call from the producer. "What," the producer asks, "have you got in there for Billy Bimbo?" Billy Bimbo is a no-talent slob who makes Harry Chesty laugh by wiggling his ears, wearing lampshades for hats and saying "ca-ca" frequently; he has been rewarded with a fat role in every Harry Chesty picture for the past twenty-seven years. If a role does not exist for Billy Bimbo it must be written in (to include his imitation of Milton Berle) no matter how badly this futzes up plot or structure. And oh, by the way, the producer adds, Miss Longlegs has a pair of sisters who need good roles written for them. It would perhaps be best to always include both of them in the same scene, seeing as they are Siamese twins. . . .

Maybe, on reflection, I'd better forget my Hollywood fantasies and stay home to write my modest little books.

> Washington
> October 1984

I am in possession of the most recent "accounting of finances" with respect to the production of that dreadful *Whorehouse* movie. The best I can translate Universal Pictures' bookkeeping hieroglyphics, the flick has grossed damn near $60 million from all sources but remains more than $15 million in the red. Though this seems passing strange to one who recalls when Universal spokesmen swore the picture would cost "only" $20 million, I am sure the figures would come as no surprise to old Hollywood hands. The biggest laugh Johnny Carson got from Tinsel Town insiders, while emceeing the Oscar telecast a couple of years ago, came when he said the producers of *Gone With the Wind* had announced it had just gone into profits; *GWTW* is, of course, one of the biggest hits of all time and has been wowing box offices for more than forty years.

See, if a picture goes into profits too quickly it can put producers into a snit and become a very expensive proposition, for then they must pay taxes on profits and otherwise share the wealth. They might be required, for example, to fork over a little money to the simple folk who conceived the story to begin with and who, perhaps, wrote the screenplay. Nothing so disgusts producers as that awful democratic prospect.

Stars and directors—though only a handful of writers—are assured of big money going in if powerful enough. Stars get handsome salaries, plus possibly a percentage of the gross off the top. Writers get up-front money that may sound large to them and to itinerant fruit pickers, but is really just a trickle from the big Hollywood hydrant. Writers get promised a share of "producer's profits." They learn after one picture that it is not advisable to hold their breath until the producer declares a profit. I once fleetingly glimpsed that rare bird the whooping crane, but have yet to set eyes on a producer-into-profits. Any accountant careless enough to permit a producer to cross over into profits shall not in the future find much use for his pencil.

There are many exotic ways for producers to avoid what they call the "profit posture." First pay a Big Star like Mr. Burt Reynolds $3.5 million up front for his alleged acting services, then wish on him an undisclosed percentage of the gross as additional compensation. Then give a second Big Star, in this case Miss Dolly Parton, $1.5 million plus a second undisclosed percentage of the gross. Right away the producer is down $5 million, plus the Lord and the bookkeepers only know how much more in mysterious gross figures. Presumably, these deficit arrangements delight producers. Otherwise, why would they keep making such deals again and again?

I do not know the arrangement managed by one Mr. Colin Higgins, director of *Whorehouse*, because Universal treats it as a secret of a magnitude equaling the Manhattan Project. If Mr. Higgins was able to swing the kind of sweet deal some directors are granted, he may have received a percentage of the *cost* of the movie in his pay envelope. This means, class, that Mr. Higgins would be a fool, indeed, to bring the picture in at a mere $16 million, say, should he find ways to spend $32 million. Yes, I know that seems a cockeyed, bassackwards arrangement to normal folks. Hollywood, apparently, thrives on cockeyed bassackwardness.

As my rheumy old eyes consider the latest swimming figures provided by Universal's money men, I see that Mr. Reynolds' production company to date has reaped $2,684,781.53; this is, presumably, in addition to his up-front payments for alleged acting. Likewise, Miss Parton's production company has been paid for billings totaling $784,783.36. Director Higgins' production company has taken out a mere $330,317.92, causing me to often fret that such a niggardly sum may not see him through the winter.

Director Higgins also receives 50 percent of the screenwriting money due the writers when *Whorehouse* is embarrassingly revealed on television, though this is exactly 50 percent less than the greedy Mr. Higgins grabbed for. One day I was sitting around the office picking me toes, see, when here comes a telegram from Universal dignitaries announcing that Peter Masterson and yours truly (coauthors of three screenplay drafts) would *not* find our names on the picture: Mr. Colin Higgins would receive sole credit as screenwriter. I originally was elated to learn that my good name would not be on such a piece of poo-poo as I imagined Universal capable of producing and as, indeed, Universal ultimately did produce. But my wife-lawyer-agent smartly rapped my knuckles in explaining I had nothing to celebrate: should Mr. Higgins be awarded all screenplay credit, he also would get all future screenwriter's television money. She said this could amount to meeny meeny thousands of pesos over the years, and that Pete Masterson and I owed it to our families to fight fiercely. Did we not wish to leave well-fixed widows and progeny?

We had ten days, from receipt of Universal's cheery telegram making us nonpersons, to file an appeal with a board of arbitration made up of members of the Screenwriters Guild. We could not merely send a telegram saying, "Hey, dagnabit, this here damn Englishman director they have hired to make a movie about Texas whores is trying to grab all our screen credit and usurp all our future TV money." Nosir, we had to prove *how* he was fouling us by comparing structure, dialogue, characters, place names and such in our scripts with that script bearing Mr. Higgins' proud name. This meant about ninety-six hours of near round-the-clock typing and legal-brief writing, in effect. We stopped only to grab a hasty cup of soup, occasionally napped for ten minutes, and twice hosed down our stinking bodies on the run. While we grubbed and sweated, Mr. Higgins—for all I know—was taking his ease with a lover over wine or having tea with the Queen. In any event, he strangely was not required to prove he *didn't* crib from us; the burden of proof, in Hollywood, always is heaped on the innocent.

During these frantic exercises we were mailed about 300 names of members of the Screenwriters Guild, from which exactly 11 personages were to be named to the board of arbitration. We were instructed to strike a "reasonable" number of individuals we did not wish to sit in judgment, though "reasonable" is nowhere defined. To me that question was moot: I did not know Aaronsko, Bruce, from Zublinski, Sally Jane; I thus had no measuring stick. Fortunately, Pete Masterson knew a bit about a few of our potential judges and, more important, he knew how to proceed: we telephoned experienced old screenwriters, friendly actors and film critics in an effort to discern the true sons of bitches and horse's asses.

"The first thing you *don't* want," said a friendly old Hollywood hand, "is any goddam Hyphenates." I said of course we didn't want any goddam Hyphenates; we wouldn't even *consider* any goddam Hyphenates. And, er, say, pray tell exactly what *is* a goddam Hyphenate?

The old screenwriter said a goddam Hyphenate is a creature who bills himself as Director hyphen Writer and tries to hog the money and credits for both jobs. Such as, for example, Mr. Colin Higgins. He said never mind that goddam Hyphenates usually had trouble composing so much as a laundry list, there was a Hollywood trend to look on them as new Shakespeares. Hollywood, he said, had long been trying to find a way to get along without bothersome screenwriters; the Hyphenate ploy was their answer. He said any other member of the Hyphenate Club who managed to sneak onto our board of arbitration would be happy to help their Hyphenate colleague take our sox and shirts.

He also warned we should shy from writers who depend exclusively for their bread on screenplays alone: they might be overly eager to impress our Hyphenate adversary with an eye toward landing future work on films he later might direct. He said we should beware all who might be cousins, in-laws or special pals of Mr. Higgins. He said since Mr. Higgins is an Englishman, we should fear the same as mad dogs all Englishmen who might go out in the midday sun to judge our case.

He said to be particularly suspicious of any screenwriter presently working for Universal Pictures, or any screenwriter who had worked for that outfit more than once—such continued servitude, he said, indicated the writer was not yet mad enough at Universal to seek secondhand vengeance by helping our cause. (Though, he said, the same would apply toward *any* studio whose anointed Hyphenate a screenwriter might take to arbitration: he was not indicating more than the usual, routine Hollywood chicaneries on the part of Universal's fine and fair-minded gentlemen.) He said if, on the other hand, we could identify a Screenwriters Guild member who happened to hate Universal Pictures, or hate Mr. Higgins, for any reason whatsoever, then we should pay bribes if said bribes would ensure that personage's serving on our board of arbitration.

So now we had to be not only lawyers but detectives. In time, we struck maybe half the 300 names before throwing our hands in the air and saying, "What the hell, it's a game of Russian roulette." Meanwhile, everybody who knows more of Hollywood than that it is west of Mississippi assured us we had absolutely no chance to win our appeal: "You are outsiders and troublemakers. Hollywood hates both breeds. The board of arbitration will unanimously award Colin Higgins your asses and fixtures, and then sleep better for it." When I ranted and raved about Justice and Free Enterprise, these wisemen laughed, rolled their eyes or sighed.

And lo! Came a telegram one day saying that by a vote of eleven to zip, Mr. Higgins was found to be 50 percent of a screenwriter; Mr. Masterson and Mr. King were found to be 25 percent screenwriters each. All future television monies due *Whorehouse* screenwriters would accrue to each of us in those exact, respective percentages.

I threw things, cussed and wished for a dog to kick. Pete Masterson, perhaps more practical, said it could have been worse. Then a strange thing happened: veteran screenwriter friends began calling to congratulate us on a stunning victory. I said, "Something is bad wrong with you boogers. Why should I rejoice that some damn interloper has purloined away half our goodies?" They said I didn't know enough of Hollywood customs, mores and practices to evaluate my good fortune; that our victory was a miracle deserving equal billing with that of the loaves and fishes.

Well, maybe so, though I'm damned if I can find it in the math; every time Pete Masterson and I split a buck, Colin Higgins gets to keep a whole one for hisself. I'd say he won the poker game, wouldn't you? Thus far I have been paid $125,000 for cowriting the original screendrafts, about $8,000 more for my pitiful cut of the soundtrack album and, at this writing, perhaps $40,000 more in TV revenues. While my little pile might loom large to a ragpicker, it don't stack up exceedingly well against Burt's, Dolly's, or even Colin's. They all came out of this sorry mess with enough money to burn a wet mule.

I know so little of the Hollywood realities that when I wrote Universal to say, "Uh, er, what is it exactly Burt's and Dolly's and Colin's production companies did to earn all that money?" I actually expected to get a response in the English language. I thought maybe some Universal Big Cheese would drop a note saying, "Well, see, they supplied the cars for the chase scenes and the bodyguards that guarded their precious high-priced bodies for us and the barbers to trim their wigs, and then there was all that cocaine everybody needed to be alert on the job," or some such. Or, maybe, they would candidly say, "Aw, Lawrence, don't worry about it, it ain't nothing but a tax dodge where Burt and Dolly and Colin bill us for production costs rather than everything in straight salaries; the arrangement only costs the taxpayers, not you, so quit your bitching and whining. Personally, Out Here, we feel like you're lucky not to be in the unemployment line while aspiring to get on welfare." Something honest like that. Instead, all I got was another copy of the same semi-incomprehensible figures that had prompted my query.

A slow learner, I again wrote Universal to say, "Uh, er, each ninety days you send an updated set of your mysterious figures. And each time it shows that all those production companies have received more fresh money since the last time. How is it, kind sirs, that they keep getting paid for new production work on a picture put in the can two years ago? Very truly yours." They mailed me a third copy of the same old financial statement.

Then I had what looked like a stroke of fortune. Old Texas friend and Washington lawyer-politico Robert Strauss sought me out at a party to brag of having just been named to the board of directors of Music Corporation of America—the parent company of Universal Pictures. I backed Mr. Strauss into a corner, stood nose to nose, poked his chest and screamed questions. As quickly as possible Mr. Strauss claimed his hat and escaped, calling back over his shoulder his intent to look into the dubious matters personally. Weeks passed.

Then Good Ol' Bob wrote a friendly note saying here, attached, was the hot scoop from Universal. I ripped his friendly note in my eagerness to flip to the long-awaited explanations. I found, of course, a fourth copy of those consarned nonrevealing figures. Six more copies and I can paper the kiddies' bathroom.

Well—you say—you ignernt fool, why don't you dispatch an accountant or two of your own to Hollywood and have them scream and poke and threaten until questions are answered in specific words rather than by abstract numbers? My sentiments exactly. Until I talked to my friendly accountant. He said sure, he'd be happy to go out there and agitate. He said it would probably take a mere six weeks to read the fine print of my contract with Universal, and Universal's contracts with everybody having a hand in the picture; his reading fee was a piddling $200 per hour. Then he would fine-toothcomb Universal's books, assuming he could get a court order to approach them without having to Mace their guard dogs, and read for several days or weeks more. *Then*, maybe, he would know what questions to ask of well-rehearsed accountants and lawyers being paid by Universal to answer questions slowly if cryptically. With luck, he might ferret out one answer per week. Meanwhile, I would be paying my accountant's and lawyer's expenses to include first-class hotels, good cigars, fine wines and perhaps the occasional chummy dancing girl. He said it would cost me no more than oh, say, $10,000 to $12,000 per week, and for how many weeks did I wish to hire them?

An old Hollywood head tried to explain how producers stay out of the dangerous "profit posture" by writing off advertising for one film against advertising for another film in mysterious package deals, and a lot of other bookkeeping flummery—which he claims is perfectly legal, no matter whether it should be—but I couldn't follow him. How can a poor simple writer be expected to understand such complexities when he fails to understand (1) how producers who have never shown a profit in their lives manage to (2) do business from grand offices while (3) owning big mansions, tooling around in limousines and Lear jets and generally living high on the hog while still (4) retaining the wherewithal to keep on buying more properties for (5) the purpose of producing more money-losing films? Somewhere in there the producer *must* be picking up a nickel or a dime, even if

I can't learn how by reading his periodic, mysterious, red-ink financial reports. I mean, if Hollywood moguls were habitually dropping dead from starvation on Rodeo Drive, wouldn't Dan Rather or Rona Barrett tell us?

Maybe some of you out there are smarter than am I about money and math. If so, please have a look at the latest report from Universal and drop me a postcard should you figure out answers to the questions I've posed:

UNIVERSAL PICTURES
A DIVISION OF UNIVERSAL CITY STUDIOS INC

PHOTOPLAY: Best Little Whorehouse in Texas
STATEMENT TO: Susannah Prod, Tejas Prod, Texhouse Corp
F-08217-20
ACCOUNTING FROM: 03-31-84 TO: 06-30-84

	CURRENT PERIOD	INCEPTION TO DATE
ACCOUNTABLE GROSS:		
SUBJECT TO A DISTRIBUTION FEE OF 30%		
United States—		
Theatrical	$ 4,631.70	$44,365,870.55
Pay Television	262,406.02	8,770,244.54
United States— Non-Theatrical	2,499.25	117,788.52
Canada	722.10	2,933,589.01
Canadian—Pay Television	46,295.86 −	38,539.31
U.S. Army/Navy	1,047.44	360,010.70
TOTAL	225,010.65	56,586,042.63
SUBJECT TO A DISTRIBUTION FEE OF 35%		
Great Britain	3,939.65	201,258.31
TOTAL	3,939.65	201,258.31
SUBJECT TO A DISTRIBUTION FEE OF 40%		
Foreign Subsidiaries	63,791.36	1,965,082.07
Outside Distributors	9,184.22	110,579.01
TOTAL	72,975.58	2,075,661.08

SUBJECT TO A DISTRIBUTION FEE
OF 15%

Outright Sales—Foreign	10,500.00	13,524.75
U.S. Trailers	—	5,254.62
TOTAL	10,500.00	18,779.37

NOT SUBJECT TO A DISTRIBU-
TION FEE

Video Disc	13,939.99	86,649.58
Video Cassette	186,157.32	541,496.20
TOTAL	200,097.31	628,145.78
TOTAL ACCOUNTABLE GROSS	512,523.19	59,509,887.17

DISTRIBUTION FEES:

30% OF $56,586,042.63	67,503.20	16,975,812.79
35% OF $ 201,258.31	1,378.88	70,440.41
40% OF $ 2,075,661.08	29,190.23	830,264.43
15% OF $ 18,779.37	1,575.00	2,816.91
TOTAL DISTRIBUTION FEES	99,647.31	17,879,334.54
BALANCE	412,875.88	41,630,552.63

DISTRIBUTION EXPENSES:

Taxes	6,917.82	128,668.25
Prints—35MM	968.98	1,946,991.17
Prints—16MM	71.86 −	97,597.17
Duping Prints, Titles,		
Foreign Versions	902.04	465,621.67
Freight, Duties, Censor-		
ship, Checking	6,863.27	269,177.62
Advertising	58.12 −	12,282,811.49
Trade Association Fees	95.74	339,409.43
Trailer Costs	378.58	20,870.96
Guild Fees	45,591.58	1,031,221.53
Other Television		
Expenses	33,696.02	105,021.40
TOTAL DEDUCTIONS	95,284.05	16,687,390.69
BALANCE	317,591.83	24,943,161.94

OTHER DEDUCTIONS:

Cost of Production		
(Ex-Interest)*	31,159.24	36,500,497.31

PARTICIPATIONS

Burt Reynolds Prod.	68,723.21	2,684,781.53
Dolly Parton Prod.	16,035.42	784,782.36
Colin Higgins Prod.	34,259.50	330,317.92
TOTAL OTHER DEDUCTIONS	150,177.37	40,300,379.12

SUBJECT TO % CALCULATION
OR LOSS— $167,414.46 $15,357,217.18 –

---

*Cost of production subject to adjustment. Interest
to be included on subsequent statements.

New York City
July 1976

Yesterday was Independence Day. July Fourth. Much hoopla in the
city. Fireworks displays. A parade. Politicians nakedly exposing their
patriotic reflexes in yahooings bordering on the obscene. The Tall
Ships sailed into New York Harbor to commemorate the nation's
200th birthday.

I feel about that old myself. Spent the entire holiday on my back,
staring at the bedroom ceiling and spouting great sighs like some fat
beached whale. I have never felt more alone or hopeless. Besides a
general crippling depression I had a granddaddy of a hangover, a
fever, a painful chest cold and a racking cough. Dr. King treated the
latter by smoking three packs of cigarettes.

I simply can't write. The LBJ book is dead, beyond resurrection
or resuscitation. The play about a Texas whorehouse lies neglected
in a corner; I think it is laughing at me. The novel, *Emmerich De-
scending*, about the tribulations of its burned-out writer-protago-
nist—guess who, gang?—started with such hope and fervor a few
weeks ago, has fizzled out. I don't know what will happen to that
damned Bobby Baker book project. I would guess not very much. I
will do the best I can by it professionally, assuming a decent contract, though personally I care not a whit for that job. It is the literary equivalent of shoveling shit in somebody else's barnyard. When
a writer feels reluctant about a project, then the work is unlikely to
be either easy or good.

Had anyone told me ten years ago I now would be scrabbling on
the magazine treadmill, I might have gone in the roofing bidness.
Oh, I manage articles well enough, and the fortnightly column for

New Times, but any long, sustaining project scares the liver out of me. There isn't enough joy or grit in my gizzard to keep me interested in anything over the long haul. I seem not to have enough inner resources to stay the course. It is rather like facing a five-mile run while knowing I haven't enough in the legs and lungs to last past one hundred yards.

As always when my work goes badly, I am finding difficulty in my personal relationships. I have been dating a few young women but can't sustain—or *won't* sustain—these beginnings. Some are silly and I can't find anything to talk about with them. Others are good people but I am indifferent to them or they want to get married and I'm afraid of becoming *more* than indifferent because of the fearful possible consequences. I can't hack a trip down the center aisle or Manhattan's version of a vine-covered cottage and the inevitable colic and baby shit. I am too broke, too old, too dispirited for that long haul; it would be as tiring and tedious and unending as writing a 10,000-page novel. My three young-adult children in their teenage years having jumped me through more fiery hoops than was good for my fur, I can't risk leaping into such long-burning flames again. This resolve makes me, I think, stubbornly matrimony-proof.

If I could just recapture the old writing drive—if I could *want* to write as I once wanted it, *enjoy* it as I once enjoyed it, *produce* as I once produced—then I think all my troubles, both personally and professionally, would largely go away. Right now that seems an unlikely prospect. I may have written my last book.

I suppose it says little for me as a human being that when my work is going well I don't need anybody—but can get along, then, with almost anyone. Conversely, when the work goes badly I need someone desperately. But, somehow, that is exactly when I can't get along with any human under the sun. In such times I challenge, agitate, place blame or transfer it from myself to others, become critical and sullen and indulge my wilder excesses. No problem *recognizing* the difficulty; solving it, though, is tougher than Chinese arithmetic.

[*Update*: Six months after writing those terminal conclusions I began dating, and soon arranged to marry, Barbara Blaine. The Baker book and *Whorehouse* successes followed. I'm a hell of a prophet, ain't I?]

New York
September 1976

It is midafternoon and I am mostly sober—only slightly pumped up by four or five screwdrivers at lunch—and it seems a good time to consider how much time and energy I waste trying to write when I am too drunk to hit the floor with my hat. Every time I wake to several pages of new gibberish I say to myself, "Lawrence, goddammit, the point at which your brain began seriously malfunctioning is *so* obvious. How did you fail to recognize it?"

Next time, I always swear, I *will* recognize when my brain short-circuits; then I will immediately quit the typewriter and stagger to bed or at least sit muttering, quietly and harmlessly, to myself. A few mornings later I wake to fresh pages of disgusting tripe. Reading them is excruciating; it makes me feel the fool that an alleged professional cannot distinguish between when he is writing well, passably well or in what might as well be pidgin Greek for all its value or coherence. Reading that crap in the noon dawn's early light brings on a psychological fatigue even deeper and more debilitating than those physiological wearies sure to result from an evening's big toot.

I know they say it is a good habit to try to write every day, no matter one's mind-set or condition. I generally agree. But this spewing of predawn shitstuff again and again is getting ridiculous. I need to grow a whistle like they put on teakettles to signal when the water's overheated.

I am often blocked these days; the longer I sit and stare at blank paper the greater the desperation and the growing conviction I'll never be able to get back on track. So, now, I pump up before sitting down to write so I won't experience that desolate panic. I begin only slightly oiled and sip as I write. Then I forget to sip. Next thing, I'm pouring the old juice down as if to put out a fire. Soon my brain is inflamed, but I don't know it. Sometimes I have a sneaky suspicion, but rationalize that some of my stuff written in a tipsy condition ain't too bad and can be salvaged after minor repairs. True enough. The problem is in knowing when *that* stage passes and the piss-down-my-leg stage arrives. I never seem to know. Perhaps writing this down, so I can refer back to it as needed, will help. But likely I attempt to fool myself once again: if I get so sloshed I need to look it up, I'll be too drunk to find it. Or, should I find it, too addled to heed its warning.

Washington
June 1983

[Perhaps the entry printed above might profit by updating.]

No, I never learned to quit trying to write when stupid drunk. I didn't cease sometimes writing in pidgin nonsense until I began trying to attain a sober state in 1980—with, let it be admitted, a few periodic early stumbles. I think, however, I ultimately adjusted after a time. Just thought, *Oh, well, there's some more of that drunk stuff*, and promptly tore it up without undue agonizing.

I used to credit liquor or pot for getting me to the typewriter when I otherwise would not have gone. Sometimes they did. But chemicals kept me away from work more times than they sat me down to it. I also believed I might be incapable of writing without help from various mood modifiers, that my creative juices would dry up. Sober and chemically unpolluted, I accomplish three times the work I did when using crutches. In retrospect I realize that my old fear—while real enough—was also self-serving. When friends concerned for my well-being pressured me to try alcoholic rehabilitation, in a time when I could not imagine life without chemicals, my defensive cry was "I'm not willing to tamper with anything that might change me as a writer." Unfortunately, this popular myth is adhered to by many writers. Until their heads are straight, however, they can't see it or won't admit it.

Perhaps some writers *can* drink or smoke dope or even snort in moderation. Perhaps a unique carousing few may be able to produce about as well as they would if remaining as straight as a Baptist fanatic, for a time, assuming they occasionally pause to sleep, eat and let their motors idle. But addiction is progressive. Those of us who tend to run rabbits and bark at the moon so long as marginally able—or past—know, for sure, that in due course there comes a day when the piper sticks out his hand and demands to be paid.

End of sermon. If, however, you are a writer who suspects yourself of crutch problems, please feel free to reread it at any time.

Washington
April 1983

My biggest disappointment is that I am not a good novelist, or even a decent one. The form seems to intimidate me. Why I can't plot novels, when I plot well enough for the stage, is a mystery. Why I love reading novels, but find them tedious to write, is another. Why I don't mind—even enjoy—writing descriptive passages in nonfiction, but abhor them in fiction, is another mystery still. Perhaps there is some vital chemistry flowing in the blood of novelists that is missing from my own.

For a decade about one-half of a pretty good novel has reposed in my trunk, but I strangely postpone trying to finish it. I eventually shall, I think, but doubt whether it will be first-rate. If one has not blossomed as a novelist at my age, and after my years of experience, one cannot count strongly on a late blooming.

Somehow (perhaps because I haven't yet actually attempted it) I think I might write fairly well in the detective or mystery genre. I once thought that about espionage novels, too, but after reading gunnysacks of spy stories admitted I could never plot all those necessary false leads, complex deceptions and ultimately provide workable solutions. Nor can a geographic ignoramus hop his people around the globe to exotic locales, peeking first into "our" camp and then "theirs." I might have it snow two feet on some mild Pacific atoll, or send monsoon seasons to chalk-dry deserts. Perhaps my novelistic problem simply is that I don't know enough about a variety of things, though I strongly suspect additional deficiencies.

Washington
November 1984

John Dos Passos once said that what he liked best about Faulkner was Faulkner's eye for detail: "He is a remarkably accurate observer and builds his narrative . . . out of the marvelous raw material of what he has seen." In James J. Kilpatrick's new book, *The Writer's Art*, Kilpatrick also stresses the importance of keen observation of the world around us; he reports that he once stood stone-still for almost two hours watching how a spider spun its web. The storing up of sights and sounds serves the writer well, Kilpatrick notes, when he needs similes and metaphors.

This is a thing I have long known but have too much neglected. I haven't the patience to watch spiders spin webs. Indeed, I am such a poor observer of nature and architecture and fashions of apparel that I often must quit the page in my typewriter for emergency readings, or to ask questions of someone more observant, before being able to proceed. Barbara is forever shaking her head when I compliment her on some "new" outfit; invariably, the outfit is three years old and she has worn it in my presence dozens of times. I just didn't notice.

I fancy that I am a good observer of people as to their physical characteristics, habits and behavioral traits. And I'll match my ear with just about anyone's. Otherwise, however, I do need to look harder at places and things: make a conscious effort to memorize them.

Washington
December 1981

Here is my word of encouragement today for would-be writers and neophyte writers:

According to *The Literary Life and Other Curiosities*, published this year, "A recent survey by Philippe Perebinossoff of hundreds of members of P.E.N., the international writers' organization, found that the median income from writing in 1978 was $4,700, with 68 percent making under $10,000 and 9 percent earning nothing."

Don't that make you want to rush to your typewriter and put in a ten-hour day?

Washington
August 1981

In those tough times when the words won't come, or when I simply suffer an acute attack of the blues-and-blahs, my antidote is to dip into Mark Twain's lighter stuff. By "lighter" I do not mean "minor"; rather, I mean to distinguish between Twain when he was truly funny and when he was merely bitterly ranting. His midlife stuff is stronger than the earliest Twain, because he knew more of the world and better how to state it; when he was old and crotchety and probably yearned to retreat incognito to Miami Beach and write "Shit" large in the sand, his dissatisfactions often showed in his work. But the best of Twain, when he was astride the world and didn't need a saddle, might uplift a man being marched in chains to the guillotine.

Humor is risky to analyze, but one of the reasons Twain was so effective was his unusual juxtapositions, his intermingling of the deadly serious and the hilariously funny. He had a talent for ordering words, common enough in conventional usage, to suddenly leap out from ambush in rare combinations we could not have guessed. He was a master at lulling us into believing he was so sincerely aroused over a given injustice he might be courting a stroke—then throwing the sneak punch by way of a line at once tongue-in-cheek, absurdly funny and yet true to the mark. Whole books have been written in anger, and long-winded orations delivered in sobs or slobbers, that failed to make their serious points half as well as Twain could with one comic, jabbing turn of phrase.

Case in point: Twain's longish essay "Fenimore Cooper's Literary Offenses." In the opening lines Twain seemingly sets out to grimly chastise Professors of English Literature at Columbia, Yale and other high-domed stations for their lavish claims in behalf of James Fenimore Cooper's art. Soon he begins enumerating why Cooper was such a bad writer; Twain lists "nineteen rules governing literary art in the domain of romantic fiction" and promptly accuses Cooper of violating eighteen of them. They are good, sound rules for the most part, but Mr. Twain does sneak in his fun: "They require that the personages in a tale shall be alive, except in the case of corpses, and that always the reader shall be able to tell the corpses from the others." And "They require that when a personage talks like an illustrated, gilt-edged, tree-calf, hand-tooled, seven-dollar Friendship's Offering in the beginning of a paragraph, he shall not talk like a Negro minstrel in the end of it. But this rule is flung down and danced upon in the *Deerslayer* tales. . . . [Cooper fails] to notice that the man who talks corrupt English six days in the week must and will talk it on the seventh, and can't help himself." Twain then quotes Cooper's dialogue to such devastating effect that I have never since been able to open one of "Fenimore's" books without going into spasms of laughter at the first sighting of same.

But where Twain utterly destroys Cooper—brutally, if uproariously—is in finding the man a wretched observer of woodsmen's lore, Indian habits and culture, nature, boatmanship, marksmanship as dictated by the limitations of the human eye—the mother-stuff of which Cooper's tales are made, and for which he earned in his time a considerable reputation. He effectively leaves poor old Cooper dead in his own forest; no human over the age of five will ever again be able to take even semi-seriously Cooper's reports of derring-do in that work collectively known as the Leatherstocking Tales.

For instance. Twain negates the method by which Natty Bumppo finds "a misplaced fort"—trailing the arrow-straight path of an expired cannonball directly to it—by recalling that cannonballs do not smoothly roll along the ground leaving convenient tracks for great distances but, instead, hop and skip and bound and rebound into the air, ricocheting off sundry objects and again hopping and skipping away on uncertain courses—rather like, I get the image, an amateur aircraft pilot attempting a disastrous first landing from which he is not even-money to walk away. Twain ridicules a scene in which a large boat comes down a curving, shallow, narrow river and he proves, with the rules of math and physics, that what Cooper said had happened could not physically have happened save for the instant repeal of gravity, time and similar laws of importance.

But he is at his cutting best in chiding Mr. Cooper for "his little box of stage properties" in which Cooper kept "six or eight cunning devices, tricks, artifices for his savages and woodmen to deceive and circumvent each other with, and he was never so happy as when he was working these things and seeing them go." Listen to the particulars:

"A favorite one was to make a moccasined person tread in the tracks of the moccasined enemy, and thus hide his own trail. Cooper wore out barrels and barrels of moccasins in working that trick. Another stage property that he pulled out of his box pretty frequently was his broken twig. He prized his broken twig above all the rest of his effects, and worked it the hardest. It is a restful chapter in any book of his when somebody doesn't step on a dry twig and alarm all the reds and whites for two hundred yards around. Every time a Cooper person is in peril and absolute silence is worth four dollars a minute, he is sure to step on a dry twig. There may be a hundred handier things to step on but that wouldn't satisfy Cooper. Cooper requires him to turn out and find a dry twig, and if he can't do it, go and borrow one."

That wonderful foregoing paragraph I often call up in my mind, never without laughing or—in inappropriate circumstances—having to conceal or smother laughter with artful snorts and coughs. I once made the mistake of calling it up to combat excessive emotion welling up at the funeral of a beloved relative, and have not been in decent odor among certain kinsmen since; when one's shoulders shake for minutes on end at a funeral, especially for a member of one's own tribe, it is best to remember that one's eyes and cheeks should not remain dry.

In my youthful admiration of Mark Twain's work, and knowing little of Samuel Clemens' personal life or habits, I assumed him the most jolly of men; more than once I lightly cursed Providence, after making sure no lightning bolts hid in the clouds, for not having permitted me to wander, laughing, at Mr. Twain's side. This was long before I had read Twain's later, bitter, posthumously published stuff or knew that he died a miserable old man full of rancor more than matching his years.

Here was a writing man who permitted his shrewish wife to excise his language, censor his thoughts and otherwise carve his manuscripts; if wifey-poo did not approve certain passages of hubby's work they went out with the coffee grounds and chicken bones. On those few occasions when Twain chose to contest his strong-willed lady, she feigned illnesses just short of leprosy or multiple sclerosis until he fell to his knees in capitulation. Twain not only permitted such bullyragging, when a crack across the snout might better have served American Letters, but seemingly encouraged it by anguished, fawning displays of guilt designed to win a dishonorable peace. Mrs. Samuel Clemens, indeed, made Mrs. Abraham Lincoln by comparison look like a shoo-in for the Miss Congeniality Award. Twain's absences from her surely made Twain's heart grow fonder of absences.

Out of fear he might lose the love and commercial support of his adoring public, Twain decreed that much of his work could not be published until he lay stretched and amoldering in the grave—long safe from mortal tweakings. Though his work often delightfully attacked or ridiculed rich, powerful stuffed shirts, it is no pleasure to say Twain often pandered to and courted such walking frauds in real life. He grew to love the Grand Life—hell, I like tastes of it myself—and those who lived it, much more than was becoming to his soul; it is a thing successful writers must guard against at the risk of losing their more acrid truths.

Had I actually wandered by Mark Twain's side, I would have witnessed petty temper fits and the occasional abuses of persons of lower station or less fortunate circumstances. I might have heard him tongue-lash his dream-addled brother, Orion, as a fool, a wastrel, a financial sponge and as a personal and social embarrassment to the family; that poor Orion *was* a bit of an ass, and a malpractor of many arts and sciences, probably made these tirades no less painful for him. My old hero dominated his daughters to the point of dictating their casual conduct and mode of dress; he forever cautioned of what high standards he—and the public—expected of "Mark Twain's daughters"; not until a ripe age did he learn his daughters had feared him all their lives. This somehow surprised him.

Twain often muttered curses against the hardships of the lecture circuit (no matter his huge fees, generous receptions and the presumed satisfaction of his own superb performances) because, he claimed, lecturing was debilitating mule work required to support the excessive demands of family and retainers. While I can easily identify with the complaint, and sometimes share it, Twain was not so quick to admit to his own costly extravagances or questionable investments—though, I suspect, he might have become an enthusiastic partner in my get-rich-quick scheme involving the Eisenhower plaques had he but been available.*

Twice Mark Twain went bankrupt because of dubious schemes better fitting the brain of the incompetent sibling Orion. First he lost a ton attempting to perfect a Rube Goldberg typesetter that never advanced much beyond its ability to smash the fingers of all who touched it; then he paid foolish sums to a broken, besotted U. S. Grant for the privilege of publishing Grant's memoirs. Despite the suspicion that Twain himself may have ghosted Grant's book, it sold on a par with cockleburr toilet paper. Twain also bought into a nonexistent silver mine pawned off on him by Julian Hawthorne, son of the writer Nathaniel Hawthorne.

---

*See "A Matter of Style," the first piece in Part Three of this book, on p. 261.

Twain was more in love—almost unhealthily so—with a daughter who tragically died than with his wife. (Though, understandably, he might have fallen more in love with a friendly salamander than with his wife, given a decent opportunity.) He sometimes took to his bed, drunk and whining and self-pitying, to write soggy diary notes or letters relating how the world had so foully mistreated him. Again, those are traits or actions not entirely unknown to this writer; one simply wishes for better from his brass-plated personal hero.

In short, I am afraid there was much in Mr. Twain that might not have made him good fun, after all, in private circumstances: hints of the tyrant, the spoiled child, the runaway egomaniac, the smiling deceiver as conscious of "image" as today's stars of stage, screen, television or the political podium.

But those are the harsh judgments of a man not having walked a mile in his victim's shoes. I have little trouble forgetting or forgiving Mr. Twain's human foibles, assuming he lurks in Purgatory awaiting my approval and prayers to free him, because in the final reckoning he left behind the gift of laughter. No matter Mark Twain's darker moods or fears, his best stuff has helped me shake off my own angst in many a melancholy moment. To that good cause, and in appreciation, I lift my tankard and sing.

Washington
January 1985

I would hate to be a writer's relative because the damn fellow would forever be embarrassing me. Writers have no decent sense of shame. They tattle on others as much as, or more than, on themselves, going public with events their kinfolks consider private property and turning the light of inspection on events that might be better left to sleep in the dark.

Of course, since I am the writer in my family I take a different point of view from that stated above. When I write of our family having starved off the farm during the Great Depression, going out as itinerant cottonpickers to live in tents and abandoned garages, someone is sure to charge that I have portrayed the family as failed, shiftless bums; *I* see it as depicting courageous parents of limited opportunities stubbornly persevering to provide for their young in the worst of times, and coming through against great odds.

When I write of that terrible five-year clash of wills and purposes with my father during the troublesome teenage years, or of my subsequent difficulties with my own now-adult progeny during their youthful escapades, someone is certain to discover a hurtful betrayal of the bloodline; *I* see it as a fair commentary on that ages-old generation gap brought on by ever-changing social mores, the innate desire of the young to fly from the family nest before they have proper wings and the concern and frustration of parents who feel an obligation to superimpose their own values in order to protect their descendants from youthful folly.

Each generation reserves a delicate balance of love for the other. Human emotions grow complex, moods mercurial, as roles shift and change in the family unit. Mistakes are made; conflicts are inevitable and built-in. To one degree or another it happens in all families, though none wants it told. I suppose conflicts between writers and their relatives are unavoidable. Families are in the protective suppression business; writers are not.

Relatives, in true anguish, ask writers, "But why did you have to tell *that*?" The writer told it, probably, because it was an integral part of his story and illustrated a pertinent point, or was so full of drama or comedy he was helpless to resist it. Writers bring to their work their best recollections and interpretations of old events; these may not mesh with the recollections, viewpoints or attitudes of others. Then the writer is charged with having seen it wrong or told it wrong. More likely, he told it too painfully truthful for others to be comfortable with it.

Sometimes there is humor in this clash of purposes or cultures. "I wish I could take an eraser and scrub out all those dirty words," my mother said on reading my novel, *The One-Eyed Man*. "Go ahead," I said. "Your copy is yours to do with as you will." My mother issued a mighty sigh: "Oh, but Lawrence, there are all those *other* copies." Aye, there's the rub: those who would be censors are not content with limited jurisdictions.

Perhaps my recitations of old foolish drunken misadventures have caused more shame or pain to my family than any other of my scribblings. I regret that, but am helpless to change it. For years my actions and utterances were greatly influenced by heavy drinking; it is a vital part of my history even if not a pretty part. A writer, especially one writing autobiographically, cannot claim to have ridden through life in a golden chariot, using the right salad fork and bestowing a gentlemanly sweetness, if he has actually come through it across rocky roads on a bareback mule while barking and howling and clawing—and he should not be expected to. False notes would clang and jangle through his work, making most discordant sounds. And if writing is not honestly delivered, it has little or no purpose.

Faulkner knew whereof he spoke when he cracked, "The 'Ode on a Grecian Urn' is worth any number of little old ladies." Writers should not forget that lesson, no matter how weighty the pressures from others and no matter how well-intended such pressures may be. I suspect that those who would censor writers are more concerned with protecting their own images, more concerned with how *they* will be considered in the eyes of others due to guilt by association, than they are truly concerned about protecting the writer from himself.

Washington
April 1982

Warren Miller. Willie Morris. Norman Mailer. John Kenneth Galbraith. David Halberstam. These, and other, writers extended helping hands when I was new to the business or struggling to move up in the pack. I have been lucky. The literary world is replete with feuds and nasty cuttings, writers forever nipping at their colleagues' asses and innards.

I really don't comprehend why this should be; just don't understand that careless private bad-mouthing by one writer against another, or those gratuitous public attacks made on writing contemporaries. Yet it is as old as our Republic: older, in older cultures.

Though I am grateful to have been largely exempt from such cannibalism, it sometimes depresses me to think it may be because I am considered such small-bore game there is no need to waste shot on me. A friend once reported that another writing friend had said loudly disparaging things of my work during a group-guzzle at Elaine's in New York; the writer who allegedly bad-mouthed me had always appeared friendly, still does, and I wonder whether he actually performed as reported. (And, if he didn't, why did the other writer so claim?) I suppose it probably happened: John Steinbeck once said that although Ernest Hemingway was nice to his face, he'd had reports of being back-stabbed when he wasn't around to see the flash of Hemingway's blade. The only working writer of note to jab me in print, to my knowledge, was Walker Percy, and his comment was more silly than vicious. Mr. Percy wrote in the *New York Times* that my book *Confessions of a White Racist* was a failure because it didn't offer solutions to the nation's ancient racial problems. Let me assure Mr. Percy I would not have withheld "solutions" had I but known them; certainly I didn't do it out of social indifference or professional sloth.

Lillian Hellman (who, yes, could be a bit tart to other writers) once remarked, "Writers are interesting people, but often mean and petty. Competing with each other and ungenerous about each other. Hemingway was [particularly] ungenerous about other writers."

For sure. Old Hem may have been the search-and-destroy champion of American letters. By the time he wrote *A Moveable Feast* (1957–1960), his account of his struggling Paris years in the 1920s, he had become a sour old man with little good to say of anyone. Perhaps those excesses might be forgiven: Hemingway then was physically troubled, aged beyond his calendar years, worried that his large talent had waned, was possibly paranoid and not far from death. But how to excuse the petty or ugly comments he made during the earlier, good years?

Early on, Hemingway seemed to delight in writing a cruel parody of Sherwood Anderson's work, though Anderson had been generous to the younger Hemingway and thought of him as a friend. On reading James Jones' *From Here to Eternity* Hemingway went into an uncontrollable rage—probably because Jones had the temerity to write brilliantly of war, a subject on which Hemingway presumed himself the ultimate authority. Hemingway fired off a blast to their common publisher: "Things will catch up with him [Jones] and he probably will commit suicide. . . . I hope he kills himself as soon as it does not damage his or your sales. If you give him a literary tea you might ask him to drain a bucket of snot and then suck the puss out of a dead nigger's ear. . . . How did they ever get a [dust jacket] picture of a wide-eared jerk (un-damaged ears) to look that screaming tough? . . . He has the psycho's urge to kill himself and he will do it." Wheah!

When I met James Jones on Long Island in the mid-1970s, seeing him several times under the auspices of our mutual friend Willie

Morris, I thought I had never known a more gentle, considerate, honest, no-horseshit person. And when I screwed up courage to ask why Jones thought Hemingway had so brutally attacked him, and sniped at him over the years, Jones only shrugged and said, "Beats me." Hemingway was by then a good dozen years dead—by suicide. Jones lived as long as nature permitted; on his deathbed he dictated the late chapters of his final novel, *Whistle,* and gave Willie Morris his plans for its conclusion so that Morris might complete the book by a lengthy summarizing. I don't suppose it's possible to be certain about such things, but I'd wager on the evidence of record that Mr. Jones was made of sterner stuff than Mr. Hemingway.

Hemingway stomped on other writers almost reflexively. On learning that Malcolm Cowley was putting together a book or books about several of Hemingway's literary contemporaries, the old hunter fired both barrels: "You could put Lionel Trilling, Saul Bellow, Truman Capote, Jean Stafford and . . . Robert Lowry into one cage and jack them up good and you would find that you have nothing. . . . [You] waste your time discussing [them] unless we want to discuss who is playing for Dallas, Texas. The Texas League is a very good one if you are playing in it but it is quite different from the big time where you actually have to play to perform what it is you do absolutely perfectly within the limits of possibility." In Hemingway's eyes Thomas Wolfe was "the over-blown Lil Abner of literature"; Dos Passos was "not a good writer"; on and on. It would exhaust a man's tolerance for invective to recount each of Hemingway's chosen victims.

The man Hemingway was hardest on over the long haul was his onetime pal and mentor F. Scott Fitzgerald. It apparently rankled Hemingway, once he had made it, that Fitzgerald in the early days had extended his helping hand; perhaps he couldn't bear being obligated. It may be, too, that the basically insecure Mr. Hemingway feared in Fitzgerald a talent burning brighter than his own. Hemingway wrote a famous paragraph in his short story "The Snows of Kilimanjaro" crediting "poor Scott" with having said, "The rich are very different than you and me," and adding that "someone" (obviously, the reader is supposed to believe that someone may have been Ernest Hemingway) had riposted, "Yes, they have more money." Hurt by the crack on reading it in *Esquire,* and knowing it to be false, Fitzgerald wrote Hemingway to ask that his name be changed if the short story reached book form. Hemingway did dutifully change it, but the damage was done; the old saw about the truth seldom catching up with the original lie is applicable. To this day, I read or hear of that "exchange" between Hemingway and Fitzgerald as if it actually happened.

The truth: Hemingway once had cracked a joke about his own rich friends to a writer named Mary (Molly) Colum and *she* responded, "The only difference between the rich and other people is that the rich have more money." Hemingway filed the remark in his mind, obviously, and later trotted it out at "poor Scott's" expense. As John Dos Passos remarked, Hemingway's jealousy of Fitzgerald not only was difficult to understand, it seemed to increase as Fitzgerald became down-and-out and least needed more troubles. Hemingway had the luck to die while still popular and idolized by many; "poor Scott" died with his books out of print and unaware he would enjoy a posthumous revival.

For most of his life Hemingway walked gingerly when it came to William Faulkner; he even wrote him atypically friendly, supportive letters. I wonder whether the bully boy of letters feared to take on Faulkner. There came a time, however, when Hemingway became furious at him. Faulkner said to a group of students that Hemingway lacked courage to go out on a limb of fictional experimentation. Word leaked out. Hemingway thereafter claimed that Faulkner had branded him "a coward"; he prompted a military general to write Faulkner attesting to Hemingway's balls and bravery under fire. Though Faulkner had in no way cast doubt on Hemingway's *physical* courage, the sage of Yoknapatawpha wrote a contrite letter of apology. I wish he had pointed out more firmly the difference between what he had said and what he was accused of saying, and then had told the bully boy to go fuck himself.

Five years later, in 1952, Harvey Breit of the *New York Times Book Review* asked Faulkner to review Hemingway's *The Old Man and the Sea*; in declining the job, Faulkner wrote: "A few years ago . . . Hemingway said that writers should stick together just as doctors and lawyers and wolves do. I think there is more wit in that than truth or necessity either, at least in Hemingway's case, since the sort of writers who need to band together willy nilly, or perish, resemble the wolves who are wolves only in pack, and, singly, are just another dog." Faulkner went on to praise Hemingway's integrity as a writer. Breit, thinking to please Ol' Hem, mailed it to him. Hoo boy, that letter pissed off Hemingway for the rest of his life! He fired a scorcher of a letter to Mr. Breit; Mr. Faulkner, of course, was the scorchee:

He [Faulkner] spoke well of me once, as you wrote me. But that was before he was given the Nobel Prize. When I read he had won that, I sent as good a cable of congratulations as I know how to write. He never acknowledged it. For years I had built him up in Europe. Any time anyone asked me who was the best American writer I told them Faulkner. Everytime anyone wanted me to talk about me I would talk about him. . . . I never told people he couldn't go nine innings, or why, nor what I knew was wrong with him since always.

So he writes to you as though I was asking him a favor to protect me. Me, the dog. I'll be a sad son of a bitch. He made a speech, very good. I knew he could never, now, or ever again write up to his speech. I also knew I could write a book better and straighter than his speech and without tricks or rhetoric. . . . You see what happened with Bill Faulkner is that as long as I am alive he has to drink to feel good about having the Nobel prize. He does not realize that I have no respect for that institution [Hemingway, however, did not reject the Nobel when offered it later, in 1954] and was truly happy for him when he got it. . . . Now he comes out with this wolves and the dog stuff and the condescension of how he rated what remains, which I take it, must include *Death in the Afternoon* etc. . . . He is a good writer when he is good and could be better than anyone if he knew how to finish a book and didn't get that old heat prostration . . . at the end. . . . I wish him luck and he needs it because he has the one great and un-curable defect; you can't re-read him. When you re-read him you are conscious all the time of how he fooled you the first time. . . .

I get fed [up] on that County [Yoknapatawpha] sometimes. Anything that needs genealogical tables to explain it is a little bit like James Branch Cabell. . . . When I read Faulkner I can tell exactly when he gets tired and does it on corn [whiskey] just as I used to be able to tell when Scott would hit it beginning with *Tender Is the Night*. But that is one of the things I thought writers should not tell out-siders. But [Faulkner] did not understand about writers sticking together. . . It is not a question of log-rolling or speaking well of each other. It is a question of knowing what is wrong with a guy and still sticking with what is good in him and not letting the out-siders in on *secrets professionnel*. . . .What got me was that he believed the majority criticism and thought that I was through and that he was being asked to help me out. Maybe because he had won the Nobel prize. It sure was a busher's reaction. Well the hell with it. . . .

It is at once amusing and a bit pitiful to see Hemingway invoking the "secrets of the club" rule against Faulkner when he, many times, had slashed and cut so many members of the lodge; his defense gives new weight to the old expression about it all depending on whose ox has been gored.

Say for Ernest Hemingway that when his ass got red it stayed red; two years after his anguished diatribe to Harvey Breit he wrote Lillian Ross, "I cannot help out very much with the true dope on God as I have never played footy-footy with him; nor been a cane brake God hopper; nor won the Nobel prize. It would be best to get the true word on God from Mr. Faulkner. . . . It is quite possible that Mr. Faulkner sits at table with him each night and that the diety comforts him if he has a bad dream and wipes his mouth and helps him eat his corn pone or hominy grits. . . . I hope Mr. Faulkner never forgets himself and gives it to the diety with his corn cob. . . . Faulkner has always been fairly fraudulent but it is only recently that he has introduced God when he is conning people. . . . I have no message to give to Mr. Faulkner except to tell him I wish him the grace of a happy death and I hope he will not continue to write after he has lost his talent. Don't give him that message. . . . But that is what I would really tell him."

Three years after the original Faulkner crime, Hemingway—still stewing—wrote, "When I get tired sometimes I imitate Faulkner a little bit just to show him how it should be done. It is like loosening up with five finger exercises. Anyone not a musician could mistake them for music." Ouch.

And—finally, again to Harvey Breit—"Mr. Faulkner has sent me, or maybe only his agents, The Hunting Stories of W/F. [*Big Woods*, 1955.] They are not dedicated [to me] so I do not have to answer. But when you see him, which is inevitible, please tell him that I found them very well written and delicately perceived but that I would be a little more moved if he hunted animals that ran both ways." Yessir, Mr. Hemingway was a formidable enemy to make.

Faulkner, himself, was not above the occasional cutting remark. Henry James, he said, was "the nicest old lady I ever met." In turn,

Faulkner received the back of Norman Mailer's hand: "Faulkner said more asinine things than any other major American writer. I can't remember a single interesting remark Faulkner ever made." Mailer, of course, has been pissed on by many a literary polecat; there is something about him that seems to bring out the savage in many of his contemporaries. Every time poet-novelist James Dickey thinks of Mailer, apparently, it is as if a painful spike has been driven into his brain; Dickey has variously written of Mailer that he is "a second-rate writer [who] will sit around wondering what on earth it is that Hemingway had that Mailer might possibly be able to get," that The Naked and the Dead is "a vastly inferior novel" and that "the bell-wether of all intellectual cuteness and overintellectualization is Norman Mailer. . . . It is a kind of substitute for literary talent, [this] battening on current events."

Mr. Dickey, indeed, seems to aspire to inherit Hemingway's old role as the Baddest Cannibal; of Robert Frost he wrote, "If I ever thought that anything I wrote was influenced by [him], I would take that particular work of mine, shred it, and flush it down the toilet, hoping not to clog the pipes." Of fellow poet John Berryman: "Berryman is a timid little academic who stays drunk all the time—it is easy to do—in order to convince himself and others that he is inhabited by the true demon, such as Rimbaud or Dylan Thomas was. In keeping with this, he tortures his poems up . . . in order to make 'an original' poetry . . . but it is all so phony and ersatz that I for one have less and less interest in it. . . . Poetry has got to be less artificial and more convincing as speech than Berryman is ever likely to become. That is beyond him; he has walled himself off with artifice, and will stay there until he and his work die." John Berryman did die, eventually, by jumping off a high bridge into dark waters; one wonders whether Mr. Dickey has since considered that the leap may have made a pretty good case for Berryman's being "inhabited by the true demon" after all, as were Dickey's heroes Rimbaud and Dylan Thomas.

This could go on forever—and almost has—but let us add two more links to the unending daisy chain of literary dirkings. Ambrose Bierce said of Bret Harte, "[He] once illuminated everything he touched. Now in shilling-shockers contracted for, years in advance at so many pounds a hundred words, [Harte] slaughters cowboys to make cockneys sit up or hashes up a short story to serve as jam between commercial sandwiches or sloppy popular magazines." Jack London then said of the aforementioned hard judge, Bierce, "[He] could bury his best friend with a sigh of relief and express satisfaction that he was done with him."

I dunno. I guess I must soon begin bad-mouthing some few writers of talent and importance, if I am to earn my union card in the brotherhood of literary backbiters.

Washington
February 1969

John Steinbeck died last December 20. I regret his death for many reasons, one of them embarrassingly selfish: I never got to meet the man.

I did spend an evening in his Manhattan apartment a few months ago, courtesy of his sister-in-law, Jean Boone, an old friend from Austin. One night after dinner on the town, Jean invited me for a nightcap to Steinbeck's place during a marvelous late-summer storm. High above many city spires and Central Park—on the thirty-fourth floor, I think—I prowled among Steinbeck's books and artifacts and drank his wine while thunder rolled, lightning flashed and rain deliciously lashed huge windows overlooking the city. The Great Man himself and his wife, Elaine [Jean Boone's sister], were in Sag Harbor, Long Island, at their country place. I told Jean how, in high school, I had discovered *The Grapes of Wrath* and almost presumed that tale of Depression-ruined and wind-blasted dust bowl itinerants had been written of my hardscrabble family. As I spewed on she said, "Would you like to meet him?" Well, you know the answer to *that*. Jean said Steinbeck wasn't feeling well but, when he returned from Sag Harbor, she would try to set it up. She did not tell me— perhaps she didn't know the seriousness of Steinbeck's illness, or perhaps she didn't want to spoil my dream—that he had been in and out of hospitals for months and was, indeed, walking steadily toward death. By the time he returned to Manhattan in November he had but six weeks left.

Three weeks after Steinbeck's death I received a letter from the Texas writer Elroy Bode. Of Steinbeck he said, "Nobody gives a shit about the man, nobody cared when he died. I was in Fort Stockton, on my way to Kerrville for Christmas, when I picked up the San

Angelo newspaper and learned about his death. I walked around in the hill country during Christmas, thinking brooding thoughts about the man—how he had done it beautifully well, and then things happened, and he gradually lost his touch, and got old, and didn't see such things as Vietnam the way the young and the liberal and what-all thought he should have seen them. So he died all but forgotten, given the backs of their hands by the newsweeklies and as far as I can tell given no kind of hand at all by *Saturday Review* and the literary crowd. He was never a culture hero, never started literary movements, was never a public figure, really, yet by God he had it: the big gift. People who don't try to write 'creatively' are so damn hard on writers who do: They don't understand how hard it is to make a living word, and expect [writers] to turn out good stuff with the ease and regularity of bowel movements."

Elroy Bode's letter inspired more than a little guilt; I, too, had grumbled of Steinbeck's Vietnam views, of his accepting the reward of supping with Lyndon B. at the White House because he had been one of few prominent writers to believe in that war. But I am a bit ashamed, now, of having at least mentally joined the packhounds who barked and howled at Steinbeck's heels. His death, the loss of him, made all that seem unimportant, and the worth of his work come back fresh and clear in memory: *Sweet Thursday*, *The Red Pony*, *Cannery Row*, *East of Eden*, *The Long Valley*, *Of Mice and Men* and, of course, the classic *Grapes of Wrath*. Perhaps he propagandized with a heavy touch for his causes—labor in *In Dubious Battle*; the Vietnam War in his late dispatches; if such a thing is possible he may even have exaggerated the Nazis in *The Moon Is Down*. But he was not the first to meld his art with his causes. When all is said and done the man was a fine storyteller, and more. He passed in and out of fashion, as is the fate of most writers if they live long enough, but critical adjustments up or down cannot change what he put on paper.

I think, here in the fresh wake of Steinbeck's death, of the honesty and beauty in his dedication of *East of Eden* to his longtime editor and friend Pascal (Pat) Covici:

> You came upon me carving some kind of little figure out of wood and you said, "Why don't you make something for me?"
> I asked you what you wanted, and you said, "A box."

"What for?"

"To put things in."

"What things?"

"Whatever you have," you said.

Well, here's your box. Nearly everything I have is in it, and it is not full. Pain and excitement are in it, and feeling good or bad and evil thoughts and good thoughts—the pleasure of design and some despair and the indescribable joy of creation.

And on top of these are all the gratitude and love I have for you.

And still the box is not full.

Sentimental? Sure. Steinbeck had the courage not to fear showing honest sentiment; not to be afraid to confront himself or to reveal his heart. And those are among the reasons John Steinbeck was such a grand old writing man.

New York
February 1976

Death, that dirty buzzard, has claimed another of my old writing idols: H. Allen Smith. I have enjoyed his comic writing since my high school days, and knew him the final years of his life. I just wish the association had lasted longer.

From almost the moment I met him, Allen Smith ranted of his misjudgment in having moved—almost on a whim—from his long-time abode in Mount Kisco, New York, to the distant village of Alpine, Texas. The last time I saw him he said, "I hope I don't die in this jerkwater town." He didn't. He died in a San Francisco hotel room, alone, while working on what must have been his one-zillionth magazine assignment. That the fates or a jesting God abruptly granted his wish not to die in that "jerkwater town" might have amused the old gent (he was seventy); Allen was quite a practical joker in his own right.

Allen Smith once had the misfortune while vacationing to pass through Alpine, a small town near the Mexican border among rock-dotted little hills, in the best part of the year and perhaps on the best day Alpine ever had. He was enchanted by the splendors of fall foliage and the clear mountain air. I suspect, as happens with many weary working writers, his periodic fantasy of escaping life's hurly-

burly—of fleeing the world for some rustic, improbable paradise—
was in full flight that day. Perhaps he'd had a nip or two and so
viewed the world, and Alpine, through rose-colored eyeballs.

Smith followed his impulse and soon uprooted in Mount Kisco to
relocate atop a bald hill overlooking the sleepy little Texas village.
He planted on that hill a prized wooden totem pole—his own likeness
carved on it as "low man"—that had been presented to him in the
long ago by comedian Fred Allen and other old cronies in celebration
of Smith's 1941 best-seller, *Low Man on a Totem Pole*.

My old hero soon discovered that Alpine in winter is windy and
barren, in summer is hot and dusty, has little or no spring and a
year-round limited understanding of a writing man's peculiar preoccupations. To many who labor on ranches or keep shops, the writing
soul appears sinfully idle. He does not produce anything that may be
worn or ridden or eaten. So what the hell good is he? "They scoff at
me here for doing 'woman's work,' " Smith told me. It must be admitted that Smith did not go out of his way to court local people or
their mores; he made fun in one of his books of the Texas custom of
awarding less-than-gentle nicknames—often based on physical de-
formities—by inventing a character called Turd-Eye. But Smith was
frustrated in his counterattacks on Alpine by the knowledge that
almost no one there read his books—or, for that matter, anyone else's.
He found a few friends at Sul Ross State College at the edge of
town, but everywhere else went unappreciated. "Faulkner had to
suffer Oxford," he said. "My cross is Alpine. I think he had the better deal."

When inadequately supervised, H. Allen Smith sometimes could
become a bit rowdy. Fred Allen once wrote of him, "He has nothing
against alcohol, save that it arouses in his breast an urge to fly kites
in two-room apartments." The grape also visited on Allen Smith a
dangerous candor. So, in New York to promote one of the last of the
thirty-three books he accomplished, Smith on a national television
talk show aired in blunt terms his discontent with his adopted hometown; *Time* magazine picked up his more caustic comments. They
were hilarious to all save citizens of Alpine. No more was required
to embroil Smith in a running feud with prideful locals. "I'd love to
sell out and move away," he said, "but these stingy-gut sons-of-bitching
Texicans won't offer a decent price to rid themselves of me."

I had discovered H. Allen Smith's work as a teenager, laughing aloud at his tall tales and wicked recountings of those newspaper days when he ran with Gene Fowler, Ben Hecht, Westbrook Pegler and other hard-bitten wordsmiths of loose habits who have passed into legend. About 1968, a couple of years after Smith moved to Alpine, I was greatly amused by another of his books—*The Great Chili Confrontation*—and wrote a long-overdue fan letter thanking the author for years of laughter. Smith responded warmly; we became regular pen pals. Now and again the one who'd had the most to drink would telephone the other late at night. I pledged to come to Alpine to visit Smith on my next Texas visit.

My lawyer friend Warren Burnett accompanied me on that first trip. Burnett and I were not innocent of drink when we arrived in Alpine. H. Allen Smith poured us a couple more strong ones, but himself strangely sipped juice with no potential. I did not then know as much of alcohol as I presumed, and boorishly kept pressing Smith to join the party. Ultimately he said, "I'm like the fella who was invited to have a drink and asked, 'What day is it?' Told it was Monday, he said, 'Oh, I couldn't possibly. I have an appointment Friday afternoon.' " Later, when I knew him better, Smith revealed that he stayed as dry as desert dirt for prolonged periods while writing his books; at book's end, he admitted to "catching up to my thirst."

This was not information I possessed, however, the second time I visited H. Allen Smith. I had telephoned him one Sunday from an Odessa hotel room when feeling such little pain that I didn't realize Smith himself was in a painless condition. The next day, horribly hungover, I braved 250 miles of burning desert sands to arrive in Alpine in midafternoon. I checked into a motel, hid getaway money from myself in the event of maximum adventures, and telephoned Allen's home. It was quickly apparent that someone—no, *two* someones—were struggling for control of the phone at the other end. Smith lost; his wife informed me that the writer was "tired," while someone sounding strangely like him bellowed in the background as if speaking to multitudes through a megaphone. Perhaps, Mrs. Smith said, I should visit her husband another time. Well, hell, you don't get to Alpine by accident from most places. I simply stayed over and called Smith early the following morning. He was cordial, if subdued, and invited me to his home.

Soon we had vastly improved our spirits, exchanging tales of the writing trade and our adventures in it; the more we drank, the more we bragged on each other as fellow artists and human beings. Until, suddenly, Allen nailed me with a mad glassy stare and said, "You goddam young piece of Texas pigshit, what the hell makes you think you're a goddam writer?" I blinked, then joked that perhaps it was the adulation of fans and critics; this lighthearted explanation only incensed Smith the more. He jumped up, doubled his fists and threatened to wipe the floor with me. I was neither embarrassed nor surprised, knowing something of the unpredictability of fermented grapes.

Mrs. Smith came running from the kitchen to hustle hubby off for a much-needed nap, then returned with profuse apologies. Allen, she said, was at a hard point in his career; most of his old friends in the literary world had retired or died; he no longer knew the prominent writers and editors of the day; his bigger fees and books were behind him. And this, she said, sometimes got to him. I mumbled assurances of the current worth of her husband's work, but my brain gave me a quick, frightening flash of what my own future probably held. As soon as possible, I escaped.

Allen and I resumed our correspondence without the incident ever being mentioned; we talked on the telephone infrequently; I saw him two or three more times, when he was in the middle of a book and eschewing drink. The past couple of years I had promised to make the trek to Alpine for another visit but had settled for good intentions. Now, of course, it is too late.

I have about fifteen of H. Allen Smith's books; it's some consolation to know I can dip into them even though he's no longer with us. Having read him so much, I always felt I knew the man better than I actually did; so I'll probably miss him out of proportion to our actual relationship. I just wish the old boy had been granted the luck to escape off that goddam hated bald mountain in Texas before his time ran out.

New York
March 1978

William Brammer (as the writing world knew him; "Billie Lee" to old friends) was found dead of drug overdosage last month in Austin. He was forty-nine. Damn.

Novelist Bud Shrake tracked me to Barbara Blaine's Washington apartment to break the bleak news only hours after Brammer's body had been found. Shrake was truly shaken; I think he was stunned by my reaction: "Well, hell, Billie Lee had been looking for it a long time. I guess he finally found it."

I didn't mean to be as cold or uncaring as it probably sounded. The comment popped out because I wasn't in the slightest surprised by the bad news: Brammer had worked life mighty close to the horns for a long, long time. And I felt, too, a quick surge of irrational anger. But even as I recognized it as such, a part of me began yelling at my old friend's ghost: *Goddammit, Billie Lee, why'd you get yourself so screwed up you only left to the world a fraction of your talent?* That talent was considerable; *The Gay Place* has been in print for almost twenty years, a mark of its worth and durability.

When we were young Capitol Hill flunkies together, Billie Lee wrote *The Gay Place* on candy bars and hot Jell-O water swigged from a milk bottle; he claimed the strange combination gave him "energy rushes." He obviously found stronger fuels later on, though I am convinced that in those distant days (1958–61) Billie Lee was no dopehead. He seemed too interested in the human comedy, had too much of the sparkle of a lively witness in his eye, too keen an appreciation of the absurdities, to go that route. Perhaps, in the end, it was Brammer's unbridled sense of curiosity and his determination to sample life in the raw—*all* of life—that led him in his fatal direction.

I've long wondered if Brammer received too much praise too soon from the literary critics. *Something* threw him off—frightened him, changed him—and I suspect that was it. Critics raved about *The Gay Place*, hailing Brammer as the new Scott Fitzgerald. That Fitzgerald was Brammer's idol and inspiration probably heightened his fear.

I'll never forget the Sunday in 1961 when I telephoned Billie Lee in Texas to read him the rave review he had received in that day's *New York Times Book Review.* He listened with an occasional pleased chuckle and a few astonished gasps. When I had finished reading he said, "Oh, Jesus, now they'll be waiting to pin my ears back if I can't do it again."

Brammer never did it again. For six or eight years I was certain he would. In the summer of 1964, in Austin, I read perhaps 150 or 200 manuscript pages of his second novel, *Fustian Days*, and thought it bordered on the brilliant. I remember saying in hot excitement,

"Goddam, Billie Lee, you're gonna become our *Faulkner* down here!" Given similar praise I might have turned cartwheels, hugged strangers and bought drinks for the house. Billie Lee just looked rattled and changed the subject. He never finished *Fustian Days*. Nor did he finish a nonfiction book on Lyndon Johnson (his Capitol Hill employer, and the inspiration for the governor in *The Gay Place*) that he originally was enthusiastic about. On the basis of random pages Brammer permitted me to read, I thought he was on the way to a great book—something that might win a National Book Award, or the Pulitzer. But that book, too, petered out.*

When Billie Lee was writing *The Gay Place* I read it in typescript as he finished each chapter. It seemed to flow so easily, and Brammer appeared so lively and energetic, I expected a stream of books from him: a veritable river of literature. Perhaps that expectation led me to be grumpy with him, and excessively judgmental of him, in later years. When a friend once lamented Billie Lee's "unrealized potential" I found myself snapping, "Don't you realize that's a cop-out? Potential unrealized is potential unproven. The promise of a talent is only as legitimate as the talent makes it." I think, too, in my brain's back country, I secretly feared that I might lose all control of that discipline a writer must have—as Brammer had lost it—to even marginally survive in a tough racket. And so when I saw Billie Lee at his idle worst, I feared to be catching future glimpses of myself.

Had Brammer received a few critical pokes and a stomping or two, as usually happens with first novelists—except when they are ignored—might he then have been motivated to prove the bastards wrong and kept on working? No way to know. But I'll die convinced that Brammer's fear of future critical expectations made him reluctant, to the point of drying him up, to let go of subsequent prose until it had attained an impossible perfection. Certainly this was indicated in many letters Billie Lee wrote me. Typical was one dated August 23, 1968:

> This is not another of them pleas begging assistance, so you should immediately relax the scrotum; lend some ease to your

---

*Brammer was *not* the LBJ staffer who promised me a look at his journals and later recanted.

careworn sac. Which is not to deny the *need* for help, God wot: wise counsel or some new miracle drug or just maybe a plain un-prettified boot in the arse: any old damn gesture is welcome cur-rently. I just this week received by mail, presumably arranged by some sadist friend, the application and capability test from the Palmer Famous Writers School of Minneapolis—and I have not yet nerved myself to hoot at the fool thing and toss it in the wastebin. . . . Writing is just so murderously hard for me in re-cent years—unaccountably so—though my skull feels livelier than ever. . . .

Wasn't that a lovely piece by C—— in your mag [*Harper's*]? I hope he can keep it up, though lately his behavior is disturbingly reminiscent of mine own: i.e., getting hung-up with attempts at over-perfection, compounded by uptight-making realization that he is really on his own and has to by-god-effing-mother *produce* as full-time free-lance typewriter fella. Goddamn! Really pains me to recollect how much I once enjoyed—and gushed very nearly to a fault—writing down words on paper. Delicious as a really well-prepared-for scarf job. Better than exorbitant Viennese analysis. Very like earning $20,000 to $50,000 a year by playing some child's game, like baseball or beach-bugger movies. . . .

Brammer's letters often offered reasons why he found it impossi-ble to produce; while still writing *Fustian Days* he claimed to be too ignorant of too much; later, he said he knew too much to put it down simple. Looking back over his letters makes it apparent Billie Lee agonized privately much more than he let on publicly during those hoo-hawing, dope-and-drink whoop-de-dos indigenous to Austin. Sometimes, there, Brammer played the befuddled clown. Maybe it was his way of hiding the agony.

Oh, shit, this is depressing! Perhaps I should only "remember the good times," as Willie Nelson sings. Billie Lee Brammer was mighty good fun-and-games for a long time; a life or two ago we laughed together and dared to dream. Brammer taught me a thing or two; at a time when I most needed inspiration by example, he provided it. I'll always owe him that. And, no doubt, I'll miss the little cuss. Shrake said over the phone a day or so ago, "I expect to look up and see Brammer come scraping and shuffling through the door saying, 'Got any speed?' I just can't believe he's gone." Right. I'll probably catch myself searching the room for him at my next Austin party.

How to summarize? "Goodbye, Billie Lee" just doesn't seem ade-quate. Wherever he is now—if there *is* any place for the dead—I guess I hope they've got an inexhaustible supply of what Billie Lee used to call his "heart medicine," and that they pass it out—free— three times a day.

Washington
May 1984

Back in February one morning I reached for my top right-hand desk drawer, to extract another sheet of typing paper—a move I have made countless times—and, suddenly, was hopping around the room howling in pain but without knowing what the deuce had happened. Shooting hot rivers of lava ran up and down my right arm from wrist to shoulder; it felt as if the inside of my right arm was being ripped out by the bone while someone poured scalding water. Over the next few days this, or something very like it, happened again and again when I made sudden reaching movements. I began to think before I dared move, and then moved like some old man fearful of slipping on ice: tentatively, carefully, afraid. I had no way of knowing what particular motion would cause the searing pain to return—forward, sideways, upward, downward, back. Nor did I know where the pain might be most severe: lower arm, upper arm, entire arm, shoulder or even back muscles.

Of course, I would not consult a physician. Something of my old father had rubbed off: he had distrusted doctors from diagnosis to treatment to fee; I had seen him attempt to mend a minor bone break with a cow-chip-and-axle-grease poultice, and cut his own swollen carbuncles with a pocketknife sterilized over a fireplace flame. Though I eschewed such drastic self-treatment, I kept hoping I would wake one morning to find the pain had magically disappeared. That did not happen. Secretly, I was certain of a new form of galloping cancer and feared having it affirmed.

By the time I consulted an orthopedist—driven to him by a wife weary of being serenaded by all-night groanings—my arm was bent almost as if to fit a sling. I could not touch my right ear, reach my right rear pocket or comb my hair. I could hardly type; writing in longhand was excruciatingly painful and out of the question. Tests and X-rays revealed old scar tissue and calcium deposits resulting from long-ago injuries, but the mystery was how I had come down with "frozen shoulder" so suddenly and painfully.

I was inclined to blame the problem on having repeatedly tossed my small son in the air, though the orthopedist and his physical therapist doubted this. One of them said, "Have you been doing for long periods anything you were not accustomed to doing?" I denied it. Then it dawned that perhaps . . . "Well," I said, "this may sound silly, but for close to a year I've been writing six or eight hours in longhand most days. And I never had done that before. When I started writing song lyrics for a new musical—I don't know, I just got in the habit of writing almost everything in longhand."

The orthopedist said, "Show me how you write." I gripped a pencil with great difficulty, flinching and whimpering as shooting pains ran up and down the arm, in exhibiting my form. "That's it!" the bone man shouted. "Look at you! You write with your entire arm in the air! You don't support your arm on the desk from your wrist upward. Your unnatural writing stance, aggravating all the old injuries, accounts for your condition." He seemed as pleased as if he had discovered a new miracle salve.

Three times per week, now, the therapist bends my arm into inventive Nazi-torture positions while I thresh, scream and curse; he also treats my back muscles with stinging jolts of electricity; thrice daily I must ice the arm and perform painful exercises at home. I am told this probably will go on for months, perhaps a year or longer, as I only had 11 percent of normal motion potential by the time I tardily sought professional help. Bet your sweet ass I won't write anymore in longhand! I've heard of people crippling themselves in fights, sports, wrecks and by falling downstairs—indeed, have done all that myself—but to do it by writing seems ridiculous. It was an occupational hazard I never considered in choosing my craft.

Washington
January 1984

Yesterday—New Year's Day—I became fifty-five years old. Damn. Fifty-five! Only a few blinks ago I was the young terror of Texas, laughing or raging from football field to oil patch to barroom to newspaper office. Certain I would live forever—or, at least, somehow never grow old. Of course, the young never consider growing old. A few years ago when my eldest son, Brad, was giving me a bunch of the usual teenage crap, I slammed him against a wall and shouted, "You think you'll always be young and slim and blond and the world will ease your passage. Look at *me*, goddammit! *I* used to be young and slim and blond!" The look of horror in the kid's eyes, as he saw what he might one day become, told that I had taught him a cruel lesson earlier than he was ready.

Like most contemporaries with whom I have discussed it, I began to doubt my eternal youth with my fortieth birthday. I became keenly aware of mortality at forty-one, on the death of my father; Rosemarie's death fifteen months later heightened that perception. One began to wonder how many good, productive years might be left and to admit that one's ranking in American letters never would reach that high rung on the ladder one had foolishly presumed reserved for one in a more innocent time. Once the first pain passes there is a certain restful ease in admitting one isn't destined to set the world aflame, but may only set the occasional random brushfire. There are moments of unintended comedy in one's assessments of life and mortality. Drinking with Bud Shrake about six years ago I said, in the utmost seriousness, that I was ready to die—just as soon as I had accomplished two more Broadway hits and a half-dozen books I wanted to write. Shrake is still laughing.

I don't feel old except when I dwell on the aging process. Such as around each new birthday. Then I recall that sixty years has always defined "old" in my mind, and now I rapidly approach that dreaded milestone. I guess I'll just have to push my definition back another decade or more. I have arranged my life with such thoughtful precision that I'll be 71 when my youngest baby, Blaine, is 17; I simply can't afford to get drooling old before dealing with the expected teenage hurly-burly.

My one large dread is the possibility of senility—sitting around slobbering and hazy and wondering who or where I am while the world passes by. Or losing such writing talents as I have years before Gabriel blows his horn with my name in mind. I would much prefer—and I guess we all would—to be suddenly seized and throttled and borne away quickly.

I suppose like many aging coots I have occasionally wondered whether I will make what Hemingway called "a good death"; I don't know what that is, exactly, but I hope to do it when the time comes. I assume it means not to go out whining and afraid. As a writer maybe I hope to say something memorable that might land me in

Bartlett's *Familiar Quotations* or serve as an honorable epitaph. Maybe I'll have the luck to utter from my deathbed such poetic last words as O. Henry issued: "Turn up the light. I don't want to go home in the dark." Or to respond with the wit and tart independence of Henry David Thoreau, who, asked by an unctuous parson if he had made his peace with God, said, "I was not aware that we had quarreled." Or perhaps issue sly, self-serving poetry as did the Irish writer Torlogh O'Carolan in requesting a final cup of whiskey: "It would be hard if two such friends should part at least without kissing." Or retain such a sense of humor as to deliver the hope expressed by Heinrich Heine, who wished that his wife might soon remarry "so at least one man will live to regret my death."

But, I don't know, the way the absurdities seem to follow me through life like barking dogs, I'll probably have the ill luck to declare something as inelegant as did the poet Walt Whitman: "Lift me up, Horace, I've got to shit."

Oh, well. Birthdays come but once a year. In the spirit of Scarlett O'Hara, let us consider that tomorrow will be better.

Part Three

BITS & PIECES

A DEFINITION

The pieces to follow, for the most part, are not so much straight journalistic pieces—"reporting" pieces—as they are "writer's" pieces. They are meant to entertain and evoke moods more than to issue news bulletins. I have done my share of hard reporting, but you will not find that work here.

When I was a rookie writer striving to get established, I roamed the nation like a hobo to chase down people and events necessary to my yarns; this is the lot of most writers breaking in as free-lances. I now may exercise my veteran's right to stick closer to home, working on books and plays. Consequently, I turn down most editors who ask me to travel extensively or profile this or that celebrity or study institutions at close range. I've done all that; now it is someone else's turn.

The following stories have two common virtues: (1) I was able to write them out of memory and personal experiences and (2) they were meant to be fun for the writer as well as for the reader.

A Matter
of Style

Jim Morgan, chief articles editor at Playboy, *called to ask me to do a piece on "personal style." He said three other writers—William F. Buckley, Jr., D. Keith Mano and Leonard Michaels—would also be asked; our pieces would appear in the issue of January 1983. My problem was that I couldn't immediately identify my "personal style." Wasn't even sure I had one. For years, however, I had wanted to write an article about a financial misadventure in which I had victimized myself, and others, but had no "peg" to hang it on. So I used Morgan's invitation to write something I long had wanted to sell, working only vaguely within his stated rules. The writer must be enterprising in the marketplace.*

My style is to get it when you can, where you can, and don't trouble to look over your shoulder with a lot of fuddy-duddy moralizing in mind. I excuse this by believing that should you permit yourself to grow up poorer than orphanshit, then you naturally will be tempted by riches early on.

Never mind I was raised a raggedy-ass yellow-dog Democrat; I wanted to be what we in Texas called "a bidnessman." Them suckers ran thangs, I observed, and hardly ever got caught at sweat work. A fascinating combination.

I did not, you understand, thirst to be the kind of mom 'n' pop store bidnessman who kept dusty ledgers and faithful hours. No, I pined to be a get-rich-quick man. I eventually discovered it was my ambition and my style to be an entrepreneur.

It took me awhile to get the hang of it. My first venture, in the fourth grade of the Putnam public school, was to write everybody's English themes for five cents the pop. Unfortunately, I used the same handwriting, tablet paper and ink color often enough to arouse official suspicions. I didn't mind the shame so much; what hurt was having to refund all those nickels.

Next I sold autographs of the famous. Business, admittedly, was slow while I depended on the signatures of local luminaries: county commissioners, preachers and such. There was a dramatic upsurge in the summer of 1939, when I made available the autographs of Tom Mix, Tarzan and FDR. When I offered the signature of Jesus Christ at fifteen cents each or two for a quarter, I suddenly found myself back in the restitution business.

The problem, I decided as I grew and matured, was that I had not thought big. In 1957, I began to think big. Real big. Quite by accident, I stumbled onto a surefire way to make $500,000 with only a minimum of heavy lifting required.

I was then working on Capitol Hill for a Texas congressman who would just as lief I not report his name. One day, I noticed a newspaper item beckoning me to riches: lumber being used to construct the inauguration platform from which President Dwight D. Eisenhower was scheduled to take his oath for a second term would be sold after the festivities to the highest bidder. Surely, such historic wood could be put to profitable use.

I approached a friend, Dr. Glen P. Wilson, an employee of Senator Lyndon B. Johnson; we got our thinking caps on. Wilson had been selected as my potential partner because he, too, thirsted to be an entrepreneur. Never mind he had failed as the inventor of a three-dimensional gameboard that boasted several clear-glass platforms permitting players to compete simultaneously at chess, Chinese checkers, mah-jongg, dominoes and, maybe, pole vaulting. Perhaps the gameboard failed because it was bigger than an oil derrick or required too much concentration for the TV generation to handle; at any rate, his large concept qualified Dr. Wilson as an Olympian thinker. I wanted him on my side in the Eisenhower-plaque bidness.

No way the Eisenhower-plaque enterprise could fail, Ike having amassed 35,000,000 votes in his second trouncing of Adlai Stevenson and being the most beloved American since Lassie. We hired a fellow with a slide rule, who calculated we could cut 550,000 little square plaques from the historic wood. Our calculations were that by selling them for $1 each, we would easily clear a cool half million—probably more. After all, our only expenses would be the lumber itself, a couple of electric saws, a gold-stamping machine, small cardboard boxes in which to ship the historic plaques, a bit of newspaper advertising, postage and rental on P.O. Box 1956, Washington, D.C. We budgeted not a dime for labor costs, figuring we would do the dirty work ourselves until the first 100,000 plaques had been sold. Then, perhaps, we might hire disadvantaged friends and illegal aliens at hourly rates so cheap the costs would be laughable to a couple of rich swells.

We successfully bid for the lumber at a cost of only $3,200 plus the interest on our bank loan. We bought two electric saws, real beauties, for a total of $1,400, and a gold-stamping machine, which would imprint in spiffy gold letters on the wooden blocks this impressive legend:

THIS HISTORIC PLAQUE IS CERTIFIED
AS PART OF THE OFFICIAL INAUGURAL
PLATFORM OF DWIGHT D. EISENHOWER,
35TH PRESIDENT OF THE UNITED STATES,
FROM WHICH HE TOOK HIS OATH OF OFFICE
ON JANUARY 21, 1957.

The gold-stamping machine was a steal at a mere $800 and change.

Dr. Wilson approached the *New York Times*, the *Des Moines Register*, the *Chicago Tribune* and many other newspapers, as well as, cleverly, the GOP national house organ. The cost of the resulting ads—tiny, and positioned at the back near the patent-medicine and truss ads in most cases—totaled a mere $4,717.36. The dignified *New York Times*, however, insisted on official assurances that our wood blocks were pedigreed. We got a letter from the Architect of the Capitol appropriately pedigreeing them. Then we had a new inspiration: perhaps we should supply our customers with small individual certificates signed by the Architect of the Capitol. These miniature numbers, on old parchment to lend a touch of class, were fashioned for only five cents each. Unfortunately, the aggregate sum for the first 20,000—we would have the remainder delivered later, from profits—strained us an additional $1,200.

We found it necessary to return to the bankers. Our total cost had now exceeded $12,000—not counting the postage we'd need. Our original banker, faced with our burgeoning capital requirements, suddenly developed an ongoing lack of enthusiasm. Through relatives and friends, we raised another $5,000. And more lectures and horselaughs than we found seemly.

Eventually, our raw lumber was delivered to the basements of our respective homes in Alexandria, Virginia. We sighed and wrote off the resulting window breakage and wall damage to future profits.

For days, King / Wilson, their wives and a few believing friends sawed, stamped and certified historic wood around the clock. As the appearance of our first ads approached, our main worry was that the 15,000 Eisenhower plaques we had readied would not suffice to meet the initial flood of orders. We hired a lawyer. For a mere $500, he pledged to stall malcontents until income exceeded outgo and we could fill orders in a timely fashion.

Came the marvelous Sunday our ads appeared across the width and breadth of the United States. Dr. Wilson and your present hero made a midnight raid on P.O. Box 1956, Washington, D.C. Zilch. *Nada*. Nothing. That was okay. We hadn't really expected to find orders that early; our visit to the P.O. was more of a dry run, for practice, like you'd conduct just before robbing a bank.

Monday's postal run proved exactly as productive as Sunday's. Well, what the hell; the mails required awhile. Tuesday morning, we discovered nine letters ordering eleven plaques. We hugged and danced and went home on our lunch hours to produce another few dozen of our hot item before the deluge. And a deluge there would be, as our first orders proved: we had counted on only *one* plaque per order and commerce was averaging better than that. We discussed whether, once our historic wood played out, we dared send common wood and just claim it to be historic. "No," Dr. Wilson said, "that would be dishonest." I wasn't bothered by that distinction so much as I feared indictment for mail fraud.

Tuesday afternoon brought a dozen letters ordering as many historic plaques. "These are only the airmail orders," we assured each other. "Wait until the regular-postage letters and postcards start coming in!" We returned, perhaps a bit apprehensively, to our saws and stamping machine.

A week later, we had sold forty-nine Historic Eisenhower Plaques. At $1 the item. Wives began to wail; friends quit volunteering their services on our assembly line; bills began to visit P.O. Box 1956, Washington, D.C.

I telephoned Jim Hagerty, Ike's press secretary, intending to say that while I admittedly was a registered Democrat, I was big enough to rise above petty partisanship: how about Ike's plugging our entrepreneurship at his next press conference, waxing eloquent about this fine example of free enterprise, and maybe letting our P.O. box number go public, or some such? Alas, the nameless secretary to the presidential press secretary coolly proclaimed that Mr. Hagerty was far too busy to be bothered and that the White House never, but *never*, endorsed commercializations of the Highest Office in the Land. *Click.*

A month later, having sold a grand total of seventy-six plaques, we began the painful process of liquidation. You'd be surprised how many people had no use for a perfectly good gold-stamping machine. Our ads in trade journals brought a single postcard, from a man in North Carolina. We hastened to call him.

"He don't do no talkin' on the phone," a woman snapped before hanging up.

We called back to beg. The lady explained that her husband didn't do no talkin' on the phone because he was "deef and dumb." We told of her husband's interest in buying our spiffy gold-stamping machine. She laughed and laughed: "He ain't got thutty-five cents. Fact is, he's a ward of the state."

"So are we," I said glumly to my partner.

We sold our marvelous gold-stamping machine at junk weight and unloaded the twin electric saws for one-third of what we had in them.

Davis Carter, a colleague on Capitol Hill, paid $300 for the unsawed remainder of our historic Ike wood and used it to build a backyard fence. He added insult to injury by adorning it with a number of those accursed plaques.

A few nights later, I hosted a to-hell-with-it party in my own backyard. Highlight of the evening was the ceremonial public burning of 15,000 little wooden plaques, give or take a few dozen. The Alexandria Fire Department came to the party, without invitation, to douse the fire. The fire marshal handed me a $50 summons for unauthorized trash burning. He was certainly right about what I had burned.

The life-style of the entrepreneur is difficult to give up, however. I always look for the main chance. When the editors of *Playboy* asked me to write this piece, I said I would do it for $1 per word.

Per word. Per word. Per word. Per word. Per word. Per word.

Mailer and Styron at Harvard

Following my Nieman season at Harvard, in 1969–70, I wrote of my experiences there for Harper's. *Editor Willie Morris rejected the section appearing here, saying it didn't mesh with the remainder of my piece. Perhaps it didn't. At the time, however, I suspected that Morris feared the piece might offend either or both of the prominent writers, who not only were his personal friends but sometimes wrote for his magazine. Writers learn to seek backup markets should their primary market fail, so I contacted Frank Rich and sold this article to the* Harvard Crimson. *I include it in this book on writing and writers because it judges two of our best wordmen as to personal styles and writing styles.*

William Styron's *Lie Down in Darkness*, published in 1951, was probably the one book that hardened my vague resolve to one day try my own writing hand; I wanted to make a book even half as good as that one. In a time when my household bills were not easily met I thought nothing of buying multiple copies of Styron's first novel, thrusting them on friends with instructions to immediately read.

Norman Mailer's early novels made their own strong impressions; unlike the critics, I was even more impressed with *The Deer Park* than with *The Naked and the Dead*. I soon came to consider Mailer the American contemporary who best understood our society as it marched crazily through the present toward that outer rim falling away to fiery voids; he foresaw bits and pieces of tomorrow more readily than others.

Fate would in time provide introductions to my contemporary literary idols, and I would be properly awed: imagine an apprentice lawyer in the presence of Darrow.

A comparison of the two, as men and artists, was inevitable. If Styron's writing was prettier, sang purer notes, then Mailer's had—for me—more of blood and tissue in it. Mailer's work was barren of the grasses of childhood, while Styron poked in the dusts of his youthful past until one sensed that it haunted him in the night, blew grain by grain through his soul; sandpapered it. Here, I identified with Styron.

Mailer wrote of sex in terms of a fifteen-round fight in which red peppers were joyously thumbed into the other fellow's eyes: he saw fucking as confrontation. Styron wrote of how sweet and good it had been before the bloom faded, preaching that the bloom would always—surely, definitely—fade. "In all of Styron's work there is an unwillingness to censure aspiring, troubled, and weak humanity," the critic Maxwell Geismar wrote, and then went on to declare that "Mailer has no confidence in human nature."

Yet it was Mailer who in a sense looked west, looked ahead, looked out to the horizon at the fiery outer rim; it was important to see who might fall off, and for what mad or ironic reasons, and in what *style* they would go over: screaming the sissy begging of pardons, or spitting and pissing into the flames? Styron looked always south, looked back to where the land was burned out or spiritually polluted or lying fallow, and empty souls stood whispering their personal regrets; for him it was more important to consider what might have been than what might yet be.

Mailer might lead you to witness an electrocution where God in a moment of fine jest caused the power lines to fail; Styron would not once think of God permitting a botched execution, though he might include Him among the later mourners at the grave: probably He would be solemn and sigh a lot.

Mailer in middle age continued to carry himself like a retired welterweight who might be thinking of a comeback, though he now pushed a bank clerk's belly. Age had performed interesting surgery on his face: cast him as a cabdriver, Chicago alderman, Irish cop, dart champion in a workingman's pub, sly old convict; his face, like that of the late Senator Everett Dirksen, told something of where he had been. Styron's face was a gentle mystery. Smooth for its forty-five years, of late it had come to appear a touch soft—though so unblemished one wondered if his secret picture, like Dorian Gray's, bled and festered somewhere in the attic. There was something of the Frat

Rat about Styron: he would come back to reunions. Mailer might have been expelled from school, and then come back to make reunion dark mischief.

Deep in their eyes, Mailer was suspiciously aggressive where Styron was aggressively suspicious. Mailer hoped to get in the first blow; Styron hoped you would not steal his pocketbook. In private moods, one imagined, Mailer threw hot coals of rage where Styron brooded and sulked. One saw Styron in repose turning inward into himself, Mailer turning outward against the world; the first was sad and the second was angry.

Mailer's easy verbal facility made listening to him hard work: required a mental mountain goat to jump from this theoretical jut to that craggy intellectual ledge. Styron was easier listening: he told you anecdotes in the familiar idioms of home, and you could rest during his pauses for verbal regroupings: he had the virtue of relaxing you more—though when you reached your bed it likely would be Mailer's words that nagged and clanged and rumbled hotly through your mind. Had heaven planted them as religious saplings, Mailer might have grown into Elmer Gantry or have taken a crack at faith-healing. Styron in his ecclesiastical maturity might have become . . . an Episcopal bishop?

At the time I bore small personal grudges against both of these old heroes. Mailer, at a Manhattan party in his honor promoting *The Armies of the Night*, when we were both silly drunk, smote me with a kidney punch—an unexpected punch—which may have been intended as some friendly he-man test, but it hurt like hell and angered me; hot words were exchanged. Styron, having written a private letter in praise of my first novel, hit me with a negative response when I inquired whether his endorsement might be converted to promotional purposes. I no longer pretend that Styron's blow was not the more painful. Still, I thought enough of both as artists and men (and owed them enough for their early inspirations) that I was eager to attract them to Harvard to speak to our Nieman group. I labored long to assure that all would go well for them in Cambridge. Neither enjoyed their best experiences.

A few days before his Harvard appearance, Styron telephoned to relate a disturbing experience at Yale: eighty-odd blacks had greeted his talk there with invectives and wild hooting, a thing he had grown to expect since publication of his controversial *The Confessions of*

Nat Turner. Black attacks on that book were painful in the extreme to Styron, who had given it seven years in the writing (and twenty years of thought) only to be accused of classic black emasculation. I assured him that such would not be the Harvard case: the audience would be racially mixed, and while he might anticipate challenges, I felt that a stimulating balance would prevail. He would have friends present as well as foes.

"Are the blacks gonna picket me?" Styron asked on arrival. My God, I hoped not. "They picket me everywhere I go," he said a bit wearily. We passed a pleasant afternoon doing equal damage to a fifth of Scotch and our respective livers. But we had no more than finished our Faculty Club ice cream when the blacks attacked. Whites at first sat in silence. Styron, more articulate on paper than from the podium, may have hurt his cause in attempting reconciliations where he might have more profitably fought. Drinks flowed, became a torrent chipping away at our brains. Voices rose. Temperatures climbed. Whites galloped to Styron's defense. Blacks increased the tempo. Instant polarizations. Curses. Shaking fists. Insanity: the black man most critical of Styron's permitting Nat Turner to secretly desire a white woman was himself escorting a stunning blonde. As moderator, I attempted to be "objective" or "fair" and became, instead, an equivocating jellyfish—and soon lost control of the crowd.

I sat there in the Faculty Club among hisses and boos, seeing in one room those tragic emotional and cultural divisions polarizing the races all across America. I had long been familiar with poisons boiling in white working-class hearts and among so-called Middle Americans, that "silent majority" so dear to the heart of Richard Nixon. I was no stranger to acid chemicals fizzing in a high percentage of blacks. At Harvard, I had learned, precious little rapport existed between black and white students. Black students insisted on standing alone, on doing their own thing, on rejecting friendly and well-meant gestures. There was something absolutely tribal about it.

White radicals thought blacks narrow in their political or sociological interests—though, out of an uptight if enlightened "white guilt," they said little on the record. More traditional whites complained that racism had taken on a darker hue. Now, supposedly sophisticated and erudite adults, hoo-hawing and blathering in the Faculty Club, made it appear that no racial reason existed anywhere in the land. My God, was Harvard no better than Mississippi? Were blacks no more tolerant than whites? In his helpless despondency, the failed moderator drank himself into a calamitous state.

At a private party, around three o'clock in the morning, Styron experienced a sudden physical collapse. Perhaps this was due to his history of high blood pressure, agitated by all-day tensions and whiskey; it may be that our guest also had stood in close proximity to clouds of Mexican boo-smoke. Whatever the causes, Styron sincerely believed himself to be dying. He declared himself able to see "the other shore," thought himself a visitor to some strange nether world and, in general, carried on like a Baptist fanatic. Rescue squads and cops came clanging and banging stretchers and doors and asking embarrassing questions. Some of the larger Cambridge-Harvard names, writers and faculty members, were attracted to the scene. It was one hell of a time to be dizzy and euphoric and bone-tired and crocked and carrying a pocketful of dope. I sat through the night at a Cambridge hospital where Styron was under cautionary observation, feeling worse than my guest *possibly* could have felt, thinking that I had Mailer, bless me, to go.

A party-crashing shaggy beard from the Harvard graduate school greeted Mailer with demands that he account for some vague, if unforgivable, "sellout"—publishing in *Life*, or something equally dreadful. Mailer awarded him a nickel's worth of evil-eye and walked away. An aggressive Nieman wife monopolized our guest during the cocktail hour, standing pelvis to pelvis with him, while everyone else stood apart to gape and shit-kick like the early Jimmy Stewart. A voice with liquor and jealousy said too loudly that Mailer was an overrated bastard. The beginnings of bad vibrations tingled my spine, and I wondered whether Styron's doctor might be on call if needed.

Mailer was surely the best actor to pay us court, the most practiced at thinking on his feet with a glass in his hand. Now and again he paused, sipping the fine yeasts of his bourbon, to regard us over a glass rim while his eyes squinted as if to flirt with a wink. Oratorically, however, he was off his game. A few weeks earlier he had read to an appreciative Harvard audience in Sanders Theatre from his new manuscript, *Of a Fire on the Moon*, scooping up questions as smoothly as a sure-handed shortstop, turning a few hecklers' hot line drives into quick double plays. This night, however, Mailer was less the athlete. He took a fighter's stance, to be sure, his left—or nondrinking—hand shooting out sharp jabs, a shoulder thrust forward, the curly graying head pulled in protectively as a close neighbor to the shoulders. He hooked the *New York Times* for its general timidity and unimaginative misinterpretations; he bloodied technology's nose for its spiritless contributions to the quality of life; he pilloried ideological liberals as impractical fools before abandoning them in a neutral corner. These were old foes he had knocked kicking on his better outings, though on this night he could not seem to care enough to expend wind in their pursuit or destruction.

Mailer had been exposed to the oft-careless ministrations of the press since fame had caught up with him in his early twenties, on publication of *The Naked and the Dead*. A few years later he would write, in *The Deer Park*, "A newspaperman is obsessed with finding the facts in order to tell a lie, and a novelist is a galley-slave to his imagination so he can look for truth." Now, at Harvard, Mailer decided to concentrate his attack on his hosts—Nieman Fellows for the most part on leave from newspapers. He began, disarmingly enough, by saying that as sorry as newspapers are, they are in some cases improved over their pasts. Then he declared that the functions of most reporters could easily be accomplished by machines, and ultimately improved the thought by calling us whores. This assault producing no return blows (and even some agreeable chuckles), Mailer lost his fighting balance. He had grown accustomed to audiences that either wildly cheered him or shouted that he could go fuck himself. Now, he appeared nonplussed by an audience regarding him in some dull Rotarian lumpishness: we had heard, at this point, enough speeches each week to properly nominate a presidential candidate, and so probably would not have been inspired had Moses appeared to reveal an Eleventh Commandment.

When our guest threw it open to questions we lobbed up fat, soft and noncurving batting-practice offerings. Mailer, reading them as clever change-ups, lunged, missed or popped to the infield. "What the hell," he finally complained, "I thought you Nieman Fellows were supposed to be tough." One was reminded of a .300 hitter who, going 0-for-5 on a horsecollar night, charges the opposing pitcher with dealing in junk stuff: Mailer wanted a high, hard one he could rip over the Nieman fence. Nobody threw it.

At a private bash afterward, Mailer originally could not relax. Still coveting his base hit, he called surviving Niemans around his feet to attempt his speech anew. By now, however, forty-odd children of the grape clamored and whooped in their private exertions. The Nieman Class Lover had eyes for a stunning visitor from the Mailer entourage, the Class Drunk stood in the kitchen loudly misquoting *Invictus*, the angry wife of a magazine editor complained that we had chuckled rather than fought when Mailer called us whores. Our guest soon abandoned oratorical attempts for hard drinking and bouts of thumb wrestling which did not, I fervently thank the powers, cause him to physically collapse.

Only footnotes remain to tidy up the record. Half of official Cambridge became angry over not being invited to my private bashes for Styron and Mailer: you must understand that in Cambridge parties are serious matters indeed. False stories made the rounds that I had poisoned Styron through dropping LSD into his Scotch; another popular lie ran that Mailer had engaged in predawn fisticuffs with this one or that. The crowning blow came when I asked a young *Crimson* editor, Scott Jacobs, for his impression of my two literary heroes. He stabbed them—and me, and our over-forty generation—with this brutal dirk: "Well, I never thought they'd seem so goddam *old!*"

We Ain't Trash No More!

I was drinking on Damyankee turf in the summer of '76 with an unreconstructed Rebel, Geoffrey Norman—an Alabama boy—when he asked me to write this piece. Then an editor at Esquire, *Brother Norman was celebrating Jimmy Carter's attaining the Democratic presidential nomination. After three dozen boozy Rebel yells he leaned across the table and said, "King, go write me a piece tellin' the Damyankees how we ain't takin' no more of their bullshid now that Jimmy Carter's rose up." For fear of losing a handsome fee, I didn't dare tell the editor that I had campaigned for Congressman Mo Udall against Mr. Carter in numerous state primaries; I just went home, sobered up and wrote the piece in two days. It was published the same month Carter oh-so-narrowly defeated President Gerald Ford. Had Ford won, then* Esquire, *Geoffrey Norman and yours truly would have had egg on our faces; sometimes writers must take risks. If permitted a small brag, I'd claim this piece proved to be pretty prophetic as to how Carter might conduct himself as President and what might happen, politically, as a result.*

The ancient vow of the South to rise again was fulfilled at that moment in Jimmy Carter's convention acceptance speech when he indicated his heart harbored a special love for all people, including—in particular—"the *Eye*-talians."

Wellsir, you just can't imagine what that familiar inflection meant to hearts bred and born in Dixie. Ol' Southern Boys around the world, recognizing the nuances and shadings of home, lurched to their collective feet, spilling right-smart amounts of bourbon and branch water over the rims of their gold goblets or jelly glasses, and with wet eyes huskily proclaimed: "We ain't *trash* no more."

Trash. That's what you Damyankee Peckerwoods been treating us like from the minute y'all won The War, just because we fired on Fort Sumter before remembering we didn't own any ball-bearing factories. You've laughed at those of us from the boll-weevil-and-pellagra belt, and mimicked us, and heaped indignities on us to include usury, occupation troops, federal marshals, and the special slander that we're born pink-eyed and don't grow decent chins because too often our mamas and daddies proved to be more than kissing cousins. You've called us everything but ladies and gentlemen: hillbillies, lintheads, woolhatters, rednecks. You've made no distinctions between those of us who produce clear fruit-jar whiskey or pale idiot children and those of us who've went to Harvard. Let us go off in a corner to have a little talk with Jesus, and you suspect us of chunking snakes, catching fevers and talking in tongues. The only time y'all have adopted or approved of one of us was when you suspected he might be finking on the rest of us—as with Faulkner or Erskine Caldwell.

When Willie Morris (who got to be a Rhodes Scholar and editor-in-chief of *Harper's* magazine) met the Yankee poet Robert Frost and belched it up that he came from Mississippi, Frost regally volunteered, "Hell, that's the worst state in the Union." Morris countered by saying, "Well, we've turned out some mighty good writers." Frost sniffed and said, "Can't anybody down there read them, can they?"

Or take the way y'all treated poor ol' Lyndon Johnson. Maybe he *did* hoo-haw right much and ate too much barbercue sauce and tugged up his shirt to show his belly scar after his operation, but hellfire, if he'd been from anywhere but Down Home then y'all would of stopped at calling him an eccentric. Never mind that Johnson was quick-minded, more complex and Machiavellian than the vast majority of his detractors, and spent most of his life in Washington at the center of power. No, he was an accidental President from the Texas boondocks who'd had the bad luck to succeed Prince Charming and so you equated him with hog callers and found him common as pig tracks.

Y'all Damyankees make one-way judgments, and we're about half tired of it. When *we* go against the grain, then the sky should fall on us and survivors should be skinned alive or cut up for fish bait. When *you* act equally asinine, then it seems like the cat gets your tongues and there's a conspiracy to look away from what's small and mean and tacky in you. Do you good Boston folk—who once sold slaves on

Boston Common—wanta step over here in the pea patch and talk to me about Louisa Day Hicks and the violence heaped on your kids while they were being bused to school? Naw, I expect you'd rather talk about George Wallace or busing violence in South Carolina a decade ago. Come over here and tell me about Bull Connor's police dogs and fire hoses in Birmingham, so I'll have a chance to drop it on you about the many race riots of Detroit City or the po-leece riots in Chicago. The sorry fact is that we've *all* been white racists, and you deserve near 'bout as much of the tarnished trophy as we sons of Dixie.

You a ill-mannered bunch, too. Eastern Seaboard hostesses of my acquaintance have blushed in mortification during seated dinner parties while I eschewed artichokes, various raw fishes, trick lettuces, suspect sauces and other outright inedibles. One, a *former* lover— bet your sweet ass—routinely announced at the beginning of each new culinary embarrassment, "Oh, *he* won't eat anything unless you can place it between two slices of bread and assure him it contains enough grease to run down to his elbow." "He" would sit there growing fire in his gut while everybody smiled as if "he" had seven toes on one foot and only three on the other, and probably couldn't count 'em proper on either one, or they edged away as if maybe "he" had a bad case of bugs and ticks. And then they wondered—after all their condescending snickers—why "he" had so much Southern Violence jangling in his blood that about the eighty-third time around "he" turned over the dinner table and poured expensive wine over the wreckage and its deserving victims. A gentleman to the core, however, "he" made nary a public judgment when his Yankee lady failed the tests of such basic staples as turnip-green pie, fried rattlesnake, or possum-and-taters. Y'all're just such *arbitrary* muthas.

We've tried real hard, now, not to get mad. Given our druthers, we've long preferred to get even. Now that ol' Jimmy Cah-tah's got it and gone with it, lemme drop a little something in y'all's ears: we're a heap more likely to reopen Andersonville prison than the Brooklyn Navy Yard. How you like *them* peanuts, good buddies?

Y'all need to understand that Jimmy Carter himself not only ain't trash no more, he never was. Nosir. Jimmy, he warn't even tacky. Maybe Daddy Carter had a little Snopes sloshing in him, but Miz Lillian, now, comes from good stock. She never let Jimmy forget his obligation to the better parts of his blood. Miz Lillian taught Jimmy such little poetry as he'd need to skim by and to excel at all things: to be that self-starting, go-getting, bright-smiling, well-rounded young man the townsfolk would owe obligatory tips of the communal hat. Miz Lillian put it in her most promising son that minor earthquakes should occur wherever he stepped, and that's why he could stand out there in front of the factory gates up in New Hampshire—where nobody knew his name, and gave him no more chance than a redbug swimming in kerosene—and say with full confidence, "I don't intend to lose." Daddy Carter, meanwhile, taught Jimmy to keep ledgers and the help in line. Yessir, Jimmy was raised real proud.

I near 'bout rolled off the bed laughing when this affluent limousine liberal New York lady (who learned 90 percent of what she knows of the South from a Rod Steiger movie [*In the Heat of the Night*] and picked up the other 10 percent in the Houston Intercontinental Airport while awaiting her flight to Cancún) asked whether I had been raised "as poor as Jimmy Carter."

I said, "Shee-eee-ii-t, honeybunch! Jimmy Cah-tah warn't never pore! Likely Jimmy carried *lightbread* to school. I doubt his ol' daddy kept hound dawgs. And if he did, he didn't let 'em run loose in the yard or feed 'em on table scraps. I bet when the Cah-tahs killed hawgs—*if* they did—they gave the headcheese to the niggahs and didn't even render the guts down for lard. Miz Lillian, now, she didn't no more make lye soap in a ol' black washpot than she scrubbed Jimmy's clothes on the rub board."

My Yankee lady's face went blank.

I said, "I bet two dollars and a dime Jimmy's folks never had a ol' rusty Buick propped up on Co'-Cola crates in the front yard, and that no Cah-tah ever drove the school bus or picked up pecans on the halves. They didn't whitewash old tires and half-bury 'em in the yard and then plant zinnias in the middle. Likely they grew *grass* in the front yard, 'stead of them sweeping it down with brooms on Saturdays. And for all his being a big 'born-again' Christian, I expect ol' Jimmy never ate off an oilcloth depicting the Last Supper in twenty-four stunning colors or owned a seventeen-inch Statue of Jesus Christ that glowed in the dark."

As clear as I had made it, the Yankee lady continued to wear her look of bewilderment. I tried again: "Jimmy didn't study no pit-bull-dog fighting. He didn't use a ten-gallon lard bucket for an otterman or make hisself window curtains out of gunnysacks. His chairs warn't even cane-bottomed. Most likely Jimmy never once drunk out of a jelly glass or used a gourd for a water dipper. Jimmy's people didn't even keep a pet black snake in the house to eat mice and rats—hell, I doubt the Cah-tahs even needed a mousetrap. They was quality folk."

Yeah. Jimmy Carter is a hard-nosed businessman—agribiz king, entrepreneur—with a soul probably closer kin to that of the old-time plantation owner than to that of any fuzzy-minded social engineer. Jimmy holds no slaves, but he's controlled sharecroppers. If he's never outright operated the classic company store, the Carters long kept the next thing to it. If you wanted to buy something in Plains, odds are you went to a Carter. Jimmy owns about two thousand Georgia acres outright, even if they ain't on the right side of the George Washington Bridge. He don't plow his place with mules, either.

Jimmy can do his Tom Sawyer bit all he wants—tromping around barefoot while draining fishponds for the cameras; playing sandlot softball for CBS News; recalling all the wonderful little pickaninnies he played with in childhood—but don't forget, back of all that Country Boy stuff, his family maintained its own tennis courts. You might remember, too, that Jimmy—in keeping with a genteel Southern tradition—went off to Annapolis to become one of those elitist officers ruling over the U.S. Navy, the most social and snobbish of the military services. Nosir, you won't find no tattoos on Jimmy and likely he didn't mail any gaudy SWEETHEART pillows home to Rosalynn from midshipman's school. Still, y'all gonna treat him like a peckerwood.

Jimmy Carter has proved he's smart and tough; I also suspect he's about half mean. This conviction is based on more than the observation that his mouth often smiles when his eyes do not. He's a "born-againer," an evangelical. You can shake every goober plant and magnolia bush between here and Stone Mountain without finding a group more wedded to its absolutes or less tolerant of dissent. Jimmy may prattle on about love and Jesus, and believe it, but at the bottom of that soft spiritual goop is a bedrock conviction that the vengeful Old Testament God, extracting eyes for eyes and teeth for teeth, is what makes the mule plow.

It may be all right for an idealistic young Jehovah to play a bit loosely with the loaves and fishes among the hungry multitude, so long as he understands that the Greater Good will one day require him to wear a crown of thorns, drink vinegar and hang by his bloody hands until his ghost is gone. Ain't no free lunch, you see. You gotta pay the piper for all dances. Jimmy Carter's creed teaches that what you sophisticated Damyankees often call fun is the sort of sinful mischief certain to be taxed—even to the extent of eternal roastings. Maybe that's why you'll never discover more than a nickel's worth of humor in Jimmy. Fun is for the frivolous, and Jimmy sees the world as a hard and serious place. Man was put here to suffer, to atone, to repent, to confess, to surrender, to witness, or else to bake until well done.

Jimmy likely won't keep any paltry little ol' enemies list as did Nixon: his assumption is that *everybody* not for him early was on the other side, and there are simply too many names to write 'em down and not enough paper. Jimmy's beholden to few, other than about a dozen ol' Georgia boys who came boiling out of the outback wearing their double-knit suits and trying not to feel sissy in feather cuts. Neither Jimmy nor his double-knit cadre will forget real quick.

Even after Jimmy won a few primaries up yonder in deep-freeze country, everybody presumed that in time the sunny-faced Georgia boy would be required to approach the old bulls of the Democratic party hat in hand. Hell, hadn't it always been that way? If you came from the South and wanted to build more than a birdhouse, you had to crawl on your knees to the New York moneymen; if you wanted to become much more than justice of the peace in Deep Gritsville, then you puckered up your lips and bought a bus ticket North and some mouthwash for afterward. So they sat back and waited for Carter to come around with his hand out, begging: *Gimme gimme / My name's Jimmy*. They're still waiting, cousin.

George McGovern's pepper-pot liberals thought they'd cut a fat hog in 19-and-72 when they excluded Chicago's bullyboy mayor, Richard Daley, from the party's official proceedings before going on to lose everything but Cambridge, D.C., and the remainder of Senator Tom Eagleton's mind. Jimmy Carter, now, he put a leash around Dick Daley's neck, had him led up to the convention podium, and there permitted him to recite a few tame passages as directed. Which tactic do you think more completely de-balled the Chicago bullyboy? There Daley stood, before God, Walter Cronkite and everybody, his gonads snared on a Georgia trotline. Just another old bull reduced to the special shame of the steer.

Jimmy knew he had the nomination locked up long before the

wheeler-dealer kingmakers suspected they were at least temporarily out of the kingmaking bidness. Governors and Kennedys and Harrimans and others accustomed to fawning supplicants couldn't understand when Jimmy wouldn't give them the time of day. They didn't understand it was Appomattox Courthouse all over again, only in reverse. Jimmy was saying, *They can keep their mules for spring plowing, but if the sumbitches want the time of day let them buy theirselves a watch.*

There's been a Down Home satisfaction in watching the frantic scramble among Eastern Seaboarders long accustomed to cuddling and cozying up to power as they (1) attempted to ignore or ridicule Carter as a no-chance nobody and (2) later stepped on each other's Guccis in the stampede to touch ol' Jimmy's hem.

The lordly pundit Scotty Reston, senior pucker-brow for the *New York Times*, poked fun at Carter as "Wee Jimmy" until the delegate count made him appear to be near 'bout tall as a silo. Averell Harriman, the patrician grand old man of the Democrats, who'd advised more Presidents eyeball to eyeball than Bernard Baruch had pretended to from a park bench, once sniffed: "How will Carter be nominated when *I* don't know him?"

Aye, *there's* the rub! That's what filled the Old Boys and the Beautiful People—the political socialites—with a dread equal to that of the grave. To suffer the extinguishing of one's flame in Washington, a one-industry town, is to smell the musk and dry rot of death on one's fingers. Not to *know* the President, not to have a shot at remaining or becoming an insider (or, at least, to foster that illusion) was too horrible to contemplate. It just couldn't happen because *I don't know him!* And if the political socialites and tail-twisters didn't know ol' Jimmy, why, then, it stood to reason he had to be no more than . . . *trash*. Just trash. Just another Willy Loman, winging it on a shoeshine and a smile, a door-to-door peddler of Southern notions and Dixie tripe.

What you Damyankee peckerwoods need to understand is that you're not dealing with any *amateur* Caesar here. Ol' Jimmy learned long ago that if you own the gristmill, then it stands to reason everybody else ain't no more than common mill hands. *Tote that barge, Scotty; lift that bale, Averell.* Yeah, sure, y'all may gang up on Jimmy and frustrate him and come back and cut him a new one four years from now. But right now, Jimmy's got the whip.

I expect ol' Jimmy's gonna mess up a lot of folks' idea of fun. Wouldn't be surprised to see him crusade against dirty movies, filthy books, people pulling off naked in bunches and clusters. It stands to reason Jimmy the Good will go after dope, gambling and other forms of recreation that keep your average Mafioso gainfully employed. He's right much the pinched-mouth prude. Likely, in the end, Jimmy won't have much luck taming the nation's major sinkholes, where sin in the aggregate will simply refuse to be jawboned away; Sin's just too profitable when you're offering it, and feels too good when you're accepting it. In Washington, however—where everybody would wear fur hats, ride wild horses, gnaw bones and smite each other with swords should Genghis Khan get to be President—ol' Jimmy's likely to superimpose his values. You can count on certain congressmen continuing to go to prayer breakfasts with liquor or nookie on their breaths, though the ambitious bureaucrat is likely to sneak his martinis and make a big thing of sending his kids to Vacation Bible School. Screwing outside the home won't become a whit less popular; with Jimmy promising to restore the integrity of American families, however, you can bet the cheating will be more cautiously planned. Mark it down that people will serve peanut butter with the main course and chase around after softballs, for Washington is a bootlick town.

Frankly, I dread ol' Jimmy's official piety as much as the next man. There's a certain species of Southerner—whether outright redneck, Good Ol' Boy or decadent son of a wealthy planter—who just naturally is inclined to run rabbits and bark at the moon. Such men want to drink when they're thirsty, dash their goblets against the wall if the mood's on 'em or cuddle sweet thangs to whom they may hold no clear titles—and they don't admire being preached at about it. But they're gonna be preached at. Oh my, yes.

Forget that the South now is part of something political scientists call the Sun Belt, that so much of it has been urbanized or homogenized beyond the old myths and images that those coonass characters populating the works of Faulkner, Flannery O'Connor, Eudora Welty, et al. are advertised as doomed species. Outside the much-heralded New South (Atlanta's high spires of finance; Miami's tinsel splendors; Houston's sprawling petrochemical complexes juxtaposed cheek by jowl with hushed corporate law offices), these remain in evidence: corncob rapists, exotic old maids, carnival geeks, seven-fingered dwarfs, snuff-dipping racists, street-corner Godlies so fanatical they blind themselves to prove their faith. We're still cursed Down Home with a sizable hellfire-and-damnation element, ever eager to meddle and censor, whether they operate from backwoods brush arbors or neon-fitted tabernacles near freeway perfumes. Their agents remain dedicated to rooting out and stomping on such fun as they discover, excluding frog-gigging or pie suppers. Bet your Yankee dollar they're happily frothing at the notion of being so highly sanctioned, now that Jimmy Cah-tah's risen and has rolled the stone away from the Southern tomb.

Likely, however, not all of us ol' home boys gonna be plumb crazy about Jimmy once the new wears off. The know-nothings and congenital tackies—drivers of mud-flapped pickup trucks, hail-fellows of huntin'-and-fishin' clubs where they burn an occasional cross when the catfish ain't bitin' or the squirrels have went into hidin'—will cuss over their long-necked beers of how they don't 'preciate Jimmy runnin' with so goddam many niggers. Calling up the hound dawgs and peeing on the fire, they'll complain because he eats supper with communists, won't whup up on them spicks over the Panama Canal or get the Jews and A-rabs to settle their disputes in a Christian manner. They may wind up feeling especially betrayed, because nothing puts their teeth on edge like a Rebel they suspect of having gone over to the other side. I can hear 'em now: "Shee-it, if it was ol' George Wallace had got it, you thank he'd be pussyfootin' like this? Nawsir, ol' George, if that Damyankee hadn't shot 'im, he'd be up there teachin' the pointy-heads how to park their bicycles."

On the other hand, home boys who've learned the difference between Pouilly-Fuissé and RC Cola, or who've had their tastes for Moon Pies replaced by cravings for caviar, may find Carter more a throwback to laissez-faire, simplistic Rotary Club solutions or even Nixonian repressions than will comfort them. Jimmy's *talked* a fair liberal game, sure. But Mo Udall wasn't just whistling Dixie when he cracked, "If Carter's elected he'll never make Mount Rushmore because there's not enough room for two more faces." Jimmy is as hard to get a handle on as a greased pig, which is about as elusive as a lightning bug.

Awright. I'm admitting my reservations. My fear is that I've seen hundreds like the man, ruling boondock courthouses and marking up prices in their shops on the square, and, yes, I gotta squirm a little bit when a humorless man grins like he's in a grinning contest. But there's this history, all this goddam haunting *history*, of the South having been shut out for so long that even us longtime expatriates defensively feel that should Jimmy Cah-tah prove to be a sumbitch, then at least he's *our* sumbitch. I understand the little old lady in East Texas who said, "I 'on't ker whut they say about Linten Johnston, he's the onliest President we ever had whut didn't have a *ak*-cent."

Jimmy, if I was to walk up to 'im and tell 'im to veto conversion to the metric system on account of it would be too blamed hard to translate what "a mess" means, he'd know where I was coming from. You and Gerry Ford and them would assume it had to do with something that had been botched. Naw, neighbors. "A mess" is a unit of measure so inexact it's not exactly possible to define. A mess of collard greens is one thing; a mess of folks is something altogether different. The same is true of that unit of measurement called "a buncha": as in, "I drunk myself a buncha beer" or "I paid a buncha money for it." Y'all just gonna have to learn by doing.

Jimmy, he'd know what a "whiskey break" is. When a Southern sheriff is up for reelection, see, he convenes the church biddies and allows 'em to clap and sang and shout hosannas, while the incorruptible incumbent—laying about mightily, as with Samson utilizing the jawbone of an ass—busts up bottles of evil bootleg whiskey alertly captured during his term. This wonderful, traditional display of official vigilance has sustained many a $3,600-per-year sheriff to the point he has grown far too rich to any longer seek the job.

Jimmy must grin a real prizewinner when he reads Yankee journalists attempting to define "Good Ol' Boys." They think *Jimmy* may be one, Jesus help the dumb bastards. Naw. Billy Carter, maybe. Billy Carter *for sure.* Billy is sometimes inclined to risk uncharted waters. Like when they rushed Billy out to the airport in a police car with its siren howling, so he could greet some visiting dignitaries come to kiss his big brother's butt, and somebody asked Billy if he'd ever before been hauled in such heady circumstances. Billy grinned and said, "Well, it was my first time riding with the po-leece in the *front* seat." Then Billy staggered off to the side and peed on the tarmac. Yeah, Billy could play in those moonshine-and-car-wreck movies starring Burt Reynolds. He's a Good Ol' Boy from scratch. Y'all got to learn that when somebody is designated a Good Ol' Boy the sentence must start about like this: "Well, now, Bubba, he may beat his wife some and burn a few barns when he's drankin', and there's the time he sorta accidentally shot his little boy's eye out with a BB gun and all that—but he sure is a *good* ol' boy."

Me and Jimmy Cah-tah, we lost a war together in 1865. We know that Tennessee Williams ain't exaggerating when he writes of delicate ladies who stare into space and hum a whole lot and always depend on the kindness of strangers. We know it's silly to pay a shrink fifty bucks an hour when you can confess your messed-up self to a whole church congregation, for free, and get hugged and your hand shook for it. We've been down with the pip and understand the importance of football. We're not ashamed to love our daddies, or cry when we've gazed on the wine a bit much and our history temporarily overwhelms us. Let one of y'all Damyankees break down and cry and everybody looks away or commences analyzing him. We just hug each other, knowing that shared misery creates a bond. It don't have all that much to do with class or economics, either. More to do with time and place and blood.

We understand, of course, that anytime President Carter drops a little more than he can pick up, then y'all Damyankee peckerwoods gonna snicker and snort like he's congenitally handicapped. We *know* that, because y'all been conditioned to it just like that Russian's dawgs drooled when them bells rung. But you know somethin', cousin? We don't have to worry about it right now. We ridin' high. We eatin' off the highest part of the hog. So piss on y'all, ya heah? We ain't *trash* no more. Nosir, by God. Nosir.

Eccentric
Americana:
Of Kinfolk
and Friends

There are stories one recites for years, and then one day it dawns, "Hey, I haven't ever written or sold that!" So, one day in December of 1980, I sat down and wrote and sold—to the Washington Post—*some of my favorite old tales of kinfolk and friends. Only the last item was too raunchy for a "family newspaper" and not published there.*

A kinsman of mine invented the stepladder.

Unfortunately, he did not get around to this until 1961. Then he wanted me to use my position as a congressional aide to ensure that the Pentagon bought them by the thousands or the millions.

"Why is your stepladder better than anyone else's?" I asked.

My kinsman said it was lighter, could be folded up and had a trick button which, when pushed, allowed the climber to climb at oblique angles. Just in case he wanted to, I guess.

I was raised to help blood kin, so I sought out the office of Army liaison. After they quit laughing over there they said, "We don't scale too many parapets in the atomic age. Besides, we've got worlds of stepladders left over from World War I."

My kinsman did not take this news well. Shortly he telephoned to say that through a magazine advertisement he had hired a "super lobbyist" who not only pledged to sell *beaucoup* stepladders to the Pentagon, but was making arrangements for NASA to use them on the moon.

"What's up there to climb?" I asked.

My kinsman said he didn't know. But whatever it was, his step-ladder would make it easier.

"What's your lobbyist's name?"

My kinsman said, "He says everybody in Washington knows him as 'Mister B.' He says he is as well known up there as the Lincoln Memorial."

I asked how much money my kinsman had paid this landmark lobbyist. He admitted to $5,000. This was back when $5,000 would fill a Cadillac with gas and leave enough in change to put a down payment on a professional football franchise.

My kinsman reluctantly gave me the famous Mister B's telephone number. I met Mister B at his third-rate motel, dressed like a bum so as not to alert him to my congressional connections. That made two of us dressed like bums. While we took turns swigging from a quart of cheap wine, I represented myself as a fresh-off-the-farm Texas bumpkin who was an enthusiastic potential partner in my kinsman's stepladder cartel. Mister B represented himself as a bosom pal of Robert McNamara, Lyndon Johnson, Sam Rayburn, the Kennedy brothers and the 87th Congress.

When he'd been given ample rope I dropped the hick act and said, "Listen, you sleazy sumbitch, *I'm* a friend of most of those people"—here flashing my House of Representatives I.D.—"and if I don't have five thousand dollars in my hands within fifteen minutes you can tell your story to the FBI, the Secret Service, the Bunko Squad and three times a day to the guy who brings the tin tray to your cell."

Within the designated time limit, Mister B had forked over $4,600 and made arrangements to restore the shortage by the week. He was damn prompt with his payments.

My kinsman was furious then and now. These days he sells door-to-door things that glow in the dark, but as recently as last summer he was still telling pals how he'd almost made a fortune in stepladders until a smart-alecky relative loused up his sweet deal.

My Uncle Fud was a bootlegger and barber, who in nine consecutive elections ran for county commissioner in his Texas hometown. He finished as high as second and as low as thirteenth: the key statistic is that in all cases Uncle Fud ran last, though in his telling of it he liked to dwell on the year he'd finished second. One election Uncle Fud got only nine votes, though he had twenty-seven blood relatives of voting age living in his precinct.

When Uncle Fud was pushing sixty years he was indicted and brought to trial for having carnal knowledge of a fourteen-year-old demented girl in a backyard chicken house. My daddy shook his head and said, "Fud sure is hard to brag on."

I took a furlough from the Army to witness the human drama of Uncle Fud's trial. Uncle Fud put on a wonderful show at his sanity hearing: if found insane, see, he could sweat a few months in the loony bin and avoid criminal contaminations. Theoretically, this would leave him eligible in the future to again offer for public service.

During his sanity hearing, Uncle Fud combed his hair with a pocketknife, chewed on a handkerchief, occasionally talked in tongues and once offered a neat little tap dance until the judge ordered him to sit down. Alas, the jury was not persuaded by Uncle Fud's theatrics and ordered him to trial by unanimous vote. Then, by the same margin, it laid three to five years on him in the state prison. At the end of his day in court, as they led Uncle Fud off in handcuffs, he sighed, "Goddammit, for nearly twenty years people wouldn't vote for me because they said I was crazy. Then when it *really counted* they changed their minds!"

About three days after Uncle Fud heard the big door clang behind him at the state prison, he wrote my father a letter. In its entirety it said: "Dear Clyde, I do wish you would try to get me out, as I am not a-tall satisfied down here."

Uncle Fud did almost four years in prison. On release, he opened another barbershop. Business was exceedingly slow, however. One afternoon Uncle Fud drank a bit, sought out the local insurance agent and bought a policy on his barbershop which valued it much above its worth or potential. As soon as it was dark enough for flames to show good, Uncle Fud slopped several gallons of gasoline in his shop and threw a match after it. Unfortunately, Uncle Fud caught fire at the same time his barbershop did. He ran wheezing and screaming into the street, where passersby rolled him in the West Texas sand until an ambulance arrived.

For a time there was talk of freshly prosecuting Uncle Fud, but the insurance company humanely decided it would be willing to forget the clumsy fire if he would. Uncle Fud under the circumstances was inclined to agree. Until he died, however, he railed against cheating insurance companies that would take a man's premium payments and then desert him as soon as he had a little bad luck.

For many years my brother, Weldon, was the undisputed fried-chicken king of Midland, Texas.

One day a representative of Kentucky Fried Chicken—the Colonel Sanders outfit—tried to buy out my brother. When he declined, the Colonel's bunch soon established their own fried-chicken hut as near to my brother's place as the property line allowed. They erected a handsome new sign: "Kentucky Fried Chicken." My brother then established a larger sign designed to appeal to xenophobics: "Texas Fried Chicken." Soon Colonel Sanders' minions retaliated with a super-large sign featuring much flashy neon announcing itself, like Joseph's coat, in many colors. A few days later my brother called and said, "I got 'em! Come by and see my new sign."

I drove up to see a simple board sign in the shape of an arrow. It began about two inches from the Colonel's fancy neon sign, pointed directly to the front door of my brother's chicken hut and said, simply, "Main Entrance."

Shortly after Lyndon B. Johnson retired from the White House to his ranch, I visited home and once again stopped by my brother's fried-chicken outlet.

After we'd exchanged pleasantries he said, "Say, I talked to an old Washington buddy of yours the other day."

"Who?"

"Lyndon Johnson."

"Sure you did," I said.

"Naw, I really did. 'Course, now, it wasn't easy to get him. I called every day for seventeen days. Finally I told his secretary, Tom Johnson, 'Look, Tom, I'm gonna call every day until you let me talk to LBJ.' And one morning he did."

"My God, what did you have to say to Lyndon Johnson?"

"Well, using national advertising and all, this Colonel Sanders outfit is eating me up. So I got to thinking that here in Texas, Lady Bird Fried Chicken—"

"You didn't!"

"Yes, I did! I told Lyndon I thought Lady Bird Chicken would make a million and that I'd be glad to market it and oversee it for a good salary and a little piece of the business."

"My God! Did he hang up on you?"

"Naw, he was pretty nice. He said, 'Well, now, we not thinkin' right now of exploitin' Lady Bird's name commercially. But if we ever do, I'll get in touch. You sound like a can-do man.' "

More to myself than to my brother I said, "Only in America! Can you imagine Winston Churchill in retirement, and making him a deal on fish-and-chips?"

Busy popping thighs and breasts into huge sizzling vats, my brother said, "Naw. That shit wouldn't sell down here."

Warren Burnett, the prominent Texas lawyer, often runs to more than the mildly sardonic.

A few years ago he was selected to give the welcoming address when the Ector County Bar Association hosted the Ector County Medical Society. The purpose of this country club social was to ease tensions between two groups of proud professionals, doctors and trial lawyers; they often found themselves at odds due to vigorous cross-examinations during those adversary proceedings necessary to courtroom disputes when big money is on the line. For days a committee, made up equally of lawyers and physicians, haggled over protocol attendant to the planned peace meeting. Even after agreements had been reached, everyone was nervous and feared some disaster.

Perhaps the preprogram cocktail session lasted excessively long. When lawyer Burnett unsteadily climbed to his feet to "welcome" the doctors, here is what he said:

"I have watched our learned doctor friends arrive here in their Cadillacs, their wives in precious stones and furs. And I have observed their expressions as they look about as if sniffing something slightly malodorous while considering superior secrets perhaps known only to themselves and God.

"I would like to remind our distinguished guests that when *their* professional antecessors were teaching that the night air was poisonous, and were setting leeches on George Washington's ass the better to bleed him, *my* professional antecessors had written as noble a document as is known to the minds of men or angels—the Constitution of the United States."

I served my country with John Saunders of Arlington, Virginia, during a time when we both held the exalted rank of Private First Class in the United States Army.

We were horsing around the company orderly room at Fort Monmouth, hoping to slick the authorities out of three-day passes, when the telephone rang. The company clerk was not at his desk, so Pfc. Saunders picked up the phone and in a most unmilitary manner said, "Hello, go ahead, it's your nickel."

There was much spluttering on the other end of the line before the calling party said, "Do you know who this is?"

"Nope," said Pfc. Saunders.

"By God, this is General Whoozit, soldier! The post commander!"

"Well, General," Pfc. Saunders said, "do you know who *this* is?"

The puzzled general admitted that he did not.

"It's a damn good thing," Saunders said, and hung up the phone just before we fled.

My old friend Norman Childress, an automobile salesman in Odessa, Texas, has never been socially housebroken. Childress loves the truth, so he would not mind my revealing that he long has been great friends with whiskey.

A semi-innocent young airline hostess once had fantasies of marrying Norman Childress. She cleaned his house after flying all day or all night, cooked meals he generally ignored, doctored his headaches and otherwise campaigned to domesticate him. One Sunday morning the would-be bride gently woke Childress for breakfast. Norman pushed back the heaping plate of eggs and bacon without taking a bite, broke the seal on a new jug and said a strong good morning to his tonsils. The airline hostess began to cry and preach. She listed the many sins and deficiencies of Childress, which took longer than to read the local newspaper. At the climax of her oration the young woman said, "And another thing: you haven't planned for the future. Norman, dammit, you made *eight times* the money I did last year and yet I saved more than you did!"

Childress regarded her in amazement. "*Of course* you did!" he said. "You don't drink, and you got your own pussy."

Hurtin' Good

An editor at the Washington Post Magazine, *Jeanne McManus, telephoned to inquire whether I knew enough of romance to write a piece for the Valentine's Day issue in 1983. "The main thing I know of romance," I said, "is that it never lasts." She immediately asked me to write a piece about the broken-heart process. Here it is.*

Don't talk any gooey Valentine stuff to me, please. My women have a way of quitting around Christmastime. When the Valentine season rolls around I'm still sobbing, threshing sleepless in my lonely bed and swearing off romantic entanglements forever.

And you know what? It's absolutely wonderful.

There never in all history was a romance worth a farthing that didn't end badly. And I'm not even counting those that ended in marriage.

Give me a blonde / brunette / redhead—truth is, she can be anything but bald—who has thrown me over, preferably for an obviously inferior replacement, then deliver me to a barstool near a jukebox equipped with plain old three-chord hurtin' country songs, and I will have such wretched fun I should pay a luxury tax.

Don't forget, please, to stack me up about $20 worth of dimes near my drinking glass: these are for calling my ex-Beloved—alternately to beg or whine, threaten or curse and finally to slobber and cry. That drill, though melancholy in its execution, is in retrospect more fun than all football and some sex. I owe undying gratitude to a lot of Annies, Lenas, Louises, Mary Ellens, Barbaras, Doras, Lindas, Alices, Maries, Sallys, Kathleens, Taddys, Dianes, Dorothys, Cindys and Helens for all the terrible things they did to tromp my heart.

I think it was the old movie actor Jack Carson who first made me appreciate how good it hurts to Lose the Girl.

Jack, for you youngsters, was an overweight, wisecracking, cherub-faced actor who through the 1940s and 1950s lost at least one girl in every picture to the likes of Farley Granger, Jimmy Stewart, Tyrone Power, Robert Preston—heck, maybe even to such lightweight dandies as Dan Dailey or Ronnie Reagan.

Carson would always introduce his Girlfriend to his Best Pal; it wouldn't be half a reel until the duo began holding hands and sneaking kisses behind poor old fat Jack's back.

Hollywood was old-fashioned then and always made it clear the Lovers were not mean little sneaky thrill-seekers; no, they were pure, honorable souls caught up in a Passion Too Great for Coping. The Lovers, between kisses, cried and bemoaned their guilty betrayal of poor old silly Jack while he, oblivious to the obvious, innocently cracked jokes and planned his wedding until the moment the Lovers took deep breaths and gave him back his ring.

In real life, the Jack Carson figure might have justifiably turned homicidal maniac; at the least, he probably would have showered the Lovers with mud pies, ancient curses and angry midnight calls. In the movies, however, Jack Carson made a brave smile and a sweet quip. The Lovers hugged him, calling him a jolly good fellow, and asked him to become "Uncle Jack" to their firstborn and please to bring it teddy bears.

Uncle Jack always walked away smiling, never looking back, presumably on the way to a teddy-bear store—a tragic, solitary figure who somehow in those final scenes managed to convey the impression of having newly developed a heroic limp.

I think I figured at an early age that Uncle Jack was going off to drink himself healed while he cried a few bittersweet rivers with the help of a good jukebox. More, I think I suspected he would at bottom *enjoy* his great loss and, perhaps, secretly rejoice in his narrow escape.

Yeah, I figured in the long run kindly old Uncle Jack would have the last laugh: he'd still be out there seeking and finding new Doris Days or Barbara Stanwycks—savoring the hot excitement of a fresh love, at least until he foolishly introduced her to a new Best Friend—while the Lovers would grow fat and bald, become surrounded by noisy children and heavy mortgages, and go out-of-their-gourds bored thanks to those built-in, obligatory and repetitious rituals of domesticity.

And you know what? I've got a wonderful gut feeling that sly old Uncle Jack *never once* showed up on anybody's doorstep burdened by teddy bears.

Here's to you, Uncle Jack!

Annie Lou was the first to smash my heart. She quit me midway in second grade when Benny Ross Everette beat me out for Cleanest Fingernails. I challenged him to fisticuffs on the playground and lost that contest, too. I was so devastated, for almost a week, it was all I could do to choke down my share of the jellybeans, jawbreakers and chocolate bars Cousin Kenneth and I swiped from his father's store.

My affair with Lena Ruth was real and deep, lasting from third grade almost through the sixth; it deserves a place in the all-time romantic rankings alongside Anthony and Cleopatra and Liz and Dick. We would meet on opposite sides of the ash heap on the grounds of our rural, wood-burning school—each bringing his or her claque of rooters and boosters—for lunch-hour wink-offs. You haven't lived until you've been winked at by Lena Ruth six thousand times a week, or received in her own hand the wonderful poem that runs: *Tell me quick / Before I faint / Is you mine? / Or is you ain't?*

Hop Bostick almost wooed her away in fifth grade by leading me for the medal in the Term Reading Contest, but blew the match on the final day when I promised him a thrashing unless he stumbled on at least three words. Hop, a frail boy, managed to enthusiastically stumble on five. I won the pewter medallion and, more, kept the love of Lena.

One ill-fated day in sixth grade, however, when the girls' volleyball team freakishly lost a ball in the high girders and distant rafters of the school gym, a little wimp named Lloyd Perkins became an instant hero by shimmying up to rescue it with the whole school looking on. Billy Royce Sweeney turned to me and said, "I betcha he got him a girlfriend while he was up there." Little did I dream it would be mine.

On the school bus that afternoon, Lena Ruth chose to sit by Lloyd Perkins and wrote *our* poem in *his* Friendship Book. That's when I first knew true betrayal and a jealous rage. Why, dammit, I had *kissed* Lena Ruth! *Twice.* Once on the sneak in the coat room on a beautiful, cold, drizzly day, and once quite publicly—causing a huge scandal and two little girls to scream and faint—out by the ash heap.

Too young to repair to a barroom jukebox, I made do with Ernest Tubb singing on the radio—"Walking the Floor Over You" and "I Wonder Why You Said Goodbye" guaranteed instant tears—and by whupping up on Lloyd Perkins so many times his daddy came to school to speak to the authorities. Lena revealed a basic lack of character by standing by her wimpy man. The old ash heap, alas, was never the same. But I learned about hurtin' good.

One Rule of Love to remember is as inviolate as any to be found in Robert's Rules of Order: *It is better for the Girl to leave you rather than the other way around.*

Absolutely no fun accrues, for the longest time, to the man who leaves the Girl. He is nagged by guilt twinges so acute he can't relax even in the arms of a seductive new companion, and he can rest double-damn-assured the Community has marked him down as a bounder and a cad, a beast and a jackal.

Somehow it is perfectly hunky-dory for the Girl to leave the Guy in the Community's eyes: "Aw hell, ol' Larry, he just lost out; I never understood what she saw in that silly jackass in the first place."

But let the Guy show the Girl the door while asking for his life back, please, and people say, "That sorry sumbitch put her on the street without five dollars and has took up with stray blondes." This does not have to be the truth to gain popular currency.

Maybe the Guy has showered the Girl with all the money he can scrape up, an apartment, help in finding a job and sincere good wishes as she starts over; perhaps she is the better educated and makes more money than a dope dealer or a brain surgeon; he, on the other hand, may be a penniless sort with no hope for the future, forever condemned to hunker in a hovel eating rat cheese. No matter. He will be treated like a child molester.

The Girl will be said to have been abandoned, betrayed, used, wrecked, ravaged, destroyed, crushed, scuttled, sacrificed, annihilated, devastated, sabotaged, razed and ruined. People will rush to the thesaurus to find new invectives to hurl against the Guy who takes a walk. No matter that it saved his life, or that he may border

on the saintly, or that the rejected lady may share much in common
with junkyard dogs or Typhoid Mary.

All you sincere Equal Rights Amendment types, if you truly care
for equal justice in your bones, will hit the streets early tomorrow
clamoring for the repeal of that particular Rule of Love.

(Memo to the Guys: Hang in there. Bite the bullet. Don't be the
one to call it quits, or you'll never hurt good. Besides, since they
started all this terrible palimony business, your freedom may not be
worth the risk and cost.)

Why is it, pray, that She never is so desirable as the day She leaves?

I have found myself weeping along with the jukebox over mousy
women, dumb women, ugly women, drinking women, fat women,
women who throw ashtrays and women who might be considered
interesting only in comparison with Oklahoma. What they shared in
common was that their values mysteriously zoomed 1,000 percent
the moment they made their final hot speeches and slammed the door.
Why should that be? I think it is more than wallowing in masochism
or indulging heartbreak songs. Somehow it seems to be akin to winning or losing a contest. Or maybe it is part of some obligatory pagan
ritual, like funerals or Lions Club luncheons.

It takes longer to heal when the good ones quit—those bright,
beautiful, lively, glittering ones who can break your heart with the
flicker of a cosmetics-counter eyelash or the crossing of silky legs.
Lord God, ain't no wound like it even in modern warfare!

You will go broke making midnight phone calls, feeding the jukebox, standing drinks for strangers and breaking things. Weight will
drop off you as if by cancer, and dark circles camp out under your
eyes. Your work goes to hell, and your friends begin crossing streets
to avoid you. You restlessly toss in an acre of lonesome bed, reaching out for someone who isn't there, and cry out in the dark for your
mama.

Sometimes, when it's hurtin' real good like that, a fellow tends to
overplay his hand. He may make one too many imploring calls to his
ex-Beloved. And when he least expects it—when he is slobbering
and wailing and making impossible careless promises—she will suddenly, and without issuing as much warning as a rattlesnake, surrender. She will commence to sob in her own right, and call him "darling"

and order him to come straight to her arms so they can Try It Again.

Well, Jesus, that ain't fair! Suppose a fellow has just poured a new jigger of Old Snort, and has found a stranger who—for a few measly drinks—is willing to listen to his life's story? Or what if he has just loaded up the jukebox again, and all that heartbreak music should go to waste? Any woman treacherous enough to pull *that* number on you is too obvious a risk. To use the logic of Groucho Marx—who said he wouldn't join any club that would admit him—something must be seriously wrong with such a woman or she wouldn't want you back.

This leads to the postulation of number two among the Rules of Love: *No matter how much you enjoy your grief, never fail to keep it well in hand.*

Losing the Girl, you see, is best in the long run for reasons other than the satisfying drama inherent in the act. The One Who Got Away may always be invoked in fantasy as the perfect mate. *She* never would have tried to change my ways, or nit-picked my few minor faults. *She* would have given me free rein and permitted me to gallop at full speed in the direction I wanted to go. *She* would have welcomed the tired old spent horse back to the stables and would have curried and groomed it and lovingly have wrapped it in a blanket after giving it great oats.

Unless one unwisely looks up the Girl Who Got Away after too many seasons have passed, she never grows thick, gray, sickly, quarrelsome, neurotic or dim. Never mind that in the long, long ago she may have charged a Rolls-Royce to your credit card just before skipping out with a flour drummer, or that she sometimes employed a vicious left hook, or that she loudly told your boss—in front of too many witnesses—to go squat in his hat. No, those were merely temporary aberrations and with the passage of time may be seen as evidence of a wonderfully high-spirited personality. Gee, she was great. How did I ever let her get away? Or the several just like her?

Some years ago, visiting a distant city of my youth, I learned through the grapevine that Bob had just left Dora. My heart sang, danced a two-step and turned a cartwheel.

I had carried Dora's torch for years. We had dated back in a time when Nice Girls just didn't Go All the Way right off. Just as I was finishing my lengthy apprenticeship and looking to my reward, Bob—curse him—came along and swept Dora off her feet in a crash court-

ship. I sniveled, begged and promised Dora—a political activist—
that if she would throw over Bob I would become President of the
United States and make her First Lady. She married Bob anyway.

Over the years, though not in the past fifteen, I had encountered
Bob and Dora at political rallies or parties. Dora continued to look
as if she could win the Miss America contest simply by showing up
in a burlap bag: tall, lithe, tanned; great, long, rich black hair; flashing eyes; legs I would have killed for; pretty painted toes I would
have sucked for far less than the minimum wage.

And now, visiting home, I learn that Bob has been crazy enough
to leave all that.

I spring to the phone. When Dora answers, I exchange pleasantries and slyly ask for Bob. "Oh, you don't know?" she says. And
tells me they have gone kaput. I shed a few crocodile tears before
suggesting drinks and dinner. She pledges to be at my hotel in one
hour.

I shower, spray, powder, starch, shine. Suck in my gut. Trim the
grayer parts of my beard. Comb my hair backward, the better to
conceal my bald spot. Decide not to wear my bifocals, though I may
stumble on a curb. All the time I am singing and dancing like I might
be Sammy Davis, Jr.; occasionally I burst into maniacal laughter.
*Dora! Whee! Thank you, Sweet Jesus! Oh, Sweet Dora! Ah, Sweet
Mystery of Life* . . .

Fifteen minutes before Dora is due, I impatiently pace the hotel
lobby and check my watch each 4.2 seconds. A state senator, a decent fellow, stops to chat; I rudely cut him off. An old friend spots
me and has difficulty getting a grudging howdy-do.

Next a short, dumpy little old lady in dowdy clothes, complete
with dowager hump, approaches with one of my books in her hand.
I unsling my trusty pen, snatch the book from her and say, "I'm-
meeting-somebody-and-I'm-in-a-big-hurry-how-do-you-want-me-to-
sign-this?"

And she says, "How about 'Love and kisses to Dora'?"

Nothing is worse than having a good friend who has been freshly
jilted.

One is obliged to hold his hand, listen to silly blather and suffer
all that heartbreak music that sounds terribly infantile and stupid

unless it is your own heart that has gone bust.

Take the case of my fellow writer Ralph, who has been madly in love with the beautiful Stephanie and plans to ask her hand in marriage. He is a little slow so doing, however, and one midday he turns up at my Manhattan apartment to say that Stephanie has met Another and has given Ralph his unconditional release. Naturally, my friend is frothing and bawling and has managed to get grass-grabbing drunk on two double bourbons and basic emotion.

Ralph is a Southerner; I know he has chosen my place because I have the greatest collection of twangy heartbreak songs to be found on the Eastern Seaboard. Such groups as the Beatles or Jefferson Airplane simply prove musically inadequate in true hurtin'-good situations. I sigh, and put on a stack of Waylon, Willie and other cowboys capable of singing she-done-me-wrong songs.

All day and all night I am Ralph's disc jockey, he finally narrowing it down to two numbers he insists on hearing again and again and again: "I'll Get Over You" and "You're Candy in the Window." He tells me and retells me how well Stephanie can hug, kiss, smile, cook, joke, laugh, sneeze, make a bed or a martini and a bunch of intimate stuff it makes me uncomfortable to hear. In the classic pattern, he alternates between giving Stephanie a clear decision over heaven's best angel and branding her the sorriest harlot west of Eighth Avenue.

On the morning of the third day I say, "Ralph, I've got deadlines and I've got to get some work done. And I can't stand hearing those two songs any longer." Ralph ignores me; he does not have work to get done: he has resigned his part-time magazine editing job, by telephone, in the middle of the second day of heartbreak so as not to disgrace his publication when he commits suicide. I rush around hiding razor blades and butcher knives.

Now I seem to have a permanent house guest, though it started with Ralph begging to crash on my couch for just one night. A week later he has neither shaved nor bathed, he has consumed all liquids in my house save my skin bracer, and those two wretched songs are still playing. By now I know more about Stephanie's body parts, and her unique uses of them, than I know of two former wives.

"Ralph, old friend," I ultimately say, "this cannot go on until doomsday. I must have my apartment and my peace of mind back. Please go let your heart break somewhere else."

Outraged, Ralph hits me in the mouth. Hard. I hit him back. We break up much furniture and each other. He curses his way out the door, vowing I am his enemy for life and—with the exception of that slut Stephanie—the sorriest human he has ever known.

I do not hear from Ralph for three or four months, though reports seep in of his overturning tables at Elaine's and publicly burning the novel in progress he had dedicated to Stephanie.

I am soon astonished to receive a wedding invitation from Ralph. He is marrying a girl who definitely is not Stephanie. I worry about this, rebound matches having a way of quickly unraveling.

These years later, Ralph and his bride have two children and apparently will live semi-happily ever after. I do not know what has happened to Stephanie, whom Ralph vowed he would never get over should he live to be one thousand and seven years old. I cautiously asked him about her a few months ago. Ralph thought for a moment, frowned, and said, "Let's see, now, was she the little blonde from Minnesota or the would-be jazz singer from Memphis?"

Thank goodness I have risen above all that love, romance, mush, poetry, roses and hurtin'-good stuff. I don't have to worry about it anymore.

I'm married. Valentine's Day don't mean squat to me.

Confessions of
an Older Father

There has been a trend in recent years for Old Geezers to marry young women and produce second families. A few years ago I would have bet my bottom dollar I never would do that; six months later I married Barbara S. Blaine and almost immediately began to do that. Texas Monthly and Parade asked me to write of the "old daddy" experience at about the same time; a sentimentalist to the core, I chose to write it for Parade because that publication pays me more money than the Texas publication. Baby, after all, must have shoes. Parade published this article in May 1983.

Four years ago, shortly after sullenly acknowledging my fiftieth birthday, I became painfully aware of a television advertisement assuring those of us "in the 50-to-80 age group" that we could buy life insurance without subjecting our presumably wrecked old bodies to physical examinations.

I am afraid I swore and threw things. I didn't mind being bracketed with actor George C. Scott or Miami Dolphin coach Don Shula—the calendar doesn't lie—but doubted whether I deserved to be considered the contemporary of funnyman George Burns.

My anxiety markedly increased when my wife, Barbara, more than twenty years my junior, announced that I was destined to become a father again. I was far from certain that I wanted to be, or that I was geared to handle paternal duties at a time when many my age had begun sneaky dreams of retirement while bouncing grandchildren on their knees.

I, too, had a grandchild. Indeed, he was graduating puberty. I worried that my three adult offspring might resent their new half-sibling—or, at bottom, speak in scandalized whispers of their foolish father's excesses. I knew that numerous of my old cronies would laugh or snort.

My primary fear, however, was that I might be too old and frazzled to keep up with fatherhood's demanding rigors and rituals.

I had been a father since age twenty-two—or, as I told people, "all my life." My first family had reached that stage where my progeny theoretically were presumed to be self-sufficient, though I knew in my heart that once one becomes a father, it remains a lifetime job. One may suffer a divorce, as I had in the long ago, but the divorce is not from the children.

I had to face the cold, statistical fact that a King child born after my fiftieth birthday faced roughly a 29 percent chance of becoming a paternal orphan before reaching age eighteen. Supposing that with luck I might live to a ripe age, was I of a temperament to enjoy—rather than merely tolerate—the pitter-patter of little feet?

I did not look forward to midnight feedings, predawn colic bouts, or that near-constant, enthusiastic noise it is the pleasure of children to contribute. I had selfish thoughts of the inconveniences children bring: reduced leisure time, interference with one's work, cost factors beginning with prenatal care and extending through baby-sitters, bicycles, jalopies and college degrees.

My mother-in-law voiced what I had only dared think in the dark and in my solitary mind: "Frankly, I don't believe I could go through all that again."

I pep-talked myself. Surely, for a variety of reasons, fatherhood would be easier the second time around.

In 1951, when my first child was born, as a neophyte sportswriter I took home a zinging $39.13 each Friday; my wife, a telephone operator, contributed a vital $18.07 per week. That was before the government had established an official "poverty level," but we did not need Washington to tell us we were poor. The pediatrician who visited our old frame rental house, indeed, worried that our firstborn might be adversely affected by cold Texas winds whistling through the cracks. Near paydays, we pooled our food with other broke young marrieds for communal meals. Well, that likely wouldn't happen again—not with a hit musical on Broadway and a wife who was prospering as an attorney.

This time, rather than depend on the largess of relatives as emergency assistants, I could hire a housekeeper and a live-in nannie. I envisioned a life where one saw one's children only when they were starched and improbably cheerful.

As a young father, I had feared approaching my infants. They might break when touched by unskilled hands. In those rare times when I gave them their feedings, the slightest off-key noise found me dangling the shocked little creatures by their heels and pounding their tiny backs to prevent choking. I was helpless in the company of a soiled diaper. Should my youngsters develop colds, or worse, I became a basket case in my own right; sometimes I disqualified myself for sick-bay duty through timely attacks of hypochondria.

Surely, with maturity, experience and more resources—including a bright, stable wife who devoured books on child care and actually enjoyed them—I would be a calmer and wiser father.

For all those hopes, I could not forget that unsettling mix of emotions felt when I had gazed on my firstborn and realized—in fear, amazement, awe, pride, consternation and confusion—that here was a fresh, untested *human being* for whom I was responsible: for her creation, comfort, shaping and future. I recall walking out of the hospital, dazed and uncertain, gazing across the Texas desert sands and thinking, *Things will never be the same.* Seized by a new appreciation for the burdens of fatherhood, I turned to my father and said, "Dad, what the hell do I do now?" I was neither assured nor instructed by his economical response: "Why, son, you just do the best you can!"

During Barbara's pregnancy, I learned that in the quarter-century since I had sired a child, more had changed than the inflation rate. Fathers-to-be actually were encouraged to participate in events of their own making! A radical departure.

In older times, I had skulked in smoke-filled, isolated rooms with other prospective fathers while our wives—in labor—were attended by strangers in hospital gowns or by female relatives. The new father was beckoned, at the convenience of others, to his wife's bedside for a perfunctory audience before being permitted a brief and seemingly grudging glimpse of a tiny stranger in swaddling clothes. Then he was herded to the admissions office to settle the bill.

This second time around, I found myself attending "prepared childbirth" classes. To my astonishment, I was taught to help my wife breathe rhythmically during labor and otherwise instructed how to coach her. One night the nurse said, "Now, dads, in the delivery room . . ." I heard no more, but spun in alarm to Barbara: "You mean they actually expect me to go in there and *help*?" Yes, and so did she. I stammered of a tendency to faint at nosebleeds.

The closer we got to D-day, the more anxious I became; it was necessary for my adult issue to assure me again that, no, they would not resent the new baby. I was unable to concentrate on the library of baby books Barbara thrust on me and began to avoid home in favor of long liquid lunches with male pals who seldom mentioned children or childbirth and long had had no reasons to. These friends I very much envied.

Came the birth. I drove Barbara to the hospital, strangely elated— considering my earlier reluctance—now that the hour was at hand. In the labor room, I breathed, coached and encouraged. Then it got down to the nitty-gritty: they tossed me a set of doctor's greens with orders to garb for the delivery room. Frankly, I had rather gone to jail. I stalled by smoking a cigarette, brushing my teeth with my finger and doing knee-bend exercises. Ultimately, however, there was no place to hide.

Amazingly, matters went wonderfully well. Lindsay Allison King reported to the world on November 16, 1979, alert and seeking. She lifted her beautiful little head to inspect us even before they cut the umbilical cord. Soon she was in my arms. In the recovery room, she studied us as if deciding whether we might be worthy of her care.

Lindsay now is moving toward her fourth birthday. She has a baby brother, Blaine Carlton, not yet a year old. Between them, those little people have taught this old graybeard a thing or three.

Even tiny babies have their own special personalities. With my first family, I missed that. Absent at work, traveling and paying scant attention to day-to-day developments, I assumed that children would not be interesting or communicative until the age of two or three years. In fact, as I have learned now that I work at home and spend time with my youngsters daily, they early learn and respond to tunes, games and other stimuli; surprisingly quickly, they attempt to imitate.

There are moments of absolute, unqualified gratification: standing over pink, innocent angels in slumber with their Annie dolls or teddy bears; Lindsay proudly exhibiting her latest nursery school painting or paste-up or memorized poem; Blaine in the chortling discovery of the miracle of toes; the two of them laughing together or sharing private mysteries portending—in the words of Saroyan—"what no man can guess and no child can remember to tell."

But don't believe for a moment that all is peaches and cream.

The notion of seeing my kiddies only when they were starched and cheerful proved a foolish fancy. Baby Blaine is persuaded that his normal playtime is midnight to 3:00 a.m.; he requires a playmate, yowling horrendously should one not be provided. Barbara is convinced she cannot function without ten hours of uninterrupted sleep; her corollary belief—that husbands best function on catnaps and cold showers—at once nominates and confirms me as the baby's nocturnal playmate. Predawn games of patty-cake and pull-Daddy's-beard sometimes are not much fun.

Lindsay has trouble with the silly notion that her father's incessant typing should take precedence over her wish to engage him in games of play school, doctor-and-dentist, dolls, or hide-and-seek. From the moment she discovered the ability to scale stairs and open doors, no hideaway has been immune from unscheduled visits. She has learned that stern lectures melt in the warmth of one magic phrase: "But Da-Da, I just wanted to give you one hug and one kiss."

"Children keep you young" is a cliché this old head often quarrels with at the end of a day when he can remember no sounds save those of crying, breakage or his own impatient orders to "stop that, quit that, put that down, don't do that, hush that." Or when his brain reels from the hundredth reading of *The Poky Little Puppy* or his joints ache from running up and down four flights of stairs to fetch toys, pacifiers, snacks or children in need of comfort, cleaning or Band-Aids. I push away those occasional dark thoughts reminding me, "If you think *this* is tough, wait till you're older and must deal with the insanities of teenagers."

Each of the children has been hospitalized for one sudden, troubling illness. Only a parent knows the helplessness and worry—accompanied by guilt when some slight or harsh word is recalled—that comes while special little people cry out in their fevers and fears. In such times, my emotions tumble over each other like trampoline artists; I promise invisible gods to be an impossibly perfect father and in the next breath rage at them—and myself—for the frightening fix I am in. I call out my defense to an unjust world: "Dammit, I'm just too old and tired for this."

Then the crisis passes, my child blooms anew with fresh smiles, and for a time I fancy that I am younger and stronger again. And until the memory of the dark time has faded, I will be all those things fathers should be but have a difficult time sustaining: patient, understanding, solid as rock.

My wife recently asked one of my grown daughters what she remembered of me from her childhood. "The main thing I recall," she said, "was that he yelled a lot." Though she laughed when she said it, it hurt. I am sure it was true. Patience has never been my virtue. I am trying to learn, when besieged by the clamor of noisy little armies clashing throughout my house, that some battles must not only be fought but tolerated. Perhaps it is not as vital whether this page is completed today or tomorrow as whether Lindsay leaves for nursery school feeling warm toward me and good about herself, or whether Blaine enjoys his special giggle while being tossed in the air before his midday nap.

(Vowing to practice what I preach, I just left the typewriter for a half-hour romp with Lindsay. Near the end, I referred to myself as "your silly old daddy." "You're not a silly old daddy!" she protested. I hugged and thanked her. Then she amended her judgment: "*Sometimes* you're a silly old daddy, but not right now." That, I presume, was my reward; it also may reaffirm the old adage that wisdom often is blurted out of the mouths of babes.)

So being an "old" daddy is a mixed bag. If there is no exact formula for being a "good" daddy or a successful one, then I think I'm at least coming closer to some marginal understanding of my father's advice that a father simply does the best he can. What he meant, I believe, was that a father owes a commitment of love and attention and effort even in the toughest times and in the face of the larger rebellions. And if he is blessed, he may know a day when his children—by then, most likely, parents themselves—will come to appreciate him a little more than nature intended, and surely more than yesterday would have believed.

Dr. Doubletrouble
Goes Straight

One morning in May 1980, I read in the Washington Post *that country-western singer-songwriter Jerry Jeff Walker would be playing in the city soon. I also had heard, days earlier, that Jerry Jeff had quit drinking and doping. I had known him, observed him and helled around with him far too long to believe it. Wondering what Walker's scam was—he'd told some people he had decided to go straight in protest of Iranian thugs having seized American hostages at our embassy in Teheran—I decided to have a personal look. Jerry Jeff Walker did, indeed, appear to have gone straight. This was such big news I decided to sell it to the* Washington Post. *Postscript: These years later, except for an occasional beer or minor brain flare-up, Jerry Jeff is still straight. Amazing. Absolutely amazing.*

The Ayatollah Khomeini admits his favorite song is "God Bless America."

President Jimmy Carter is releasing all his delegates so that Democrats may choose their leader in a free and open convention.

While you slept last night, hell froze over in a hailstorm. The needle was found in the haystack.

But all that is very small potatoes, indeed. The Big News this morning is that Jerry Jeff Walker has gone straight.

I ain't kidding you. Jerry Jeff has quit dope cold turkey. He eats health food. He runs four or five miles each morning. He drinks only the infrequent beer. He shows up on time for his concerts and knows what town he's in. He hasn't had a fistfight in four months, or thrown his guitar at an autograph seeker, or pitched backward—in mid-song—onto a set of drums.

Cut to last week in Arlington, Virginia.

Jerry Jeff is sitting in his traveling trailer, parked behind Eskimo Nell's, ignoring all the pot and booze passing back and forth. "Naw," he says, "I haven't found God or anything. Last January fifteenth I realized I'd hit bottom. It was time to change directions."

Walker's pretty wife, Susan, had left him, taking along their three-year-old daughter. He'd missed a few show dates, which had led to legal complications; there was no new record album in the works. Jerry Jeff had gone five or six twenty-four-hour days without sleep except for catnaps on barstools, in front of urinals or at red lights he decided to honor.

Came, as Jerry Jeff says, January 15. He bleakly called his accountant with instructions to transfer "all my money and property to Susan's name." This would be the first step to woo back his wife. The accountant said, "You mean your pickup truck and car?" Jerry Jeff said, "Naw, fool! Everything!" The accountant said, "That *is* everything, Jerry Jeff. You don't have any money or property. And you're twenty-six thousand dollars in debt." Jerry Jeff sat there stunned, in the old country house a few miles out of Austin, and decided he simply had to clean up his act.

Boy, it took a lotta scrubbing. For years and years ol' Jacky Jack Doubletrouble—as his long-suffering friends called him—had wandered in a crazy daze. His main hobby was causing riots. Like the time he walked into a motel room full of drunk cowboys, during the National Rodeo finals in Oklahoma City, and very shortly inspired them to stomp a mudhole in his ass. Jerry Jeff looked up from the floor, while dripping blood and surrounded by broken furniture, and sneered: "Y'all ain't so bleepin' tough. I been beat up worse than this by motorcycle gangs."

Once I was hosting this sedate cocktail party at Princeton, see, for delicate literary academicians and their proper wives, when Jerry Jeff Walker, who'd been playing a club in New York, appeared very much unannounced and uninvited. He was dressed like a buffalo hunter and looked like three months on field bivouac complicated by the blind staggers. Jacky Jack Doubletrouble immediately lived up to his nickname by imitating the walks and lisps of sherry-sipping academicians; he crashed about stepping on long gowns and howling for Lone Star beer. He asked a highly placed faculty wife her relative expertise in an exotic sexual discipline and generally cleared staid old Maclean House as efficiently as a drunk with a switchblade. He left in a snowstorm, at supersonic speed and—unknown to me—in a rental car charged to my American Express card. The car eventually was found abandoned in midtown Manhattan, long on traffic tickets and short on operable parts. Jerry Jeff's explanation was that he couldn't remember being in a car that night. . . .

One night at Castle Creek Saloon, in Austin, Dr. Doubletrouble showed up at eleven-twenty to play the eight o'clock show. His audience, having paid a heavy cover charge for more than three hours of silence where they had expected to hear music, greeted him with catcalls and obscenities. Jerry Jeff gave as good as got and then some. When he wearied of cussing he grabbed a live armadillo from a bystander and flung it toward ringside tables. Then he seized the microphone and invited everybody to come onstage and fight. Two or three or more did. After order had been restored, Jerry Jeff started singing, through a split lip, a tender number called "Pissin' in the Wind." Halfway through it he began to stagger backward and didn't stop until he'd crushed his poor drummer's equipment to smithereens. He lay there, snoring, while management churlishly chunked refunds and caught abuse.

Jacky Jack rarely slept in those days. "I don't dream, man," he'd explain. "See, if I ain't dreamin' nothin's happenin'. It's like bein' dead. So if I'm asleep I miss things." Quite obviously, the solution lay in never sleeping. Dr. Doubletrouble simply quit going to bed.

Jerry Jeff's insomnia policy was hard on his friends; he got insulted should they want to sleep. If you sacked out when Walker didn't approve, he would wake you quite suddenly by spraying you with a water hose or holding a spoonful of cocaine under your nose until you choked. "Why do you put up with that crazy man?" more than one lady-friend asked me. I'd tell 'em it was because he was more interesting than your average Rotarian and, besides, I didn't want to miss it when somebody decided to kill Jerry Jeff.

Ol' J.J. sleeps four to five hours a night now, though he still complains that he never dreams.

Between shows at Eskimo Nell's, standing by his trailer while signing autographs and hugging pretty girls, he says, "Say, man, I got up early this morning in North Carolina and ran four miles. You believe that?"

"No," I say.

Jerry Jeff shows me what little is left of his potbelly and urges his band members to confirm his running yarn. They do. He beams, sticks his tongue out and says, "Lookit that. Cleaner than a baby's. And every morning I drink about a quart of hot saline solution. And guess what, man? My shit comes out clear as club soda."

Jerry Jeff has arrived at Eskimo Nell's, an Arlington club located in a shopping center of no particular distinction, fresh from a concert at P. B. Scott's in Blowing Rock, North Carolina. It is the front end of a month-long tour that will take him to such places as Grandaddy's in Ames, Iowa, and Gunter Hill in Greeley, Colorado, and to Skip's in Ellis, Kansas. The man who will play those clubs once wowed 'em at the Village Gate and the Lone Star Café in New York City, to say nothing of Madison Square Garden and—dig this—Carnegie Hall. Then came all those missed concerts, and lawsuits, and a lotta breakage and . . . well . . .

Onstage at Eskimo Nell's, when a microphone momentarily malfunctions, Jerry Jeff goes to another one and says to the crowd, "I just play these joints, I don't pick 'em. But don't worry, y'all can get as sloppy in here as you want."

Jerry Jeff certainly had not picked Eskimo Nell's. He'd been booked to play the Ontario Theatre in D.C., but forty-eight hours before the gig management had canceled because of slow advance sales. That kinda burned old J.J. "Hell," he scoffs, "I told them people my fans don't buy *nothin'* in advance. They just show up loose and ready." But the Ontario people got nervous and shifted the booking to a place nobody much had ever heard of.

A huge man named Charley, who weighs about 300 pounds and works for Eskimo Nell's, says, "They called me two days ago and offered Jerry Jeff Walker. Frankly, I'd never heard of him. Then they told me he'd wrote that song 'Mister Bojangles.' What the hell, that's all I hadda hear. And look at this crowd!" Charley is delighted. Near to 400 people have crowded in for the first show; long before the second one, hundreds more are shoving for position in a long line that swoops and stretches and curves. Everybody is buying drinks like Prohibition is coming back at midnight. It is a happy crowd— real hard-core Jerry Jeff fans who cry for his old familiars like "Redneck Mother," "London Homesick Blues," "L.A. Freeway," "Desperadoes," "Mister Bojangles"—and they whoop and stomp and guzzle and can't spend their money fast enough. Big Charley says happily, "He gets all the door money, but we get all the booze and food money.

It's gonna work out real neat for everybody. Walker'll take away—oh, three thousand dollars plus, maybe close to four." He beams at the crowd and says, "*Jeeze!* And we just fell into this thing."

Crowded around the bar at Eskimo Nell's are three foot-pattin' lovelies, with wonderful names and hometowns, all of whom work for Texas congressman Charles Wilson. Wilson, better known as "Goodtime Charlie," was supposed to be at the concert himself, but he got to having such a good time elsewhere he didn't show up. There was Amy Sue Trites of Cut 'N Shoot, Texas. (I swear to Christ: there *is* a Cut 'N Shoot, Texas. Roy Harris, who once unsuccessfully tried to take away Floyd Patterson's heavyweight title, comes from there.) And there was Julie Ann Booty of Farmers Branch, Texas. And Karen LaNell Webb of Conroe, Texas, a young yellowhair with a home-fried accent bordering on parody. Karen LaNell says, "I tol' mah frens in *Con*-roe I was gonna come see ol' Jerry Jeff do his thang and git commode-huggin' drunk." She didn't think it unusual to have flown from Texas to Washington to see a Texas-based performer. "I jes' cain't git enuff of him sangin' that 'Pissin' in the Wind,' " she sighed.

It has been many years since Jerry Jeff Walker broke into the New Orleans jail on charges of rowdy conduct and there met an old black man who inspired him to write "Bojangles." Probably only God and the auditors know how much money that song has made for J.J. Even so, the song has long been a sore spot with him. He is expected to sing it everywhere he goes, maybe three or four or five times in one night, and back in his hellion days he'd occasionally punch out somebody simply for requesting that song. You can still get a rise by ragging him about Richard Nixon once having named "Bojangles" as his favorite tune. Somehow, Jerry Jeff finds a certain shame attached to that. "Dammit," he says, "ol' Nixon just liked that song because his tame little buddy Sammy Davis Junior sang it."

Three or four years ago Jacky Jack staggered into the Austin home of author Bud Shrake one night at God knows what time. "He was scratched and bleeding," Shrake recalls, "but I just thought somebody had beat him up again." But after a few minutes Shrake noticed that Walker seemed uncommonly quiet, and began quizzing him. "I just had a wreck in my jeep," Jerry Jeff said. "It's down the road in a ditch, turned over, and I can't remember—I don't *know*—if anybody was with me." Shrake telephoned Walker's home but Susan did not answer. Fearing the worst, he followed Jerry Jeff back to the wrecked jeep and they poked around in the dark calling "Susan" over and over. And after awhile J.J. began to cry.

They went back to Shrake's house to call for medical help and a bigger search party. As they entered, the phone rang. It was Susan, hunting her husband, mad as hell because she hadn't heard from him in several hours or maybe days. Jerry Jeff was so relieved he kept laughing all through her muleskinner tongue-lashing and telling her how he loved her and how he would go out and pluck her a star from the sky if she would pick one out. . . .

Ol' Jacky Jack was really wailing last week. There he was in clean clothes, with a haircut and not even wearing his usual dirty cowboy hat; he sang with more vigor and competence than he has in a long while and played the bejeebers out of that scarred ol' guitar. "It helps a little," he grinned, "to be able to remember the words." The crowd at Eskimo Nell's cheered and screamed and it was like old times.

I guess the man is back. Now that word is around he is actually honoring his contracts, Walker has been booked for appearances at the Felt Forum in Madison Square Garden, at the Lone Star Café in Gotham, at the Paradise Club in Boston and at Ontario Place in Toronto. He's even started writing songs again, something he has neglected for ages.

And oh yeah, to end on a big upper—whoops, excuse me, J.J., I nearly forgot you'd quit taking 'em—Susan and the baby have come back home.

I ain't booking any bets on how long the "new" Jerry Jeff will stay straight; I know too much history. But give him this: anybody who could get born in Watertown, New York, as Ronald Clyde Crosby, and somehow turn out to be a singing Texas outlaw named Jerry Jeff Walker, will always have a few resources to call on.

That Terrible
Night Santa Got
Lost in the Woods

This Christmas tale, of old-fashioned values and old-time courage, is one I often heard as I grew up. Chuck Conconi, then an editor of the Washington Post *"Style" section, asked me to write him a Christmas story in 1980; the* Post *published it on Christmas Eve of that year. The following year, in a slightly longer version than appears here, this story was brought out as a limited-edition book by William Wittliff of the Encino Press in Austin, Texas, and featured line drawings by the award-winning cartoonist Pat Oliphant.*

Franklin D. Roosevelt had been in the White House less than a year, and I was only four, when Christmas rolled around in 1933. That Christmas would become a colorful part of our family lore. I heard about it so many times, in such detail, that my memory attempts to trick me by claiming to recall more of it than could have been possible.

We lived on a hardscrabble dirt farm in Eastland County, Texas, in a time when much more than one-third of the nation was "ill-housed, ill-clad, ill-nourished." In that bottoming-out year of the Great Depression the King family owned no automobile, no telephone, no electric lights, no indoor plumbing, no running water and no cash.

The only heat in our farmhouse was provided by a rude stone fireplace in the living room and a wood-burning stove in the kitchen. On bitter nights—and it does get very cold in certain parts of Texas, Sun Belt myths to the contrary—my mother wrapped hot irons or hot bricks in layers of cloth as foot warmers. On frozen mornings, my parents broke the ice in a large kitchen bucket to wash the sleep from their eyes and to brew bracing coffee. Later, when the kitchen had warmed, but still before sunup and sometimes before first light, I would crawl from my chilly bed and dash to the fire in anticipation of hot biscuits, gravy and—after hog-killing time—home-cured sausage, ham or bacon.

At four years of age I knew nothing of unemployment, depressed farm prices, instant hobos riding the rails in search of work, the daily economic woes and fears of my parents. That would come soon enough, but in December of 1933 I innocently assumed the visit of a Santa Claus of generous spirit and limitless gifts.

"Your momma had ordered your Santa Claus doo-dads from a mail-order house that year like she always done," my father would many times recall, "but for some blame reason it never come. She met the mailman every day for a week, fussing and fuming at him, but it never done no good.

"When your Christmas hadn't come by Christmas Eve day, Cora rung the dinner bell on the porch to call me in from work. I recollect I was chopping wood and stacking it to haul to Cisco to sell for three dollars a cord. Well, I put down my ax and went to the house. Cora met me on the porch so you wouldn't hear her."

"Clyde," my mother said, "if that boy's gonna have any Santa Claus you're gonna have to go to town and buy it."

The old man (I think of him that way though he was short of his forty-sixth birthday, six years younger than I am now) asked a direct and simple question: "What with?"

"You can ask Will Gaddis for credit."

Her husband shook his head and mumbled; he thought credit buying unwise, unmanly and probably unforgivable by heaven. There was a shame attached to a man's not being able to make his own way on a cash-and-carry basis. When he said nothing more, she issued an edict: "Clyde, there's not any choice. We can't disappoint that boy. Christmas is for children."

"It was god-awful cold," my father would recall, "and getting colder. I could tell the clouds had snow in 'em. It was about six miles over to the little town of Scranton—had two stores there, a couple churches and a post office—and I didn't waste time trying to hunt down a horse in the pasture to saddle. Figured I'd strike out walking and maybe somebody would come along and pick up. At the least, I figured to run into somebody in town I could bum a ride from coming back home.

"I wrapped up in my heaviest old work jumper, put on heavy socks, long johns and struck out afoot. Didn't cut through the fields and pastures, which would of saved me more'n a mile and a half, on account of I had hopes of a car coming along. Well, I'll just be plagued—none did. Before I'd went a mile the snow was falling so thick and fast I couldn't see but a few steps ahead of myself. The wind was blowing so hard I had to lean into it, which made mighty tough walking. Time I got to Scranton, I was snow head to toe and half-froze."

Not much was doing in the little crossroads Texas settlement on a Christmas Eve afternoon. The country folks were at home: trimming trees they'd likely cut off their own land or a neighbor's, making popcorn balls, wrapping such few presents as they could afford, cooking the Christmas feasts that were so much a part of the holiday tradition.

One old couple was in Gaddis Brothers General Mercantile, which sold everything from axle grease to large sacks of flour to horse collars to patent medicines. In season, the Gaddis boys stocked a few toys and special items for Christmas.

"Me and Will Gaddis had been boys together, but I hated to ask him for credit worse than sin. I sure didn't want them other people hearing me. So I warmed my backside by the stove there in the store. When Will asked what he could do for me, I said, 'Let me thaw out first, Will.' Well, consarn that old couple, they asseled around in there, must of been a good hour, buying their little dab.

"Soon's they left I said, 'Will, my woman sent a money order to a mail-order house up in Chicago to buy my boy his Christmas, but it never come. I need to buy him a few things, but I flat don't have no money. It's all in Chicago.' I went on to tell Will I'd pay cash when I could. Or, if he'd druther, I'd work it out around his store or on a farm him and his brothers owned. Will said, 'Aw, Clyde, don't worry none about that. I know you good for it. You go on ahead and take whatever you want.' I appreciated that. Still and all, I couldn't help but feel little."

My father selected a half-dozen oranges, an equal number of apples, some nuts and hard candy, a small pocketknife and a child's little red rocking chair. "I don't know if you recollect that chair," he said in later years, "but you was plumb foolish about it. You used to set down in it and play like you was some big boss"—he laughed an old man's cackle—"and the rest of us would have to come ask you for our wages. And you'd make us tell what we'd did to deserve our pay before you'd give it to us—or play like you did.

"Anyhow, I'd carried a gunnysack to town with me. I put that red rocker and other Christmas things in it, told Will I was much obliged, and started to leave the store."

"Lord God, Clyde," the storekeeper said, "you don't want to go out in that danged blizzard! Somebody's bound to come along in a car directly."

The snow was getting thicker, the wind was howling fiercely; my father decided his old friend was right. Probably he secretly delighted in the rare opportunity to escape his daily labors and the isolation of his poor farm: he loved to talk, to tell stories, to crack dry jokes. The two men sat by the potbellied stove, Dad smoking roll-your-own cigarettes and Gaddis chewing tobacco, through much of the afternoon. I am sure they talked of crops and hard times and the Bible and men a long time dead.

"Wellsir, it got later and later and still nobody come to town. And the way that snow was swirlin' and bankin' up, I figured wadn't nobody likely to. The old roads was all dirt in them days, wadn't paved, and I guess folks figured they'd be mean to travel. So along about dusk I told Will Gaddis I'd just as well move on."

"Clyde, you better let me drive you over to your place," Gaddis said. "You can't walk six or seven miles in this mess."

But my father refused. Will Gaddis lived but a few hundred yards from his store, and such a wayward trip might be an imposition. "No, Will," he said, "you've done enough for me as it is."

My old man hoisted his gunnysack full of Santa Claus goodies on a broad shoulder and started the long trudge home through the storm. For a mile or so he stayed on the road, still hoping for the luck to hitch a ride.

"Then I thought, 'Thunder, ain't nobody in his right mind gonna come out in this blizzard.' So I cut through a plowed field, which crossed into some woods over about the old Biggerstaff place.

"Wellsir, outside of voting for Herbert Hoover, that was about the biggest damnfool thing I ever done. Ten minutes after I got in them woods it was pitch dark. I hadn't thought to bring a lantern, it being the middle of the day when I'd left home. Snow had covered up any markers I might have recognized, you see, and there I was bumping around in them blame woods getting myself or that gunnysack tangled up.

"Didn't bother me much at first. I figured I knowed which way I was heading and I'd come out on the road again, up by Ernest Weed's old place, if I walked true. And from there it wadn't but a mile, a mile and a quarter maybe, on home.

"But I walked and walked in that storm, until I finally knowed within reason I'd overshot Ernest Weed's place. So I started backtracking. But in the dark and that blowin' snow, all that done was get me turned around and twisted. I didn't have no notion where I was at. You couldn't read the stars—it was overcast and the moon was blotted out. And that snow was falling so thick it was hard to breathe.

"Well, I admit to it, I commenced feeling scared. It was cold enough that night a man could get frostbite or worse. I hadn't never seen a blizzard like that, and never seen another 'un. I knowed if I lost my head I'd be worse off than I was. Tried to follow my old tracks back to the road, but in the dark and with new snow falling I couldn't track myself. I tell you, I was between a rock and a hard place."

My mother usually picked up the story at that point. "When it got good dark and after, I was worried sick. It just wasn't like Clyde to lay out that way. He didn't drink; he was always particular to be on time and not worry me."

Mother and my older sister, Estelle, walked the floor of that old unpainted farmhouse, "wringing our hands and wondering." I was darting about underfoot, too excited by the prospect of Christmas and the proximity of Santa Claus to think of sleep. Not wanting to alarm me, my mother cautioned Estelle against emotional outbursts or tears.

"I thought it would be better if we had something to occupy our minds," my mother recalled. "We all went in the kitchen and popped popcorn and roasted a big pan of peanuts. You had a good time eating, rattling on about Santa Claus and asking questions about when he'd be there and what he fed his reindeer and such. I tried to act natural, but I just knew something was terrible wrong. I felt like I had to do something. So I told Estelle to stay with you, sing you songs or play little games to keep you occupied."

Telling me she was going to the barn to gather eggs for our

Christmas breakfast, my mother bundled warmly and collected three kerosene lanterns we kept for predawn farm chores.

"It was the only thing to do," she said. "The nearest neighbors was nearly a mile away. I was afraid to try to go there in the storm—and they had a yard full of big dogs I was afraid of. I set out walking to the main road, about a quarter of a mile from our old house, to set out lanterns. If your daddy was lost in the storm, I thought he might see their lights. All I could imagine, if somebody hadn't knocked him in the head or he hadn't been run over by a car, was that he'd got lost in that storm.

"It was all I could do to get up our lane to that main road and back—I later heard it snowed way over a foot. And there was drifts that was waist-deep. I know, because I fell in two or three. But I kept on until I got those lanterns lit and set out. I placed 'em in a row right in front of our gate.

"When I got back to the house you'd gone to sleep in Estelle's arms. When we tucked you in bed, you woke up mumbling about Santa Claus. But I sung you back to sleep. Then I said, 'Estelle, I can't think of but one other thing we can do.' So we dropped down on our knees and prayed."

Back to my father's tale. "I don't have no notion how long I stumbled around in them woods. Had to be hours and hours. I was wore out, hungry, cold to the bone—but I knowed if I stopped to rest I might go to sleep despite all I could do, and then I'd freeze to death. I'd heard of it happenin'.

"After awhile I got mad. I'd been raised on that same farm we lived on then. I'd hunted in that country all my life, walked them woods with dogs, worked fields. And it made me want to bump myself that I was lost and couldn't find no landmarks. I might as well a-been in China. But gettin' mad and gettin' to where I wanted to go was two different things."

He found himself thinking that if he could stumble onto a cow he could grab the animal, throw it to the ground and trace its brand with his fingers in the dark—thus learning whose land he was on. Surely then he would be able to chart a homeward course.

"I knowed cattle clumped up in deep woods and turned their backsides to the wind during a storm," he said. "Ever little bit I'd stop walkin' and listen for cattle millin' around, mooing and such. But all I could hear was the wind. 'Course, now, if I *had* found cattle I'd probably of spooked 'em and they'd of scattered in the dark. But I couldn't afford to let myself think about that."

He knew that he should have crossed one, possibly two small creeks that meandered through the countryside and was puzzled as to why he had not. He didn't think they would have frozen so solid that he might have walked across them without knowing it. No, likely he would have plunged into a sudden icy bath. Somehow it had not happened. "I studied on it and decided I'd never come to them creeks because I'd probably been wanderin' around in one big circle. I reckon that was when my spirits dropped just about as low as they could go."

By then he was scratched, bruised and bleeding. Tree limbs, heavily weighted by snow, had lashed his face; he had stumbled face or head first into a number of trees; he had fallen when surprised by deep snowdrifts or by tangling his feet in small bushes, none of which could be seen in the country dark. City slickers have no idea how dark is country dark on a blind and moonless night. There are no lights reflecting from traffic or highways or towns; one literally cannot see one's hand before one's face. In those conditions, my father most feared breaking a leg or an ankle. "I knowed if that happened I was a gone goose. I'd flat freeze layin' out there in the woods." Occasionally he stopped, cupped his hands and shouted *"Ha-low! Ha-low!"* But there was only the answering wind, and it might have been easy to imagine that it mocked him.

My old man's feet became so cold and wet they were but two dully aching lumps. He decided he must warm them. "My notion was to build a fire if I could scrabble up enough dead wood in all that snow that wadn't too wet to burn. Wellsir, I dug around and found a few pieces wadn't much more than twigs. Figured if I could could get 'em lit, I might find more dead wood by the light of the fire. Wadn't no use in thinking of stripping limbs off a tree unless it was a dead one. Green wood won't hardly burn even if it ain't wet."

When he searched himself for matches he found only three—kitchen matches, long and slender, the kind with which he had fired many a fireplace, campfire, kitchen stove, cigarette. One his numb hands dropped in the snow and was lost, despite his searches and curses. A second he foolishly attempted to strike on his wet shoe sole; the sulfurous matter crumbled. The third he managed to strike by popping the match head with his thumb. But when he tried to light the skimpy pile of wet twigs the flame fizzled and went out. "If I had been a woman," he said, "I would of cried right then."

He propped against a tree trunk, took off his heavy denim jumper, and after removing his shoes and wet socks he wrapped his feet in the rough garment. "After a little bit my feet commenced to sting, so I knowed I wadn't dead yet. I cussed myself for not rolling a cigarette before I struck my last match. I swear it, I'd of give a ten-dollar bill for a smoke."

He opened the gunnysack, ate one of the apples he had bought for me—"It was hard and cold, but juicy"—and popped open a few walnuts. These made him thirsty again, so he ate snow.

"I knowed I had to move on, because I was gettin' drowsy." He briefly considered trying to burrow into the snow, building something of a rough igloo, but decided that "not bein' no Eskimo I didn't know enough about it. It might cave in on me."

Shivering without his jumper, he squeezed out his wet socks—which had stiffened from direct exposure to the cold air—and painfully got back into his high-topped, soaked work shoes. Then he wrapped himself in the jumper again and resumed his lonely, aimless walk.

"Maybe it was a hour later I blundered into a barbed-wire fence. Hadn't seen it until I hit it. Wellsir, I knowed a fence had to lead *some*place and was likely to be decently close to a house or a road. I naturally decided to follow it.

"Only thing, I didn't know which direction to go. By then I barely knowed up from down. Sure's I followed that fence one way, the right way would prove to be the other 'un. By then I was just hopin' to stay on my feet till daylight. I knowed blamed good and well I'd be all right when mornin' come.

"When I tried to start off again—I'd kinda sagged against that fence to rest a spell—my durned jumper had got caught on them barbs and I couldn't pull loose. Had to fish for my pocketknife and cut myself aloose with my hands half-froze. Seemed like it took a week and a day.

"I followed that fence by feel. Carried the gunnysack in my left hand and slid my right one along the wire. Them barbs cut that hand up somethin' awful. Maybe it was twenty to thirty minutes later, I dunno, I broke out into a open field.

"It was still pitch dark and the wind was blowin' worse than in them woods, but it felt good to be out in the open even if I didn't know where I was at."

He stood perfectly still, listening. He heard creaking sounds, metal blowing against something in the wind. Carefully he made his way toward the rasping sound, stopping periodically to make certain he wouldn't lose it.

"It was a old cabin, hadn't nobody lived in it for years and years. What I'd heard was a piece of the old tin roof blowin' against what was left of the chimney.

"When I got up to it, I recognized it as a cabin Joe Lee Brown had lived in when he first married maybe thirty years before. Well-sir, it looked better to me than a palace. I knowed exactly where I was. I meant to say, 'Thank you, Lord, for answerin' my prayers,' but the words that come out of my mouth was 'It's about goddam *time*!'"

Though still almost two miles from home, so great was his relief at knowing the spot of ground he occupied in God's dark and bound-less universe that he celebrated by eating another apple and yelling *Yahoo!* several times.

"I et that second apple in the shelter of that old cabin, stompin' my feet to get circulation goin'. Didn't stay long, though, knowin' your momma would be standin' on her head worryin' about me.

"I set out from that cabin towards the way I knowed the road was, walkin' as true a line as I could. When I found that ol' road I wanted to kiss it. I turned left and started steppin' it off a mile a minute, feelin' like I wanted to sing."

A couple of hundred yards from the gate leading down to our farmhouse, he saw through the slackening snowfall a grouping of lights. At first he thought he was hallucinating, that the mental strain and physical drain of the long dark night of cold and fear had caused his senses to betray themselves.

"Then I thought, 'Thunderation, that's a blamed search party lookin' for me.' Wellsir, the notion of gettin' lost on my home grounds made me so ashamed of myself I went back in the woods again—just the edge, now, you can bank on that—and squatted down. Figured I'd let whoever it was go on by, then I'd sneak on home. I just couldn't stand to think of people guyin' and hoorawin' me about gettin' lost like some damn tenderfoot.

"But them lights, after awhile, hadn't come no closer. I got back on the road and walked down there, where I found them lanterns Cora had set out. Well, goddurn, be damn if I didn't hull down and cry." And telling it, in later years, his eyes always puddled up when he reached that point in the tale. Then he would chase the tears away with an abrupt laugh and say, "Them durn lanterns, they looked better to me than a fried-chicken dinner. I blowed two of 'em out and put 'em under the culvert there by our gate. Then I hung the other one on my arm and stumbled on towards the house."

It was a bit after four o'clock in the morning. My mother, sleepless and sitting in front of the fireplace with a patchwork quilt thrown over her legs, saw a tiny blob of light moving raggedly down the lane toward the house. At first she thought she, too, was seeing things. "Then I realized it was Clyde, that he'd found the lanterns." Now it was her turn to cry.

"I had already decided your daddy was dead or bad hurt. At first light, I planned to walk to Tal and Ola Horn's place and get help to start looking for Clyde. But in my heart I'd come to believe we'd find him in a bad way. I was sitting there wondering how to prepare you kids for it when I looked up and seen that lantern bobbing in the lane."

Dad was, she remembered, "an awful sight"—covered with frozen snow from crown to toe. Her hand flew to her mouth when she saw his swollen, bloody face and the hand so cruelly ripped by barbed wire.

My father grinned at her and said, "Breakfast ready yet?"

And somehow that made my mother mad. Perhaps she had anticipated some more dramatic utterance, for she was not without drama in her own nature. Or maybe it was a reaction against having sat home, helpless and unknowing, while her man knew an adventure she could neither share, imagine nor describe. Perhaps, more practically, in her lonely solitude she had permitted herself a fearful glimpse of what might be her future, with children and only a sixth-grade education, left to make her way in what then was very much a man's world. At any rate, she gritted her teeth at her man and said, "*Clyde King, where in the world have you been?*"

"I ain't got any idea," he said. "But I sure ain't going back without no breakfast."

She embraced him then, helped him out of his wet, stiff clothing and wrapped him in a blanket before attending his cuts, lumps and scrapes. He dozed by the fire while she hurried to brew coffee, and he later remembered that as he fitfully slept—awakening with sudden jerks and starts before dozing again—he was aware of her singing hymns of praise to Jesus.

While Dad drank the coffee and ate hot buttered biscuits, I rolled out of bed—full of a tingling, four-year-old awareness of a Christmas that, as usual, had taken forever to arrive—and romped into the living room to see what surprises Santa had left under the Christmas tree. Even in his weary state, my father had removed my rocking chair from the soaked, frozen gunnysack and placed it under the tree; he also had patiently stuffed my hanging stocking with the oranges, apples, nuts, hard candy and small pocketknife.

I fancy to recall that scene dimly, though probably I do not. Certainly I don't recall my contribution to what came to be known as the Christmas Daddy Got Lost in the Woods, though it was the part of the story my old man most enjoyed telling.

"There I set feelin' half dead," he chuckled, "and you runnin' around all hot about your Christmas presents and squealin'. But after a few minutes you looked over at me—after all I'd been through to be sure ol' Santa Claus come to see you—and you said, 'Dingbust it! Old Santa never brought me no stickhorse and cowboy suit like I asked him for. I ain't ever writin' to that old fool again!' "

And the old man would laugh and laugh and laugh until tears came into his eyes and, later, as he aged and as I matured, into my eyes as well.